BLACK GENDERS AND SEXUALITIES

THE CRITICAL BLACK STUDIES SERIES

FOUNDING EDITOR: MANNING MARABLE

INSTITUTE FOR RESEARCH IN AFRICAN AMERICAN STUDIES

Edited by Shaka McGlotten and Dána-Ain Davis
Columbia University

The Critical Black Studies Series features readers and anthologies examining challenging topics within the contemporary black experience—in the United States, the Caribbean, Africa, and across the African diaspora. All readers include scholarly articles originally published in the acclaimed quarterly interdisciplinary journal *Souls*, published by the Institute for Research in African-American Studies at Columbia University. Under the general editorial supervision of Manning Marable, the readers in the series are designed both for college and university course adoption, as well as for general readers and researchers. The Critical Black Studies Series seeks to provoke intellectual debate and exchange over the most critical issues confronting the political, socioeconomic, and cultural reality of black life in the United States and beyond.

Titles in this series published by Palgrave Macmillan are as follows:

Racializing Justice, Disenfranchising Lives: The Racism, Criminal Justice, and Law Reader
 Edited by Manning Marable, Keesha Middlemass, and Ian Steinberg

Seeking Higher Ground: The Hurricane Katrina Crisis, Race, and Public Policy Reader
 Edited by Manning Marable and Kristen Clarke

Transnational Blackness: Navigating the Global Color Line
 Edited by Manning Marable and Vanessa Agard-Jones

Black Routes to Islam
 Edited by Manning Marable and Hishaam D. Aidi

Barack Obama and African-American Empowerment: The Rise of Black America's New Leadership
 Edited by Manning Marable and Kristin Clarke

New Social Movements in the African Diaspora: Challenging Global Apartheid
 Edited by Leith Mullings

The New Black History: Revisiting the Second Reconstruction
 Edited by Manning Marable and Elizabeth Kai Hinton

Black Genders and Sexualities
 Edited by Shaka McGlotten and Dána-Ain Davis

BLACK GENDERS AND SEXUALITIES

EDITED BY

Shaka McGlotten and Dána-Ain Davis

First published in 2012 by PALGRAVE MACMILLAN® in the United States—
a division of St. Martin's Press LLC, 175 Fifth Avenue, New York, NY 10010.

Where this book is distributed in the UK, Europe and the rest of the world, this is
by Palgrave Macmillan, a division of Macmillan Publishers Limited, registered in
England, company number 785998, of Houndmills, Basingstoke, Hampshire RG21
6XS.

Palgrave Macmillan is the global academic imprint of the above companies and has
companies and representatives throughout the world.

Palgrave® and Macmillan® are registered trademarks in the United States, the
United Kingdom, Europe and other countries.

ISBN: 978-1-4039-8399-2 (hardcover)
ISBN: 978-1-4039-7775-5 (paperback)

Library of Congress Cataloging-in-Publication Data is available from the Library of
Congress.

A catalogue record of the book is available from the British Library.

This book is printed on paper suitable for recycling and made from fully
managed and sustained forest sources. Logging, pulping and manufacturing
processes are expected to conform to the environmental regulations of the
country of origin.

Design by Scribe Inc.

First edition: December 2012

10 9 8 7 6 5 4 3 2 1

For Manning Marable

CONTENTS

INTRODUCTION

Shaka McGlotten and Dána-Ain Davis

WE OPEN WITH THREE EVENTS, ONLY TWO of which bear an obvious relationship to one another. The first are the killings of two young black people, Sakia Gunn and Trayvon Martin. The third is a controversy that erupted in the wake of provocative blog posts about eliminating black studies programs written by conservative commentator Naomi Schaefer Riley on the *Chronicle of Higher Education* website.

On May 11, 2003, Sakia Gunn a 15-year-old black "aggressive"—female bodied but gender nonconforming—was stabbed and killed at a Newark bus stop after she and her friends rebuffed the sexual advances of older men. The story of her murder circulated in the lesbian, gay, bisexual, transgender, and queer (LGBTQ) press and among some rights-based organizations. But Gunn's story, and the vigils and antiviolence demonstrations held in the wake of her death, went largely unreported by the mainstream media (Pearson 2006). At first glance, the killing of Trayvon Martin on February 26, 2012, seems different insofar as his death has provoked a widespread national discussion. These discussions center on antiblack violence, racial profiling, and the indifference or outright violence of state police and other state agencies. Yet, importantly, Martin's case only gathered the nation's attention weeks after his killing as the result of the work of three black male journalists, Trymaine Lee, Charles Blow of the *New York Times*, and Ta-Nehisi Coates at the *Atlantic*, who refused to allow Martin's murder to become another example of what is sometimes called in newsrooms, "a garden variety killing" (On the Media 2012). Trymaine Lee, who writes for *The Huffington Post*, observed that while the local Florida media was covering the case and that the story was circulating widely on social media like Facebook and Twitter, the national media wasn't paying much attention. But Lee, along with Blow and Coates, helped ensure the story gained a wider audience. Each had a personal connection to the case by the very fact of being black men, either because they had been subjected to racial profiling themselves or because they had known other black men who had been the victims of violence. They refused to submit to the increasingly matter-of-fact assumption that black men are doomed to violent fates.

The differences between the deaths of these two young people, and the national response to them, are striking. Perhaps talking about death in the introduction of a book ostensibly about black gender and sexuality is startling.

But the death of both of these young people and the responses to their murders turn on the particular ways differences of gender and sexuality matter in black life. Trayvon Martin's death has, at least for a time, galvanized the nation to the recognition (once again) that black men are disposable and that black masculinity continues to pose a kind of existential threat to the American imaginary. Sakia Gunn's death shows us that gender nonconformity incites murderous violence and an equally murderous silence and forgetting insofar as her death was not recuperable to the lobbying efforts of LGBT policy groups or antibullying campaigns. After all, she was no Matthew Shepard; she was black and poor and "aggressive," and she fought back rather than wait for things to "get better." Black lives, these killings remind us, are more than precarious; they simply don't count for much. In the differences in media coverage, one might conclude that a black woman's life is patently less important than that of a black man; that a lesbian's death—particularly a butch's death—does not warrant the same outrage as that of a presumably straight young man. But neither of these conclusions would be the only point here.

The real point is that the awkward scenes of subjection of black gender and sexuality both prevail in policy and in the popular imagination (see for example, among many others, Alexander 2012; D. Davis 2004; Harris-Perry 2011; Hartman 1997). The black body remains a site of pathologized difference: the black gendered body is typically cast in hyperstereotypical form, violent, muscled Bucks and inviting, sassy, bootylicious Jezebels are pervasive throughout various media. Blacks also cast a shadow in the policy speeches of the Republican nominees for president in the 2012 primaries, who repeatedly invoked tired tropes about welfare moms and other forms of public aid in which race and class are often conflated. Mitt Romney, for instance, has argued that poor moms should be required to work outside of the home in order to receive public aid, to experience the "dignity of work." We know he is referring to black and Latino women, although he does not say it. Black bodies continue to be easily yoked into some titillating space of hypersexualization and/or abjection. Black lives are ultimately viewed as politically expedient but ultimately disposable; after all, how does anyone help a people so prone to the internecine violence that result from drugs, poverty, or whatever.

This sense of black disposability is what animates Naomi Schaefer Riley's dismissal of black studies as a discipline. In a widely derided post in the *Chronicle of Higher Education* blog "Brainstorm," Schaefer Riley dismissed the work of emerging black studies scholars (Schaefer Riley 2012). Her post responded to an earlier article written by Stacey Patton (2012), "Black Studies: 'Swaggering into the Future.'" In her article, Patton examines what she regards as the third wave of black studies, focusing predominately on Northwestern University's program. Her assessment is that while earlier black studies scholars wrested their knowledge in a particular discipline, like history or sociology, newer graduate students are benefitting from an interdisciplinary approach to the study of the ongoing salience and reproduction of race. Patton expressly notes how black studies has grown as a field and solidified its place in higher education, evidenced by the now 11 doctoral programs that can be found around the country.

In a bald failure to apply even the most basic standards of intellectual or journalistic rigor, Schaefer Riley's rationale for dismissing black studies rested on a fundamentally erroneous premise: the irrelevance of the dissertation research of a few doctoral students in the Northwestern program. Their dissertations, Schaefer Riley asserted, amounted to "a collection of left-wing victimization claptrap." Her evidence? Although her post's title, "The Most Persuasive Case for Eliminating Black Studies? Just Read the Dissertations," points readers to the dissertations specifically, she hadn't bothered to read them herself. Apparently she only needed to read the titles to know that the work amounted to nothing. And from the titles, she concluded, the discipline itself must be antiquated and out-of-touch. The work of the students she identified focused on natural childbirth, histories of housing policies and their effects on blacks, and black conservatives' rolling back of civil rights gains. Of course, as commenters on her blog, students she attacked, faculty at Northwestern, and many others observed, all of these continue to be pressing issues in the larger tapestry of black life, indeed American life generally. For Schaefer Riley, these varied projects amount to left-wing claptrap because these students blame white racism for the problems that face black people. But since she didn't read the work, how would she know? Since being fired from the blog, Schaefer Riley has gone on a range of conservative media, in increasingly familiar ways, to claim that she wasn't victimizing anyone but is herself the victim of intolerant politically correct liberals, a point made repeatedly by commenters defending her original post and follow-up.

Schaefer Riley is not the first, nor will she be the last, to denigrate black studies. In 2002, for example, Candace de Russy, a trustee of the State University System of New York was prominently featured in an article on the state of black studies programs (Evans 2002). She criticized black studies on several grounds, saying that they lack rigor and amount to little more than "feel good" programs. In de Russy's opinion, black studies programs have an anti-American bias and do little to advance "real" knowledge (D. Davis 2011). De Russy, like Schaefer Riley, is connected to organizations whose ideologies and aims include the dismantling of public higher education and, indeed, many of the tenets of a liberal education. In a generous reading of their views, they seem to want to return to what Stuart Hall calls, skeptically, "the grand narratives of history, language and literature" (Hall 1993, 107). In other words, the classics. But increasingly, right-wing attacks go much further, arguing that public funding for any "soft" fields of knowledge, including sociology, English, or history, much less women's or black studies should be eliminated. Public funding, this argument goes, should be restricted to more "useful" disciplines, to hard sciences like engineering, mathematics, and the like. They say this without irony, even as they simultaneously form alliances with other culture warriors who attack the very foundations of the scientific method and rigor in disciplines like biology or environmental science, arguing instead for a faith-based approach to our shared material reality in which evolution and global warming are unproven theories that have become doctrine through the conspiracies of a tight knit cabal of leftists.

In her closing argument, Schaefer Riley notes that "there are legitimate debates about the problems that plague the black community from high incarceration rates to low graduation rates to high out-of-wedlock birthrates. But it's clear that they're not happening in black-studies departments." We agree with Schaefer Riley that these are real and pressing issues. We disagree that this work isn't taking place in black studies departments; in fact, it is often from such departments that this kind of work is most likely to arise, even if it doesn't appear in the three dissertations whose titles she read. Schaefer Riley's assault on black studies and by extension on the black community is a form of violence. It is likely that her original blog post was simply intended to create debate, to "stir the pot" as one commenter put it and increase traffic for the *Chronicle*'s website. This sort of provocative disruption is like the online practice known as "trolling," which often uses highly charged racist, sexist, and homophobic language to incite another's response. Then when the victim of trolling responds, the troll takes further pleasure in observing the victim's hurt, anxiety, and anger. The best response to trolls is no response at all (in Internet slang, "do not feed the trolls"). Of course, for people whose lives are always already marked by violence, ideological and otherwise, it's not so easy to shrug off attacks like Schaefer Riley's. In her desire to end black studies, she does a disservice to its history, to the knowledge produced by it, and to the transformations it has effected in both intellectual life and larger social spaces. From Schaefer Riley's perspective black (and likely queer, gender, and Latino) studies are all about victimization. This mistakenly understands that the only use of, say, a black studies department, is to either soothe the beast or uncover solutions to the pathology of the beast. The victimization trope is an idea for intellectual babies. Indeed, Schaefer Riley's condemnation reflects and reproduces forms of antiblack violence and thereby clearly points to the need and continued relevancy of blackness as a worthy subject of interrogation, precisely what black studies, as well as gender and sexuality, programs continue to do.

The black intellectual tradition has currents that are over two centuries old. In periodizing this tradition, Manning Marable (2000) notes that the conceptual period of black studies occurred between Reconstruction and the Great Depression. In this period, which included W. E. B. Du Bois, Charles S. Johnson, Horace Mann Bond, St. Clair Drake, Zora Neale Hurston, and Carter G. Woodson, among others, black intellectuals merged their "scholarly production to the lived experiences of black people" (Marable 2000, 20). Marable further notes that after World War II, African American studies broke from its confinement in racially segregated institutions to "a vibrant curriculum and hundreds of programs" (21). One of the most salient observations that Marable offers is that the purpose of the black intellectual tradition has "always been descriptive, that is presenting the reality of black life and experiences. Second, it has been corrective; that is Black Studies has challenged and critiqued racism and stereotypes that have persistently cropped up in mainstream discourse of white academic institutions" (Marable 2000, 17) Finally, Marable argues that the black intellectual tradition has been prescriptive. He says, "Black scholars . . . have often proposed practical steps for the empowerment of Black people" and that "there is a practical connection between scholarship and struggle, between social analysis and social transformation" (Marable 2000, 18).

These are the foundations of black scholarship. And in the tradition of Marable, who viewed scholarship as potentially transformative, we offer this edited volume as an intervention and a trenchant counterpoint to those who have a vested interest in ending black studies, queer studies, gender studies, Latino studies, and the like. We seek to protect and advance the vitality and variability of the study of black life and cultures. The essays included in this book illustrate this commitment. They cut across a range of disciplines (anthropology, history, sociology, public health, cultural studies) and methods (textual analysis, ethnography, and surveys). Taken as a whole, the work collected here represents a more realistic, albeit still very partial, snapshot of work by emerging scholars across race and ethnicity. Many of the authors who first appeared in the *Souls* issues we edited three years ago, with Vanessa Agard-Jones, have already made significant contributions to black and queer studies. Among the recent contributions they have made are a special issue of *GLQ: A Journal of Lesbian and Gay Studies*, edited by Jafari Sinclaire Allen, whose work appears in this volume. Two other contributors, Marlon Bailey and Rashad Shabazz, are coediting a forthcoming special issue on blackness and gender for the journal *Gender, Place, and Culture: A Journal of Feminist Geography*. Other participants in this project have forthcoming books, many of which, like the articles here, were based on dissertation projects, giving truth to the lie that new work in black studies is out-of-touch or commercially unviable.

This anthology, like the examples we cite previously, represent an attempt to mark black gender and sexuality as fields that are special without being inevitable. That is, we do not seek to consolidate or reproduce many of the most widely circulated iterations of black bodies and desires or to situate them in stable locations (filial, political, geographic). This is not to suggest that past or present studies of black genders and sexualities have only reproduced stereotypes or fixed the range of identifications and practices that fall under the rubric of gender and sexuality. Indeed, the past three decades have given rise to challenging, critical scholarship on questions of gender and sexuality throughout the African diaspora, as we argue previously. Yet, in unlikely agreement with Schaefer Riley, we have been struck by the way so much of the scholarly literature on black gender and sexuality is focused largely on racism and especially on the ways racism operates as both cause and effect, at once determining black gender and sexual deviance and emerging as an effect of that deviance. Are the range of black gender performativities, affinal bonds, emotions, and sexual practices, and their links to larger US political economies, necessarily overdetermined by racist ideologies? We can gesture here toward a range of work that cuts across historical and interdisciplinary sites (Cosby and Poussaint 2007; Gilman 1985; Moynihan 1965). Let us be clear: we are attuned to the ongoing salience of racism—given the everyday impacts of violent antiblack racism that takes shape in murders like the ones we discuss previously or mass incarceration, politicians' and pundits' barely veiled rhetoric, and the proliferation of more explicitly antiblack discourse online. It's impossible not to attend to the ways racism continues to shape American life. Our point, though, is that we did not explicitly seek out work that grappled with racism as its central analytic lens. Rather, we sought to capitalize on what we view as an ongoing disruptive momentum in black studies and emergent black queer studies. The goal was to locate the strongest new scholarship in black gender and sexuality both in the United States and abroad. And while normative het-erosexualities certainly fall under this rubric (see the following), we were more interested in, among other things, new definitions of the alphabet soup: lesbian, gay, bisexual, transgender, queer, and intersexed (LGBTQI); critical approaches to activism and sexuality; neoliberalism and black sexuality; race, sexuality, and affect; sexual citizenship; and/or gender and performativity.

To say that we were interested in work that didn't reproduce black genders and sexualities as overdetermined by racist ideologies is not to say that we were espe-cially interested or invested in what is increasingly, though sometimes mistakenly, called a postracial politics. Rather, we sought lateral movements away from those trends in which black bodies and desires have been made congruent with, or in resistance to, cultural pathology and social deviance. We sought to sidestep some of the limits of representational analyses that have plagued scholars and critics of black experiences. The problems attendant in these representations led Hortense Spillers (2003) to make her comment that "black women are the beached whales of the sexual universe, unvoiced, unseen, not doing, awaiting their verb. Their sexual experiences are depicted, but not often by them, and if by the subject herself, often in the guise of vocal music, often in the self-contained accent and sheer romance of the blues" (153). The equation of black sexuality with pathology has led others to engage in an ambivalent politics of refusal, in which representation is blocked, as in Lorna Simpson's famous image "Guarded Conditions" in which a black woman stands with her back to the camera. Of course the limits of the refusal to represent are painfully clear: if no image of black gender or sexual difference can fully escape the weighted history of racial violence, then the only "good" image is no image at all. Therefore, while engagements with, or refutations of, the equivalences between black genders and sexualities and pathology or shame are necessarily ongoing, we do not want to revisit those key and still informative (if often only of the anxieties and desires of white cultural imaginaries) controversies about fractured black fami-lies, promiscuity, welfare, sexual precocity, and penis size.

This is not to say, of course, that we were unaware of the work that has been done in this area since the 1970s (or earlier, depending on how you periodize black studies more broadly—obviously folks like Ma Rainey and James Baldwin had quite a bit to say prior to the black cultural nationalisms of the '60s and '70s). Our efforts here, like those of so many others, owe a good deal to those who have gone before us, especially the pioneering work done by black feminists and other feminists of color (A. Davis 1983; Hill Collins 1999; hooks 1999; Hull, Scott, and Smith 1982; Moraga and Anzaldúa 1983), as well as the work that has emerged over the last two decades that has documented a growing synergy between critical race and what has come to be called critical queer studies (Cohen 2001; Eng 2001; Ferguson 2004; Holland 2000; Johnson and Henderson 2005). Like many of the cultural producers parenthetically listed previously (an admit-tedly truncated list), we had taken seriously the call for intersectional approaches proffered by Kimberlé Crenshaw (1991), while also recognizing the ways inter-sectionality continues to prove so elusive to realize (McGlotten 2012). Thus even if we've resisted framing our intervention as one that begins and ends with racism, race is obviously not incidental to the studies of genders and sexualities these articles offer. Our point, though, is that black sexuality does not belong only to public policy or to racist or antiracist discourses; black sexuality, like sexuality writ large, is so important and interesting (to think about or even to do), in addition to being so analytically difficult, because it is effectively everywhere, permeating all aspects of cultural life, including the spheres of mainstream political and popular culture and transnational black diasporic spaces.

Rather than begin, then, from what might be called a position of "racial paranoia" that would shape and guide our efforts only in relation to racism, we began from a reparative one (Jackson 2008; Sedgwick 2003). Eve Sedgwick, in an important essay, "Paranoid Reading, Reparative Reading," argues that the "hermeneutic of suspicion" in which most intellectuals and academics are trained has mutated into an injunction to be paranoid, a methodological imperative. Yet as she puts it, "For someone to have an unmystified, angry view of large and genuinely systemic oppressions does not intrinsically or necessarily enjoin that person to any specific train of epistemological or narrative consequences" (Sedgwick 2003, 124). That is, the fact of racism is not the only thing that might make black genders and sexualities special. And knowledge of the metacultural power of racism doesn't necessarily lead to critiques that take it as a point of departure and arrival. Reparative reading, in contrast, might be about healing—echoing many of the calls that accompany calls for reparations—but it is also about what Sedgwick evokes as "queer possibility" (147). In a series of ongoing and forthcoming works, José Esteban Muñoz (1999, 2009) offers astute and hopeful critiques of the queer possibilities and art of making do that are embedded in ordinary life in ways that don't necessarily undo or even directly contest the oppressive structures (racism, gender normativity) that so preoccupy paranoid thinking. Many of the essays in this issue share this sensibility, tying black genders and sexualities to everyday (if also interstitial) spaces without fixing them, offering partial views into the ways identities and practices tied to gender performativity or sexual practice are dispersed throughout larger social fields, crystallizing in particular places and time, particular bodies or networks. In short, the essays included here often gesture toward a something or somewhere else, another site in which genders and sexualities congeal without foreclosing other possible iterations. The openness that accompanies the utopian impulses of queer possibilities leads us to speculate that the emphasis on hopeful possibility might be as much a black cultural value as a queer one.

The queer of color critique in which our work is situated, then, remains both an emergent and ongoing project, one that continues to proliferate even as it resists neat categorization or institutionalization (something that is both wishful and unlikely given the degree to which so few queer theorists, after more than two decades at the "cutting edge," have yet to find institutionally stable homes). We hope that this volume might contribute in its own way to this body of work by offering new scholarship that seriously and creatively evidences and explores the mutual imbrication of categories of difference like gender, sexuality, nation, race, and class, among others. The emergent scholarship on black genders and sexualities across the diaspora that we offer here locates these axes of differences within broader fields of knowledge, politics, and history. Put plainly, we looked for and found important new work that operates both to queer black studies and to orient this queering toward local and transnational politics and practices, activist, academic, and otherwise.

Three works examine aesthetic and popular culture texts. Simone Drake explores the meanings of black gender and sexuality projected onto the screen and on canvas. In her chapter "Craig Brewer and Kara Walker: Sexing the Difference and Rebuilding the South," Drake looks at filmmaker Craig Brewer's and artist Kara Walker's examination of the South. She seeks to root experiences of US racial melancholia that both artists explore in a particularly southern sensibility. For Drake, memory and place are organizing themes for both artists, and they gesture toward a reconciliatory or recuperative vision for gender and racial differences. C. Riley Snorton explores the "ghettocentric imagination" at play in R. Kelly's episodic musical soap opera, "Trapped in the Closet," while Guy Mark Foster critiques the documentary on black boxer Emile Griffith, *Ring of Fire*, for the ways it eludes a serious contextualization of his identity as a black Caribbean man in favor of the established narrative of the "the closet." Arguing that the model of the closet that the film employs is inadequate, Foster instead situates the film against the backdrop of what Jasbir Puar (2007) calls "homonationalism," the complex interaction between nationalism, racial difference, sovereignty, and a national heterosexuality that includes homosexuality as a mark of national exception(alism). Snorton likewise argues that in Kelly's (still?) ongoing saga, black sexuality emerges as a congeries of class and gender relations, performatively enacted affective scenarios, the musically saturated history of black expressive culture, and a meditation "that inextricably ties black sexuality to queerness in the popular imagination" (this volume, p. 16). If Foster pushes against the limits of the closet metaphor, Snorton multiplies its meanings.

Drawing on ethnographic methods, the chapters by Aimee Cox, Tanya Saunders, and Marlon Bailey examine the interface of performative gender identities with state-run agencies, female masculinities, and as an "intravention," respectively. Cox's essay "Thugs, Black Divas, and Gendered Aspirations," draws on her experiences working in a Detroit Fresh Start social service agency and interviews with residents with whom she worked. Cox looks at the ways neoliberal social service policies "constrain the possibilities for self-identification and sexual expression" among poor and working-class women (this volume, p. 86). At the same time, she highlights how these women find creative ways to negotiate these gendered aspirations, including the enactment of a range of oppositional masculine stylings. The themes addressed in this chapter are critical to considerations of how state institutions and neoliberal models of social service shape, albeit unevenly, the possibilities for self-identification and sexual expression among individuals living in underresourced urban communities of color.

The performance of female masculinities is taken up by Tanya Saunders who explores the relationship between female masculinities, normative models of gender, and the state. In her article, she documents the strange life of Grupo OREMI, a lesbian social services group originally funded by the Cuban government. This state support was later withdrawn when the success of the program became too visible and the increasingly large gatherings of women, especially poor and non-gender-conforming women, exceeded socially acceptable bounds of propriety and tolerance. In the chapter "Performance as Intravention: Ballroom Culture and the Politics of HIV/AIDS in Detroit," Marlon Bailey argues that ballroom community members deploy forms of "intravention," strategies for HIV/AIDS prevention that are created by and emerge from within the ballroom community, a so-called high risk community.

Autobiography and biography are the focus of three other essays. Examining the production and expression of interiority and exteriority of the self through literature, historian Doreen Drury offers a critical biography of lawyer and civil rights activist Pauli Murray. Drury's essay "Love, Ambition, and 'Invisible Footnotes' in the Life and Writing of Pauli Murray" looks at the threat that Murray's status as a woman, her love of other women, and her preference for masculine style posed to her dreams of becoming a civil rights leader. This chapter considers Murray's efforts to resolve her conflicts through several means, including the research and writing of her family history, *Proud Shoes*. Included are also two first-person narratives, one a polemic and the other a remembrance of clubbing that also engages debates in queer studies about futurity and the figure of the child. In the former, Ashon Crawley's "Can You be Black and Work Here?," Crawley draws expressive traditions of black aurality to reflect on his departure from a gay and lesbian nonprofit and the consternation his departure, as well as his communication with leaders in the organization, generated. Crawley's work is an experimental and experiential account of black queer embodiment in conflict with white gay homonormativity. The second personal narrative "For 'the Children' Dancing the Beloved Community," by Jafari Allen, develops an epistemology that conjures the history of black gay intimacies and the spaces through which they move. Allen's essay draws on his own experiences in black gay clubs to reflect on life and freedom for black queers. At the same time, he engages recent debates in queer studies about politics and futurity, challenging ideas that queer politics are or should be dead. Indeed, for Allen, even the melancholic nostalgia that informs his memories of the black queer clubs he frequented are important ontological and political resources for contemporary black feminist and queer studies and other democratically or utopian-minded political projects.

One of two new essays that appear in this book, H. Sharif William's "In the Heat," sits between the intimate autobiographical/autoethnographic essays previously mentioned and the more traditional research projects we outline shortly. Williams's essay mixes social science research on black men who have sex with men with evocative reflections on the ways black men experience intimacy with one another. Four other pieces relate findings from research projects and one offers commentary on a conference. Annecka Marshall and Donna-Maria Maynard's "Black Female Sexual Identity: The Self-Defined" shares findings from a questionnaire survey distributed to female university students in Barbados and Jamaica to reveal diverse attitudes about female sexualities in the Caribbean. Participants acknowledge that at the same time that Caribbean societies are undergoing positive changes about sexuality as a consequence of globalization and the mass media, degrading notions that women are promiscuous and viewed as sex objects, persist. Renee McCoy's research "Ain't I a Man: Gender Meanings among African American Men Who Have Sex with Men" illuminates the meaning, identity, risks, and cultural beliefs of twenty African American men who have sex with men (MSM) and the consequences that labeling men as "gay" or on the "down low" has on HIV/AIDS interventions. Ana Paula Da Silva and Thaddeus Gregory Blanchette's "Sexual Tourism and Social Panics" details how these two anthropologists came to be involved in working with the Brazilian Prostitutes' Network, an advocacy group that has increasingly come to challenge the ways state policies position prostitutes as victims of sexual tourism, an identification that in fact makes them more vulnerable to surveillance and police harassment. The commentary by Zethu Matebeni, "Feminizing Lesbians, De-Gendering Transgender Men: A Model for Building Lesbian Feminist Thinkers and Leaders in Africa?" examines the 2008 Feminist Leadership Institute held in Mozambique. The Institute sought to develop African lesbian feminist thinkers and leaders and was attended by diverse participants, which facilitated an interrogation of African feminisms. At the same time, it highlighted issues around sexuality, particularly same-sex sexuality, as well as contentious issues about gender. Reflecting on this institute foregrounds many of the challenges posed to a model of African feminism used to negotiate sexual orientation, race, class, and gender.

Three pieces explore black masculinity. Ethan Johnson and Roberta Hunt's essay, "Race, Sexuality, and the Media: The Demotion of Portland, Oregon's Black Chief of Police," the second of the new essays that appear in this volume, focuses on the newspaper coverage of a sex scandal involving Portland's black chief of police. They crucially point to the differences in coverage between the mainstream and black presses. The public geographies of black gender and sexuality are astutely critiqued by Rashad Shabazz's chapter, "So High You Can't Get Over It, So Low You Can't Get Under It: Carceral Spatiality and Black Masculinities in the United States and South Africa." Shabazz looks at the ways in which carceral or prison space, and the techniques that make prison punishment possible, shape black living and working space and how in turn they influence black masculine performance. Using the Robert Taylor Housing Projects and South Africa's mining compounds as case studies, he examines the carceral logics that underwrote these spaces, specifically focusing on the practices that seek to fix blacks spatially.

Taken as a whole, this volume, which was made possible by Manning Marable, Elizabeth Kai Hinton, and the Souls Editorial Working Group, illustrates some of the powerful political struggles and structures that shape black gender and sexuality as ideological, epistemological, and spatial articulations and assemblages. It features established and emergent scholars who cross disciplinary boundaries in the ongoing process of tracing the lineaments of black gender and sexuality across local, national, and international frameworks. And the book frames black genders and sexualities as special, in the ways they are embedded in the ordinary texture of life yet tied to larger social imaginaries, institutions, and ideologies, rather than only as a special "problem." Finally, we hope that our efforts here operate to do some modest justice to the discursive and material violences black people experience as well as to the resilient vitality and creativity of black life in and outside the academy.

REFERENCES

Alexander, Michelle. 2011. *The New Jim Crow: Mass Incarceration in the Age of Colorblindness.* New York: The New Press.

Cohen, Cathy J. 2001. "Punks, Bulldaggers and Welfare Queens: The Radical Potential of Queer Politics?" In *Sexual Identities, Queer Politics,* edited by Mark Blasius, 308–11. Princeton, NJ: Princeton University Press.

Cosby, Bill, and Alvin F. Poussaint. 2007. *Come On, People: On the Path from Victims to Victors.* Nashville: Thomas Nelson.

Crenshaw, Kimberlé. 1991. Mapping the Margins: Intersectionality, Identity Politics, and Violence against Women of Color. *Stanford Law Review,* 43: 1241–99.

Davis, Angela. 1983. *Women, Race, & Class.* New York: Vintage.

Davis, Dána-Ain. 2011. "Constructing Fear in Academia: Neoliberal Practices at a Public College." *Learning and Teaching in the Social Sciences* 4(1):42–69.

———. 2004. "Manufacturing Mammies: The Burdens of Service Work and Welfare Reform Among Battered Black Women." *Anthropologica* 46(2): 273–88.

Eng, David L. 2001. *Racial Castration: Managing Masculinity in Asian America.* Durham, NC: Duke University Press.

Evans, Martin C. 2002. "Reviewing Black Studies: Legitimacy of Discipline Taken to Task." *Newsday,* February 4. http://www.goacta.org/press/Articles/202Articles/02-02-04ND.pdf.

Ferguson, Roderick A. 2004. *Aberrations in Black: Toward a Queer of Color Critique.* Minneapolis: University of Minnesota Press.

Gilman, Sander L. 1985. *Difference and Pathology: Stereotypes of Sexuality, Race, and Madness.* Ithaca, NY: Cornell University Press.

Harris-Perry, Melissa. 2011. *Sister-Citizen: Shame, Stereotypes and Black Women in America.* New Haven, CT: Yale University Press.

Hartman, Saidiya V. 1997. *Scenes of Subjection: Terror, Slavery and Self-Making in 19th Century America.* Oxford: Oxford University Press.

Hall, Stuart. 1993. "What Is This 'Black' in Black Popular Culture?" *Social Justice* 20(1–2): 104–11.

Hill Collins, Patricia. 1999. *Black Feminist Thought: Knowledge, Consciousness, and the Politics of Empowerment.* New York: Routledge.

Holland, Sharon P. 2000. *Raising the Dead: Readings in Death and Black Subjectivity.* Durham, NC: Duke University Press.

hooks, bell. 1999. *Ain't I A Woman.* Boston: South End Press.

Hull, Gloria T., Patricia Bell Scott, and Barbara Smith, eds. 1982. *All the Women Are White, All the Men Are Black, but Some of Us Are Brave.* New York: The Feminist Press.

Jackson, Jr., John L. 2008. *Racial Paranoia: The Unintended Consequences of Political Correctness.* New York: Basic Civitas.

Johnson, E. Patrick, and Mae Henderson, eds. 2005. *Black Queer Studies: An Anthology.* Durham, NC: Duke University Press.

Marable, Manning. 2000. "Black Studies and the Racial Mountain." *Souls: A Critical Journal of Black Politics, Culture, and Society* 2(3): 17–36.

McGlotten, Shaka. 2012. "Ordinary Intersections: Speculations on Difference, Justice, and Utopia in Black Queer Life." *Transforming Anthropology* 20(1): 45–66.

Moraga, Cherrie, and Gloria Anzaldúa. 1983. *This Bridge Called My Back: Writings by Radical Women of Color.* New York: Kitchen Table Press.

Moynihan, Daniel Patrick. 1965. *The Negro Family: The Case for National Action.* Washington, DC: United States Department of Labor, Office of Policy Planning and Research.

Muñoz, José Esteban. 1999. *Disidentifications: Queers of Color and the Performance of Politics*. Minneapolis: University of Minnesota Press.

———. 2009. *Cruising Utopia: The Then and There of Queer Futurity*. New York: New York University Press.

On the Media. 2012. "Why the Trayvon Martin Story Took So Long to Gain Traction." *On the Media*, March 23. http://www.onthemedia.org/2012/mar/23/why-trayvon-martin-story -took-so-long-gain-traction/transcript/.

Patton, Stacey. 2012. "Black Studies: 'Swaggering into the Future.'" *The Chronicle of Higher Education*, April 12. http://chronicle.com/articleBlack-Studies-Swaggering/131533.

Pearson, Kim. 2006. "Rethinking News Coverage of Hate Crimes against GLBT People." In *News and Sexuality: Media Portraits of Diversity*, edited by Laura Castañeda and Shannon Campbell, 159–90. Thousand Oaks, CA: Sage.

Puar, Jasbir K. 2007. *Terrorist Assemblages: Homonationalism in Queer Times*. Durham, NC: Duke University Press.

Schaefer Riley, Naomi. 2012. "The Most Persuasive Case for Eliminating Black Studies? Just Read the Dissertations." *The Chronicle of Higher Education* (blog). http://chronicle .com/blogs/brainstorm/the-most-persuasive-case-for-eliminating-black-studies-just -read-the-dissertations/46346.

Sedgwick, Eve Kosofsky. 2003. "Paranoid Reading and Reparative Reading, or, 'You're So Paranoid, You Probably Think This Essay is About You.'" In *Touching Feeling: Affect, Pedagogy, Performativity*, 123–52. Durham, NC: Duke University Press.

Spillers, Hortense. 2003. *Black, White, and in Color*. Chicago: University of Chicago Press.

CHAPTER 1

TRAPPED IN THE EPISTEMOLOGICAL CLOSET

BLACK SEXUALITY AND THE "GHETTOCENTRIC" IMAGINATION

C. RILEY SNORTON

R. KELLY'S WIDELY POPULAR, EPISODIC OPERA *TRAPPED in the Closet* (*Trapped*) begins with the protagonist, Sylvester (Kelly), waking up alone, noticeably disoriented, in the bed of a presumed one-night stand. His sexual partner, Cathy, soon returns to the bedroom to inform Sylvester that her husband Rufus is coming up the stairs. First considering jumping out of the window, Sylvester decides to hide in the closet to avoid the inevitable confrontation. A few seconds later, Rufus arrives, and the couple begins to engage in foreplay until the untimely ringing of Sylvester's cell phone interrupts them. After searching other parts of the apartment, Rufus approaches the closet to find Sylvester waiting inside, with a Beretta in hand.

Backing away from Sylvester, Rufus turns his anger toward Cathy at the realization of her infidelity. Sylvester, eager to get home to his wife, threatens to shoot both Rufus and Cathy if they do not let him leave. Rufus, however, somehow manages to make Sylvester stay in the apartment in order to meet the other half of Rufus's own adulterous affair, Chuck, a deacon at the church where Rufus is the pastor. In an effort to silence the escalating assertions of betrayal, the competing claims to moral superiority, and finally a declaration from Rufus that he intends to marry his lover, Sylvester climatically shoots the gun into the air. Sylvester, after effectively silencing the room, calls his house and hears an unidentified man. The third chapter ends with Sylvester quickly exiting Rufus and Cathy's house, hoping to catch his wife in her own affair. The succeeding 19 chapters are a slow crescendo on the foundational themes of infidelity, concealment, and the inextricability of blackness and queerness in the popular imagination.

Part of the appeal of *Trapped in the Closet* lies in its ability to visualize the interplay among and between many of the most persistent and compelling stereotypes of black masculinity—the minister, the ex-con, the cop, the "down-low" brother, the pimp, and the hip-hop star, setting them against the backdrop of a postindustrial black urban landscape. As S. Craig Watkins argues, popular media culture serves as a terrain on which scholars might understand the processes of social and political struggle in "constant operation."[1] For Watkins, the "black ghetto" is a cultural object that serves as a location for ideological struggle and maps the epistemological terrain of postindustrial black space and its inhabitants, thus producing a "ghettocentric imagination."[2] Positing her own cartography in *Epistemology of the Closet*, Eve Sedgwick argues that the crisis of "homo = heterosexual definition," emblematized by the metaphor of the closet, produces myriad binaries that have served to structure culture invisibly in the twentieth century.[3] Drawing on Sedgwick and Watkins, I examine how *Trapped in the Closet* uses affect-laden imagery and music to interrogate, complicate, and even deconstruct the binaries of knowledge = ignorance, urban = suburban, and homosexual = heterosexual that structure and maintain a ghettocentric imagination.

Mirroring the form of my principal object of analysis, this essay is structured episodically in an attempt to address the complexities of Kelly's work. The first section attends specifically to how *Trapped in the Closet* was received, anatomizing audience responses, including critics, fans, and the broader artistic community, and highlighting the way the series effaces traditional distinctions between high and low art. The second section is devoted to the relationship between the form and content of *Trapped in the Closet*. The third section focuses on the artist, R. Kelly, his celebrity persona and personal life, legal dramas, interviews, and performances to offer a few ways in which we might understand Kelly as figured on the "down low." Pitched specifically as an intervention in hip-hop scholarship, the fourth section focuses on the spatial landscapes and secondary characters, which structure and queer Watkins's concept of the "ghettocentric imagination" and converse with Mark Anthony Neal's writings on gender politics in "postsoul" hip-hop and R&B. This section is particularly interested in how *Trapped* sheds light on the complex relationships between and among concepts, like the "ghetto," "race," and "sexuality."

In the final section, I draw on my analysis of the content and popularity of *Trapped* to explain the cultural purchase of this work and the concept of "down low" more generally as instantiations of the structuring metaphor of the "glass closet" in epistemologies and representations of black sexuality. By glass closet, I refer to the simultaneity of hypervisibility and opacity that characterize representations of black sexuality in which the closet is both "obviously" transparent and a space for subterfuge. The glass closet, for those who inhabit it, is a space of containment that comprises the possibility for constraint and the possibility of possibility itself. Moreover, the trope of the glass closet produces the context for the creation and promulgation of the "down low" as a narrative to explain the further demonization of black sexuality, and black masculinity more acutely, in media and public health discourses.

READING CLOSET DRAMA

Described by *New York Magazine* as "the cultural event of the year,"[4] *Trapped in the Closet* has become somewhat of a darling among critics. Since the premier of the first five episodes in the summer of 2005, Kelly's magnum opus has attracted a great deal of attention. In her *New York Times* article, journalist Kelefa Sanneh attributes the popularity of *Trapped* to the rise of YouTube and the series' status as a viral hit.[5] Kelly produced and codirected the first 12 episodes, which were released on DVD in November 2005. In August 2007, the Independent Film Channel (IFC) aired ten new chapters of the series on its cable station and day-by-day online.[6] In an interview in *Variety* magazine, Kelly stated that he "thought of 'Trapped' as an independent film."[7] IFC General Manager Evan Shapiro, in a press statement, cited two reasons for the collaboration. Shapiro writes, "Perhaps . . . it's the way that Kelly pits the most influential, stereotyped elements of black pop culture . . . against each other in an irreconcilable moral conflict. Perhaps . . . it's because Trapped takes the traditional production values of a music video and turns them on their head. There's no hit single; there's no cute hook or catchy lyric . . . The focus is on story and character, usually at the expense of a hummable tune."[8] In other public statements, Shapiro compares Kelly to director John Waters, stating, "'Trapped,' like many of Waters' films . . . exists on the fringe of mainstream culture, but also on the forefront of the current (or next) cultural shift."[9] Shapiro's statements, however, do not acknowledge a history of black sexuality in the United States that includes both a legacy of slavery and a positioning of black sexuality as "other" to white Victorian sexual norms.[10]

Commentators have also compared Kelly to Charles Dickens, Homer, Shake-speare, and Tyler Perry. In many ways, *Trapped* has become a cultural product that proves Kelly's status as auteur. As one blogger suggests, "it represents raw artistic vision at its best—which is to say, at its most willfully ignorant."[11] This ignorance, as the blogger puts it, seems key to the series' success. As much of the criticism suggests, part of the popular interest in *Trapped* owes to its ability to exploit numerous potent stereotypes of black masculinity and sexuality. In this way, Dave Chappelle is another interlocutor in a conversation on the themes of Kelly's work. Like Chappelle, Kelly pushes buttons around race, in what John L. Jackson Jr. has described as a contemporary climate of "racial paranoia."[12] Similarly, as the title of Sanneh's article, "Outrageous Farce from R. Kelly: He's in on the Joke, Right?" suggests, there is a political investment in believing that Kelly (like Chappelle) control these representations. Sanneh argues that many of the biggest fans of *Trapped* "seem to think they're laughing at Mr. Kelly, not with him, as if the whole thing were some sort of glorious terrible mistake."[13] The condescension discernable in the interactions between Kelly and IFC News anchor Matt Singer lends credence to her argument. However, as Ien Ang notes in her study of the television drama *Dallas*, popular consumption of melodrama is rife with tensions produced by mass-culture ideology, which would assign low value (a classist formulation) to melodramatic form and the pleasure produced by watching. *Trapped* serves as another example of what Ang calls a "bad object," such that the pleasure audiences derive from viewing is rhetorically reconciled through claims that they take pleasure in the absurdity, ridiculousness, or "bad-ness" of the series.[14]

Kelly adds another layer of rhetorical embellishment in interviews about the series, when he often states that he has no idea how to explain *Trapped in the Closet*. In an *Entertainment Weekly* article, Kelly states, "I can explain all my other songs, but this is an alien to me."[15] It is difficult not to view Kelly's comments as anything but a form of posturing, given the history of his music on similar themes. Previously recorded songs like "Down Low (Nobody Has to Know)" and "Down Low, Double Life" demonstrate an ongoing interest in examining themes of infidelity, mistaken identity, sexual "indiscretion," and the precariousness of black sexuality figured on the "down low," reminiscent of the themes of blues and soul music to which Kelly's style is so deeply and explicitly indebted.

If mimicry is the highest form of flattery, *Trapped in the Closet* has received a significant amount of praise. In 2005, the writers of the animated comedy show *South Park* produced an episode, "*Trapped in the Closet*," that parodied the series. In the same year, Tichina Arnold, Tisha Campbell, and Duane Marin performed a live parody at the BET Comedy Awards. *MADtv* also aired a parody called "Trapped in the Cupboard," which playfully evokes the introduction in chapter 8 of *Trapped*, "Big Man." *Saturday Night Live*, "Weird Al" Yankovic, and even a Chicago-based Shakespearean troupe performed their takes on the enigmatic series. In 2006, a parody from No Film School called "Out of the Closet" began to circulate over the Internet, in which the creators splice audio from *Trapped in the Closet*, Kelly's other songs, and Dave Chappelle's "Piss On You," a comedic sketch on Kelly's statutory rape and child pornography trial, to produce a narra-tive eerily reminiscent of Kelly's recently concluded legal epic and suggests that Kelly might have been forecasting his possible future of same-sex sexual relations in prison. "Out of the Closet" vocalizes a significant aspect of popular readings of Kelly's text. However, I would argue that rather than contemplate whether *Trapped in the Closet* is Kelly's thinly veiled coming out story, we might view *Trapped* as a narrative that inextricably ties black sexuality to queerness in the popular imagination.

STRUCTURING THE CLOSET (SPOILER ALERT!)

Although many critics have tried, it is virtually impossible to describe accurately and comprehensively in a phrase the form and musical structure of *Trapped in the Closet*. Jody Rosen, in an article for *Slate,* describes the piece as a "psychedelic chitlin-circuit soap opera,"[16] while others have used less colorful descriptions situating Kelly's work in the tradition of the "hip-hopera," a term that high-lights the interplay between hip-hop sound and operatic form.[17] In many ways, *Trapped in the Closet* reminds viewers of B. Ruby Rich's definition of "new queer cinema": "There are traces in all of them of appropriation and pastiche, irony, as well as reworking a history with social constructionism very much in mind. Definitively breaking with previous humanist approaches and the films and tapes that accompanied identity politics, these works are irreverent, energetic, alter-nately minimalist and excessive. Above all they're full of pleasure."[18] The pleasure audiences derive from *Trapped in the Closet* is partially explained by the narrative form of the content and musical structure of the storytelling. The signature melodic strain of synthesized strings in the first episode (and several subsequent chapters) sonically conjures the experience of watching a 1950s melodrama. As Peter Brooks suggests, melodrama is a "mode of excess" with a fundamental drive toward "expressivity"; its principal mode is that of "uncovering, demonstrating, and making operative the essential moral universe in a postsacred era."[19] Daphne Brooks, citing the mutual constitution of melodrama and minstrelsy in nineteenth-century American popular culture, explains that the "moral ethics of melodrama produced 'racial legibility' in addition to an apparently clear moral code."[20] Similarly, *Trapped in the Closet*, in its deployment of the cinematic codes of melodrama, audio-visualizes the excesses of black sexuality and stages its epistemological unincorporability.

The serialization of *Trapped in the Closet* is reminiscent of the format of soap operas, serial novels, or the Spanish-language telenovela. *Trapped* employs the structural characteristics of these genres in order to highlight the spatial dynamics of character interaction. The site of Rufus's church hosts some of Kelly's most potent messages about the relationships between sexuality and race as well as the consequences of its contradictory, histrionic representation. As Ang explains, the "psychological credibility" of soap-opera characters is "subordinated to the functioning of these characters in melodramatic situations," a fact that emphasizes the series' emotional effect.[21] The imagined situations depicted in *Trapped in the Closet* as melodrama are constituted and surrounded by cultural myths and fantasies of "race" and "class" among other forms of identification, which draw less on the "bare facts of these situations than on the metaphorical role they play in the popular imagination."[22] *Trapped* is structured as a recitative, a musical declamation that hovers between song and ordinary speech, and in a traditional opera provides an exegesis of the scene before the song begins. While the operatic recitative is usually marked by roboto (having no tempo), Kelly's recitative includes a driving beat. A two-measure progression of chords, which moves from diminished to E-major, a transition coded in Western music for staging tension, sets up a hypnotic loop. The stasis, caused by the repetitive chord progression, allows Kelly to spin out the storylines in a through-composed lyrical narrative, which in addition to the beat further connects the piece to a recognizable hip-hop sound. The instrumentation is minimal and includes synthesized strings, keyboard, and tympani.

Inexpensive to produce and drawing on the generic codes of melodrama, opera, musical theater, and silent film, Kelly's instrumental accompaniment is principally about highlighting the "drama" of the narrative. One could argue that the instrumentation, which draws on well-known, well-rehearsed musical codes, is meant to be understood not at the level of cognition but affectually, since each production convention works to minimize and invisibilize its function. The instrumentation also centers Kelly's virtuosic vocal performance, as he becomes a modern-day Uncle Remus telling the story of sexual "indiscretions" in urban and suburban Chicago. Common vocal strategies in Kelly's storytelling include elision, whereby Kelly begins his next line before finishing out the last, stylistic changes in his ventriloquisms of the numerous gendered, racialized, and queered characters,[23] and the use of polyphonic vocal clusters to draw attention to key terms and phrases in the narrative, such as "closet," "get on the line," and "the package."

The narrative is intricate and to detail every chapter would exceed the boundaries of this essay. However, here I will provide my own idiosyncratic rendering of *Trapped in the Closet*, focusing on its settings and the complex, spatially inflected relationships that constitute the drama. The series begins with Sylvester waking up in the bed of a presumed one-night stand. Within the first three chapters, Cathy (a.k.a. Mary), Rufus, and his lover, Chuck, are introduced in a developing narrative about sexual infidelity as Rufus and Cathy's apartment sets the tone for what ensues at Sylvester's suburban estate. Upon Sylvester's arrival home, both the protagonist and audiences come to understand the cause of the unexpected male voice that responds to his call and the possibility of his own wife's extramarital sexual activity.

Following a dysfunctional sex scene, Sylvester finds the evidence of his earlier suspicions: a used condom buried in the sheets of his bed. Sylvester confronts his wife, Gwendolyn, who then reveals that she knows that he has cheated as well. The episode then takes a rather strange turn as Gwendolyn, in response to Sylvester's demand to know the name of her lover (whom Sylvester has already met on his drive home), provides a string of names and connections to characters previously seen and not yet introduced. Gwendolyn states (as told through Sylvester's subjective lens),

> Wipes her nose and asks me about a girl name Tina I thought to myself, said, "It sounds familiar." Then said, "I'll probably know her if I seen her." Then I said "Anyway girl what the hell does that got to do with this man?!" She said, "He know my girl Roxanne"
> I said, "Who the hell is Roxanne!?" Then she said, "Roxanne is a friend of mine who know this guy named Chuck" "Chuck's cool with this guy named Rufus" And I'm sitting there like what the fuck. Then she says, "Rufus' wife Cathy, we both went to high school She introduce me to the policeman that stopped you."[24]

This surprising exposition works in at least three ways: it serves to structure the core characters of the drama, foreshadowing the action in scenes for the succeeding ten chapters; it demonstrates the imbrications of "heterosexual" and "homosexual" relationships within the narrative; and it gestures toward the abilities of sexual relationships to collapse spatial and economic boundaries. Audiences later understand that Gwendolyn's friend Roxanne is Tina's lover (chapter 16). Tina is also the "baby's mama" of Twan, Gwendolyn's brother who has been recently released from prison (chapter 15). And Gwendolyn's lover, Officer James, also knows Chuck and Rufus (chapter 11); the context of this revelation suggests that perhaps Officer James might also act on his same-sex attraction.

Following Gwendolyn's soliloquy, Sylvester and Gwendolyn quickly make up, sharing laughter over their recent choices, resignifying them as "drama" created by the craziness of other people. Across the 22 episodes, a recurring response to moments of sexual revelations is laughter. This emotional response from the characters is also often misrecognized as in the instance when Officer James mistakes Gwendolyn and Sylvester's laughter for the evidence of domestic violence. James confronts Sylvester; Twan, Gwendolyn's brother, comes home, and the narrative comes to another climatic moment in the only shooting of a person. Reminiscent of the dramatic climax in *West Side Story*, Twan is shot in the arm as he intervenes in the duel between James and Sylvester. The commotion arouses the suspicion of Rosie, referred to as the "nosy neighbor," who provides comic relief to the scene when she rings the doorbell armed with a spatula. While Rosie lightens up the story line, she also signifies a particular class anxiety that remains a subtext within the series. Many of the characters in *Trapped in the Closet* appear to be middle class, although they are negotiating problems associated with urban poverty.[25] Her spatula emblematizes intraracial class anxieties, which, similar to the logic of bringing a cooking tool to intervene in gunplay, is hopelessly unable to control the potency of fantasies about black deviance or the possibility of black people behaving "poorly."

Chapters 8 through 12 stage the story unfolding in three distinct locations: Cathy and Rufus's apartment, Sylvester and Gwendolyn's suburban home, and the house in which Officer James and his white wife, Bridget, live. In these episodes we learn that Bridget has also been having an affair and that her lover has fathered the unborn child she carries. Cathy, over the phone, reveals to her high-school friend Gwendolyn that she slept with Sylvester. Cathy and Rufus continue to argue about Rufus's affair, as Cathy suggests that Rufus has now put her at risk of contracting HIV. While Cathy's argument signifies a typical response (one that dominates the framing of "down low" in the media) to the revelation of Rufus's same-sex desire, the narrative of *Trapped in the Closet* does not allow the audience to view her as blameless victim. In fact, the audience later finds out in chapter 13 that Cathy promised to pay Sylvester to sleep with her that night.

Chapter 8 also marks an innovation in Kelly's storytelling as he creates a new role for himself as omniscient narrator, no longer voicing the subjectivity of Sylvester, and perhaps increasing the role of a traditional anthropological gaze. The scene is particularly striking as it stages two instances of men contained by closets of sorts. At James and Bridget's home, the narrator emerges, materializing from thin air, from the kitchen closet while Bridget's lover, a little person named "Big Man," emerges from the kitchen cupboard. The choice to have the narrator emerge from the closet seems to literalize Sedgwick's argument in that the relationship between knowledge and the structure of the closet are inextricably linked. However, the staging of two competing closets complicates Sedgwick's work and demonstrates its blind spot around race. As a counternarrative, *Trapped* audiovisualizes the contained black male body as purveyor of knowledge and ignorance. Big Man's cupboard, like Sylvester's earlier closet, serves as a form of protection in its ability to hide the materiality of indiscretion, although it is never a stable hiding place for long. Rather, the cupboard = closet functions for the black male body as a space of inevitable discovery (and the functions of knowledge) and escape (the embodied opportunity to opt out of epistemological scripts through misrecognition).

Chapters 13 through 22 mark the next installment of Kelly's series. It begins by staging a meeting between Cathy and Sylvester at a restaurant that Tina and Roxanne manage. The restaurant scenes are among the first to visualize the urban landscape of Chicago, a point that is emphasized narratively by Twan's conversation with his friend Streetz, who informs Twan that his co-conspirators in the drug bust that put Twan in jail are right inside the very same restaurant. In a high moment of melodramatic tension, Twan attempts to kill Tina and Roxanne for testifying against him in the court proceedings that sent him to jail for drug possession. In this scene, audiences learn that Tina is having Twan's child and is currently in a relationship with Roxanne. The knowledge of this same-sex relationship causes Twan and Sylvester to lose their tempers, and Sylvester initially plans to shoot them until he remembers (vis-á-vis the structuring logics of patriarchy and homophobia) that he loves watching women make out. Sylvester is also able to persuade Twan to relent by reminding his brother-in-law that any action would jeopardize his parole.

The narrative then takes another striking turn as the audience follows the narrator to church. The church scene marks the first time that diegetic music is performed, as it is the first moment where the source of sound originates from action in the film's world. In many ways the church becomes the central location for the narrative, as Chuck reveals to Rufus over the phone that he's in the hospital with "the package." The audience also witnesses an interaction between multiple characters all performed by Kelly, in which Kelly, playing visiting minister (Reverend Mosley James Evans) at Rufus's church, attempts to convert Pimp Luscious, also played by Kelly, to Christianity. This scene is particularly important in my discussion on R. Kelly in the third section. Chapter 20 features another instance of a character trapped in the closet. In this episode, O'Dale, the church janitor, Rosie's husband and Sylvester's neighbor, and still another character played by Kelly, is eavesdropping on Chuck and Rufus's conversation from a nearby closet at the church. O'Dale's eavesdropping and subsequent conversation with his "nosey" wife sets the context for the last episode of the series so far. The final chapter, a riff on the "Goin' Steady" number in *Bye Bye Birdie*, visualizes the relationships between all the characters introduced over the course of the 22 episodes as they make and receive phone calls about Pastor Rufus's sexual "indiscretion" and the possibility of the pastor having "the package." As the subtitle of the full 22-episode DVD—"The Big Package"—makes clear, *Trapped in the Closet* is concerned with the dangerous enormity of fantasies that surround and construct black masculinity and sexuality.

THE DOUBLE LIVES OF R. KELLY

As journalistic speculations and its artistic derivatives emblematize, popular discourse on *Trapped* often seeks to find some referent in Kelly's life to account for the outlandishness of the narrative. In an interview with performance artists Neal Medlyn and Kenny Mellman (Kiki and Herb) featured in *New York Magazine*, Mellman typifies this sentiment when he states, "I just picture him alone in a studio with that same track playing over and over and over and over, and he's quietly going crazy, and he's so excited, and suddenly he realizes that he might be going to jail. And suddenly the story takes a turn and we learn why Twan went to jail. I mean, is it autobiography? Are all the characters just different parts of Kelly's personality?"[26] There are several narrative elements in *Trapped* that seem to correlate to Kelly's life, namely, that the drama is set in Kelly's hometown of Chicago; its main character takes Kelly's middle name, Sylvester, as his moniker; and the theme of sexual indiscretion comes only a few years after Kelly's June 2002 indictment for child pornography.[27] Moreover, the focus on the church in later episodes not only asks us to remember his popular hit "I Believe I Can Fly" but also signifies Kelly's vocal training under renowned gospel composer and music teacher Dr. Lena McLin. The song Kelly performs as Rev. Mosley James Evans, a version of Chicago-based Rev. George Allen Jordan's "Jesus Can Work It Out," further emphasizes Kelly's roots in the Chicago church.

The action of the church scene (chapters 18 and 19) also provides significant insights into how R. Kelly is figured on the "down low." Opening with Rev. Moseley (Kelly) singing a spirited version of "Work It Out," the audience soon follows Rufus into his church office where he has been summoned away to take a phone call from his lover, Chuck. In this moment, the audience witnesses one of the most emotional and tender scenes of the series, as Rufus and Chuck discuss the effects of not having seen one another in some time (presumably not since the temporal era of chapter 3). Rufus then attempts to break things off with Chuck, who blackmails Rufus by claiming that he will go to the media. When Rufus offers to meet with Chuck again, Chuck explains that he is in the hospital (which later the closeted, eavesdropping figure O'Dale interprets as Chuck having the "package").

The audience then returns to the main action of the sanctuary. In this scene, Kelly plays both the visiting Reverend and a near-converted sinner, Pimp Luscious.

(Reverend Evans) Pimp Luscious, you have been on my heart Hallelujah, thank you Jesus, and I looked at you and got a word from God mmmmm now Pimp . . . Luscious God is tellin' me you don't wanna pimp no more he sayin to me he saying you wanna stop pimpin' aaaahlllll these hoes

(church man) Amen (Reverend Moseley) and turn your life around Ha Ha (church man) just turn it around, Luscious (Reverend Evans) Now if you want it, God will do it for you, yes he will

(church man) Yeah (Reverend Evans) come on choir help me sing it, come on (Reverend and choir) You can do it Pimp Luscious (Reverend Evans) just stop pimpin' (church man) just stop pimpin' (Reverend) Luscious (choir) you can do it Pimp Luscious (Reverend) just cut it loose, let it go (choir) you can do it pimp Luscious (Reverend) I believe, oh I believe. Now ya'll just come on saints and give Pimp Luscious a hand as he leaves the stage. Come on give him some of that agape godly love. Then young Bishop Craig says are you seriously gonna stop pimpin' and give your life to God? And Pimp Luscious stops dead in his tracks and says, shhhhh, shhhhh, shhhhhhhh Then Pimp Luscious says, "I, I ai—ai-ain't ee-ee-ever go-go-gonna s-s-s-stop p-p-p-pimpin', pimpin's for life. T-tt-tell you what c-cc-cousin. C-church, church (directed to choir and congregation). (Turning back to his friend and sidekick Bishop Craig) The only thing a p-ppimp don' caught up in here is the ho-ly ghost. Now let's go-g—go get out of here and m-make this m-mmoney.[28]

As the lyrics describe, Kelly stages his personal moral antagonisms (also evidenced in the wide variations in his song choices throughout his career) to confront himself about his pimpin'. And although Reverend Evans makes a valiant attempt, it is also clear that Pimp Luscious remains unchanged. Mark Anthony Neal, in his analysis of Kelly's earlier hit "Bump 'n' Grind" aptly describes the dynamics at work here. Neal writes, "Kelly's collapse of the sexual and the romantic—really a collapse of the public and the private dimensions of African-American sexual relations—naturally suggests that many of these narratives and artists simply represented a pool of resources that Kelly could appropriate to articulate his own existential concerns, while also acknowledging the constraints placed on previous generations of artists in terms of how they coded sexual innuendo in a language that could be widely distributed."[29] Kelly's career, as Neal rightly suggests, may be another form of "pimping" in its ability to widely distribute sexually charged music and imagery that reference his personal sexual dramas. In other words, Kelly's musical persona, public = personal sexual drama, and music figure him as trapped within a glass closet.[30] Moreover, the precise location of the church as both the scene of Pimp Luscious's intervention and Chuck and Rufus's attempts at reconciliation encourages further speculation about Kelly's double lives, as he locates these emotionally charged moments in the birthplace of "down low" culture in the popular imagination.[31] The doubling of narrative structure in which both sets of men (Chuck and Rufus, Reverend Moseley and Pimp Luscious) fail to come to a moral reconciliation on sexuality serves as metaphor for Kelly's life, as the pairs stand in for the artist's inability to unshackle his sexual proclivities from his musical morality tales. Kelly, and the figure of the "DL" brother more generally, therefore explicitly produce anxieties about the intermingling of the sacred and the secular, marriage and infidelity, and private sexual relations and public personas.

"A GHETTO LOVE IS THE LAW THAT WE LIVE BY"

Watkins, in a discussion of 1990s black urban cinema, writes that one of "the foremost themes that resonates throughout the ghetto action picture is the idea that poor black urban communities are locations of entrapment and repression."[32] R. Kelly's work asks us to think about what is precisely trapped and repressed in urban = suburban black communities. Many of the characters in *Trapped* are middle class: the minister, the restaurateurs, the police officer. However, *Trapped* also shows the way alternative and criminalized economies (and particularly economies based on sex work) intersect with black, middle-class modes and mores. Big Man, Tina, Cathy, Pimp Luscious, and his sidekick Bishop Craig are all tied to alternative sexual economies. And Sylvester gets drawn into the drama of the closet as a result of agreeing to have sex with Cathy for money. Later chapters of *Trapped* also reveal that Sylvester utilizes his ties with the mafia (chapter 21) to support his impeccable taste for fine suits, expensive cars, and mortgage of his suburban estate. *Trapped* also forces us to rethink the tenor of critical discourse in hip-hop scholarship. Focusing on Watkins and Neal, I suggest that we must think through sexuality (and the spectral quality of queerness) as another vector of identity that constitutes a "ghettocentric imagination."

Watkins and Neal both focus on the "(dis)organization of black familial life" as a major theme in black urban cultural production and a frame with which to more clearly understand black urban space.[33] Watkins writes, "The notion that black familial life is largely responsible for ghetto poverty pervades the cultural landscape" of black entertainment.[34] Although *Trapped* is certainly concerned with black familial life, as the love triangle between Cathy, Rufus, and Chuck epitomizes, the connection between sexuality and economics is better described by a politics of disidentification and disavowal than a crisis in a heteronormative, nuclear family structure. Rather than seeing the drama around sexuality and the family as idealizing or privileging heterosexuality, *Trapped* demonstrates a wide range of sexual activities and desires, posited as inescapable in the narrative.

Moreover, *Trapped* helps us rethink relationships between men and women, particularly as they have been discussed in Neal's chapter, "Baby Mama (Drama) and Baby Daddy (Trauma): Post-Soul Gender Politics."[35] In *Trapped*, the core characters function as couples and siblings, not as parents or children.[36] However, even as *Trapped* presents one case of "mama's baby, papa's maybe,"[37] evidenced by the James–Bridget–Big Man triangle, other vectors of identity—namely, race and corporeal difference—complicate reading this subplot as simply a failure of traditional family values. Bridget, the first white character featured in the series, is ventriloquized with a heavy southern accent and visualized as obese. All of these forms of difference obfuscate the notion of black family politics as Neal and Watkins might imagine them by demonstrating a resistance to presenting typical scripts of black female and male coupling. Furthermore, the ubiquity of queer relationships in *Trapped* forces us to acknowledge that gender politics must exceed an examination between men and women to include the relationships occurring between men and between women. While *Trapped* admittedly does not focus much critical attention on the dynamics of the queer relationship between Tina and Roxanne, the existence of their relationship spurs an extended conversation on black masculinity between Sylvester and his brother-in-law, Twan. Moreover, the issue of Tina's unborn child queers a narrative about the need for a heteronuclear family. Instead Roxanne, with her kiss and declaration, "I'm f—king her now," performatively enacts a space for queer families.

The portrayal of Rufus and Chuck's relationship is in large part what is most compelling to me about the series. At first glance, it seems that the series, like other popular representations of "down low," demonizes the couple's desire. Cathy and Sylvester's initial reactions support that reading. However, *Trapped* does not vest Cathy or Sylvester with moral authority; rather, it encourages the viewer to think about how each character interacts with the structure of the closet, literally and metaphorically. *Trapped* also suggests that we think about the various functions of the closet, adding a crucial nuance to Sedgwick's theory by highlighting how the closet not only structures knowledge (about the self and the world) but also has particular ramifications for the constitution and maintenance of "class," "race," and "gender." In the "Special Features" section on the *Trapped in the Closet* DVD,

R. Kelly reveals that another figure lurks in each of the closets, which alternatively contain Sylvester and O'Dale: a set of Rufus's golf clubs. It is not simply Rufus's sexuality that might be structured by a closet but also his class status and the expression of classed leisure. Reflecting on its entirety, *Trapped* pretends to be an urban drama but focuses on the way sexuality effaces the distinctions between the urban and the suburban and exposes the false dichotomy between the black middle class and underclass. Kelly's "outing" of middle-class sexual improprieties prevents the kind of behavioral bracketing enacted in middle-class assessments of the underclass (where out-of-wedlock births, suicide, and even drug use are screened off from scrutiny).

TRAPPED IN THE EPISTEMOLOGICAL CLOSET

Understanding the glass closet not only may help us refigure our understandings of black geopolitics but also points to reasons why there is a transpolitical (that defies categories such as conservative or liberal) investment in the notion of the "down low." Fanon, among others, demonstrates how blackness becomes the object of (white) ways of knowing. As an object, blackness becomes the thing we always already know—that is, the opposite of white. And as both Du Bois and Sedgwick allude to in their prescriptions of the twentieth century, the problem of this period is fundamentally tied to a crisis in visibility. *Trapped in the Closet* encourages us to think precisely about how race, class, gender, and sexuality, both popularly and epistemologically, are structured by the space of the glass closet. Moreover, the popularity of *Trapped* urges us to consider how the concept of the "down low" functions as an ideograph, which requires racist fantasies about black masculinity and sexuality to infer its meaning.

Since the mid-1990s, we have witnessed the ascension of the "down low," a term that is generally used to describe the experiences of black men who have sex with other men (and women) and do not identify as gay, in black popular discourse. Two major conceptualizations or explanations have emerged to describe this "subset" of black culture. The identification model, typified by the series *The DL Chronicles* and Keith Boykin's *Beyond the Down Low: Sex, Lies, and Denial in Black America*, suggests that "down low brothers" are victims of excessively homophobic black communities, which are unable to make room for gay and lesbian identities within blackness. The second mode of explanation, as seen in Oprah Winfrey's special on the "down low" with self-appointed expert J. L. King, relies on fantasies about black masculinity that mark black men as inherently dangerous, deceptive, and prone to trickery. Both explanatory models make invisible the nature of sexuality as a dynamic, fluid process constructed, at least in part, at the intersections of space (actual and imagined) and desire.

Trapped offers a different mode to explain the popularity of the down low by highlighting its ideographic nature, akin to Raymond Williams's "structure of feeling," which he defines as "firm and definite as 'structure' suggests, yet it operates in the most delicate and least tangible parts of our activity."[38] Trapped audiovisualizes the manner with which emotion and sexual desire are partially derived from broader structural forces, including economic shifts, migration, and negotiations with (urban = public) space. As the golf clubs in Rufus's closet suggest, discourses on the down low mask class-based anxieties about blacks behaving badly (read: poorly) and middle-class fears regarding the contagion of inappropriate sexual relations. Examining the trope of the glass closet and its structuring relationship to epistemologies of black sexuality, therefore, allows for the examination of black sexualities as historically situated, culturally embedded, and dynamically produced. Moreover, understanding the "glass closet" helps situate the "down low" as one string in a broader symphony of epistemologies and representations of black sexuality.[39]

While numerous scholars have looked to popular culture to discuss representations of race, gender, and sexuality, studying these moments of signification allows us not only to apprehend broader cultural and social forces in operation but also to perceive how the process of representation mirrors processes of identification— namely, in its ability to articulate relationships between meaning, language, and culture. As *Trapped in the Closet* evidences, the "down low," as it appears in popular representations, signifies a process and paradigm that signals a gap in the critical literatures of sexuality studies as well as an absence of epistemological frameworks that are able to address the complexity of black sexual expression. The discursive formation of the "down low" is the presence of that absence.

ACKNOWLEDGMENTS

Thanks to the guest editors of *Souls*, Elizabeth Kai Hinton, Herman Beavers, John L. Jackson Jr., Mark Anthony Neal, Marc Lamont Hill, Camille Charles, Sunny Yang, Benson Gilchrist, and Jasmine Cobb, for comments on this article. Special thanks to Guthrie P. Ramsey Jr. for assistance with analysis of the musical form of *Trapped in the Closet*.

NOTES

1. S. Craig Watkins, *Representing: Hip-Hop Culture and the Production of Black Cinema* (Chicago: University of Chicago Press, 1998), 197.
2. Ibid. The term "ghetto" has relatively recently acquired a pejorative quality in black speech. That quality certainly reflects tensions that have long been present in the black community, but it also reflects the more recent—and constantly growing and rigidifying—gap between the underclass and the middle class. To articulate the existence of a "ghettocentric imagination," then, is also to articulate that this is a cultural imaginary whose performative characteristics are assumed to refer to only one segment of the black community.
3. Eve K. Sedgwick, *Epistemologies of the Closet* (Berkeley: University of California Press, 1990), 11. Sedgwick's assessment of one key crisis in the twentieth century comes roughly eighty years after W. E. B Du Bois's prediction that the "problem of the twentieth century is the problem of the color-line—the relation of the darker to the lighter races of men." I envision this article, and my larger dissertation project, as an opportunity to examine exactly how Sedgwick and Du Bois's declarations describe black sexuality in the twenty-first century.
4. "*Trapped in the Closet*' Chapter Fifteen: Up in Smoke," *New York Magazine*, August 15, 2007.

5. Kelefa Sanneh, "Outrageous Farce from R. Kelly: He's in on the Joke, Right?" *New York Times*, August 20, 2007.

6. Jive Records also released a DVD of episodes thirteen through twenty-two on August 21, 2007.

7. Steven Zeitchik, "IFC Climbs into 'Closet' with R. Kelly," *Variety*, July 11, 2007, http://www.variety.com/article/VR1117968393?refCatId=14.

8. J. Kimball, "The Independent Film Channel's GM on R. Kelly's TitC," *The Listenerd* (blog), August 12, 2007, http://thelistenerd.com/2007/08/12/the-independent-film-channels-gm-on-r-kellys-titc/.

9. Evan Shapiro, "Reeler Pinch Hitter: Evan Shapiro, IFC," *Screening Gotham* (blog), August 2, 2007, http://www.thereeler.com/the_blog/reeler_pinch_hitter_evan_shapiro.php.

10. Countless scholars have made this claim. Instructive to my work is Daphne A. Brooks's *Bodies in Dissent* and Fred Moten's piece, "Preface for a Solo by Miles Davis," *Women & Performance: A Journal of Feminist Theory* 17, no. 2: 217–46. Both Brooks and Moten theorize the relationships between race, space, and sexuality and focus in part on the condition of containment. Fanon's canonic *Black Skin, White Masks* (New York: Grove, 1967) is also deeply instructive on these issues.

11. Sanneh, "Outrageous Farce."

12. John L. Jackson Jr., *Racial Paranoia: The Unintended Consequences of Political Correctness* (New York: Basic Civitas Books, 2008).

13. Sanneh, "Outrageous Farce."

14. Ibid.

15. C. Schonberger, "R. Kelly Returns to the 'Closet,'" *Entertainment Weekly*, July 27, 2007.

16. Jody Rosen, "R. Kelly Gets the Joke Why *Trapped in the Closet* Is a Brilliant Career Move," *Slate*, August 22, 2007, http://www.slate.com/articles/arts/music_box/2007/08/r_kelly_gets_the_joke.html.

17. A notable example of the "hip-hopera," includes Robert Townsend's MTV made-for-television movie *Carmen: A Hip Hopera*, which featured R&B and pop darling Beyoncé.

18. B. Ruby Rich quoted in D. Contreras, "New Queer Cinema: Spectacle, Race, Utopia," in *New Queer Cinema: A Critical Reader* (New Brunswick, NJ: Rutgers University Press 2004), 119.

19. Peter Brooks, *Melodramatic Imagination: Balzac, Henry James, Melodrama, and the Mode of Excess* (New Haven: Yale University Press, 1976), 15.

20. Daphne Brooks, *Bodies in Dissent: Spectacular Performances of Race and Freedom, 1850–1910* (Durham, NC: Duke University Press, 2006), 37.

21. Ibid., 64.

22. Ibid.

23. The vocal stylization of each character becomes more pronounced in the latter part of the series.

24. *Trapped in the Closet, Chapters 1–22: The Big Package*, chapter 5 (Zoomba Films, 2007).

25. The characters' lifestyles might also signify the ways that "ghetto fabulous" constitutes a replication of middle-class consumption and a new configuration of poverty, whereby the relatively easy access to cable TV, cell phones, and other cheap audio and visual technology allow for a much higher standard of living than one might find in rural poverty, even as it is a highly unstable economic circumstance.

26. *Trapped in the Closet*, chapter 15.

27. Another reading of *Trapped in the Closet* may be that R. Kelly has created his own version of a story akin to Humbert Humbert's subjectivity in Nabakov's *Lolita*. Here I am thinking particularly about the dynamic between Humbert and Clare Quilty.

28. *Trapped in the Closet*, chapter 19.

29. Mark Anthony Neal, *Soul Babies: Popular Culture and the Post-Soul Aesthetic* (New York: Routledge, 2002), 17.

30. Michael Jackson is another figure that exemplifies this paradigm, although his music speaks less consistently to these issues than R. Kelly's.

31. J. L. King, in his part-memoir, part self-help guide, and part-exposé, suggests that the church is one of the primary cruising grounds for "down low brothers."

32. Watkins, *Representing*, 198.

33. Ibid.

34. Ibid., 219.

35. Mark Anthony Neal's use of "postsoul" seems to correlate to Mark A. Reid's suggestion of postnegritude as a temporal and political category of analysis. Neal writes, "I use the term post-soul to describe the political, social and cultural experiences of the African-American community since the end of the civil rights and Black Power movements" (3).

36. One possible exception is that Sylvester calls his neighbors "mommy" and "daddy," although the narrative is not particularly clear on whether O'Dale and Rosie are his biological parents.

37. Hortense Spillers, "Mama's Baby, Papa's Maybe: An American Grammar Book," in *The Black Feminist Reader*, ed. Joy James (Malden, MA: Blackwell, 2000).

38. Raymond Williams, "The Analysis of Culture," in *Cultural Theory and Popular Culture: A Reader*, 2nd ed., ed. John Storey (Athens: University of Georgia Press, 1998), 53.

39. In his article "Preface for a Solo by Miles Davis," Fred Moten cites Theodor Adorno's theory on radio symphony, which is similar to how I regard the relationship between the down low and black sexuality. Adorno writes, "The particular, when chipped off from the unity of the symphony [as trivia, quotation, reductively expressive detail], still retains a trace of the unity in which it functioned. A genuine symphonic theme, even if it takes the whole musical stage and seems to be temporarily hypostatized and to desert the rest of the music, is nonetheless of such a kind as to impress upon one that it is actually nothing in itself but basically something 'out of' something else. Even in its isolation it bears the mark of the whole" (238).

CHAPTER 2

CRAIG BREWER AND KARA WALKER

SEXING THE DIFFERENCE AND REBUILDING THE SOUTH

SIMONE C. DRAKE

> Places, places are still there . . . it will be there for you, waiting for you . . . Because even though it's all over—over and done with—it's going to always be there waiting for you.
>
> —Toni Morrison, *Beloved*

THE MEMORY OF A PLACE AND ITS history never dies, as the epigraph drawn from Toni Morrison's *Beloved* observes. Morrison's rendering of memory as an eternally powerful force is perhaps especially true of the American south, with its history of racial violence and segregation—whether during slavery or Jim Crow. The South is the "it" that Morrison insists will always be there waiting for all Americans, producing a *rememory* that like a vortex will pull Americans into that eternal place. For white American film writer and director Craig Brewer and African American visual artist Kara Walker, an unlikely duo for comparison, the segregated South is still there. Both artists attempt to produce art that make the history and memory of the South relevant for contemporary audiences. The themes and settings for both artists' work resonate with moves in the academy to develop a literary and cultural studies subfield of new Southern studies, and the themes and settings also resonate with the reverse migrations to cities like Atlanta, Nashville, and Houston that were catalyzed in the late twentieth century. These intellectual and migratory developments inform Brewer and Walker's investment in remembering the social, political, cultural, and economic history of the South in order to encourage contemporary audiences to "look south."[1]

Brewer and Walker intertwine memory, geography, and history to interrogate what I identify as a national, racial melancholia that is rooted in the pervasive visual economies of sexual difference. Both artists, working in different media, present depictions of how racial inequalities and a history that haunts the present create a melancholic bind for white America, a bind that forces white America to share racially marginalized people's racial melancholia. In this essay, I draw on Robyn Wiegman's work on comparative anatomies and theories of sexual difference and Wahneema Lubiano's introduction to *The House That Race Built*. I draw on these texts to demonstrate how Brewer and Walker's art contributes to critical race and gender discourse and how their art is more than the spectacle and titillation that frames the popular perception of their work. Brewer's films *Hustle & Flow* and *Black Snake Moan* and Kara Walker's antebellum silhouettes reveal an investment in challenging popular representations of the ways in which black and white bodies have been raced and gendered in American culture. Their investment is ultimately an effort to make Morrison's "there"—the past, the South, slavery—an inhabitable space both literally and figuratively for US citizens across racial lines.

DEVELOPING A BLUES SENSIBILITY

The films of writer and director Craig Brewer call upon scholars of black culture to consider critically the intersections of race, class, memory, and geography. The first two installments in Brewer's music series, *Hustle & Flow* (2005) and *Black Snake Moan* (2007), do far more than indulge in the raunch and spectacle that could be quickly assumed by previews and clips from both films that capture a gritty, rawness of Southern life today in Memphis and Mississippi. But this is not why Brewer's work should be viewed as more than trite indulgences in the raunch and spectacle that US audiences clamor to. His work demands critical analysis because it presents a perverse depiction of how what scholar Anne Anlin Cheng refers to as the United States' "exclusion-yet-retention" of racialized others creates a shared racial melancholy between the dominant white racial order and its racial others.

Attention to race relations in the antebellum South often focuses solely on the master-slave relationship. This focus perpetuates an image of the slave experience as a plantation experience, with slaves either toiling in the fields or working in the "big house." *Hustle & Flow* and *Black Snake Moan* call upon viewers to look beyond the plantation to the cities and the rural spaces where both free and enslaved blacks and poor whites encountered one another, sometimes with animosity, sometimes socially, and sometimes as allies. Through contemporary relationships between black men and white women, in particular, but not exclusively, Brewer repeats the lesser attended to black-poor-white relationship that has roots in slavery. In addition to his remembering of that relationship, Brewer also reverses the stereotyped raced and gendered constructions of black men and white women. His male protagonists shed the hypersexuality that is all too often forced on them by Hollywood, the media, and themselves, all most to the point of impotency. Brewer's white female protagonists, in turn, are literally sluts and whores, hypersexualized, poor white women who are not Southern belles. These female protagonists defy every tenet of the cult of true womanhood, and when class is combined with their blatant disregard for social conventions, they, too, defy the image that Hollywood and the media presents of white women. The reversals that Brewer makes are framed by a rememory of lesser-noted cross-racial relationships that are framed by music.

In interviews, Brewer often explains his commitment to producing a set of films that are rooted in music that is indigenous to the South. His first film, *Hustle & Flow*, is immersed in crunk. His sophomore production, *Black Snake Moan*, is entrenched in a blues matrix, specifically outlaw blues. His upcoming film, *Maggie Lynn*, attends to country music, and he promises a fourth music film that is all about soul. Music operates in Brewer's films as a Southern vernacular art form that is not raced or gendered. In fact, Brewer insists that *Hustle* and *Black Snake Moan* are biographical, depicting his own struggles with economic hardship and debilitating anxiety attacks. Crunk and the literal "black snake moan" are the lyrical routes to his own escape from the various demons that possess him. Brewer uses music and counternarrative, then, to repair his own racial melancholia, and in doing so, he signifies on key tropes in such antebellum and postbellum narratives as, Harriet Beecher Stowe's *Uncle Tom's Cabin*, D. W. Griffith's *Birth of a Nation*, William Faulkner's *Sanctuary*, Richard Wright's *Native Son*, and Tennessee Williams's *A Streetcar Named Desire*. Brewer's films, however, function as signifying structures of intertextual revision with a complicated twist. The complication arises from the fact that Brewer is a white writer/director who relies heavily on the African American signifying tradition in order to deconstruct popular, preferred images of the South and of black men and white women.

Brewer's turn to art to repair himself is nothing new. The type of art that he turns to and how he positions himself in that art form, however, alludes to George Schuyler's ideologies about race, region, and art in his well-noted essay "The Negro Art-Hokum" (663), while simultaneously demanding a critical inquiry into the limits and fallacies of the "blackness of blackness" that Henry Louis Gates Jr. and so many other scholars assign exclusively to black culture.[2] The shift from the national discourse that Gates's assessment is rooted in to a postnational discourse that dismisses notions of authenticity and identity politics, much like Schuyler's 1926 assertion, provides a space to understand Brewer's work as not simply exploiting the raw, taboo elements that are implied in *Black Snake Moan* when Lazarus (Samuel L. Jackson) intends to "cure" Rae (Christina Ricci) of her promiscuity by chaining her half-naked body to his radiator. When Brewer constructs narratives around black and poor-white relations in the contemporary South, Brewer acts out Cornel West's assertion that the post-9/11 United States is "at a moment now in which a blues nation has to learn from a blues people" (18+). Brewer has what West calls a "blues sensibility"—a commitment to democracy and equality and the ability to respond to wrongs without vengeance, but instead to respond through the pursuit of justice. West draws on an observation by Toni Morrison when he notes that "there's no vengeance and bitterness in the blues, even though there's a dogged determination"—a determination that enables "blues folk" to "say it's about justice and it's about looking beyond so you don't reinforce the cycle."[3]

The "blues sensibility" that Brewer has apparently learned from a blues people and a blues geography is produced by the racial melancholia or the melancholic bind that Cheng insists is shared between dominant and marginalized racial groups. Brewer's racial melancholia forces him to be invested in a certain type of justice, a justice that uses a blues sensibility in order not to simply remember a particular history but, while remembering that history, to also rebuild the South both literally and figuratively. Brewer works toward a literal rebuilding of the South when he refuses to use a set for his films and insists on filming in Southern locales. His contract with Paramount includes a concession that his studio office be located in Memphis instead of Hollywood. When possible, he casts Southern-born actors like Samuel L. Jackson, D. J. Qualls, Justin Timberlake, David Banner, Isaac Hayes, and Taraji Henson. These concerted efforts do more than simply pour money into the Southern economy; these efforts also force viewers to be exposed to rural and urban Southern geographies that often are not the settings of Hollywood productions.

In a figurative sense, Brewer rebuilds the South through rememory. A buzz was created around *Black Snake Moan* due to the preview poster image of Samuel L. Jackson standing over Christina Ricci, who is on her knees at his feet, tethered to the chain that he holds in his hand. In an interview in *Mean Magazine*, Jackson and Ricci are asked what the chain a metaphor is for. Both actors respond that it is nothing more than a chain; it is nothing more than a utility, something that keeps Rae from leaving Lazarus's house. The chain figures so prominently in the previews and the film itself that it is difficult to imagine it being simply a chain and not symbolic of slavery and vengeance. This is especially difficult to dismiss because of the subject position reversals that Brewer performs with Rae and Lazarus—Rae being a white, promiscuous woman ravaged by an abusive past and Lazarus being a cantankerous, older black man tormented by an unfaithful wife and a brother who betrayed him by sleeping with his wife.

In spite of Jackson and Ricci's assertion that the chain is nothing more than a chain, the chain is indeed a sign. The chain signifies how black and white Southerners are tethered together by history and geography. Rae's pain is Jackson's pain and vice versa, and their shared pain is encapsulated in the film tagline, "To save his soul, he must save hers." The chain, then, is in their rememory. And it is the permanence of place and its inextricable relationship to both the literal and figurative chains of slavery that Sethe warns Denver about in *Beloved*: not only are places always there waiting for you but you must never go to those places, lest "it will happen again; it will be there for you, waiting for you. So, Denver, you can't never go there. Never. Because even though it's all over—over and done with—it's going to always be there waiting for you" (Morrison 36). The racial trauma that has occurred in the South, whether during the antebellum period or after emancipation, has not died. The chain in *Black Snake Moan* is not some juvenile reversal of slavery and racial terror wherein the black man is now tormenting the white woman; the chain symbolizes how both their futures are bound together.

The way that Brewer approaches rememory is much different than how Sethe understands it. Unlike Sethe's admonishment to Denver to never go to that place, Brewer is determined to go to that place and to make that place inhabitable. The rugged determination of Brewer's blues sensibility is driven by a desire to locate a place that is framed by what Paul Gilroy calls a radical nonracial humanism, a progressive ideology that provides an alternative language to the language of antiracism that always already polarizes and perpetuates the ontology of race. The interracial partnerships in both films are invested in taking up Gilroy's instruction "to become more future-oriented" (334) and, hopefully, in doing so, retrieve some of the promises of democracy that raciology has stripped from US citizens across racial lines.

Like the chain in *Black Snake Moan*, there are also signs in *Hustle & Flow* of Brewer making an effort "to become more future-oriented." Scholar Robyn Wiegman has noted the analogous wedding of blacks and women in nineteenth-century political and social discourse. She points out how black men and white women occupy a shared space in the race house where they are bound by their status as nonpersons and property at various historical moments (Wiegman). *Hustle & Flow* reifies existing stereotypes of black men and narratives of white women as vulnerable, which has historically rendered these men and women inferior. Black men and white women, then, have been hustled—simultaneously pimped and hoed by white men, the architects of what scholar Wahneema Lubiano refers to as the "race house." *Hustle & Flow* identifies the ways in which white women and black men continue to be pimped and hoed by race and racism in the United States.

Hustle & Flow opens with Djay (Terrence Howard) and Nola (Taryn Manning) sitting in the front seat of a late model Chevy as Djay recites a seemingly inane pontification on the difference between dog and man. His monologue, however, proves to be a colloquial articulation of Wiegman and other scholar's arguments about how in certain historical situations, black men and white women have been bound together—much like the figurative interpretation of Lazarus and Rae's chain in *Black Snake Moan*. So like Rae and Lazarus, Djay and Nola are bound together in an economically depressed and disenfranchised position. Djay explains to Nola, "And when I say 'man,' I'm talking about man as in mankind, not as in men . . . I mean you a woman and all, but we man." He explains that men share the base qualities of dogs—territorial, crude, and driven by basic instincts. "But man . . . he know about death. Got him a sense of history. Got religion." What Djay is ultimately saying is that *man* controls his destiny whereas *men* do not. He and Nola are man—agents who control their future and thus he is encouraging her "to become more future-oriented," particularly at the end of his monologue when he concedes, "So when you say to me, 'Hey, I don't think we should be doing this,' I gotta say, baby, I don't think we need to be doing this neither, but we ain't gonna get no move on in this world, lying around in the sun, licking our ass all day."

In order to get Djay and Nola to that future space, or at the very least, to remember the South that weds them together, Brewer troubles the gendered subjectivities that black men and white women occupy. It might seem that as a pimp and aspiring rapper Djay is the embodiment of stereotypes, except for the fact that he is a rather peculiar pimp/wannabe rapper. Djay exhibits no sex drive throughout the film, unless if his unprecedented and awkward kissing of Shug before going to meet Skinny Black counts. Otherwise, Djay shows no interest in sexual pleasure or in performing masculinity through a virile sexuality, as pimps and rappers often do.[4] Ultimately, Brewer suggests that through their transgressive alliance, Djay and Nola can "repair" one another, and in the end, save one another from the bonds of the race house. Their reciprocal act of salvation is repeated when Lazarus and Rae purportedly repair and save one another in *Black Snake Moan* when the literal chain that links them in the present signifies on the metaphorical chain that linked them in the past and produced their melancholia, or as Brewer depicts it, their blues.

An additional peculiarity about Djay's character is that Brewer breaks away from the stereotypical "bling" and glamour of pimping. Through most of the film, Djay is clad in a wife-beater and Dickies. He looks dirty, sweaty, and unkempt. His pressed hair is often returning to its roots under the oppressive Memphis heat. He lives in a three-room house with Nola; Shug, a pregnant prostitute; and Lexus, a stripper, and her toddler son. There is nothing glamorous about Djay's life or occupation, and in interviews Brewer steadfastly points out that there is a difference between pimping and hustling; Djay can hardly be called a pimp—he is a hustler, always trying to sell anything he might have—women, weed, a keyboard—in order to make ends meet.

As a white prostitute who is being pimped by a black man, Nola troubles whiteness as property, and especially virtuous white womanhood. Nola is the only white woman and the only income-generating prostitute in the film. Multiple times throughout the film, Djay insists that Nola is his "primary investor" in his rap career taking off, which will allow him to escape the dismal reality of black urban life. He explains, "Shit, baby, you my whole operation. You might be what they call a . . . like, a primary investor, you know? Making this shit happen one trick at a time." The return on Nola's investment is an escape for her as well. Just as Djay envisions Nola saving him from dreams deferred, he claims that he saved her when he found her trickin' at a truck stop and he rescued her, offered her protection. It is, of course, problematic to propose that prostitution is a form of salvation but that is how both Djay and Nola look at the situation. Thus in a reversal of the plantation structure, Nola's body is the property of Djay, but this reversal ought not to be interpreted as trite. Just like the role of Djay as a pimp is more complicated than one might initially think, this reversal is complicated too. Maintaining the line between white and black during slavery was of paramount importance. Cheryl Harris explains, "because whites could not be enslaved or held as slaves, the racial line between white and black was extremely critical; it became a line of protection and demarcation from the potential threat of commodification, and it determined the allocation of benefits and burdens of this form of property" (Adams 8). In relationship to Harris's point about whiteness as property Jessica Adams makes the point that the understanding that "the essence of whiteness is that, though it can be owned as property, it cannot be sold" became undone during the Progressive Era when the "dual rise of urban life and consumer culture and the attendant renegotiation of women's role in society" created hysteria over "white slavery" (6, 8). Brewer signifies on this Progressive Era hysteria around white women being forced into prostitution, "white slavery," as he simultaneously signifies on the white womanhood that Griffith called upon white men to protect from black male savagery in *Birth of a Nation*.

The investment Nola makes in Djay's rap career and the reversals that Brewer plays with in this film do, however, become problematic. As Djay's primary investor, Nola becomes the primary, in fact, the only investor in Djay recovering his (black) dick. And who better to hold that investment than a white woman who can stand in for, and in regards to Nola's precarious class status, disrupt the "Southern lady" iconography that lynch mobs purported to protect from hyper-sexual, black brutes. Brewer's reconstruction falls flat because although he strips Djay of the hypersexuality that plagues historical and popular constructions of black masculinity, he does so in order to recover a respectable white womanhood for Nola. Djay forgoes his sexuality while Nola appropriates Djay's definition of "man" by using her (white) sexuality to sell rap. When Djay is being arrested for assaulting Skinny Black at the juke joint, he gives Nola instructions, telling her that he wants to "hear [his] shit in the yard" and insisting that she is his partner and she is in charge. Taking Djay's instructions seriously, Nola takes up a new form of prostitution, soliciting every radio station in Memphis and appropriating Djay's definition of man, "We can't lay around licking our ass all day like a dog, you know? I mean, we man. I mean, I know I'm a girl and all, but we mankind." In the end, Nola is in charge and Djay must defer to her. Placing all the power in Nola's hands is a troubling move for several reasons.

Ultimately, Brewer depicts a "white-trash" woman selling a degenerate black masculinity in order to fill the pockets of the rich, white male music industry. The fact that Nola's marketing and sales, her "come-up" so to speak, is intricately linked to perpetuating white male dominance hearkens back to the rift between black men and white women that was produced by the analogous nineteenth-century wedding of blacks and women. When black men received the vote before white women, many partnerships and alliances were dissolved, revealing the hegemonic relationship that white women have with white patriarchy, even if it is a subordinate position. This is not to say that Djay, himself, ought to have been in charge, but there is a critical point to be made about Brewer needing to be mindful of the intricacies of the histories that he remembers. In this sense, the white-female, black-male stereotypes that he reverses ultimately become repetition without a difference.

This repetition without a difference is further emphasized by the fact that repairing the image of the black woman apparently has no role in rebuilding the South. The blues sensibility that fails to imagine black women as participants and recipients of the justice and democratic ideals that West asserts a blues nation is in search of is predictable, almost a cliché. In spite of Anna Julia Cooper's well-noted foreboding that "only the black woman can say where and when I enter . . . and there the whole Negro race enters with me," the black woman consistently remains doubly marginalized on the periphery of critical race and gender dis-course (31). In other words, Brewer's failure in this regard is indicative of a much larger national crisis in the United States that is not dictated by racial lines. In the analogous wedding of blacks and women, black still means black men and women still means white women.

The challenge Brewer faces with incorporating black women into the rebuilt South is evident in both films. There are two compelling instances in *Hustle & Flow* where this perpetual exclusion is most pronounced. Djay refers to Nola as his "primary investor" and later as his partner. Although Nola is indeed the only income-generating prostitute, Djay does acquire income from Lexus, whose primary source of revenue seems to be earned from stripping. In spite of her contribution, Lexus (Paula Jai Parker) is not an investor in Djay gaining a virile masculinity. She is not an investor because unlike Nola, she demands an equal return in the investment, and in the process is explicit about Djay's impotency when she taunts him, "Know what? Matter of fact, I think I feel like making me some money right now. Feel like popping my pussy, maybe shaking my ass. Go on, boy. Go on, get my car for me. You heard me. Go on, now, little bitch." Lexus expects a partnership that is equal, or at least has a worthwhile return. As a result of her demand in which she articulates the reality of the economic structure at work in the film, a reality that further emasculates Djay, she is violently expelled from the home. Lexus, then, is the stereotypical Sapphire who is punished for being a castrating bitch.

Shug (Taraji P. Henson), the pregnant, black prostitute, does not fare much better than Lexus. While she is meek and submissive, catering to Djay's every need and empathizing with his impotency, her character also does not stray from popular and preferred images of black women. And like Lexus, Shug is denied a partnership; apparently, there is no space for her in the rebuilt race house. This reality is evidenced by the fact that although Shug sings the hook that distinguishes the track that later becomes a hit, she receives no reward. She is not left in charge, and she is not a partner. Instead, she is presented as a welfare queen, a woman who just gave birth to a baby with "a ho for a mamma and a trick for a daddy, that nobody even know where he at;" a woman who leaches off of (white) society and embarrasses respectable black society. Her baby, Keisha, will be no different, as Djay explains to Key (Anthony Anderson): "You know that little girl Keisha, right? One day she gonna dream big, the way kids do, you know. And she gonna come to me and ask me when she grow up, can she become president? Now, I know that little girl got a ho for a mama and a trick for a daddy, that nobody even know where he at. But I tell you something. I'm gonna look her right in the eye . . . and I'm gonna lie."

POLICING THE BLACK WOMAN'S BODY

In order to make sense of Brewer's failure with black women, it is useful to consider what I call his "church ladies," Yvette (Elise Neal) in *Hustle & Flow* and Angela or Ms. Angie (S. Epatha Merkerson) in *Black Snake Moan*. These women are not prostitutes, Sapphires, or welfare queens. They are respectable, pious, and chaste middle-class women. Yvette is married to Key, and Angela is a pharmacist who sings in the church choir and is sweet on Lazarus. In addition to serving as models of respectable black womanhood, both women impose a moral consciousness on their men. Yvette is quick to question Key's association with Djay when Djay arrives at their home without invitation and his working girl entourage. Angela likewise expresses concern about Lazarus's relationship with Rae, albeit more through facial expression than vocally like Yvette. In the end, however, Key and Lazarus maintain the troublesome relationships that Yvette and Angela object to and these women acquiesce to their men's agendas.

Brewer uses church ladies to correct the image of the oversexed black Jezebel that has its roots in the antebellum period and migrated with black women to the North during the Progressive Era. The church-lady image as well as her willingness to acquiesce to her man's agenda, regardless of the danger it could potentially bring to the black home space, is a way for African Americans to counter not only the lascivious black Jezebel image but also the constructions of the black family as a pathological, matriarchy-ruled domestic space that always already sets the black family outside of middle-class social values, and thus, outside of the nation. Brewer signifies heavily on the antebellum and post–World War II ideologies that constructed black women and the black family as pathological, and in doing so, it becomes difficult to always see the line between signifying as an act of correction and signifying as an act of patriarchal reordering. Yvette and Angela's positive representation is therefore complicated and complex.

In order to understand why it is complicated and complex, I want to consider how the premise of Hazel Carby's essay, "Policing the Black Woman's Body," can be reversed in the context of *Hustle & Flow* and *Black Snake Moan* in order to understand why Yvette and Angela remain outside of the scope of democracy and justice. In "Policing," Carby analyzes the response of dominant culture to the migration of Southern black women from the South to the North and the purported threat to a moral social order that the black migrant woman posed upon black urban life (738–55). What happens when the contemporary black woman is repositioned in the South instead of the North? In Brewer's films, what happens is that respectable black women's bodies are depicted as being simultaneously in danger and reformed.

In Brewer's films, not only does the South become a geography that not only repairs black manhood, rescuing it from sexual deviance, but the South also operates as a geography that can offer the same repair for the black womanhood that was vulnerable in the North. Coming home, returning to a primordial US geography acts as a cure for the racial melancholia created in that space during slavery. Coming home also offers a cure for the social and sexual improprieties that became associated with Northern migration, particularly for black women, during the late nineteenth century and through the first half of the twentieth century. Hazel Carby points out that black women's migration created a "moral panic" that produced "a series of responses, from institutions and from individuals, that identified the behavior of these migrating women as a social and political problem, a problem that had to be rectified in order to restore a moral social order" (740). The result of this moral panic is an effort to do what Carby refers to as "policing the black woman's body." By positioning Yvette and Angela as respectable examples of black womanhood, Brewer participates in the same kind of policing that Carby notes became a phenomenon during the 1920s, the only difference is that he does so through a Booker T. Washington type of ideology that imagines the South as the ideal space to support a return to a moral social order.

In response to the licentious Jezebel images of black women that framed the antebellum landscape, Brewer offers the "reformed" black woman in both films. Yvette and Angela are both respectable, middle-class, God-fearing women who cook and garden—women who call to mind the club women of the late nineteenth and early twentieth century. Brewer responds to the precarious position black women's bodies occupied in the antebellum South in two specific ways. First, in *Hustle & Flow*, Brewer depicts the legacy of that historical positioning and how it manifests in the contemporary selling of hot (black) pussy, as bell hooks calls it. But perhaps, more interesting than the juxtaposition of Yvette's respectable middle-class body to the morally depraved bodies of Lexus and Shug is what happens in the absence of that kind of foil in *Black Snake Moan*.

A critical aspect of the "repair" project that Brewer presents as a tool for rebuilding the south in *Black Snake Moan* is to subvert the marriage plot. At its root, Brewer's subversion of the marriage plot disrupts the Southern bourgeoisie ideals of womanhood, manhood, and heterosexual marriage that continue to be central to literature, but particularly to film and television plots. From Lazarus's initial point of contact with Rae, he determines that he must cure her of her lascivious nature. He chastises Rae, proclaiming "God seen fit to put you in my path, and I aim to cure you of your wickedness . . . we gonna break the hold the devil got on you." The cure he concocts involves chaining her to his radiator, but it also involves transforming her into respectable marriage material. Lazarus is appalled to learn that Rae has no domestic capabilities, especially her lack of culinary skills, and it is with urgency that he replaces her cut-off top and panty ensemble with proper clothes. He explains to the sales clerk, "I'm lookin' to get some things for a woman . . . but they gotta be nice things—you know—proper things for a woman—you know—things that make a woman feel like a woman and not look like a, a, hussy or a floozy." The result that Lazarus works toward is that Rae will be transformed into a domestic, pious, chaste, and submissive young woman who will make a good wife for her man—a wife who is not susceptible to the vices—adultery and abortion—that his wife succumbed to.

Lazarus's vision and Brewer's vision are not one in the same, however. In order to truly rebuild the South, Brewer must deconstruct the social and cultural ideals that frame the South. He, therefore, resists the marriage plot, and although there is a wedding at the end of the film, there is nothing romantic or entertaining about the marriage it produces. As Rae and Ronnie (Justin Timberlake) drive off to Knoxville after completing their marriage nuptials, Ronnie experiences an anxiety attack and viewers are given the clear impression that perhaps nothing has been repaired, and, indeed, the past is not even past. This doomed marriage stands in contrast to the marriage that never happens. Lazarus and Angela function as Rae's surrogate parents when they plan (or impose) and host her wedding. In spite of the romantic interest that Lazarus and Angela share for one another—a romantic interest that is represented as much more sustainable than Rae and Ronnie's relationship—Lazarus and Angela are not written into the marriage plot. Instead, they operate as foils for Rae and Ronnie, standing in as the historical asexual Mammy and the faithful Tom.

Brewer's whiteness and the privilege it entails makes it difficult to assess his acts of signifying. Is he indeed invested in repairing black women alongside black men or do black women simply become fodder? Brewer could very well be signifying on what Candice Jenkins refers to as "the salvific wish . . . a black, largely female, and generally middle-class desire—is a longing to protect or save black women, and black communities more generally, from narratives of sexual and familial pathology, through the embrace of conventional bourgeois propriety in the arenas of sexuality and domesticity" (14). Jenkins's explanation makes it plausible that Brewer extends this salvific wish to the South in general, suggesting that such respectable disciplining will rebuild the South as the idyllic antebellum space that was the cradle of a "healthy" nation. It is important to note that it is only when black women and black men are situated in their Southern roots and when they embrace the cultural values inherent in those historical roots—hard work, a connection to the land, Christianity—can they be freed from the past that haunts the present, creating a happy space where black and white can live side-by-side. But what is to be made of Lazarus and Angela's exclusion from the marriage plot? Is Brewer signifying on the absurdity of the convention? If there was a space in the rebuilt South for sexually deviant black women, as there is for sexually deviant white women, then I could be comfortable interpreting Brewer's films as signifying texts. Because that is not the case, I am compelled to make the point that this exclusion suggests that black women are indeed fodder for creating a nonracial patriarchal order that uses Jezebels and church ladies as foils while disciplining white women who do not recognize their privileged position as an extension of white patriarchy.

"I Sell the Shadow to Support the Substance"[5]

Kara Walker's antebellum silhouette art provides a compelling theoretical framework for interpreting Brewer's acts of signifying and the way in which black women appear to be cultural fodder for the Southern nation he is working to rebuild. Walker's antebellum silhouettes respond to the various negative images and caricatures of black womanhood that frame the national and, indeed, global imaginary—an imaginary that Brewer must surely be conscious of but one that he nonetheless found challenging to tackle. For a little over a decade, Kara Walker has produced art in various mediums that cause controversy and sometimes outrage.[6] Her antebellum silhouette installations that I focus on here have been at the center of the controversy. Using what Gwendolyn DuBois Shaw calls "nostalgic postmodernism" as a tool to reinterpret and signify on antebellum plantation life, Walker's antebellum silhouette imagery is intentionally grotesque, carnivalesque, transgressive, and titillating (5). My interpretation of Walker's art and how it can provide an understanding of Brewer's challenge with black women relies on positioning Walker's work in a continuum of black feminist criticism and in the African American call and response tradition. Criticism on Walker's antebellum silhouettes has clamored toward rather flat analyses that see it as signifying through intertextual revision of white texts like Harriet Beecher Stowe's *Uncle Tom's Cabin*, Thomas Dixon's *The Klansman*, and Margaret Mitchell's *Gone With the Wind*. Walker does in fact signify upon these texts, but she also signifies on the black club woman's and, later, the black feminist's call for black men to support black women socially and politically, and in doing so, signifies on both the dominant culture's subjugation and oppression of black women as well as the black man's role in black women's subjugation.

I want to avoid the "Walker debate" because her usefulness to my argument here has little to do with assessing whether her renderings of black people are stereotypical or postmodern. I am instead interested in how the infusion of a black feminist criticism in her antebellum silhouettes allows for a comparative analysis of Brewer's films, offering an explanation for why the black woman occupies such a precarious and policed position in what Walker's father called "the New South" when he announced his family's move from Stockton, California, to Stone Mountain, Georgia, when Walker was 13. Walker's silhouettes conjure up images and memories of the antebellum South that are at odds with the harmonious contemporary images that Brewer depicts in his films. Brewer indirectly suggests that in spite of slavery, harmonious black-white relations always have existed in the South, especially within the lower social classes. But more than countering Brewer's memories of the Old South and his rebuilding of a New South that is not so new, Walker's art imagines a Southern black womanhood that is framed by agency—her ability to act for herself and make her own choices—an agency that is not allotted to black women in the repair work that Brewer performs.[7]

Amid the violence and debauchery of the silhouettes, Walker analyzes what Kimberly Springer calls "postfeminism's racialized agenda" by making her primary goal the recuperation of an antebellum black female agency that is just as relevant to contemporary (mis)representations of black female sexuality as to antebellum representations.[8] By giving the black slave woman agency, Walker in effect positions contemporary black women as part of a legacy of resistance and acting for one's own self, which is ultimately a deeply personal pursuit for Walker. In interviews, Walker consistently explains the evolution of both her black consciousness and her feminist consciousness. After being perplexed by the type of racialized and race conscious art she was expected to produce in her art classes at the Atlanta College of Art, Walker enrolled in the master's degree program at Rhode Island School of Design. During this time, Walker discovered black feminism and its demand for a critical gender consciousness. Her work, which focuses on granting black slave women agency, then, also maps an evolving feminism that was only named feminism in the late twentieth century.

How the political becomes personal for Walker is perhaps exemplified most profoundly in the various personas she creates in the titles of her work that are directly linked to herself—nigger wench and Missus K. B. Walker are two examples. Walker notes that these personas are drawn from cultural texts from the nineteenth century, like Thomas Dixon's *The Klansman* and the titles and frontispieces of slave narratives, but they also evolved from her discovery of Barbara Smith's 1983 anthology *Home Girls: A Black Feminist Anthology*. Walker notes, "The book was so new for me, in a way" (Als 75). Encountering the black feminist concerns in *Home Girls* enables Walker to understand the conflicted and alien space she was thrust into as a teenager in Georgia. She explains this understanding in an interview with Silke Boerma in 2002, "'One of the most interesting reversals of cultural prejudice . . . comes from the old notion that black women represented the lowest possible moral standard for any (white supremacist patriarchal) nation or state'" (Als 75). This assertion echoes one made by one of Walker's black feminist idols, Michele Wallace, when Wallace insists that the black woman is the "'other' of the 'other'" (74). Walker counters these ideologies of inherent inferiority and otherness through images of black womanhood that refuse to imagine her "otherness" without agency. The images that result from Walker's black feminist positionality depict highly sexualized beings by virtue of the many sex acts Walker incorporates into her installations, yet they are not Brewer's Lexus or Shug who *chose* to work in the sex industry, and they are not the pious and chaste Yvette and Angela who acquiesce to black patriarchal orders regardless of how nonsensical the situation.

Walker has many images of black women resisting through acts of violence or implied acts of violence, but there are two images in particular that interest me most, and they interest me because the acts of agency are not circumscribed by violence. In *The End of Uncle Tom and the Grand Allegorical Tableau of Eva in Heaven* on the far left of the installation there are three women suckling one another with a baby on the lap of the third woman, attempting to suckle as well. This act of mutual sexual gratification, Gwendolyn Dubois Shaw, asserts is Walker's way of deconstructing the stereotype of the mammy, as "Walker's women do not focus their attention outward, seeking the satisfaction of white others, but toward each other instead" (47). Shaw's analysis is echoed in psychoanalytic interpretations of this scene that also argue that Walker works to deconstruct notions of mothering and nurturing as they relate to the black female body.[9] Thus the three black women in this scene act as their own agents, *choosing* when and with whom they will be sexually gratified. In this manner, they clearly differ from DJay's prostitutes who had no choice about when or with whom they performed sexually. They also differ from Yvette and Angela whose sexuality and sexual desire is "policed."

A second piece that exhibits strong agency and offers a theoretical framework for understanding the dilemma Brewer encountered with black women and the race house is *You Do*. Like *The End of Uncle Tom*, *You Do* also draws on a black feminist sensibility to present black women as their own agents. Unlike *The End of Uncle Tom*, however, *You Do* is explicitly engaged in deconstructing a whole host of stereotypes. The silhouette is composed of two, large black cutouts of black women standing back-to-back with their buttocks touching, forming what looks like a pedestal table that their oversized buttocks rest on. Their hair is composed of four Mohawk-styled, braided spikes that also touch along the backside of their heads. Both women have large lips that are slightly agape and they are both bare-breasted, revealing very modest-sized breasts. At the waist, they are clothed in what looks like grass skirts and grass bracelets adorn their ankles. The woman on the left is holding out in front of her a crude cutout of a baby that looks more like a bug sprawled on it back. The woman on the right mirrors the other woman's posture but is holding out in front of her a white man dressed in a coat and top hat who looks like the extremely diminutive white man who is standing at the foot of the woman on the left, wearing the same attire and holding a long disciplining rod.

This image and its title are loaded. The title, *You Do*, suggests the imperative command, you do as I say, which is a reversal of the power constructs between antebellum black women and white men. The contrasts in size are exaggerated: the miniature white man not only has no power over the giant black woman but is subject to her whim. The phrase "you do" also calls to mind marriage vows and the repetition of "I do." But this marriage of sorts is just as twisted and sadistic as the US slave institution. Both the miniature white man and the bug-baby are held just below the women's oversized mouths, as though the women are contemplating devouring them. *You Do*, therefore, insinuates the cultural cannibalism that Oswaldo de Andrade espouses in his Brazilian modernist treatise, "Anthropophagite Manifesto." *You Do* depicts the oppressed implying the consumption a white body in order to transform it from taboo to totem, and it is through that absorption and the creation of a new social organization that the two giant women can be empowered (de Andrade). The power and fear that is generated by the women's immensity coupled with the primitivism indicated by their bare breasts and grass skirts invokes an Amazonian image of black women that fuels the cannibalism/anthropophagy implied in their gestures. Furthermore, power dynamics and reversal of the Hegelian master-slave dialectic is further accentuated by the women's skirts, both of which are cut in such a manner that it suggests each woman has two phalluses, whereby they not only absorb the oppressor in his entirety but become the oppressor, explaining the baby that also is under the threat of being consumed.

In contrast to Walker's depiction of agency in her black female characters, her black male characters are depicted in the opposite manner, without agency and often times as complicit in white people's exploitation of black women. In spite of her assertion in an interview in *The New Yorker* with Hilton Als that "the black male figure—generally a slave, sometimes engaged in homosexual acts with a white slave owner—has special meaning for her," I do not see the black male figure in her antebellum silhouettes ever being depicted with the least sense of agency. It is interesting, then, that Walker admits to Als that as a woman constructing black male figures, "I've consulted 'official' black men. I look to my father and brother" (73). Arguably, when juxtaposed to the helpless and supplicating positions her black male figures occupy, this peculiar statement could offer a way of understanding the less than becoming representations of black men as reflective of the way black men recognize their marginal position in a white patriarchal nation. Walker's understanding, nonetheless, does not explain the ways in which her black men are represented as complicit with the acts of rape, violence, and general defilement that black women experience at the hands of white men. I want to examine three specific scenes that present black men as either complicit, helpless, or disinterested in the violence that is being acted out upon black women. These scenes not only will further explain Walker's commitment to constructing black women as their own agents but also will provide a way to see how Walker's contemporary work is in dialogue with the images of black women that Brewer wrestles with and that are rooted in a slave past. It will also ultimately reveal how like Brewer, the efforts by Walker to rebuild the race house encounter similar challenges with intersectionality.

An Abbreviated Emancipation (from The Emancipation Approximation), an installation produced at the University of Michigan Museum of Art in 2002 includes a scene in which a nude, young black boy is crouched on the ground, one knee bent with his leg beneath his buttocks that also touches the ground and the other knee bent with his foot resting on the ground to support the weight of a white man who is seated on the boy's head and shoulders as though he is sitting on a chair. The white man who is seen in profile shares an uncanny resemblance to George Washington. The white man's legs merge with the body of a black woman who is on her knees in front of him, prepared to fellate him. The woman's formal dress that is marked by the bustle that is cut with detail stands in stark contrast to the boy's nakedness. This scene, then, invokes two similar yet different types of complicity. The first and more obvious complicity is that of the boy complying with the demands of his master, assisting in the violation of the black woman. The second type of complicity is that of the black woman perhaps not being particularly opposed to the service she provides her master. This complicity is implied through not only the woman's dress that is not indicative of standard slave attire but also the fact that her hair is neatly coiffed in a bun at the nape of her neck and not in braids or covered. Her attire and hair suggest that she is a slave mistress. In the case of this particular scene, the *approximation* of the emancipation is not just due to prevailing postslavery white supremacy but also due to certain blacks who were complicit in maintaining white supremacy. Despite the mutual complicity depicted in this scene, the black boy's collusion with his master stands out as the greater evil because he fails to protect the black woman.

In *Gone: An Historical Romance* the black man once again fails to protect the black woman and is thus also complicit in the sexual mayhem that is exacted in this installation. While the standard Walkeresque scenes of debauchery prevail in this installation—a slave girl fellating a white boy, a slave child potentially being impaled by a white *gentleman's* sword, and a second set of legs emerging from under a white *lady's* skirt—what is hard to miss is the naked black man floating in the sky, being kept afloat by his penis that is so large it is nearly equal to his body length and wider than his girth. He, too, is not protecting black womanhood. In contrast to the hypermasculinity indicated by the inflated penis of the black man in *Gone* that stands in for perhaps a contemporary inflated ego, the adult, black male figure in *The End of Uncle Tom* is feminized. In *The End of Uncle Tom* the black women—girls and adult women—have taken it upon themselves to protect themselves in the first half of the installation through mutual suckling (when viewing from left to right) and a slave girl has positioned a stake behind a white girl who is wielding an ax above her own head. While these women are ensuring their own protection, to their immediate right an obese, one-legged white man is penetrating a black girl from behind as she hangs onto a stalk of corn and while the man uses a saber stuck through the chest of a young child to balance his weight. In the meantime, a black man has his hands clasped and raised to the sky, head tilted up toward the sky, and pants pulled below his buttocks as a baby with umbilical cord attached falls from his anus. This father who is praying for deliverance from his unnatural condition alludes to the critique made by Daniel Patrick Moynihan in *The Negro Family: The Case for National Action* that the black family was "a tangle of pathology." Directly in front of him is an image of a woman pointing a chastising finger at him as a child's head protrudes from beneath her skirt. Here, then, is the father who will not be a father, and the castrating black matriarch who is to blame for the dire situation Moynihan asserts the black family is in when his findings were released in 1965 (US Department of Labor).

A REQUIEM FOR THE BLACK MALE FIGURE?

A recurring motif in Walker's antebellum silhouettes is that black women must act as their own agents because they only have themselves to seek for protection. Is Walker signifying on the fact that black men had little ability to protect black women during slavery or is she indicting black men as being passive and complicit in black women's oppression during slavery? Many of the African American artists who participated in Betye Saar's letter writing campaign against Walker and her art made her personal life, particularly her marriage to a white, German artist, evidence of her art being undermining to black progress as well as evidence of her work catering to white desires to see and reward black duplicity. I have no interest in using Walker's personal life choices to judge her artistic intentions. I will assert, however, that I think Walker is too smart, too well versed in theory to present such a flat correlation: black men are passive and fail to protect, therefore black women must protect themselves, therefore that is why she likes white boys (and hates black men). Perhaps, one of Walker's more recent exhibitions at Sikkema Jenkins & Co.'s studio can be helpful for answering the questions posed previously as well as engage her troubling assertion that she consults "'official' black men" when constructing the black male figure—an assertion that is steeped in middle-class politics and social essentialism.

In contrast to the spotlighting of the black female antebellum experience that pervades the antebellum silhouettes, the color paper cutouts in *Bureau of Refugees, Freedmen and Abandoned Lands-Records, "Miscellaneous Papers" National Archives M809 Roll 23* that shows in *Search for Ideas Supporting the Black Man as a Work of Modern Art / Contemporary Painting; a Death without End, and an Appreciation of the Creative Spirit of Lynch Mobs* foregrounds the experiences of black men in the Reconstruction South. Drawing their titles from the actual records of the Freedmen's Bureau these cutouts depict the violence and racism that black men encountered during Reconstruction. Oddly, or perhaps not so surprisingly, this exhibition has not received the media or critical attention that the titillating and grotesque antebellum silhouettes received. Like the grind house raunch that Brewer's films promised viewers, the antebellum silhouettes inevitably strike at viewers' more base emotions at the same time that the images shock viewers. *Bureau of Refugees* share more in common with James Allen's *Without Sanctuary*, a traveling exhibit of photographs and postcards of lynching in America, than with the titillating spectacle of Walker's previous work or Brewer's films.

Walker's recent exhibition interrogates the spectacle of racist atrocities committed in the postemancipation South and leaves no space for titillation or jocularity. Using language taken directly from Freedmen's Bureau records in their titles, these pieces only invoke discomfort and painful, forced recollection of a South that is not so far in the past. *Bureau of Refugees: Cut in a Most Shocking Manner* exhibits the body of a black man who is nearly decapitated at the head and waist. *Bureau of Refugees: Mulatto Hung by a Grapevine near Road Side between Tuscaloosa & Greensboro* depicts a lynching. *Bureau of Refugees: May 29 Richard Dick's Wife Beaten with a Club by Her Employer. Richard Remonstrated—in the Night was Taken from His House and Beaten with a Buggy Trace Nearly to Death by His Employer and 2 Others* depicts just what the title says. There is no play here, just hardcore brutality and hatred. These cutouts do not suggest complicity. In fact, their refusal to make a spectacle of the debauchery of slavery reveals why they, themselves, have not become the international spectacle that the antebellum silhouettes almost immediately became. Viewers and critics are quick to note that the antebellum installations make you want to look at what you know you ought not to want to see, but these *Bureau of Refugees* pieces force you to look at what you do not want to remember, what is painful to see, and worse, to acknowledge what occurred.

It makes sense that Walker's work on slavery would have an investment in redemption for the black woman's pain and suffering because historical documents like slave narratives and contemporary black feminist criticism has focused so much attention on the fact that black women were violated sexually during slavery (and after). It also makes sense that Walker's attention to the Reconstruction and post-Reconstruction eras would focus on black men and the violence they experienced as a result of lynch mobs and white fear of "negro domination." The Reconstruction silhouettes, with their exhibition of black men's limited agency and the dire price paid for acts of agency—*Richard Dick's Wife Beaten with a Club by Her Employer. Richard Remonstrated—in the Night was Taken from His House and Beaten with a Buggy Trace Nearly to Death by His Employer and 2 Others*—speak to the image of black men in the South that Brewer wrestles with when he depicts Djay and Lazarus's characters as impotent. Their impotency reverses the white supremacist representations of black men as hypersexual brutes that were used to justify the atrocities that Walker remembers in her *Bureau of Refugees* collection. What becomes evident in both Walker and Brewer's art, then, is that that "place"—the antebellum and segregated South—is still there when Brewer and Walker migrate to the South from California. They both bump into Morrison's "it," and their encounter with the undying past that haunts the Southern landscape is the impetus for their art that insists on remembering the past in order to better navigate the present and to perhaps imagine a future space that unlike Sethe's "there," we can go to and retrieve some of the promises of democracy that raciology has stripped from US citizens across racial lines.

WORKS CITED

Adams, Jessica. *Wounds of Returning: Race, Memory and Property on the Post-Slavery Plantation.* Chapel Hill: U of North Carolina P, 2007.

Als, Hilton. "The Shadow Act: Kara Walker's Vision." *The New Yorker* 8 October 2007: 75–79.

Carby, Hazel V. "Policing the Black Woman's Body in an Urban Context." *Critical Inquiry* 18.4 (1992): 738–55.

Cheng, Anne Anlin. *The Melancholy of Race: Psychoanalysis, Assimilation, and Hidden Grief.* New York: Oxford UP, 2001.

Cooper, Anna Julia. *A Voice from the South.* New York: Oxford UP, 1988.

Copjec, Joan. *Imagine There's No Woman: Ethics and Sublimation.* Cambridge: MIT P, 2002.

de Andrade, Oswaldo. "Anthropophagite Manifesto." *Antropofagia.* 1 May 2008. 4 Oct. 2008 http://www.antropofagia.com.br/antropofagia/en/man_antropo.html.

Gilroy, Paul. *Against Race: Imagining Political Culture Beyond the Color Line.* Cambridge: Harvard UP, 2000.

hooks, bell. "Selling Hot Pussy." *Black Looks: Race and Representation*. Boston: South End, 1999.

Jenkins, Candice. *Private Lives, Proper Relations: Regulating Black Intimacy*. Minneapolis: U of Minnesota P, 2007.

Lubiano, Wahneema, ed. *The House That Race Built: Black Americans, U.S. Terrain*. New York: Pantheon, 1997.

Johnson, E. Patrick. *Appropriating Blackness: Performance and the Politics of Authenticity*. Durham: Duke UP, 2003.

Morrison, Toni. *Beloved*. New York: Plume, 1987.

Schuyler, George. "The Negro Art-Hokum." *Nation* 16 June 1926: 662–63.

Shaw, Gwendolyn Dubois. *Seeing the Unspeakable: The Art of Kara Walker*. Durham: Duke UP, 2004.

Springer, Kimberly. "Divas, Evil Black Bitches, and Bitter Black Women: African American Women in Postfeminist and Post-Civil-Rights Popular Culture." *Interrogating Postfeminism: Gender and the Politics of Popular Culture*. Ed. Yvonne Tasker and Diane Negra. Durham: Duke UP, 2007

US Department of Labor. "The Negro Family: The Case for National Action." *US Department of Labor*. 4 Oct. 2008 http://www.dol.gov/oasam/programs/history/webid-meynihan.htm.

Wallace, Michele "Variations on the Negation and the Heresy of Black Feminist Creativity." *Heresies* 6.2 (1989): 69–75.

West, Cornel, and Toni Morrison. "Blues, Love and Politics." *Nation* 24 May 2004: 18+

Wiegman, Robyn. *American Anatomies: Theorizing Race and Gender*. Durham: Duke UP, 1995.

NOTES

1. Both Walker and Brewer migrated to the south from Northern California. Walker's family moved from Stockton, California, to Stone Mountain, Georgia, when she was thirteen. Brewer's family is originally from Memphis but he grew up in Chicago and Vallejo, California and moved to Memphis in 1994.

2. In his definition of a black signifying tradition, Gates identifies acts of agency through trickery, repetition, reversal, confrontation, mediation, and linguistic prowess that by his estimation are uniquely black cultural forms.

3. There is a strong essentialism inherent in West's claim, but I draw on it, nonetheless, because Brewer shares a similar sensibility of the blues and blues folk that not only informs his art but also informs how he understands his own politics.

4. A contrast is exemplified in Tyrone's character (David Banner) in *Black Snake Moan*. Tyrone is the hypersexual and threatening black male who defiles white womanhood. While his behavior is not punished or corrected in the film, Tyrone is a minor character and the celibacy and ultimate impotency of Lazarus is privileged.

5. Walker points to this Sojourner Truth quote when she explains to Gwendolyn Dubois Shaw that making silhouettes "kind of saved me. Simplified the frenzy I was working myself into. Created the outward appearance of calm" (Als 75–79).

6. After Walker won a MacArthur award, Betye Saar, an African American sculptor, launched a letter-writing campaign against Walker and her art, arguing that Walker was a young and foolish artist who produced images of blackness that were degrading and sexist.

7. In *Appropriating Blackness: Performance and the Politics of Authenticity*, E. Patrick Johnson addresses the white privilege that is central to my critique of Brewer, explaining, "Thus, when white-identified subjects perform 'black' signifiers—normative or otherwise—the

effect is always already entangled in the discourse of otherness; the historical weight of white skin privilege necessarily engenders a tense relationship with its Others" (4).

8. In "Divas, Evil Black Bitches, and Bitter Black Women: African American Women in Postfeminist and Post-Civil-Rights Popular Culture," Springer notes that liberal feminism consistently fails to recognize that it cannot call for gender equality without also including racial analysis, which in essence raises the same issues that black feminists placed at the forefront in the 1970s, over thirty years ago.

9. See Joan Copjec's chapter on Walker in *Imagine There's No Woman: Ethics and Sublimination.*

Chapter 3

Race, Sexuality, and the Media

The Demotion of Portland's Black Chief of Police

Ethan Johnson and Roberta Hunte

Introduction

The coherence and solidarity created through legal discrimination that defined black people's experience in the United States up until the civil rights era created an abundance of indigenous institutions that black people relied on for their survival and that simultaneously served as spaces where resistance was practiced and developed (Cohen, 1999; Morris, 1984); one of which was the black press. The black press has historically and contemporarily contested the representation of black people in the mainstream, white press (Cohen, 1999; Dates, 1990; O. Davis, 2005; Huspek, 2005a, 2005b). While prior to the civil rights era the power of racial oppression obscured the significance of alternative identities that black people experienced, today, analysis must take into account how social class, gender, sexuality, culture, and other identities shape how people of African ancestry experience the world (Cohen, 1999; Collins, 2005; McGruder, 2009; Nagel, 2003).

If the black press has played and continues to play such an important role for black people in opposing the white/mainstream press and constructing an alternate view of the world then within the present moment, the black press must begin to take into account the complexity of blackness. We want to encourage the black press to adhere to their original mission because of their value to the community as a site of resistance. This is critical because research continues to demonstrate that the mainstream/white media represents black people in stereotypical ways and there is no indication that this is going to change any time soon (Cohen, 1999; Collins, 2005; Huspek, 2005a). While recent scholarship has given greater focus to the significance of the multiplicity of blackness, few scholars have applied this critical lens to the black press, particularly regarding issues that intersect with sexuality (Cohen, 1999; O. Davis, 2005; McGruder, 2009). Furthermore, we highlight the need to locate the analysis of the mainstream and black press's treatment of race and sexuality within the specific sociohistorical context in which it occurs (Cohen, 1999).

In April of 2006, the second black person appointed chief of police in the city of Portland, Derrick Foxworth, was accused of sexual harassment and seven other related charges by Angela Oswalt, a white female civilian desk clerk working for the Portland Police Bureau. This occurred in the whitest large city in the United States (Abbott, 2003) where exogamy rates by black people are among the highest in the nation (Oregon Center for Health Statistics, 2005). In addition, research indicates that black people and other minority groups in Multnomah County, where Portland is located, experience a particularly "toxic" form of racism (Curry-Stevens, Cross-Hemmer, & Coalition of Communities of Color [CCC], 2010). At the same time, Portland is often considered one of the most politically progressive and livable cities. We suggest that the uniqueness of how race is experienced in Portland deserves consideration in order to more fully understand how the black and mainstream press treated this case.

Central to this case is the representation of black male sexuality in the media, which requires consistent critical analysis because of the historically specific ways it supports and has supported the criminalization of black males (Jones, 1993; Saint-Aubin, 1994). In this essay, we explore how the *Oregonian*, the paper with the largest circulation in Oregon and whose main office is in Portland, characterized Foxworth. We demonstrate that the *Oregonian* characterized Foxworth as a moral and sexual deviant, moving him from an "embraceable" leader to an "unembraceable" black male (Page, 1997). The strategic use by the *Oregonian* of explicit sexual imagery made it impossible for Foxworth to recover politically from this scandal even though the city's official investigation found him not guilty. We also examine how the black press challenged the representation of Foxworth and the case against him in the mainstream press. We claim that the *Skanner* and the *Portland Observer*, while they did contest the *Oregonian*'s representation of this case, failed to provide a place to engage in discussions of black sexuality and their significance at the local level. The mainstream's and black press's treatment of this case disconnects the significance of the ways race and sexuality are inextricably intertwined in the reproduction of racial inequality in the United States and elsewhere.

Historically, the black press has served as a key site of opposition to the dominant stereotypes of black people in the mainstream news media, albeit not without its contradictions. Sexual deviancy has served as an important element in the racial oppression of black people, and in response many black institutions and leaders have historically not provided and/or limited the space in which discussions and analysis of issues of sexuality and morality can occur and at times have themselves policed black sexuality (Cohen, 1999; Collins, 2005; McGruder, 2009; West, 1994). However, these practices can contribute to the reproduction of racial discrimination and inequality within the present context of the new or color-blind racism where divisions within and among black people have taken on greater significance. While the Foxworth case was not a national news story, we contend that it provides the opportunity to demonstrate areas in which the black press could have extended its oppositional position because of the provocative ways it addresses the intersections of race, gender, and sexuality.

SETTING THE STAGE

On April 6, 2006, Derrick Foxworth, the second black person appointed chief of police in the city of Portland was accused by Angela Oswalt, a white, female civilian bureau clerk, of sexual harassment. Her claim sparked an investigation of the chief for the misuse of city resources, sexual harassment, retaliation against a whistleblower, favoritism, alcohol use on the job, discourteous treatment, disclosing information, and unprofessional conduct. Their relationship took place from April 2000 to September 2001. Foxworth was married at the time to a black woman.

When Oswalt placed her complaint with the city, her attorney also leaked a series of intimate emails to the press that Foxworth wrote to Oswalt. Excerpts of these sexually explicit emails were published in the print, Internet, and television media from April 6 through 11, 2006. Showcased email excerpts included references to sexual acts Foxworth would like to perform with Oswalt and racialized comments about their respective bodies. Mayor Tom Potter stated that he suspended Foxworth from his post as chief on April 12, 2006, largely because of the distraction the case was causing within the bureau. Rosie Sizer, a white woman, was appointed as interim police chief. Oswalt's response emails to Foxworth were not shared publicly or given as evidence in the sexual harassment case against him.

On June 1, 2006, the investigation into the allegations against Foxworth were completed, and on June 17, it was announced that seven of the eight charges against him were dropped. The only claim substantiated by the investigation against Foxworth was that of unprofessional conduct, which was based on an email he wrote to Oswalt that shared his opinion about an internal bureau case regarding, ironically, sexual harassment. Shortly after his demotion, interim chief Rosie Sizer promoted Foxworth to commander of the Southeast Precinct, which she had left to take on the position of chief.

In October 2006, Foxworth filed an intent to sue the city claiming that he was wrongly demoted and reprimanded because he was a black man involved in an affair with a white woman. He claimed that there was no city legislation against workplace dating, thus the consensual affair was not improper. Foxworth's attorney asserted that the reasons given for Foxworth's dismissal were not the actual reasons.

In a discussion of racial profiling within the police force (on October 30, 2007, at Portland State University), Foxworth discussed his experiences of being pulled over by his white peers when he was working undercover. Prior to his stint as chief, Foxworth rarely spoke publicly about race and the police. As chief he did push for the recruitment of minorities to the force and recognized a need to positively influence the negative image of the police among minority communities. He was responsible for hiring the first black women assistant chief of police. Foxworth began working for the bureau as a police officer approximately 25 years prior to the case coming out against him.

THE POLITICS OF BLACK SEXUALITY, THE
NEW RACISM, AND THE BLACK PRESS

The myth that black people are sexually deviant is arguably the cornerstone of historical and contemporary racial discrimination and inequality (Collins, 2005; hooks, 2001; Nagel, 2003; West, 1994). Racial oppression during slavery and the Jim Crow era vilified black people as hyperheterosexual in order to justify and perpetuate their exploitation (Collins, 2005; A. Davis, 1983; Nagel, 2003). Collins (2005) captures how black people's understanding of the role of sexuality shaped the civil rights movement, where lynching as a public spectacle done to black men became the centerpiece through which racial struggle was framed. She states, "In a climate of racial violence, it was clear that victims of lynching were blameless and murdered through no fault of their own" (p. 223). In this way, the struggle against the clear and present danger of lynching prioritized the masculinity of black men and challenged the myth of black sexual deviancy. Within communities of black people, this prioritizing of the racial oppression of black men has contributed to the neglect of the significance of ideologies of gender and sexuality in reproducing racial inequality and discrimination (Cohen, 1999; Collins, 2005; Crenshaw, 1995; Hammonds, 2004).

One of the most insightful examples of prioritizing black men's oppression to the neglect of black women's is the Anita Hill case. Here, it becomes evident the ways that gender and sexuality have been largely silenced in communities of black people as a political strategy. Many black people felt it was more important to support Clarence Thomas's nomination to the Supreme Court than to discuss the significance of sexual impropriety within communities of black people even though many believed Hill (Collins, 2005). This case also speaks to the bifurcation of feminist and antiracist strategies, where each, through their neglect of the intersection of race and sexuality, contribute to the oppression of black women (Crenshaw, 1995).

Both the response to lynching and the Anita Hill case reveal the ways that a system of sexualized racism has shaped how black communities and their leadership resist oppression (Collins, 2005). On the one hand, in order to avoid the stigma of sexual deviancy placed upon them, black people resisted Jim Crow largely through the state sanctioned policy of lynching. The issue of rape of black women by white men was neglected within this strategy. This strategy, while diminishing the power of the myth of black sexual deviancy, simultaneously obfuscated the significance of the sexualized racism that oppressed them and rescued the masculinity of black men. Within a heteronormative framework, racism became equated as something done to black men both internally and externally (Collins, 2005; Crenshaw, 1995). We suggest black communities and leadership carried these strategies into the post–civil rights era and is evident in the black press when they address issues of sexual impropriety within the black community.

Within the present post–civil rights era, demonstrating how discrimination and inequality happens has become more difficult. Various concepts have been applied to the current era—for example, *covert* (Coates, 2008), *color-blind* (Bonilla Silva, 2006; Monahan, 2006), and *new racism* (Collins, 2005)—that help elucidate the key elements of the changing context. In particular, scholars have focused on how the mass media serves as a new site for the justification for the disproportionate number of black people experiencing poverty, incarceration, and premature death (Coates, 2008; Collins, 2005; Monahan, 2006). Coates (2008) writes of the new era of racism, "As a consequence, the media as an instrument of covert racism serves to preserve the relative boundaries of racial identity. One of the primary vehicles by which and through racial identities are preserved is through the mass media's manipulation of racial etiquette" (p. 222). Not only are the archetypes of black male and female sexuality alive and well in today's media and popular culture (Collins, 2005; Hewlett, 2005; Leonard, 2004), but the mainstream media's greater provision for a space for black people and other racialized groups gives the impression of integration. However these images speak more to a rhetorical integration rather than real efforts to address racial injustice (Cloud, 1996; Collins, 2005; Steinhorn & Diggs-Brown, 2000; West, 1994). The Jim Crow era has been replaced with a contemporary rhetoric that is based on the denial or minimization of race (Bonilla Silva, 2006; Collins, 2005). While evidence of the new racism can be seen in multiple arenas of mainstream media—that is, movies, sports, music, and talk shows—the treatment of cases of sexual impropriety between black men and white women are particularly revealing. Responses to instances of alleged sexual assault by black men upon white women in the mainstream media continue to be pathologized in comparison to their white male counterparts (Markowitz, 2006; McGruder, 2009; Page, 1997), though statistically white and black men commit sexual assault crimes in relatively equal numbers and overwhelmingly within the same racial group (National Institute of Justice [NIJ] & Centers for Disease Control and Prevention [CDC], 1998).

Where the black press often avoids the significance of gender and sexuality within cases of sexual impropriety, the white/mainstream press demonstrates a hyperfascination with the sexuality of these cases coupled with a denial and silencing of the significance of how race and sexuality have and continue to play a role in the oppression of black people (Leonard, 2004). What is important in the analysis of the white/mainstream press is to reveal the strategies they use to simultaneously criminalize black sexuality and avoid claims of racism, particularly in a context where there exists powerful discourses claiming racism has ended in the United States. Through an intersectional analysis of the white/mainstream press we can demonstrate how their denial of the significance of race in cases of sexual impropriety contributes to the reproduction of racial inequality.

The black press has historically and contemporarily been shown to provide a discourse that contests how black people are often represented in the white/mainstream press (Cohen, 1999; Collins, 2005; O. Davis, 2005; Huspek, 2004, 2005a). Cohen (1999) writes, "Thus, the black press has functioned as a source of information formulated from the perspective of black Americans as distinct from white Americans. It has also served as a source of perseverance and resistance used to build self-esteem, a sense of community, and a common historical narrative of struggle—all necessary components of collective political action" (p. 190). Furthermore, because of the often-local focus of the black press, it has the added benefit of addressing geographically specific issues communities of black people face (Cohen, 1999). However, Cathy Cohen (1999) demonstrates that the black press has also played a role in marginalizing those most marginalized within communities of black people, particularly in the post–civil rights era, by constructing or defining blackness in ways that highlight what is similar between white mainstream values and the black community and by disparaging and/or making absent that which is not in order to align blackness closer to the status quo. Cohen's scholarship, which focuses on the ways that race, gender, and sexuality intersect within communities of black people, addresses directly Olga Davis's (2005) call for research that examines how the black press manages the construction of identity in the post–civil rights context. Davis (2005) states, "Today of course our communities are increasingly more diverse and complex, and this gives rise to such issues as interracial relationships, same-sex marriages, black sexuality, homophobia, the reconstructions and redefinitions of family, borderland considerations, and the diasporic dilemma accompanied by the contentious debate over 'who is black?'" (p. 30). In other words, the black press needs to employ intersectional politics (Collins, 2005) in its reporting that acknowledges the powerful ways race and sexuality are implicated in the oppression of black people. Specifically, cases of accusations of sexual impropriety by white women on black men need to be considered as opportunities to make connections to how historically such claims have and continue to substantiate the myth of the black male sexual deviancy. Additionally, while the guilt or innocence of the individual being charged is significant, reporting should also focus on how the sensationalization of these cases in the mainstream media diverts attention away from the more substantial issues within black communities, such as interracial intimacy, sexual impropriety, and sexuality in general; each of which, in regards to the Foxworth case, are critical. Finally, the black press needs to acknowledge that black men and women experience sexuality differently, otherwise the significance of gender in cases of sexual impropriety involving black people will be neglected.

Through discourse analysis, we examine the ways the *Oregonian* characterized Foxworth and the case against him and how the black press contested the *Oregonian*'s representation of Foxworth. We also provide a constructive critique of the black press by analyzing how it treated intersections of race, gender, and sexuality. In the current context of the new or color-blind racism, where overt forms of racial discrimination have been made largely illegal and morally reprehensible, racism can be revealed and demonstrated through discourse analysis that focuses on the more nuanced ways it is expressed in print and the spoken word. We demonstrate how the *Oregonian* within the context of the new racism perpetuated the myth of black male sexual deviancy. We also show how the black press contested the *Oregonian*'s narrative, however, we argue that the black press was largely silent concerning how the Foxworth case spoke to issues of sexuality and gender within communities of black people. In conclusion, we offer a constructive critique of the black press by suggesting ways they could have expanded their reporting to engage the ways race, gender, and sexuality are implicated in the Foxworth case particularly concerning the specific racial sociohistorical context of Portland.

METHODS

When we began research into this study, we did search for a discussion of the Foxworth case in the area of virtual media because, as other research has shown, these are important sources to consider when examining racial representations (O. Davis, 2005; Leonard, 2004). We looked, for example, on white supremacist websites for discussion of the Foxworth case but found none. We did find two blogs that are explicitly dedicated to the experiences of black people in Portland, however, upon review, we found that they receive relatively little attention and found no discussion of the Foxworth case[1]. We suggest that because of Portland's relative geographical isolation, because of its small population of black people, and because the Foxworth case was not about a nationally known figure the primary source for discussion and information about this case was limited to the print media in the Portland Metro Area.

This research is based on analysis of published articles by the *Oregonian, Skanner*, and *Observer* written between the period of early April to October of 2006. We read every article that each of these newspapers published that was related to the case during this period. In total, we read over one hundred articles written by the *Oregonian* and 18 written by both the *Observer* and the *Skanner*. The smaller amount of articles published by the black press can largely be accounted for because they are weekly presses, whereas the *Oregonian* is a daily paper. Through a close reading of these articles we found that the black press and the *Oregonian* reported on the case very differently. On the one hand the *Oregonian* presented the case as a clear instance of sexual impropriety while ignoring the contemporary and historical significance of race at both the national and local levels. On the other, the *Skanner* and *Observer* were concerned with the impact this case would have on the black community while ignoring the significance of sexuality. Building on Crenshaw's (1995) analysis, this bifurcation of race and sexuality limits the ability of black people to challenge its leadership in cases of sexual impropriety and address such issues as domestic violence and homophobia in their communities. The primary question driving our analysis was how was race and sexuality constructed within each of these papers? Furthermore, we ask as a result of how these papers constructed the relationship between race and sexuality, how are readers encouraged to think?

THE *OREGONIAN*: FOXWORTH THE FREAK

In this section of the essay, we focus our analysis on how the *Oregonian* treated the Foxworth case. We contend that the *Oregonian*, in their representation of Foxworth, reproduced the archetype of black male sexual deviancy while denying the significance of race. While the Foxworth case did not receive the national attention of the Kobe and O. J. cases, due both to Foxworth's relatively low stature as a public figure and the less serious degree of the charges against him, in many ways the mainstream media responded in the same way. That is, the case became a spectacle through which America's fascination with inter-racial relationships between black men and white women could be examined.

Furthermore, this case helps elucidate how treating cases of sexual impropriety through a color-blind lens contributes to the reproduction racial inequality (Collins, 2005; Crenshaw, 1995).

Within the first week of the case, from April 6 to April 11, the *Oregonian* produced 14 articles, 6 of which were editorials, until mayor Potter suspended Foxworth on April 12. These articles relied heavily on printing racially and sexually charged excerpts from Foxworth's emails to Oswalt. For example, on April 6, the front-page article,[2] "Accuser of Chief Details E-Mails, Threats," states the following regarding the emails: "One is described as among the 'highly solicitous and sexually disgusting' emails she regularly received from him. In it, he boasts about how well endowed he is, how he wants to expose her to his 'naked brown chocolate body' and how he longs for her tan sexy body. He details how he wants her to gratify him sexually, the type of clothing he daydreams about her wearing and the sex acts they should perform." The excerpts the *Oregonian* chose to print in this article and others focused on Foxworth's references to his and Oswalt's race, that is, "chocolate" and "blond," and words that expressed power such as "submissive." While the *Oregonian* strongly suggested that Foxworth's motivations for his relationship with Oswalt were racial, they completely ignored the historical meaning of race this case is embedded in regarding America's hyperfascination with black/white sexual relations (Collins, 2005; Leonard, 2005).

Sexual deviancy in the United States is located upon black men and women (Collins, 2005; Leonard, 2004; West, 1994), and in regards to contemporary charges of sexual impropriety by a black man upon a white woman, the historical relationship between lynching and charges of rape must be taken into account. Leonard (2004) writes, "White fears of Black rape have historically resided at the center of this constructed vision of Black male (and White female) sexuality. The White imagination has justified state violence as part of an effort to protect the pure and innocent White female body from the Black predator. Linda Williams (2001, p. 14) argued that the 'White female suffering at the hands of the hypersexual Black male' has a long-standing place within America's racial discourses" (p. 293). Just as important in this case is how the *Oregonian* characterized Oswalt in relation to Foxworth. From the Scottsboro case to more contemporary cases of white women and men making false claims of black male sexual and criminal deviancy, it is evident that the media and the criminal justice systems have longed presumed the innocence of white women in order to inflict sanctioned violence on communities of black people (Hutchinson, 2000; Leonard, 2004; Rome, 2002).

In the beginning of the case, the *Oregonian* treated Oswalt as the innocent that had been sexually abused by the powerful and cunning black man. For example, the *Oregonian* repeatedly printed Foxworth's sexually charged emails, while providing little space for the significance of Oswalt and her lawyer not making her corresponding emails available. In addition, during the first week of the case the *Oregonian* wrote that Oswalt received "racial and demeaning taunts" by other officers during her relationship with Foxworth, which suggested that she was the victim in this case. Much like in other more high-profile cases, the white /mainstream press refused to consider the possibility that Oswalt's charges may have been false[3]. Within the first week, this quick deployment of racial sexual archetypes limited the possibilities for critical public discussion of sexual harassment and the ways that race is implicated in cases of sexual impropriety (Crenshaw, 1995). The *Oregonian* seemed to not care or understand the implications of their approach to reporting.

After the first day, the *Oregonian* began to interview numerous "experts" and make references to "similar" cases. In fact, the *Oregonian* interviewed no less than ten "experts" from April 7 to April 11. For example the article "What Was He Thinking?," written on April 9, cites four "experts" and four "similar" cases. Edward Hill, who works for the US Equal Employment Opportunity Commission as a deputy field director in Seattle is quoted as stating, "I'm amazed about the dinosaur brains out there," regarding sexual impropriety in the workplace. Victor Kisch, a lawyer that represents employers in sexual harassment cases in Portland remarked, "This is just a fundamental lapse in judgment," concerning the Foxworth case. Then the article compared the Foxworth case to four "related" cases: those of US Senator of Oregon Bob Packwood, former chair of the Portland Development Commission Matt Hennessee, Oregon Congressman David Wu, and former Governor of Oregon Neil Goldschmidt. Packwood was found guilty of sexual abuse and assault of no less than ten women (Graves & Shepard, 1992); Hennessee (Learn & Griffin, 2005) sexually abused a minor over a period of years; Wu both admitted to and was disciplined by officials at Stanford University for "inexcusable behavior" he committed while attending college there as an undergraduate (Miller, 2004); and Goldschmidt admitted that he sexually abused a 14-year-old girl while he was mayor of Portland (Rosen, 2004).

This article went on to cite two more "experts." James C. Foster, a political science professor at Oregon State University that teaches courses on gender in the work place, stated, "They may be pillars of the community in one area and then behave abominably in another," and Deborah Rhode, a Stanford law professor that writes on sexual discrimination in the workplace, commented that some men "can't process the fact that their attention might be unwelcome. And some people just have difficulty accepting of a relationship being over." Although these statements speak to the sexual behavior of men generally, they are addressing the Foxworth case specifically. Without the investigation even starting, Foxworth had been characterized as "abominable" and compared to four other more egregious cases that have each been substantiated.

The *Oregonian*'s characterization of this case as simply a case of sexual harassment with no relevance to race contributes to the reproduction of racial inequality because it ignores how race is implicated in cases of sexual impropriety. As research has demonstrated black women and men receive different treatment than white women and men in the criminal justice system, media, and social science research due in large part to structural, political, and cultural reasons (Crenshaw, 1995; Kapsalis, 2002; Roberts, 1997). For example, the criminal justice system and the media at times discount or diminish claims of sexual impropriety by black women, such as in the Anita Hill case. Black women may also remain silent regarding domestic violence more than white women because of the pressure to deflect claims of dysfunctionality within communities of black people and in order to convey racial solidarity. In addition, research has demonstrated that black men receive harsher sentences for raping white women than for raping black women. Hence in the United States, to address sexual impropriety without engaging the significance of race leaves these inequalities unquestioned and uncontested (Crenshaw, 1995). The *Oregonian's* treatment of this case through a color-blind lens makes it complicit in the reproduction of racial inequality because the color-blind lens does not take into account that black people experience and perceive sexual impropriety differently.

On April 16, the *Oregonian* ran the editorial "Coverage of Police Chief: Readers Voice Fairness Concerns" in which the newspaper addressed readers questioning the possible bias of the reporting of the case. After citing various criticisms that were sent to the *Oregonian*, the article quoted the managing editor for the news stating, "It is hard to find comparable situations, she said, without going back decades." To be fair, this was in reference to Portland's history in particular, not at a global or national level, but in comparison to the four previously cited cases, each of which fall within her suggested timeframe, and she cannot find other cases that were at least as worthy of this type of coverage? Nevertheless, the article goes on to explain that within the newsroom "a fairness alarm went off" regarding its coverage and this is the context in which we would contend the articles written after Foxworth's suspension on April 12 should be considered. That is, the paper realized that it did appear biased in its coverage of the case and as a consequence the reporting took a noted shift. Specifically, the newspaper no longer printed sexually charged excerpts from Foxworth's emails, although they did continue to reference them.

However, as the *Oregonian's* own reporting demonstrates, the court of public opinion had found Foxworth guilty. For example, an article written on April 12 suggested that Foxworth's suspension was based on the distraction the case was causing within the police department due to the intense interest by the media. Without quoting Foxworth's emails directly, the article stated in reference to the original charges against Foxworth that "the documents contained lurid emails purportedly from Foxworth to Oswalt detailing how he wanted her to gratify him sexually, the type of clothing he daydreamed about her wearing and the sex acts they should perform." The article ended with various city officials giving their opinion of the case and/or the suspension, one of which repeated the following joke a city commissioner heard an emcee make at a black tie event in Portland: "We just got an email from Derrick Foxworth. I'd like to read it to you, but I can't." The city commissioner that repeated the joke went on to state that people "either shake their heads or roll their eyes" apparently to demonstrate that Foxworth has lost the public's respect.

On June 1, the *Oregonian* reported that the investigation into the charges against Foxworth had been completed and on June 17, the *Oregonian* announced in the front-page article, "Serious Lapse in Judgment Costs Foxworth's Chiefs Job," that all the charges against Foxworth had been dropped except the minor charge of unprofessional conduct. The article also reported that mayor Potter was demoting Foxworth to the rank of captain. Three days after his demotion, interim chief Rosie Sizer promoted Foxworth to commander of the precinct she had left to take on the position as chief. Upon his promotion to commander, the *Oregonian* ran an article on July 5, "Emails Reveal Help by Foxworth," that attempts to show that Foxworth used his power as precinct commander when he was having an affair with Oswalt five years ago to have Oswalt's shift changed so it would accommodate their relationship better. Although the investigation had been judged to be "thorough, impartial and fair" (June 8) by an outside auditor, the *Oregonian* seemed to be unwilling to accept the results especially since he was promoted to commander. However, what is revealing about this period of the case and up to Foxworth's filing of his intent to sue the city for racial discrimination in October is that the *Oregonian* printed two articles that focused on the significance of race.

The first was the front-page article, "Foxworth Tale Raises Race Question," written on June 18. The article asked, was race a factor in the outcome of the case and why are there so few black public officials in Portland? This article represents the first time since the case began in early April that the *Oregonian* interviewed experts on race. Darrell Milner of the Black Studies Department at Portland State University was asked about the small number of black people in high profile positions and explained that "the fact that there are no blacks in those positions now will cause a little soul searching." This article went on to consider Foxworth's role in healing relations between the black community and the Portland Police Bureau in relation to a number of unarmed killings of black people. The article also recognized Foxworth's attempts to diversify the bureau. The article went on to cite Mayor Potter claiming that race played a role in the media's coverage of the case and ended with a comment by race and ethnicity consultant Floyd Cruz claiming that the city of Portland lives the myth of a progressive city in regards to issues of race.

After Foxworth announced his intent to sue the city for racial discrimination on October 11, the *Oregonian* wrote another piece focusing on race called "Race and the Foxworth Lawsuit." Here, the *Oregonian* provided space to various leaders of the black community in Portland to express their thoughts on the case. The article begins by stating, "For months, race had been the uneasy undercurrent in a scandal that gripped the Police Bureau," which represents the first time the paper has admitted overtly that race should be considered in terms of how people are making sense of the case. Through the words of various representatives of the black community the article suggested that Foxworth was treated unfairly not only because he was a black man but also because his accuser was a white woman; that internal politics within the police department also played a role; that media representations of black sexuality should be considered; and that Foxworth was, through his lawsuit, taking advantage of resentment among black people due to the history of and contemporary experience of racial discrimination and inequality in Portland. In regards to the significance of race and sexuality, the article, through an interview with Portland State University sociology professor Jose Padín, addressed miscegenation laws and current perceptions of interracial dating.

While the previous piece acknowledges many of the issues that an intersectional politics of race and sexuality should employ, as a narrative taken in its entirety up to this point, readers of the *Oregonian* have been provided with a relative mountain of "evidence" suggesting that Foxworth is morally and sexually deviant in comparison to information corroborating the role race plays in cases of sexual impropriety regarding black people. Of more than one hundred articles written about the case, only two considered race as a factor. Here, the level of detail and space provided as "proof" of Foxworth's sexual and moral deviancy deserves to be juxtaposed with the neglect of race as a factor in the case. Moreover, the case against Foxworth had already been decided, thus, for the *Oregonian* to address race cost the paper very little at this point. Indeed, the provision of a space for a consideration of the significance of race was convenient for the paper, that is, it served as a face-saving gesture and maintains Portland's socially progressive reputation. This face-saving gesture or "'positive self-representation" is a strategy used in order to dispel or avoid accusations of racism (Van Dijk, 1993). Van Dijk (1993) writes, "Such strategic moves may have a strong influence on readers' models of ethnic events, because they allow readers to develop negative opinions about minorities without feeling guilty of racism. The model, thus structured, does not violate the social norms of tolerance" (p. 120–121). This article provides a way for the *Oregonian* and much of its readership to deny accusations of racism in its treatment of Foxworth while leaving in place their characterization of him as a sexual and moral freak. Again, the dominant color-blind lens through which this case was told in the *Oregonian* implicates this paper in the reproduction of racial inequality because it does not acknowledge the significance of the intersection of race, gender, and sexuality in social science research (McGruder, 2009), the criminal justice system, and the mainstream media. Furthermore, requesting or urging that the *Oregonian* employ an intersectional analysis in future cases within its current leadership would seem a futile effort, as its attempts to save face strongly suggests they do what they do consciously. Consequently, we place more of our hope in challenging the black press to employ an intersectional politics as it has consistently served as a site of intervention opposed to the white/mainstream press.

THE BLACK PRESS

In this section of the essay, we focus our analysis on how the black press treated the Foxworth case. In the *Portland Observer* and the *Skanner*, Portland's black newspapers, we found 18 articles that focused on the case against Foxworth. In contrast to the *Oregonian*'s daily runs, these papers print weekly, which explains their limited coverage of the case. However, other factors may have contributed to this relative small quantity of articles considering that between the two papers there were approximately sixty issues printed from when the case first broke in April of 2006 until Foxworth announced his intent to sue the city in October of 2006.

In our analysis, we found that the black press on the one hand treated this case almost exclusively through the lens of race by focusing on the significance of Foxworth to the community of black people in Portland. On the other hand, the *Skanner* and the *Observer* avoided the issue of sexuality almost completely. Even though this case was about sexual harassment and sexuality is inextricably linked to racial discrimination and inequality, the black press was virtually silent on this issue. In effect, Foxworth was presented within the black press as asexual. We suggest that the *Skanner* and *Observer*'s limited coverage may also have been related to the significance sexuality has in the perpetuation of racial inequality. That is, the *Skanner* and the *Observer* may have limited the coverage of this case in order to avoid the stigma of deviant sexuality that has been placed on black people by the larger society. Hence while the black press contested how the mainstream press told this story, it missed an opportunity to discuss how sexuality was implicated in this case, particularly in relation to black masculinity and interracial relationships.

When the story first broke in early April of 2006, the *Skanner* was the only paper of the two to address the case in an article titled "Foxworth Accused of Sexual Misconduct" written on April 6. Besides the absence of printing excerpts from the racially and sexually explicit emails in the *Skanner*'s initial article, this piece also countered the white press's version of the story by limiting their coverage to what was known at the time. For example, the *Skanner* article quoted the mayor regarding his decision not to suspend or fire Foxworth, "The city of Portland is investigating all allegations of misconduct made against Portland Police Chief Derrick Foxworth." The article also states that Foxworth did not deny that he had a relationship with the claimant. He is quoted stating, "I regret I cannot go into detail or provide you with anything, as much as I would like to, regarding a brief personal relationship that took place five to six years ago." This initial article by the black press stands out as subdued in contrast to the *Oregonian*'s sensationalized reporting. It does not consider or suggest anywhere that Foxworth may have committed an act of sexual impropriety.

The next week in mid-April the *Skanner* printed another article, "Foxworth Placed on Administrative Leave," which explained that Potter initially stated that he "would wait for the human resources bureau to finish its investigation before making any decisions about the Foxworth case." The article reveals that Potter had denied requests made by city union officials for Foxworth's suspension, but due to the high level of interest in the media, he relented and felt he had no choice because of the distraction it was causing within the police department. Again, in juxtaposition to the *Oregonian*'s articles focusing on printing sexually explicit excerpts, interviewing "experts," and referring to other "related" cases, this piece highlights the black press's reluctance to engage in a discussion of sexuality.

The *Observer*'s article, "Community Support for Police Chief," written on April 12, and the *Skanner*'s "Could There be Other Casualties?," written on April 20, besides repeating the strategy of not reprinting the sexually explicit emails and being silent on the issue of sexual impropriety, each suggest that race played an important role in this case at two levels. First, the articles claimed racism motivated the charges against Foxworth. Second, these articles focused on the significance Foxworth's loss will mean to the black community. That is, Foxworth is characterized as an embraceable asset to the black community because of his power as chief of police combined with his upstanding moral character. For example, the *Observer* article stated, "Friday's gathering showed a weary but strong group, facing the potential downfall of a man they call their chief, advocate, neighbor, and family. It was clear they will stand by Foxworth." The article went on to quote one of the meeting's participants concerning the charges against Foxworth, "The bullseye could have been on any of us said Reverend Robert Richardson, church elder from Emmanuel Temple Full Gospel Pentecostal Church." The *Skanner* article stated, "The hope that surrounded Foxworth's appointment makes the allegations about his conduct all the more poignant. What ever other casualties may arise from his case, the whole city feels the loss of another police chief's promising tenure brought short." In contrast to the *Oregonian's* clear representation of Foxworth as a sexual deviant, the black press has countered this portrayal by claiming racism and the significant role he played for the black community.

Highlighting again the black press's claims of racism and the significance of the loss of Foxworth to the black community, the *Observer* article cited previously referred to the era of the previous chief of police Mark Kroeker, during which there were two high-profile police killings of black people that paralyzed the already tense relations between the black community and the Portland Police Bureau. The article states that "to Foxworth's credit—the external review and revision of the bureau's policy on the use of deadly force that occurred during Foxworth's watch is a model of citizen-government collaboration." The *Observer* also ran another article, "Police Shuffle May Stifle Minority Voice," written on May 3, that reveals that when the mayor selected Rosie Sizer as the interim chief of police when Foxworth was suspended, she asked Dorothy Elmore to step down from her position as assistant chief of police. The article states, "Foxworth appointed Elmore last October as the first African American woman assistant chief." Besides Elmore's appointment, it was common knowledge that Foxworth was actively attempting to increase the racial and cultural diversity of the police department. Clearly these articles challenge the *Oregonian's* portrayal of this case through their claims of the significance of race and racism. However, it should be noted that these newspapers continued to remain virtually silent on the issue of sexuality. This article was the only one we found by the black press to be openly critical of Foxworth's behavior. It stated, "The public will likely never know the whole truth of the matter, but it seems clear that at the very least, he exercised poor judgment and acted in a way unbecoming a high-ranking police officer." Besides this sentence, there was no critique or discussion of the how this case is related to sexuality, that is, sexual impropriety, interracial relationships, and black masculinity.

The next phase of the story revolves around the findings of the investigation and Foxworth's demotion to captain by Mayor Potter and promotion to precinct commander by Interim Chief Sizer four days later. In June, the investigation cleared Foxworth of all claims except the minor charge of unprofessional conduct. "Charges Failed Test" was the title of this most straightforward and succinct piece released by the *Observer* regarding this phase of the story. It contained only the following paragraph, "City investigators identified and concluded an investigation on eight allegations of misconduct against Chief Derrick Foxworth in connection with a sexual affair he had with a desk clerk six years ago while commander of the Northeast Precinct." This piece ended in bullet format of each allegation followed by "unsubstantiated" except for "unprofessional conduct," which is followed by "substantiated." Sticking to the known information, this piece attempts to lay the case to rest in no uncertain terms.

On the same day the *Observer* ran another article, "Foxworth's New Command," which explained the mayor's decision to demote Foxworth, "Taking full credit for his decision, Potter concluded that Foxworth's ability to effectively lead as chief was damaged by the affair and a series of sexual emails he sent during the period of the relationship from April 2000 to September 2001." As in the previous article the piece then reports that only one of the charges against Foxworth was substantiated. This article highlights that though Foxworth was cleared of the egregious claims against him, his image remained unembraceable within the court of public opinion. Foxworth's image could not recover from connection to a consensual affair.

Finally, on October 18, 2006, both the *Skanner* and the *Observer* ran articles speaking to Foxworth's intent to file a discrimination suit against the city of Portland that claims he was demoted because he was a "black man who was involved in a relationship with a white woman." These pieces each review the history of the case regarding the release of the emails, finding the charges unsubstantiated, and Mayor Potter's claim that the city will "vigorously defend itself against any allegation that he was treated unfairly or inappropriately." In addition, the *Observer* also asks readers to consider why has "a mayor that has been seen as a civil rights activist when he was police chief in the early 1990s" now stating that Foxworth's suit was unfounded? Mayor Potter has suggested on several occasions up to this point that the mainstream media's racialized portrayal of Foxworth contributed to the outcome of the case.

Even though this case is squarely located at the intersection of race and sexuality at multiple levels, the black press remained silent on the significance of sexuality. Foxworth's sexual behavior was rarely questioned or critiqued. The black press did not ask the question: Why did a black man that had worked for decades to reach the pinnacle of his profession engage in such risky behavior? This speaks to how black men are at times beyond critique by their community concerning their sexual behavior within the black community and their relationships with white women. Interracial relationships, a site at the intersection of race and sexuality, was also neglected by the black press considering the tensions and anxieties that exist within the black community concerning the history of lynching, miscegenation laws, and the current "lack" of available black men for black women. Additionally, we would add the particular context of interracial relationships in the Pacific Northwest deserved some discussion. For example, black exogamy rates in the region are much higher than other parts of the country, which cannot be disconnected from the specific racial history of the Pacific Northwest.

CONCLUSION

Our objective in this essay has been to examine, through discourse analysis, how the mainstream and the black press treated the Foxworth case. We found that the *Oregonian* characterized Foxworth as a moral and sexual freak, which undermined the possibility for Foxworth to receive a fair trial in the forum of public opinion. The *Oregonian*'s treatment of Foxworth cannot be disconnected from the historical and contemporary myth that black people are sexually deviant that has served as the cornerstone of racial oppression in the United States of America. Finally, the *Oregonian* chose only to address race substantively when it no longer mattered indicating this move was largely a face-saving gesture to protect the newspaper from claims of racism. We reiterate that research continues to demonstrate the bias of the mainstream/white press and this is why we spend more effort providing a constructive critique of the black press.

The *Skanner* and *Observer* told a story that contested, through the lens of race absent any connection to sexuality, how the mainstream press told the story. They did this by emphasizing that the black community would be losing its leader, advocate, and protector. In addition, the black press suggested that the mainstream press was racist in its treatment of Foxworth. Nevertheless, the Foxworth case provided the opportunity for the black press to deconstruct how discourses of sexuality play a role in the reproduction of racial discrimination and inequality. The sexual harassment claim against Foxworth fit squarely into the long documented history of criminalizing black male sexuality as predatory, especially concerning white women. The *Skanner* and *Observer* both made reference to the media frenzy that was occurring, revealing their awareness of the link between race and sexuality, but they went no further than this.

Analysis of this case reveals how it is linked to a "sexualized system of racism" (Collins, 2005, p. 98). The black press in providing little or no space to examine the link between blackness and sexuality does not reflect the diversity of black sexual experience and limits critical reflection concerning issues of sexual impropriety within communities of black people (Crenshaw, 1995; Hammonds, 2004). In order to gain and maintain access to the mainstream and/or because of the internalization of the "sexualized system of racism," black elite discourses may lack the ability or sufficient nuance to critically engage complex intersections of race, gender, and sexuality.

Additionally, black leadership's silence inadvertently contributes to the reproduction of the racial hierarchy when male public leaders are linked with alleged sexual deviance (Nagel, 2003; West, 2001). Allegations of this sort bring up negative stereotypes of an unbridled black masculinity. Due to the history of lynching black men for their perceived interest in white women, black leadership in the United States have shied away from publicly linking themselves with black male leaders accused of sexual impropriety, especially with white women, because even when proven innocent, they are stereotypically judged as sexually deviant. Hence black leadership often attempts to portray itself as asexual to maintain status and political legitimacy. This strategy of a "politics of respectability" (Collins, 2005) or an "acceptable blackness" (Cohen, 1999), in this case the appropriation of an asexual black masculinity in order to appear more acceptable to mainstream society, does not take into account mass media's perpetuation of black masculinity as a dichotomy. One can be either the asexual black male historically represented as "Uncle Tom" or the hypersexual black male or black brute figure, which circumscribe the possibilities for black male sexuality and discussions of healthy sexual behavior within the black community.

The other aspect of this case that again the black press was silent on is the issue of the significance of interracial relationships within communities of black people (Collins, 2005; Nagel, 2003). The dominant discourse of black female and male sexuality has provided more space for black men to transgress the racial romance divide because their sexuality was more overtly sanctioned (Collins, 2005, p. 262). The stigma of race traitor is lessened due to the increase in masculinity afforded black males when they transgress the racial romance border. Today, with perceived lack of eligible black men due to high rates of incarceration and low academic achievement coupled with the discourse of the strong black woman, black women as "overbearing or not knowing their place" finds a place for reproduction when they critique black men for having interracial relationships. Treating the Foxworth case as if gender did not matter in the perceptions and experiences of interracial intimacy in the black community neglects these critical ways black men and women experience sexuality differently. Furthermore, within this dilemma, the role of white women is left unexamined, as if there is no place for analysis of their role in "taking" black men (Collins, 2005; Nagel, 2003) or of their claims of sexual impropriety. The black press needs to understand how the application of an intersectional politics can simultaneously deconstruct the white/mainstream press's representation of cases of sexual impropriety that silence the significance of race and speak to critical issues that are creating cleavages within the black community along the lines of gender and sexuality.

Finally, the black press had the opportunity to address critical aspects that are specific to the region. While the lack of economic possibilities as compared to other large West Coast cities may have contributed to the small population of nonwhite racial and cultural groups, it appears that race played an equally if not more important role in contributing to the small population of black people in Portland. Oregon is the only state to join the Union with an exclusionary clause in the state constitution (Berwanger, 1967). Indeed, the black exclusion laws were in place in the state's constitution until 1926. Further testament to the unwelcoming attitude Oregon presented to black people is revealed in the Oregon legislature's rescission of the Fourteenth Amendment in 1869, which was not reratified until 1973 (Brooks, 2006). Historian Carl Abbott suggests that as a result of this history, "Portland is White—demographically and culturally" (Abbott, 2003, 26). Abbott also points out that due to the small population of black people and other racialized groups, Portland has not experienced the development of large racially segregated, poor areas. Considering the lack of segregation relative to how it is experienced in other large metro areas and the small population size of black people may help explain the significantly higher rates of exogamy among black Oregonian men and women that occurs at a rate of 65 percent and 44 percent, respectively (Oregon Center for Health Statistics, 2005). Arguably, the forces shaping the lives of black people in the Portland Metro Area, where the overwhelming majority live in the state, makes for a qualitatively different experience than compared to other large urban areas in the country.

We contend that the black press missed an opportunity to address the complexity of the intersections of race with sexuality and gender, generally, and in the Northwest, specifically, that continue to shape the experiences of black people. We suggest that if the black press is going to continue to be a key site of resistance to the mainstream, it must begin to acknowledge the significance these issues play in communities of black people. Silence on the importance of gender and sexuality within communities of black people is an unsustainable position because it limits critical discussions of the diversity of sexual experience and behavior within black communities.

REFERENCES

Abbott, C. (2003). White like us. *Arcade (Architecture and Design in Northwest)*, pp. 25–26.

Associated Press. (2006, October 18). Foxworth announces intent to file suit against city. Retrieved from http://www.theskanner.com

Beaven, S. (2006, June 18). Foxworth tale raises race questions again. *The Oregonian*, p. A01.

Bernstein, M. (2006, April 6). Accuser of chief details e-mails, threats. *The Oregonian*, p. A01.

Bernstein, M. (2006, July 5). E-mails reveal help by Foxworth. *The Oregonian*, p. B01.

Bernstein, M., & Griffin, A. (2006, April 12). Foxworth goes on leave, waits for inquiry results. *The Oregonian*, p. A01.

Berwanger, E. H. (1967). *The frontier against slavery: Western anti-negro prejudice and the slavery extension controversy*. Champaign, IL: University of Illinois Press.

Blount, S. (2006, April 12). Community support for police chief. *The Portland Observer*. Retrieved June 23, 2007, from http://www.portlandobserver.com

Blount, S. (2006, May 3). Police shuffle may stifle minority voice. *The Portland Observer*. Retrieved May 3, 2006, from http://www.portlandobserver.com

Blount, S. (2006, June 21). Foxworth's new command. *The Portland Observer*. Retrieved June 23, 2007, from http://www.portlandobserver.com

Bonilla Silva, E. (2006). *Racism without racists: Color-blind racism and the persistence of racial inequality in the United States*. Lanham. MD: Rowman and Littlefield.

Brooks, C. (2006). Politics of forgetting: How Oregon forgot to ratify the 14th amendment. *Oregon Humanities. fall/winter*, 1–11.

Charges failed test. (2006, June 21). *The Portland Observer*. Retrieved from http://www.portlandobserver.com

Chuang, A. (2006, October 30). Race and the Foxworth lawsuit: Some say it's tempting to see race as the issue. *The Oregonian*, pp. A01.

Cloud, D. (1996). Hegemony or concordance? The rhetoric of tokenism in "Oprah" Oprah rags-to-riches biography. *Critical Studies in Mass Communication 13*(2), 115–137.

Coates, R. (2008). Covert racism in the USA and globally. *Sociology Compass, 2*(1), 208–231.

Cohen, C. (1999). *The boundaries of blackness: AIDS and the breakdown of black politics*. Chicago, IL: University of Chicago Press.

Collins, P. (2005). *Black sexual politics: African Americans, gender and the new racism*. New York, NY: Routledge.

Could there be other casualties? (2006, April 20). *The Skanner*. Retrieved from http://www.theskanner.com/article/view/page/2/id/1186

Crenshaw, K. (1995). Mapping the margins: Intersectionality, identity politics, and violence against women of color. In K. Crenshaw, N. Gotanda, G. Peller, & K. Thomas (Eds.), *Critical race theory: The key writings that formed the movement* (pp. 357–383). New York, NY: The New Press.

Curry-Stevens, A., Cross-Hemmer, A., & Coalition of Communities of Color (2010). *Communities of color in Multnomah county: An unsettling profile*. Portland, OR: Portland State University.

Dates, J. (1990). Print news. In J. L. Dates & W. Barlow (Eds.), *Split images: African Americans in the media* (pp. 343–387). Washington, DC: Howard University Press.

Davis, A. (1983). *Women, race and class*. New York, NY: Vintage Books.

Davis, O. (2005). Vigilance and solidarity in the rhetoric of the black press: The Tulsa Star. *The Journal of Intergroup Relations, 32*(3), 9–31.

Foxworth accused of sexual misconduct. (2006, April 6). *The Skanner*. Retrieved from http://www.theskanner.com/article/view/page/3/id/1065

Foxworth placed on administrative leave. (2006, April 13). *The Skanner*. Retrieved from http://www.theskanner.com/article/view/page/2/id/1123

Frank, R. (2006, June 8). Potter gets report on Foxworth today. *The Oregonian*, p. D07.

Frank, R., & Griffin, A. (2006, June 17). Serious lapse in judgment' costs Foxworth chief's job. *The Oregonian*, p. A01.

Goldschmidt, N. (2004, May 7). Statement by Neil Goldschmidt: Text of the statement. *The Oregonian*, p. A01.

Graves, F., & Shepard, C. (1992, November 22). Packwood accused of sexual advances; alleged behavior pattern counters image. *Washington Post*, p. A1.

Hammonds, E. (2004). Black (w)holes and the geometry of black female sexuality. In J. Bobo, C. Hudley, & C. Michel (Eds.), *The black studies reader* (pp. 301–) New York, NY: Routledge.

Hewlett, A. (2005). Reproduction of narrative myth versus strategic uses of race ideology: Early press coverage of the police killing of Malice Green. *The Journal of Intergroup Relations, 32*(3), 89–104.

hooks, b. (2001). *Salvation: Black people and love*. New York, NY: William Morrow.

Hortsch, D., & Rowe, S. (2006, April 16). Coverage of the police chief: Readers voice fairness concerns. *The Oregonian*. Retrieved from http://www.oregonlive.com

Huspek, M. (2004). Black press, white press, and their opposition: The police killing of Tyisha Miller. *Social Justice 31*(1–2), 217–241.

Huspek, M. (2005a). Black press contributions to advances in civil and human rights: Introductory comments. *The Journal of Intergroup Relations, 32*(3), 3–8.

Huspek, M. (2005b). From the standpoint of the white man's world: The black press and contemporary white media scholarship, with emphasis upon the work of W. Lance Bennett. *The Journal of Intergroup Relations, 32*(3), 67–88.

Hutchinson, D. (2000). Gay rights for gay whites?: Race, sexual identity, and equal protection discourse. *Cornell Law Review 85*, 1358–1391.

Jones, J. (1993). The construction of black sexuality. In M. Diawara (Ed.), *Black American cinema* (pp. 247–256). New York, NY: Routledge.

Kanziger, L. (2006, May 17). Double standard at play [letter to the editor]. The Portland Observer. Retrieved from http://www.portlandobserver.com

Kapsalis, T. (2002). Mastering the female pelvis: Race and the tools of reproduction. In K. Wallace-Sanders (Ed.), *Skin deep spirit strong: The black female body in American culture* (pp. 301–320). Ann Arbor, MI: University of Michigan Press.

Learn, S., & Griffin, A. (2005, November 4). Civic leader accused of sex abuse. *The Oregonian*, pp. D01.

Leonard, D. (2004). The next M. J. or the next O. J.? Kobe Bryant, race, and the absurdity of colorblind rhetoric. *Journal of Sport and Social Issues, 28*, 284–308.

Markovitz, J. (2006). Anatomy of a spectacle: Race, gender, and memory in the Kobe Bryant rape case. *Sociology of Sport Journal, 23*, 396–418.

McCall, W. (2006, October 18). Former chief cites emotional distress, harm. *The Portland Observer*. Retrieved from http://www.portlandobserver.com

McGruder, K. (2009). Black sexuality in the U.S.: Presentations as non-normative. *Journal of African American Studies, 13*, 251–262.

Merle, R. (2005, March 8). Boeing CEO resigns over affair with subordinate. *Washington Post*, p. A01.

Miller, D. (2004, October 12). Rep. Wu apologizes for "inexcusable behavior" as college student, *New York Times*.

Monahan, M. (2006). Race colorblindness and continental philosophy. *Philosophy Compass*, *1*(6), 547–563.

Morris, A. (1984). *The origins of the civil rights movement: Black communities organizing for change*. New York, NY: Free Press.

Nagel, J. (2003). *Race, ethnicity and sexuality: Intimate intersections, forbidden frontiers*. New York, NY: Oxford University Press.

National Institute of Justice & Centers for Disease Control and Prevention. (1998). *Prevalence, incidence and consequences of violence against women survey*.

Oregon Center for Health Statistics. (2005).

Nielsen, S. (2006, April 9). What was he thinking? *The Oregonian*, p. D01.

Page, H. (1997). "Black male" imagery and media containment of African American men. *American Anthropologist*, 99(1): 99–111.

Roberts, D. E. (1997). *Killing the black body: Race, reproduction and the meaning of liberty*. New York: Pantheon Books.

Rome, D. (2002). Murderers, rapists and drug addicts. In C. R. Mann & M. S. Zats (Eds.), *Images of Color Images of Crime*. Cary, NC: Roxbury.

Rosen, J. (2004, August/September). The story behind the story: How a 30-year secret involving one of Oregon's most powerful figures finally came to light, how a feisty alt-weekly made it happen, and how the state's dominant newspaper stumbled along the way. *American Journal Review*. Retrieved from http://www.ajr.org

Saint-Aubin, A. (1994). Testeris: The dis-ease of black men in white supremacist, patriarchal culture. *Callaloo, 17*, 1054–1073.

Steinhorn, L., & Diggs-Brown, B. (2000). *By the color of our skin: The illusion and the reality of race*. New York, NY: Plume Books.

Van Dijk, T. (1993). Discourse and cognition in society. In J. Stanfield (Ed.), *Race and ethnicity in research methods* (pp. 92–134). Newbury Park, CA: Sage.

West, C. (2001 [1994]). *Race matters*. New York, NY: Vintage Books.

Williams, L. (2001). *Playing the race card: Melodramas of black and white, from Uncle Tom to O. J. Simpson*. Princeton, NJ: Princeton University Press.

NOTES

1. They are http://blackamerican.blogspot.com and http://goldenwest.wordpress.com.

2. The first day the case was made public, the *Oregonian* printed four articles about the case.

3. However, as the case unfolded and did not fit into this narrative, the *Oregonian* switched to the lying, troubled white women narrative, which is revealed in the *Oregonians* printing of a number of articles suggesting Oswalt was psychologically unstable. Either simplification of Oswalt's character requires that white women be protected from their attackers or themselves.

CHAPTER 4

Love, Ambition, and "Invisible Footnotes" in the Life and Writing of Pauli Murray

Doreen M. Drury

AFRICAN AMERICAN LAWYER PAULI MURRAY APPLIED FOR a research job in 1952 with an international law project based at Cornell University. Her potential employers thought highly of her qualifications, which, in fact, were exceptional. Few women and fewer black women still had attained Murray's academic and professional standing. She was a graduate of Hunter College in New York and the Howard University School of Law, and she held a master's degree in law from the University of California, Berkeley. In 1945, the National Council of Negro Women recognized her as "one of the twelve outstanding women in American life for the year."[1] In 1946, Murray served as deputy attorney general for the state of California, the first black woman to hold such a post. Her first book, *States' Laws on Race and Color*, was published in 1951. Yet Cornell did not hire her for the position. A university administrator wrote to Murray, according to her posthumously published autobiography, *Song in a Weary Throat*, "[T]here were some questions concerning your past associations which . . . might place the University in a difficult situation."[2]

Murray wrote that Cornell's rejection appeared to hinge on questions about her communist and socialist associations. In those years of political backlash, as hearings on "un-American activities" continued and Senator Joseph McCarthy "fanned the flames of suspicion into a national hysteria," as Murray put it, her earlier involvement with many leftist political projects, including the Workers Defense League, the March on Washington Movement, and the Negro People's Committee to Aid Spanish Refugees, would have caused alarm at Cornell.[3] Murray had also engaged in groundbreaking civil rights activism, including sit-ins at lunch counters in Washington, DC, in the early 1940s, and she had been arrested and jailed for refusing to move to the back of a bus in Virginia in 1940.

Yet Murray knew that there were other "past associations" that could just as easily cause her to lose such a position and even end her career. These were her romantic relationships with women and her experimentations with masculine gender presentation, subjects she never publicly discussed, but that are detailed in letters, diaries, photos, and notes in her private papers.[4] Many of these documents survived her own efforts to "sanitize" her files in the mid-1970s and again close to her death in 1985.[5]

In January 1953, in the aftermath of her rejection by Cornell, Murray wrote in her diary that she feared what might be exposed through such a "loyalty investigation." Scrutiny of her "intimate private life," she revealed, was more threatening than scrutiny of her politics:

> [A] loyalty investigation [is] a harrassing [sic] experience. One feels frightened, inse-
> cure, exposed. One thinks of all the personal errors, the deep secrets of one's life
> unrelated to political activities. One is apprehensive that all of the details of one's
> intimate private life will be spread on the record to be read, sifted, weighted, evalu-
> ated and judged by strangers—some vicious neighbor with a gossipy tongue will
> be visited by an investigator and will glibly spread one's goings and comings on
> the record. One worries over one's private indiscretions and errors of judgment for
> which one has already paid in regret, remorse, but which may now endanger one's
> economic security.[6]

Murray was terrified that her relationships with other women could come to light and threaten her reputation as well as her always-tenuous ability to finan-cially support herself and members of her extended family. She was certainly not alone in fearing persecution on the basis of her same-sex relationships since "homosexuals" were targeted perhaps even more often than suspected commu-nists during this period.[7]

Murray's diary entry described not only her fear of discovery but also her remorse for "indiscretions" and "errors" for which she had already paid dearly. In addition to losing the Cornell position, Murray had suffered other experiences of rejection and marginalization, including her near dismissal from Howard because of a relationship with an undergraduate woman. Yet Murray recorded more than self-reproach in her private papers. She also recounted joy and pleasure in her "boyish" persona and in her love of women. On the whole, Murray's story is one of struggle to reconcile her aspirations to the opportunities and prerogatives of men, in love, career, and style—with expectations that she would fulfill family and community dreams of respectable achievement as a feminine, heterosexual woman.

This article briefly explores the astute ways that Pauli Murray navigated gender and sexuality while she worked toward a self-determined future. Scholars have variously described her as a lesbian, a homosexual, or as a transgender person or have written about her as if her gender and sexual preferences had no bearing on her politics. These assessments have generally not integrated race and class analyses into the reading of her issues around gender and sexuality and, therefore, fail to illuminate the complexities of Murray's identity strategies. Furthermore, such treatments miss the central place of gender and sexuality in her political evolution and in her contributions to twentieth-century thought and politics. I argue that Murray's reckoning with her gender and sexual desires cannot be understood apart from her particular family history, racialized and gendered discourses of respectability and normalcy, and her engagements with medicine and psychiatry as well as with leftist and feminist analyses of race and sex inequalities.

As a twenty-something-year-old in the early 1930s, Murray studied and participated in leftist politics and culture in New York City, experimented with self-representation in writing and photography, and fell in love. By the late 1930s, however, the heartbreak of young romance, the deep fears about the meanings of her gender and sexuality, the financial strains, and the needs of her family back in North Carolina began to take their toll. While Murray worked and attended law school through the mid-1940s, she searched for a creative medical solution to what she saw as her central problem: that the life that she wanted, in terms of love, family, and career, was really only available to heterosexual men. Eventually, however, she came to the conclusion that medicine could not help her "locate the seat of [her] conflict" because the problem was in society rather than in her body or psyche.[8] Taking note of this broad set of concerns, I discuss Murray's research, writing, and publication in 1956 of her book *Proud Shoes: The Story of an American Family* as playing a critical role in her clearing of an emotional, intellectual, and political path for the second half of her life. While telling the story of her maternal grandparents and arguing against the use of race (and sex) categories to demean and disenfranchise, just below the surface, *Proud Shoes* asserts that the "dignity of the individual" necessarily includes the freedom to love without restriction.

A daughter of the African American middle class, Murray was raised in the segregated world of Durham, North Carolina. She came of age infused with a commitment to representing "the best of the race." Since both of her parents died when she was young, she developed a keen sense of herself as having a special responsibility. Not only did she expect to fulfill her own destiny, but she also felt that she must fulfill her *parents'* destiny because their lives were cut tragically short.

In the late 1920s, Murray relocated from Durham to New York City, and for the next decade, she was relatively able to chart her own course without undue concern for the imperatives of black, middle-class, heterosexual womanhood. During the 1930s, as a college student and a worker in New York, Murray moved more or less freely through the world—aspiring to be a poet, learning about radical politics, sometimes passing as a young man, and engaging in intimate relationships with other women. In this period, Murray also literally renamed herself, replacing her birth name, Anna Pauline, with the gender-ambivalent name "Pauli," by which she was known for the rest of her life.[9] In New York, first based in the women-only environments of the Harlem YWCA and then Hunter College, she became actively engaged in new communities of intellectual, political, and adventurous women and men. Together with a multiracial, multiethnic group of friends and "fellows," Murray traveled widely, defied the conventions of gender, and lived a very different life from the lives of her mother and aunts. And certainly she loved differently.

Like other young people during the Great Depression, Murray benefited from and contributed to women-centered, black, and leftist (and black leftist) projects and communities. While by the early 1930s Stalin and the Communist Party in the Soviet Union rejected homosexuals,[10] queer progressive people in US cities made space within leftist communities to connect with each other politically and socially. The Left's antiracist, antifascist politics and analysis of capitalism and imperialism inspired and facilitated the carving out of space for the expressions of same-sex love and sexuality, gender nonconformity, interracial love, and critical analyses of sexism.[11]

New Deal programs also offered settings for like-minded women to meet each other and pursue their interests together. In 1934, at a temporary relief camp for unemployed women in New York, Murray met Peg Holmes, a white woman. They formed an immediate bond. In the company of Peg, Murray wrote poetry, participated in radical politics, and sometimes presented herself as a young man. With Peg, she also explored an adventurous life that she referred to as "tramping," including hitchhiking, hopping freight trains, and camping.

Murray recorded her journeys in letters, poetry, and short stories and creatively represented her transgressive boyishness and homoerotic desire in several photo albums. One album titled "The 'Life and Times' of an American called Pauli Murray" contains a carefully organized and captioned section labeled "A creature of many moods and facets—my 'id.'"[12] Both introspective and playful, this series documents important aspects of Murray's identity in those years, including several of her masculine personae. Murray labeled these snapshots "The Poet," "The Dude," "Peter Pan," "The Vagabond," "The Acrobat," "Game of Tennis," "The Imp!," and "The 'Crusader.'" In six of the photos, short hair slicked back, Murray is wearing what would be considered male attire—jackets, shirts, long pants or knee-length pants tucked into knee-socks, and boots—posing in what we might call "unwomanly" stances. In most of the photos she is grinning at the camera. The album also includes photos of Pauli, sometimes called "Pete," and Peggie. These chronicle Murray as the strong, romantic Pete enjoying life on the road with the more feminine appearing Peggie.

In "many moods and facets," Murray's delight and proud self-possession in her boyishness is complicated by "The 'Crusader.'"[13] Here, Murray is dressed as a professional woman on a New York street, wearing a dress or skirt with stockings and lady's winter coat, carrying a hat and briefcase. By including this particular photo, strikingly different from the others, Murray surfaces one of the central tensions of her life: could she pursue her ambitions to become an influential writer and civil rights leader on her own terms—that is, as a lover of women who sometimes styled herself in a masculine way and who identified with the privileges of men? Or would any "crusading" have to be done as an apparently conventional woman, who would be cast in a supporting role or relegated to second-class status?

The Pauli Murray who celebrated what she referred to as her "'boy-girl' personality"[14] also contended with deep social disapproval of same-sex love and "gender inversion," both in the larger society and within the black community. Murray was deeply troubled by the fact that her love of women was characterized as abnormal by dominant discourses of the times and in particular that they violated black, middle-class norms of respectability. Over and against white ideas about African American sexuality and gender arrangements, black communities developed ideologies of respectability and race uplift that included strict codes of conformity to gender roles, to heterosexuality, and to patriarchal, nuclear, monogamous family life. Especially for black women, who frequently worked outside their homes to support their families, there was a heavy burden in terms of comportment and reputation.[15]

In this context, Murray entered psychiatric hospitals several times, apparently beginning in the late 1930s, as she coped with breakdowns brought on by what she described as a "longstanding emotional and mental conflict, popularly known as homosexuality."[16] In December 1937, suffering deeply over the loss of—or the impossibility of—a relationship with another woman, most likely Peggie, Murray sought help at the Long Island Rest Home. In notes she made during her hospital stay, Murray struggled to understand her "very natural falling in love with the female sex" and why she succumbed to "[t]errific breakdowns after each love affair that has become unsuccessful."[17] While she noted that her "conflict" was "popularly known as homosexuality," Murray rejected that identity for herself, pointing out that she had little in common with the negative characterizations of homosexuals, often also attributed to black people. She emphasized her restrained piety, sobriety, and belief in science as signs of her respectable nature. When she wondered why she "[could not] accept the homosexual method of sex expression, but insist[ed] on the normal first," the implication was that she could not accept it because she was *not* "homosexual."[18] During a subsequent hospitalization, Murray lamented that homosexuals did not have the "opportunity to express such an attraction in normal ways—sex life, marriage, dating, identification with the person and her environment."[19]

As much as she craved a "normal," respectable life, Murray was very clear about the kind of normalcy she desired. Despite the encouragement of doctors, she rejected any "adjustment" to heterosexual femininity.[20] Instead, Murray developed her own theory about her problem and its potential cure. Drawing on medical literature about hermaphroditism, as well as newspaper reports on the treatment of "effeminate males" with "synthetic male hormones" that "cured" their homosexuality, Murray theorized that she might have a hidden male element inside her body and struggled to persuade her doctors to search for—and if found, treat—this source of her "maleness." Her idea was that if a gland, for example, were located, male hormone therapy could be used to bring her hidden maleness to fruition. This way, she hoped, she could be classified as a normal, heterosexual male and be allowed to love freely, style herself in the ways that she preferred, and pursue professional and leadership opportunities open to men.[21] Murray's goal was to legitimize her feelings and the self-understanding she had developed and, perhaps even more crucially, *to be understood by others*, including some of the women she fell in love with, as *not* deviant, as *not* degenerate. In response to her request that she undergo exploratory surgery and treatment with male hormones to enhance what she saw as her own virility, her doctors offered her psychological treatment and hormones to strengthen her femininity, both of which she steadfastly refused.[22]

In our present moment, the appeal of claiming Murray as an early "transgender warrior" is perhaps understandable. Yet this framework obscures key features of Murray's life and politics, as does the unproblematic identification of her as "lesbian" or "homosexual." While there are competing understandings of transgender identity today, a dominant, popular narrative maintains that one's body doesn't fit with one's *true* self, one's *true* gender, hence the focus for some people on bringing the body into line with the felt gender, through dress, hair style, name change, hormones, and often surgery.[23] Although Murray sought "experimentation on the male side"[24] for several years, she came to believe that it was not her body that needed to change, but the confining limits of oppositional sex/gender and race identity categories. She also devoted much of the rest of her life to ending the subordination of "women" and "Negro" people—as a lawyer, a professor, a priest, and a theologian.

During the early 1940s, as a law student and burgeoning feminist, and informed by her leftist politics, Murray began to develop a recognition of the social forces that impeded her ability to act on her desires while retaining the respect of her peers and wider society. In 1943, while at Howard Law and recovering from a breakdown related to her relationship with an undergraduate woman, she described the social disapproval she faced in a letter to her maternal aunt. Exposure of the relationship had "endangered . . . everything I've worked for for two years at Howard." She continued, "Where you and a few people understand, the world does not understand nor accept my pattern of life." In language that evokes what she would later write about Cornell's investigation, Murray recounted feeling defenselessness in the face of potential enemies—because "the laws of society" offered no protection—and the agonizing impasse between her happiness and "society's standards." She also noted that, once again, her professional success was in jeopardy: "[T]o try to live by society's standards always causes me such inner conflict that at times [it's] almost unbearable. I don't know whether I'm right or whether society (or some medical authority) is right—I only know how I feel and what makes me happy. This conflict rises up to knock me down at every apex I reach in my career. And because the laws of society do not protect me, I'm exposed to any enemy or person who may or may not want to hurt me."[25] Over the next several years, Murray continued to wrestle with the question of how best to move forward given the painful reality of social limits. As she developed even more fully her conviction that a person, whether regarded as "man" or "woman" or as "Negro" or "white," should be able to live, love, and work as they chose, she also finally underwent abdominal surgery in 1947. The surgery did not reveal the gland or tumor that she thought might be "secreted" inside her, and Murray seems to have ended her quest for a medical resolution. She turned instead to writing, a practice that throughout her life often served as her "only safety valve against frenzy."[26]

The writing project through which Pauli Murray advanced a new understanding of her right to her desires and to her place in the world was *Proud Shoes:*

The Story of an American Family.[27] Immediately after Cornell's rejection in 1952, and as reactionary forces continued to rise in the United States, Murray began researching and writing in earnest the history of her mother's side of her family. Published in 1956 and still taught in colleges today, *Proud Shoes* fired back at McCarthy-era assaults on democratic values, challenged American racism and the politics of exclusion, and asserted a politics of radical humanism, a radical respect for the individual. While Murray did not openly discuss her sexuality or gender identifications in the book, *Proud Shoes* must also be read as an encompassing argument for the right to pursue her love and ambition.

Repudiating Cornell's dismissal on the basis of her "past associations," Murray wrote many years later that *Proud Shoes* demonstrated that her brave and righteous family members "were actually my earliest and most enduring 'past associations'" and that her family "had instilled in [her] a pride in . . . American heritage and a rebellion against injustice."[28] Indeed, in a key moment in *Proud Shoes*, Murray explained the dissonance between the demeaning assertions commonly made about African American character, constitution, or capability—and the stories she was raised on about her free-born, mixed-race grandfather, Robert G. Fitzgerald (1840–1919). Her grandfather's heroic service in the Union army during the Civil War, his education and work as a teacher of freed men and women, his economic independence, and his respectability all served Murray in her youth as "invisible footnote[s]" on the racist, poisonous textbooks she read and the degrading experiences she and her family prevailed against.[29] As Murray wrote, "A Negro was forever on trial, carrying always a heavy burden of proof that he was not by nature degraded or inferior, for he stood against the accumulated weight of words, laws, customs and the sanctity of judicial precedent."[30] Against this backdrop, her grandfather's life was a potent reminder that there was *no truth* to the depravity assigned to black people by the white world.

The granddaughter of a soldier, Murray carried a similar burden, not only as a woman of color, but also as a queer person in a world where pathologizing discourses on same-sex desire and "gender inversion" were extremely difficult to escape. *Proud Shoes* encoded a layer of "invisible footnotes" about Murray's struggles to manage *that* "heavy burden of proof"—that her unwomanly career aspirations, her sexual and romantic desires, and her masculine identifications were not effects of her degradation or inferiority. In other words, *Proud Shoes* did double or triple duty for Murray. The book's manifest content locates it within the field of racial and political protest, challenging any claim that the sources of her politics or heritage are suspect. It is radical for its open embrace of multiracial heritage and of love across the color line, commonly considered at the time a form of sexual deviance. In its defense of the individual against any fixity of status by birth, *Proud Shoes* also insists that the meaning of freedom in the United States necessarily includes the right to love, to work, to be . . . without regard for gender and sexual prescriptions.[31]

Murray described the book as using the story of her grandfather to contest unfair charges against black people, and in particular, to disprove charges of sexual degeneracy. These accusations and Murray's responses to them paralleled and informed the book's subtextual defense against judgments of degeneracy commonly attributed to same-sex love and unconventional gender expression. Shortly before the book's publication, Murray told Elizabeth Lawrence, her editor at Harper Brothers, that her focus on the Civil War experiences of her grandfather "refutes *in the story of an individual* the distortions of many historians about the role of Negroes on behalf of their cause" (emphasis in original). She added, "anything said for 'us poor Negroes' to show that we are neither degenerate [nor] rotting with venereal disease is all to the good, me thinks."[32]

While Murray makes a powerful case for radical respect for the individual in *Proud Shoes*, this political vision is clearly hard-won, and at times, unsettled. She grapples in the text, as she did in her life, with authoritative notions of hereditary depravity and inferiority on the basis of race and sexuality. *Proud Shoes* is a tale of heroism and nobility, as well as a search through sorrow, shame, and illegitimacy. Ostensibly a story about the "proud shoes" in which her maternal grandfather walked, the book inevitably circles back to slavery, to rape, and to violence. We find Murray working to come to terms with these painful aspects of her family history and of the nation's collective past as well as their meaning for her own loves and aspirations.

Some of the deepest scars hidden under Murray's pride in her family history are events of great emotional pain in her own lifetime, which she truly feared could be the result of hereditary insanity.[33] These are stories she does not tell in *Proud Shoes*, but they have been preserved in her private papers and to some extent in *Song in a Weary Throat*, published some thirty years after *Proud Shoes*. Not only was Murray herself hospitalized in psychiatric facilities several times, but her mother, who died suddenly (of "apoplexy") when Murray was three, was rumored to have committed suicide, suggesting that she had succumbed to mental weakness. A few years later, her father was committed to a psychiatric hospital where he remained for many years until his death at the hands of a white attendant in 1923. A sister and a brother also suffered emotional breakdowns and psychiatric hospitalizations. These traumas—in a world where people could literally be driven crazy by racism and injustice—were undoubtedly at the forefront of Murray's thinking as she told the stories of her grandparents and endeavored to take control of the meaning of her own "associations."

Murray wrote that the adversity of her family history was mitigated by the family's legacy of heroism and the conviction that they, and she, in particular, perhaps, had inherited the pride and fortitude to fight for respect. "Because of [grandfather] we felt that we belonged, that we had a stake in our country's future, and we clung to that no matter how often it was snatched away from us . . . I was never allowed to forget that Grandfather had been a soldier and that I was a soldier's granddaughter."[34] Always fending off the threat of being treated as less than, she wrote that he taught her to never speak like "ignorant riffraff."[35] He told her, "I won't have any grandchild of mine sounding as if he is a nobody and came from nothing."[36]

Great-grandfather Thomas Fitzgerald, who is described as "a half-Irish mulatto," and great-grandmother Sarah Ann Burton Fitzgerald, a white woman whose ancestors were "Swedish and French," also provided legacies of struggle and rebellion that sustained Murray.[37] Thomas Fitzgerald promoted an inclusive

Christianity that valued every individual and made "[e]very member of the household . . . feel important in the eyes of the Almighty and [know] that he had his place in the universe."[38]

In a passage that evokes the vulnerability Murray often felt about her gender and sexuality, she describes the magic of the legends of the Fitzgerald ancestors.

> Fitzgerald ancestors from County Kildare, Ireland, was a lilting and magical phrase which sounded well in my ears. It strengthened the growing shell of pride used to protect the soft underbelly and wobbly legs of a creature learning slowly to navigate in a cruelly segregated world. But, more than anything else then, it kept me from acceptance of my lot. I would always be trying to break out of the rigid mold into which I was being forced. I would always be in rebellion against crushing walls until people no longer needed legends about their ancestors to give them distinctiveness and self-respect.[39]

The "wobbly creature" of herself, which notably has no gender, is just learning to protect itself in the harsh world, to understand what is possible and perhaps impossible. Her "soft underbelly"—the profound truths about love and selfhood at the core of her life—had already been used against her and she continued to pay a high price for them. As much as Murray bravely struggled to create an alternative path for herself and her aspirations, and as much as she had accomplished, she had also lost so much—in time, in health, in self-confidence, in opportunities to serve and lead social justice battles. However, by the time of the writing of *Proud Shoes* and through its composition, she was fighting her way back through the construction of this "growing shell of pride." She did not accept the reduced ambitions and "rigid mold" of how to be a black woman, how to love, and how to lead. The Fitzgerald history helped Murray "gather . . . strength to combat" what she called "an almost intolerable present" that did not yet affirm the full scope of her personhood.[40] Of course, the language here of "an almost intolerable present" resonates with the language Murray used during her recovery from a breakdown in 1943 to describe an "almost unbearable" present.

Murray also disarmed notions of black, and sexual, depravity in *Proud Shoes* through her recounting of the story of the rape of her great-grandmother, Harriet. In this section of the book, Murray grappled with some of the most unforgivable assaults on black (and native) women and she appeared to accept the possibility that there *may* be some biological degeneracy—in the case of *white men*, that is. Murray offered as an embodiment of true wantonness Sidney Smith, the "evil little man" who was her white great-grandfather, the father of her maternal grandmother, Cornelia Smith Fitzgerald (1844–1924).[41] She asserted that rape and slavery were the true "sickness[es]" and suggested that if there was a degree of madness in Harriet and Cornelia, it was a result of the trauma they suffered.

Murray noted in *Proud Shoes* that some people held Harriet responsible for Sidney's rape of her, because she was so "alluring," but that it was Sidney who must be held fully responsible for his violation of her. Harriet, the mother of Cornelia, was a slave in the Smith household, described by Murray as "three-fourths white and one-fourth Cherokee Indian."[42] Sidney's crimes, his "dark, sinful acts," were also, she suggested, evidence of *his* "wild blood."[43] Clearly, Murray reversed the paradigm: not black women and men or queer people, but rather white, heterosexual men represent depravity and danger. Harriet developed "a wild look in her eyes" and "a silent smoldering hatred" only *after* she was attacked by Sidney.[44]

Complicating this narrative, and pointing toward Murray's sense of entitlement to the male professions, is her description of how her grandmother, Cornelia, also took enormous pride and even "joy" in Sidney, her father.[45] Cornelia remembered Sidney as nurturing in her "a rebellion against everything Negro slavery encompassed. He instilled in her the idea that she was inferior to nobody."[46] Murray wrote that she, in turn, inherited not only her grandmother's nervousness but also her rebelliousness, her constant struggle to "shak[e] off a restraining hand to get on with what she was doing."[47] Cornelia was well aware of the tension between her dual white legacies of shame and accomplishment,[48] between the shame of Sidney's assault and, as Murray put it, "everything desirable in life—power, wealth, privilege and respectability" that whiteness represented to Cornelia.[49]

Following her grandmother, Murray developed an attachment to her roots in "southern [aristocracy]"[50] and drew on this legacy in shaping her aspiration to the "highest" vocations, which were represented in the professional achievements of her white male Smith ancestors: "doctors, lawyers, judges, and legislators."[51,52] Murray was certainly haunted by Sidney's evil. Yet faced with his horrible acts, she claimed her connection to white men's *best* legacies as a birthright. She could claim these legacies because, in the first place, she had already claimed the legacies of bravery, compassion, generosity, and humility from her grandfather and the other black soldiers he fought with in the Civil War.[53] These virtues led her not to hate, she wrote, but instead to pick through the white legacies for what was worthy of carrying forward.[54]

Her knowledge that she was the great-granddaughter of a lawyer and legislator, a "very smart man" in her grandmother's estimation, helped stimulate Murray's pursuit of a career in civil rights law when such an ambition was improbable and often considered improper for a woman. Many years after *Proud Shoes*, in a 1968 interview, when asked why she decided to become an attorney, Murray replied, "I have a feeling [that] first it was an unconscious choice. My great-grandfather, Cornelia Smith's father, was a lawyer in the slave-owning Smith family. I saw him through her eyes. He was supposed to be a very great, very smart lawyer. This was grandmother's image of him. I think that image challenged me."[55] Murray's experiences in law school, recounted in her autobiography, help explain why she might have felt she needed this challenge and justification. Murray described her frustrations with the diminished role she was given as a woman, even when she had made her way to Howard University Law School, one of very few women enrolled in law schools in 1941. At Howard, despite a progressive dean, who apparently supported her application and helped her gain a scholarship, she was subjected to "ridicule" as a woman, rarely called on in class, and excluded from "the fraternity of lawyers who would make civil rights history."[56]

In *Proud Shoes*, Murray interpreted Cornelia's "uncontrollable pride in blood," pride in her white father, as alleviating "the frustrations of her later years—the barrenness of her existence . . . and the blighted life she led in a world where she had no place."[57] Yet how much of Cornelia's rage could have been alleviated when she felt unrecognized and ended her days in relative poverty despite her father's wealth? In the mid-1950s, as a queer, middle-aged woman of color struggling personally and professionally in the aftermath of Cornell's rejection, Murray was equally frustrated and outraged by the accumulated weight of her own marginalization. As she wrote in her autobiography, the loyalty investigation by Cornell "stripped me of individuality and discarded me like unwanted refuse."[58] But in writing *Proud Shoes*, Murray launched herself into her future, wrapped in family pride and perhaps more secure in the knowledge of her utterly complex, nonconforming self and her impossible to reconcile heritages. She began to find her way forward by defining freedom for herself and viewing her trajectory as similar to that of newly freed people in 1865. Freedom in America, Murray wrote toward the end of *Proud Shoes*, meant "the end of being nobodies."[59] Even when you had nothing to call your own and few prospects, it meant something in you that could not be destroyed. "Freedom was not something you could hold in your hands and look at. It was something inside you that refused to die, a feeling, an urge, an impelling force."[60]

Not surprisingly, the freedom to find *love* is central to the meaning of freedom in *Proud Shoes*. Murray was not only thinking about Peg Holmes during the writing of the book but was inspired by memories of their time together so many years before. As she wrote to Peg in a letter in the early 1970s, it was she who prompted a passage in the book on freedom as the opportunity to embark on what Murray called an "unending quest for loved ones."[61] The invisible footnote on this passage is certainly Murray's own quest to be able to have her love, her desire, safely, freely, with "no curbs" or "restraints" of any kind.[62,63]

Pauli Murray found other loved ones and created for herself what Jean Humez has described as a "'beloved community' of women," including Ella Baker, Maida Springer Kemp, Caroline F. Ware, to name only a few of the many women (and some men) who were her intellectual, political, and spiritual comrades on the journey.[64] In 1957, the year after the publication of *Proud Shoes*, Murray met Irene Barlow when both women worked at a law firm in New York. Murray and Barlow developed a "special" relationship that lasted until Barlow's death in 1973.[65] In the years after *Proud Shoes*, Murray also found and immersed herself in women's liberation and feminist thought. She worked for women's rights with the President's Commission on the Status of Women and the ACLU and was one of the founders of the National Organization for Women. Although it does not seem that she felt she could—or needed to—publicly discuss her complex relationship to gender and sexuality, her fierce feminism enabled her to develop her critique of constraints based on race and sex. Until her passing in 1985, Murray wrote and spoke often, elaborating a radical humanism grounded in an intersectional black feminist analysis.[66]

It is remarkable that at the age of 66, Pauli Murray was ordained as one of the first women Episcopal priests. She concluded her autobiography, *Song in a Weary Throat*, describing herself as "a symbol of healing" at her first mass in Chapel Hill, where her maternal grandmother, born and raised in slavery, was sent to the balcony as a little girl. In the mid-1970s, rejecting any essentialisms—whether based in race, sex, or status—and this time from her position of almost ultimate authority, *as a priest*, Murray wrote, "All the strands of my life had come together. Descendent of slave and of slave owner . . . I was empowered to administer the sacrament of One in whom there is no north or south, no black or white, no male or female—only the spirit of love and reconciliation drawing us toward the goal of human wholeness."[67]

NOTES

1. Pauli Murray, *Song in a Weary Throat: An American Pilgrimage* (New York: Harper & Row, 1987), 297.
2. Ibid., 297.
3. Ibid., 294.
4. Pauli Murray Papers (MC 412), Schlesinger Library, Radcliffe Institute, Harvard University (hereinafter cited as PMP).
5. On sanitizing her files, see, for example, Murray to Peg, March 18, 1973, f. 1688, PMP.
6. "Diary Notes," January 31, 1953, f. 27, PMP.
7. David K. Johnson, *The Lavender Scare: The Cold War Persecution of Gays and Lesbians in the Federal Government* (Chicago: The University of Chicago Press, 2004).
8. "Questions prepared for Dr. Titley," December 17, 1937, f. 71, PMP.
9. Throughout her life Murray was often addressed as "Mr. Pauli Murray." See, for example, Stephen Vincent Benét to "Dear Mr. Murray," October 3, 1939, f. 1621, PMP. And at least once, in 1974, she was called "Father" while working as a hospital chaplaincy intern. See "Dear Ruth," June 23, 1974, f. 1689, PMP.
10. John D'Emilio, *Sexual Politics, Sexual Communities: The Making of a Homosexual Minority in the United States, 1940–1970* (Chicago: The University of Chicago Press, 1983).
11. On radical black women's gender critiques see Dayo Gore, *Radicalism at the Crossroads: African American Women Activists in the Cold War* (New York: New York University Press, 2011). On social and political connections between gays and the Left, see Daniel Hurewitz, *Bohemian Los Angeles and the Making of Modern Politics* (Berkeley: University of California Press, 2007).
12. "The 'Life and Times' of an American called Pauli Murray," f. 24vf, PMP.
13. "The Imp!" is also an important and complicating figure in Murray's self-presentation, but space constraints prevent a discussion of this figure.
14. "Dear Mother," June 2, 1943, f. 253, PMP.
15. See Cheryl D. Hicks, *Talk with You Like a Woman: African American Women, Justice, and Reform in New York, 1890–1935* (Chapel Hill: University of North Carolina Press, 2010); Deborah Gray White, *Too Heavy A Load: Black Women in Defense of Themselves, 1894–1994* (New York: W. W. Norton, 1999); Kevin Gaines, *Uplifting the Race: Black Leadership, Politics, and Culture in the Twentieth Century* (Chapel Hill: University of North Carolina Press, 1996); and Hazel Carby, "Policing the Black Woman's Body in an Urban Context," *Critical Inquiry* 18 (1992): 738–55.
16. "Memorandum on P.M.," July 13, 1942, f. 71, PMP.
17. "Questions prepared for Dr. Titley."
18. "Questions prepared for Dr. Titley."
19. "Summary of Symptoms of Upset," March 8, 1940, f. 71, PMP
20. On "adjustment," see "Summary of Symptoms of Upset." Regarding her dis-identification with "homosexuals," see "Interview with Dr. _____," Dec. 16, [1937], f. 71, PMP.

21. Two books have been especially helpful in my understanding of Murray's engagement with medical science: Jennifer Terry, *An American Obsession: Science, Medicine, and Homosexuality in Modern America* (Chicago: The University of Chicago Press, 1999) and Anne Fausto-Sterling, *Sexing the Body: Gender Politics and the Construction of Sexuality* (New York: Basic Books, 2000). My analysis of Murray's engagement with medical science differs from that presented by Nancy Ordover in *American Eugenics: Race, Queer Anatomy, and the Science of Nationalism* (Minneapolis: University of Minnesota Press, 2003).

22. I am at work on a book manuscript that includes an extended analysis of these issues, but I first discussed them in my dissertation, "'Experimentation on the Male Side': Race, Class, Gender, and Sexuality in Pauli Murray's Quest for Love and Identity, 1910–1960," (diss., Boston College, 2000).

23. See, for example, Henry Rubin, *Self-Made Men: Identity and Embodiment among Transsexual Men* (Nashville: Vanderbilt University Press, 2003).

24. For "experimentation . . . ," see "Questions prepared for Dr. Titley."

25. See "Dear Mother," June 2, 1943, f. 253, PMP. This letter also explores concerns about family financial issues.

26. Murray, *Song in a Weary Throat*, 391.

27. Pauli Murray, *Proud Shoes: The Story of an American Family* (New York: Harper Brothers, 1956). All page references appear in the text and refer to the 1987 Perennial Library edition of *Proud Shoes* (New York: Harper & Row). Hereinafter designated in the text as *PS*.

28. Murray, *Song in a Weary Throat*, 298.

29. Murray, *Proud Shoes*, 104.

30. Ibid., 108–9.

31. My analysis is informed by Claudia Tate's *Psychoanalysis and Black Novels: Desire and the Protocols of Race* (New York: Oxford University Press, 1998). In contrast to Murray's encoding of her concerns, Rebeccah Welch notes that by the early 1960s Lorraine Hansberry's "sexuality worked to expand her understanding of the interrelated nature of oppression" and that she "*explicitly* framed 'homosexuality' as a 'question of human rights'" (emphasis added) in "Spokesman of the Oppressed? Lorraine Hansberry at Work: The Challenge of Radical Politics in the Postwar Era," *Souls* 9, no. 4 (2007): 318n54.

32. Murray to Lawrence, January 9, 1956, f. 1377, PMP.

33. Murray, *Song in a Weary Throat*, 13.

34. Murray, *Proud Shoes*, 24.

35. Ibid., 5.

36. Ibid., 6.

37. Ibid., 56.

38. Ibid., 73.

39. Ibid., 59.

40. Ibid., 157.

41. Ibid., 42.

42. Ibid., 38.

43. Ibid., 37, 158.

44. Ibid., 44.

45. Ibid., 35.

46. Ibid., 51.

47. Ibid., 7.

48. Ibid., 158.

49. Ibid., 50.
50. Ibid., 16.
51. Ibid., 33.
52. Murray also ran for local office in New York in 1949 (Murray, *Song in a Weary Throat*, 279–82).
53. Murray, *Proud Shoes*, 145–46.
54. Ibid., 52.
55. Interview with Murray by Robert Martin at Howard University, August 15, 1968. Audio tape number 2574, PMP.
56. Murray, *Song in a Weary Throat*, 184.
57. Murray, *Proud Shoes*, 35, 54.
58. Murray, *Song in a Weary Throat*, 298.
59. Murray, *Proud Shoes*, 167.
60. Ibid., 168.
61. Ibid., 168.
62. Ibid., 167.
63. Murray to Peg, March 18, 1973, f. 1688, PMP.
64. Jean M. Humez, "Pauli Murray's Histories of Loyalty and Revolt," *Black American Literature Forum* 24, no. 2 (1990): 333.
65. Murray, *Song in a Weary Throat*, 316.
66. Robin D. G. Kelley interprets Murray in the tradition of Anna Julia Cooper, Alice Walker, and many other black feminist and womanist theorists. Referencing the work of Patricia Hill Collins, Kelley puts it this way, "This radical humanism . . . has been a consistent principle of black feminist thought." See Robin D. G. Kelley, "Identity Politics and Class Struggle," *New Politics* 6, no. 2 (1997): 89. See also Patricia Hill Collins, *Black Feminist Thought: Knowledge, Consciousness, and the Politics of Empowerment*, 2nd ed. (New York: Routledge, 2000), 42.
67. Murray, *Song in a Weary Throat*, 435.

Figure 5.1   "Michelle" from Cryptofemme series by Chloé Zetkov

CHAPTER 5

THUGS, BLACK DIVAS, AND GENDERED ASPIRATIONS

AIMEE COX

YOUNG, LOW-INCOME BLACK WOMEN IN DETROIT, BY definition, live at the intersection of age, class, race, gender, and place. Positioned on the wrong side of these socially constructed identity markers, these young women must negotiate the boundaries of respectability and deviance most often erected in the space where race and sexuality meet. In addition to their network of family, friends, and coworkers, many of these young women are also immersed in a web of social service institutions that inform the way they perceive the possibilities not only for achieving social mobility but also for defining and expressing their identities.

This essay presents ethnographic data from over four years of fieldwork with the young female residents of the Fresh Start homeless shelter in Detroit to contextualize an analysis of how the sexual identities of low-income, young black women are framed by the racialized and class-based expectations of nonprofit community organizations, the welfare system, and vocational training programs. Young black women living in postindustrial Detroit must navigate these overlapping social service networks daily and, in the process, discover the most efficacious strategies for achieving their self-defined measures of success. This current work emerges from a larger book project that considers more broadly how an ideology of self-improvement, embedded within the context of leveled opportunities, impacts the shelter residents' ability to get ahead. Here, I am concerned with how the young women rework, maneuver within, and disrupt identity categories in ways that demonstrate their sophistication in subverting the race and gender hierarchies that threaten their life chances. In claiming ownership of their ability to define and continually redefine their sexual identities, while staging performances of self in public and private spaces, the young black women of Fresh Start reveal their understanding of gender and its expression as inherently dynamic and unstable. I also discuss how different notions of normative sexuality and gendered respectability among black girls and women are promoted in the client—social worker relationship. The themes addressed in this article are critical to considerations of

how state institutions and neoliberal models of social service constrain the possibilities for self-identification and sexual expression among individuals living in
under resourced urban communities of color.

   Divas, *thugs*, and *wannabes* are labels that both residents and staff at the Fresh
Start shelter attached to certain shelter residents to define their gendered behaviors,
relationships to men, and assumed sexuality. Like all tropes, these identifications
were imperfect, ill-fitting terms rooted largely in stereotypes and, in this case, the
possibilities for who and what young black women could be within certain social
and institutional settings. Within Fresh Start, *divas* referred to young women
who cultivated hyperfeminine personas through their style of dress and grooming, which often included form-fitting trendy clothing, air-brushed acrylic nails,
and well-maintained elaborate hairstyles. In addition, divas kept up a reputation
for having simultaneous multiple boyfriends that they juggled and manipulated
to meet their material and emotional needs. *Thugs* were the shelter residents who
openly claimed a lesbian identity and whose oversized clothes, close-cropped or
unstyled hair, and "hard"[1] demeanor led the Fresh Start staff and other residents
to assume that they were performing a version of masculinity. The *wannabes* were
residents who were thought to be mimicking the physicality and appearance of
the thugs, while pretending to be attracted to women, so as to gain some of the
respect and deference the thugs were afforded both within and outside of the
shelter setting.

   Certainly, these three identity types in no way fully define the young women
placed under each banner nor do they account for the wide spectrum of diversity
found among the nearly 150 young women who resided at Fresh Start for varying lengths of time during the course of a calendar year. My intention in focusing
on the divas, thugs and wannabes is to highlight the ways of being in the body,
in both the corporeal and behavioral sense, that were most salient at Fresh Start
as meaningful and socially productive (or destructive) types. The legibility of the
divas, thugs and wannabes as physical types with corresponding desires, motives,
and actions highlights the race and gender discourses that establish the parameters within which young black women of a certain class must negotiate processes
of self-identification. The status of diva, thug or wannabe represents the limits to
understanding young black women's full personhood and complicated positionality within social services. However, these tropes also provide room to consider
how young women, often perceived as marginal and ineffectual, actively rework
and reconstitute the social contexts, institutional spaces, and urban geographies
that are usually identified as unilaterally defining their existence. This reciprocity between constituting bodies and constructing spaces is a critical relationship
to explore. This is especially true if our political goals include propelling the
theoretical discussion of power into a realm where the everyday, and seemingly
mundane, individual acts of oppression that take place within state-sponsored
projects can be identified and eventually disrupted. In the introduction to *Black
Geographies*, McKittrick and Woods urge scholars to uncover how "black human
geographies are implicated in the production of space"[2] and where these geographies "disclose how the racialized production of space is made possible in the
explicit demarcations of the spaces of *les damnés* as invisible/forgettable at the

same time as the invisible/forgettable is producing space—always, and in all sorts of ways."[3]

McKittrick and Woods's discussion of black geographies and the mutually constituting nature of spaces and bodies is especially relevant in thinking about how all the young women in spaces like Fresh Start, not just those who appear to fit the label diva, thug, or wannabe, are constructed within neoliberal social service models of self-improvement, while they also both consciously and unintentionally subvert these models. Situating space more prominently, which in this ethnographic case means paying attention to the implications of Fresh Start's geographic and ideological location as a homeless shelter serving an overwhelmingly African American female population in the city of Detroit, provides additional avenues for comprehending the performances and practices of gender, sexuality, race, age and class. What Judith Butler calls "the system of compulsory heterosexuality" and its reproduction and concealment through the "cultivation of bodies into discrete sexes with 'natural' appearances and 'natural' heterosexual dispositions"[4] is, then, more clearly revealed as constructed and reproduced when space and location, and not just individuals and bodies, are more carefully read. Thus here I present the actions of the divas, thugs, and wannabes and Fresh Start staff as made up within, responsive to, and comprising the local and global institutions in which their actions take place.

I tell the stories of the divas, thugs, and wannabes through the experiences of residents and staff when I was conducting fieldwork from 2000 to 2004. During two years of this period, I was also the Fresh Start shelter director. I continue to be connected to the shelter administration, staff, and many of the young women and their families who participated in both the Fresh Start and the larger Give Girls a Chance (GGC) organization, of which Fresh Start is a part. I include this project in the tradition of black feminist research, as outlined by Leith Mullings[5] and am particularly concerned with exploring methodologies and writing strategies that enable the perspectives of working and low-income women's voices to come to the forefront in the discussions that frame their experiences. This is extremely vital to black feminist researchers' continued academic and activist commitments to work that investigates the new and emerging ways intersectionality impacts women's lives. Therefore, I have kept intact, as much as feasibly possible, the stories of these young women from the one-on-one informal interviews that occurred both on-site at Fresh Start and in the community. In addition, considering my embedded role in the shelter beyond researcher, I believe that maintaining the ethnographic detail that reveals my relationship to the residents and staff and my own problematic readings of and reactions to the way the young women represent themselves contributes to the tradition of demystifying the assumed infallible authority and invisibility of the researcher. This active tradition, established by minority scholars in the social sciences interested in interrupting hierarchies of knowledge production, is also a central part of my praxis.

THE FRESH START SHELTER

Fresh Start is a homeless shelter and transitional living program for young women between the ages of 15 and 21. The shelter is located in Detroit and is part of a larger nonprofit organization called Give Girls a Chance that is home to three additional programs: an after school academic and cultural enrichment program for middle school and high school age girls; a street outreach program that trains and hires teenage young women labeled high-risk to provide peer-to-peer education workshops and street counseling to other high-risk young women on issues such as safer sex, alcohol, tobacco and other drug use, and self-esteem; and the *New Pathways* program that assists adult women who live and make their living on the streets as sex workers in addressing drug addiction and making the transition to legal, safer employment. The Fresh Start shelter, however, is the largest of the three programs, receiving a little over two million dollars in federal, state, and private foundation funding out of the total agency annual funding stream of approximately three million dollars. The shelter provides room and board to up to 25 parenting and nonparenting young women (including a maximum of ten children under the age of six). Residents may choose to stay for a brief emergency period of up to two weeks if they need just minimal assistance in getting back on their feet or may apply to become a participant in the transitional living program (TLP). In the transitional living program participants receive full case management services along with access to the employment readiness, educational goal setting, and the self-care curricula. The average TLP participants stays in the shelter for four to six months and continues to receive supportive services for up to a year after moving out of the shelter and into their own independent living situation.

The overarching service delivery philosophy guiding the shelter and TLP program is based on the concept of youth development, which includes focusing on the young women's strengths rather than the characteristics that qualify them as part of an at- or high-risk target population, including the young women as much as possible in program planning and implementation, and training staff to celebrate individual differences while practicing nonjudgmental attitudes in case management and group workshop facilitation. Additionally, the staff is prohibited from exhibiting any faith-based leanings or discussions of church, God, and religious-based morality in their interactions with the residents. These ideal program principles are not so easily or directly translated in day-to-day program delivery, however. At the time of my research, approximately one-third of the 12-member hourly shelter staff, or resident advisors, were former Fresh Start program participants themselves and all, with the exception of one woman who identified as Puerto Rican, were working-class and low-income African American women. The salaried case managers were considered by the other employees in the organization, as well as themselves, to be well above the resident advisors in the agency hierarchy due primarily to their college degrees and nonexempt status. These women, whose wages and residential living situations put them in the lower-middle class to middle class, were also predominantly African American. Although the resident advisors and case managers found themselves in conflict and disagreement around many issues, they tended to be in agreement on what expressions of sexuality were acceptable by the young, predominantly black women in the program.

The relationships between the shelter residents and staff members were grounded in the expectations developed through intimate, daily interactions in the residential setting. These interactions, though based on firsthand personal knowledge, were, nonetheless, always mediated by larger narratives of young black womanhood. Thus what was considered allowable, unacceptable, normal, or deviant in terms of the residents' appearance and behaviors was tied to the discourses that framed their visibility as social beings or, as Butler states, "the social conditions by which people become intelligible."[6] In locating the shelter resident and staff dynamics within discussions of young black women in hip-hop culture, the welfare system and codes of respectability, I am connecting the meaning making and expressive capacities of the shelter residents' bodies to the history that constrains this creative, and perhaps even disruptive, potential.[7]

DISCOURSES OF YOUNG BLACK WOMANHOOD

Young black women's legibility as both human and sexual beings in mainstream society is framed by stereotypes of black womanhood that are emphasized in popular culture and discussed in the scholarship and policy initiatives that speak to and around their absence. Black feminist scholars have demonstrated how the familiar historical representations of the promiscuous, insatiable Jezebel and the overly aggressive and hot-tempered Sapphire find contemporary counterparts in the video vixens and faceless booty-shaking bodies that populate hip-hop and R&B videos. As the aesthetics and cultural references of hip-hop become increasingly ubiquitous, young black woman, whether they relate to these black female image in commercialized hip-hop or not, must contend with what these particular constructions of race, gender, and sexuality allow, sanction, and validate in terms of young black women's assessment and treatment in larger society. Here, I want to remind us that hip-hop culture, like all cultural manifestations, is shaped by history and tethered to larger economic interests. Therefore, the blame and condemnations that have been hurled at the young, primarily black male artists ignore the historical degradation of black female identity that has been instrumental in bolstering the Western white ideal of femininity and in providing a ready and available platform for the commercialization of misogyny in the black community. Since slavery, black women's roles in the home and community, out of necessity, have straddle the gendered boundaries of motherhood and the domestic sphere on one hand and participation in the labor market outside of the home on the other. This boundary crossing has been made required work for black women because of racial and gender oppression while also posing a threat to racial and gender oppression as black women's very beings stand in opposition to white patriarchy and female dependency on men for material and emotional support.

The narrative of low-income black women that emerged in the 1960s, when reforms to welfare were made to eliminate the discriminatory exclusions and standards that largely prohibited black women from receiving federal ADC (Aid to

Dependent Children), capitalized on the stereotypical image of black women as sexually irresponsible, slovenly, lazy, and poor mothers. These characterizations blatantly denied the realities of black women's presence in the labor force and comparatively small numbers on the welfare rolls. This discursive shift from welfare recipients as *worthy mothers in need* to *greedy societal parasites* directly reflects the broader inclusion of black women in federal benefit programs and the conservative political ideology that establishes an ahistorical case for making the links between poverty, black motherhood, and urban environments seem natural and inevitable. Questions of respectability become important in these discussions and in the lived experience of the young black women like the residents of the Fresh Start shelter.

During the Great Migration, codes of respectability[8] related to ways of being and living in the world, from style of dress and mannerisms to home maintenance and interactions in public spaces, were enacted in both overt and unspoken ways by more established members of the black middle class to ease newer black Southern migrants' assimilation into the norms of white Northern mainstream society. Performing respectability was, then, a strategy for achieving some level of acceptance and mobility within urban industry as well as civic and social life. In many ways, respectability was (and still is) a way for marginal members of society to establish grounds for claiming their rights as full citizens and was exceedingly important for the new black middle class trying desperately to hold onto their precarious status as well as for newly arriving working and lower-class blacks wanting to move up and out of poverty. Women, assumed to be the keepers of home and family, were especially held to the mandates of comportment and decorum that respectability demanded. Women working in and maintaining the domestic sphere while their husbands worked outside of the home was symbolically important for maintaining the private and public divide on which all forms of identity management hinge. Lower- and working-class black women, however, simply by the economic realities of their lives that necessitated their work both within and outside of the home, were automatically excluded from being respectable—no matter how sincere their efforts. This, perhaps, is why the performance of middle-class status and normative gendered behavior is so critical for determining the possibilities for social mobility for low-income women.

The young women of Fresh Start, who are working to create stability, success, and comfort in their lives, encounter contemporary codes of respectability not only within the shelter setting but also within the public school system, training programs, welfare agencies, and other social service agencies where the hidden charge seems to be focused on "improving" the physical appearances, attitudes, and overall public presentation of self by these young women. The intersection of race, class, and gender highlighted in issues of respectability and self-management, as in the past, take shape through discourses of sexuality. Within social services and the welfare system, this has meant a "performance of authority" over black female bodies whereby sex and the expression of sexuality become signs that they are undisciplined, irresponsible, and potentially dangerous. Thus the question of whether a young woman is deemed "committed to achievement" and "really working the program" or thought to have a "bad attitude," be "too grown to help," or "not ready for success" is largely determined in these institutional settings by the performance of a raced self that gets read through gender and class norms that have been shaped by ideas regarding appropriate expressions of sexuality. What is deemed sexually "appropriate" in these programs is usually the absence of expressions of sexuality in the case of single, young black women living in poverty. In the Fresh Start residents' case, their status as unemployed, or low-wage worker, single mother and young adult means that sex for them exists outside of the nuclear family and, more important, disconnected from dependence on a male wage-earner. Therefore, sexuality is predefined as taboo, improper, and degenerate. Surveillance and judgments of young, low-income black women's sexuality by the state and other public institutions is by no means a new phenomenon. We need only to look at the dehumanizing constraints placed on black women's procreation during slavery and the behavior modifications trends in welfare reform policy to understand this. It is, however, important to consider what it may now mean that these policing acts are often enacted by other working and low-income black women who work in case management and administrative positions in social service agencies. These women have similar experiences of economic marginalization, and their own conflicted understandings of how the limitations and freedoms in the expression of sexuality and gender identities impact success in the mainstream.

Representations of young black women in mainstream hip-hop culture, within the imaginary of welfare policy legislators and in relation to respectability, are not the only dialogues that shape popular characterizations of low-income, young black females. They are, however, the dialogical sites most commonly referenced in the conversations the staff and young women have within the shelter both within and between their respective groups. This makes sense considering the central role each discursive space plays in the lives of women at Fresh Start. Popular culture entertains and provides escape via television, radio, and the Internet during the few hours of down time the young women have between work, school, and caring for children; the frustrations of navigating the local welfare office are daily topics that often warrant strategic conversations and therapeutic venting sessions; and respectability is always the underlying subtext in conversations ranging from protocol in romantic relationships to the reasons for not getting hired.

Beyond the familiarity and accessibility of these particular popular, legislative, and theoretical discourses in the context of Fresh Start, I am interested in how they establish realms of exclusionary inclusion[9] for low-income women of color. In an essay on the status of black Caribbean women within the inclusions and exclusions of migration policy in Canada, Jenny Burman describes black women's nonstatus positions in society as being "expelled within the nation" where they operate as both insiders and outsiders, citizens and noncitizens. Burnam tells us that "through social-spatial regulation—which is underwritten by racial-sexual mappings on and of the body—black women are cast as assimilable stock figures in need of sympathy, help, corrective discipline, lessons in family values and so forth."[10] Like the black Caribbean women in Burnam's work, the young women of Fresh Start spend the majority of their days moving through nonprofit organizations and welfare agencies within the neoliberal state. While these institutions ostensibly provide service, resources, and care, they are governed by policies, goal plans, and training curricula focused on behavioral management and self-improvement strategies disconnected from the structural obstacles in these young women's lives.

While other scholars have discussed the self-governing turn in state services and social policy,[11] I find Burnam's focus on redemption and black women's liminal status on the borders of citizen, noncitizen, and salvageable semicitizen critical here. Although the young black women of Fresh Start are not migrants, their homeless status, age, blackness, femaleness, and ambiguous sexuality locate them within "geographies of exclusion." Their primary, though implicit, work within various systems of care then becomes proving their rights to occupy space and be included as true citizens of the state. This work most overtly takes the form of becoming employed in the low-wage labor force and striving to replicate the familial and gender norms of the heterosexual nuclear family, therefore finding social redemption in a sense. Within popular hip-hop culture,[12] young black women see themselves centrally as subjects in the imagery and content of much of the music and literature they consume but less so as producers and authors of this commercialized lifestyle; they are inside yet excluded. Remembering the reciprocity between bodies and spaces, geographic and discursive sites and individuals, we should not envision these practices of exclusion as unchallenged and unmitigated processes. All actors within the Fresh Start site—not just the divas, thugs, and wannabes—shape and subvert the physical and philosophical space of the shelter as well as the corresponding narratives that support Fresh Start's reputation in the community as a "place that helps and improves troubled girls."[13] Even though the ruptures that the young women manage to create may be viewed as relatively small and accomplished within the strict parameters of historical conventions and predetermined scripts, they nonetheless provide a view into what may be possible in the contexts of seemingly untenable situations.

DIVAS

The Fresh Start shelter staff's overall view of the residents' sexuality reflects their perception of the young women as a collective target population in need of protection from the dangers in the world outside of the shelter while also posing a threat to social order. With backgrounds that included sexual abuse, sex work, and exploitation and violent boyfriends, the Fresh Start residents' possibilities for experiencing sex and expressing their sexuality were quite often limited to the contexts of victimhood and violence. In this construction of the young women's sexual lives, the staff focused on encouraging the residents to refrain from relationships with men at all ("just be by yourself and focus on getting a job") or to be alert to what were made to seem inevitable instances of physical and/or emotional abuse and betrayal. Considerations of love, care, and comfort were rarely explored in staff conversations with the residents unless it was part of the assumption that they were carrots on a stick men used like subterfuge and weaponry to make the young women vulnerable to their devious schemes.

There was also, aside from these narratives of danger and precaution, the narrative that followed young women labeled divas. The residents who focused on dressing provocatively and talked openly in the shelter about their sexual experiences with men were divas. Divas were also generally considered physically attractive and, at least superficially, charming. In the common spaces such as the dining and television rooms, the divas dominated conversations with colorful stories of their multiple boyfriends and the various ways they were using or "getting over" on them to get money, clothing, and even support for their family members outside of the shelter. Although the actions and self-presentations of the divas pigeonholed them in a contemporary Jezebel-Sapphire stereotype, the other residents were conflicted in their reactions to the divas who garnered a lot of attention, both negative and positive, inside and outside of the shelter. They seemed intimidated and envious of the divas' brazen attitudes about men, sex, and money (all easily accessible, fluid and fleeting), but most often expressed judgmental disdain for their actions. The staff generally felt as if the divas' materialistic perspectives and strategically casual relationships with men negatively influenced the other residents and also undermined the core mission of Fresh Start's mission to help young women "make positive choices in their lives" and get ahead through hard work and diligent goal planning. The bold, proactive sexuality of the divas inspired a staff narrative of young black female sexuality that highlighted morality and ethical behavior. In this case, young women were seen as the perpetrators of improper and immoral sexual relationships and the victims of what the staff believed to be their poor upbringing, low self-worth, and lack of positive female role models. The divas sex lives were categorized as vulgar extensions of survival sex—materialistic sex.

These narratives align with Michelle Fine's findings in her research on the most common discourses of sexuality found in the public school system: victimization, violence, and morality.[14] Fine argues that missing from these discussions of adolescent sexuality is the discourse of desire. In the Fresh Start shelter, the narratives of protection, victimization, violence, and morality were bumping up against and overlapping one another in ways that proved confusing for both the staff and residents. For instance, the narrative of morality and respectability most closely associated with the divas was used to caution all young women, and the divas' risky relationships were sometimes tumultuous and violent, landing them in the category of potential victim in need of reminders of the emotional and physical dangers of sex. Desire is not the only theme missing from these discussions, however. Also absent is the belief that these young women are more than targets or uncritical actors. The Fresh Start residents make decisions about how they chose to define and express their sexuality based on considerations that they believe have the greatest potential to improve their chances for happiness, holistic health, and economic stability. The divas, although outwardly, through appearance, hyperfeminine, thought of themselves as playing a very masculine game. They would discuss how their ability to control their relationships with men was "flippin the script" or, in other words, reversing what they saw as the traditional gender dynamics in male-female relationships. In this way, the divas were behaviorally riffing on masculinity.

The overemphasis on self-improvement and self-presentation in the context of the economically devastated metropolis of Detroit where the jobs that would require mastery of these codes of respectability are few and far between for young, underskilled black women creates frustration among the Fresh Start staff and resentment among the residents. The stress and demoralization that accompanies the daily process of navigating the few employment options available within the deindustrialized, highly segregated city space creates a situation where attempting change at the individual level seems a welcome prospect compared to the large-scale social transformation really needed for Fresh Start residents to see a difference in their life chances. Under these conditions, social service providers (somewhat subconsciously) revert to an overemphasis on respectability so that they may see some progress and transformation in the outcomes for their program participants. The young black female participants, however, are more concerned with respect.

The hourly shelter staff workers, in particular the resident advisors, led lives outside of Fresh Start that were parallel to the residents. Their wages (just barely above minimum wage) were often equal to and sometimes lower than the pay the young women received in their various jobs. Although the residents' were required to save a percentage of their earnings toward moving out into their own apartments, the fact that they did not currently have to pay for rent or food meant that they had more disposable income then the resident advisors to purchase logo-covered bags, designer sweat suits, and other objects of conspicuous consumptions that the staff coveted but could not afford. The resident advisors talked about juggling work, childcare, continuing education, and social life with the residents as both peers and mentors. In many ways, the aligned lives of the RAs and residents supported the development of other mother[15] relationships based on the staff members' genuine care and concern for the young women. This was especially true for the young women who resided in the shelter for longer periods (between four to six months) and eventually graduated from the TLP program.

The contempt of familiarity was also a part of these familial like bonds. In my interviews with the resident advisors during the course of my fieldwork and work with them as their supervisor in my role as the shelter director, I listened to all the RAs at one time or another express their frustration with the inability to protect the young women from the emotional pain of having to deal with conniving boyfriends, disrespectful bosses, absentee fathers. and drug-addicted family members. As one RA, named Rhonda told me, "Most of us have been there and done that. They are just babies, even though they try to act grown. If we can tell them something and get them to listen to us, it's worth beating a dead horse."[16] On the other hand, RAs complained about the privileged attitude of the girls and the need to enforce more punitive policies and restrictive shelter entry guidelines. The line between the resident as victim and the resident as parasite was regularly drawn based on assumptions about the young women's respectability. Residents who failed to conform to the RA guidelines for respectability were thought to be promiscuous and/or not willing to "work the program"—that is, get a job and comply with shelter rules; divas often fell into this category.

It is interesting that the resident advisors would overtly categorize the young women's sexual practices as an infraction of shelter rules. Fresh Start's program philosophy of nonjudgmental advocacy and support for young women's right to make independent, informed choices did not support the RAs' condemnation of the divas. The welfare system that the divas and a majority of the RAs had ongoing experience with, did, however, systematically pry into their sexual behaviors and intimate relationships and make resource allocations based on lifestyle assumptions. The fact that the resident advisors would empathize with the diva's complaints about disrespectful, nosy welfare caseworkers and then exhibit the same punitive measures in their own roles demonstrates the conflicted nature of their placement in the Fresh Start hierarchy. The resident advisors were keenly aware that they had a reputation among the Fresh Start social workers and employees in the other branches of the GGC organization for being "ghetto" and "indistinguishable from the residents."[17] Calling for stricter policies served the purpose of making visible the resident advisors' authority (and, therefore, respectability) in the agency and distinguished them from the residents, even though they were essentially "perpetuating hierarchies that constrain them both."[18] Within Catherine Kingfisher's study on the relationship between welfare workers and welfare clients, she identifies the relatively low status of the workers within the welfare system and their responsibility for implementing as opposed to developing policies as key factors in feeding worker-client tensions.[19] The similar tensions I witnessed in the shelter concealed a pervasive sense of inefficacy among the RA staff and contributed to their need to demonstrate some level of control in their jobs through an overemphasis on rule enforcement.

THE REPLICATING RESEARCHER

During my time as shelter director the resident advisors were quite open with me about their discontent within the GGC organizational structure and the contradiction that they felt in being held accountable for life and death matters in the shelter[20] without having any real authority in their roles. Their status as gatekeepers and enforcers, although sometimes validating, was ultimately experienced as a position of powerlessness. The fact that the resident advisors did not see me as responsible for this structural set up but still felt I was in control of its perpetuation speaks to the complicated and continually shifting nature of privilege and accountability in our relationship. Prior to my appointment as director, the position had been vacant for over two years. The shelter caseworkers and RAs were forced to divide up administrative duties during this time while still maintaining their hands-on duties within the day-to-day schedule. The added responsibilities of completing grant reports, attending the state-mandated social service networking meetings, and keeping the shelter up to licensing code created a monumental strain in their already overburdened workloads. At the time the search for a director began, I was working in the after school program and had just begun my ethnographic research in the organization. I had contact with the shelter staff at least twice a week during the creative arts workshops I facilitated for the residents and became close enough to them to be taken into their confidence. They heard that the CEO of the agency was recruiting me to be the new director and were encouraging me to take the job. Since I was sympathetic to their issues with the upper-level administrations constant surveillance of the shelter coupled with a lack of support for their difficult and emotionally draining work, they thought I would be a good advocate for their needs.

The reasons why I ultimately decided to take the job reflected my uncertainty regarding what my obligations and alliances should be as a black woman, university-affiliated researcher, and youth advocate in the context of a homeless shelter serving and employing a predominantly black female population in Detroit. Many researchers from the surrounding universities had come to the shelter before me so my ethnographic work was not foreign to the staff. I was, however, the first black woman researcher—which in all of our minds meant something very different. The staff expected that I would do much more than collect data and write a report and verbalized the belief that my work would include direct hands-on interventions. This expectation was supported by the fact that I was already working in the GGC organization, and thus, crossing the traditional researcher boundaries. In addition, my own desire as an outsider within[21] to transgress the script of the distanced ethnographer impacted the shelter staff's perception of me. I felt deeply connected to the both the shelter staff and the residents and reasoned that my identity as a black female and orientation as a scholar-activist mandated my participation in a very different way. I didn't see, at the time, how I could not agree to take on the role of shelter director. My middle-class background, non-Detroiter status, and relatively young age (described as assets by the shelter staff before I took the position) soon became the explanations for decisions I made or policies I implemented with which the staff did not agree. I struggled to maintain a balance between supporting the resident advisors and insuring the best interests of the residents while working to create an environment where the two were not directly opposed. In this concrete, real life setting where the lives of young women were at stake in some way daily, my readings of feminist and critical race theories were challenged by both the immediacy of and limitations within the situations before me.

My intentions to implement the Fresh Start official philosophy of empowering, providing positive choices, and creating a space for the young women to direct the course of their own lives was frequently at odds with my compulsion to keep them physically and emotionally safe. In this way, I understand how difficult it was for the resident advisors to avoid other-mothering and gate-keeping tendencies. I wanted to find a way to replicate and share the lessons I learned in my two-parent, Midwestern, middle-class home in the context of this urban homeless shelter. This included relaying the standards of decorum, gendered respectability, and expressions of sexuality that were passed on to me as, I was often told, fundamental for gaining acceptance and respect as a black woman in America. I realized that these standards would and should not translate to the Fresh Start residents' lives. Nonetheless, in the back of my mind, I considered them privileged strategies for mobility that the residents should have access to as another way of performing and presenting themselves in the world. Operating under a separate set of behavioral expectations for the residents felt like dumbing down to me in a way. After all, I reasoned, don't most successful middle-class black women inherently understand that performing respectability is just part of living through the limited social scripts we have available to use to our advantage, even as they diminish and often undermine us? But still, as imperfect strategies, would not sharing them be an additional disservice to the shelter residents? This logic denied the fact that the residents were already keenly aware of respectability's codes and actively engaged in revealing their futility.

I bring up my position here for three significant reasons. First of all, it is important that in interrogations of social service and welfare agencies the low-wage worker does not become the scapegoat or primary frame of reference for understanding how systems of oppression are reinforced by the oppressed. There are multiple overlapping interests involved at all levels of bureaucracy; we must identify the points where individual motivations and personal relationships collide in professional caregiving settings to more carefully consider how people simultaneously transform and are transformed within systems. Second, a consideration of my multiple roles and conflicting interest in the shelter brings emotion and intentionality to the forefront. This makes the call for a deeper interrogation of the socially constructed nature of feelings, desires, best interests, and care as critical components in understanding how power plays out in the context of social service delivery. Lastly, my struggles as shelter director concretely demonstrate how historical conventions and social norms (even, or especially, those that are the most oppressive) are carried not only on our bodies but also as emotional baggage that shapes the nature of the social spaces we inhabit.

In my last year as Fresh Start director, I convened a team of resident advisors to work independently on restructuring the life skills curriculum and policy guidelines in an effort to capitalize on their hidden knowledge[22] and intimate understanding of the residents' life experiences. In this new role, the RAs were able to see past their professional insecurities and develop more balanced relationships with the residents. From the new communicative space that emerged for the staff and young women, they collectively created a sexual education curriculum called *Sex, Lies and Love*. This new curriculum moved beyond the discourse of sex as purely functional (the mechanics of procreation and perpetuation of the heterosexual family structure) or dangerous (highlighting only transmittable disease and their prevention). Two residents known as divas spearheaded *Sex, Lies and Love* by developing the program structure based on interviews with their peers. The resulting workshops included the themes of love, emotional self-care, and alternative ways of establishing supportive family environments, concerns previously not considered a relevant part of educating around "sex" in this setting. This resident-and-staff-led program suggests the spaces that may be opened up when self-reflection and critical dialogue among all members of the social service community become a part of the intervention.

AMBER

This tension between the staff and resident notions of respectability, identity management, social mobility, and sexuality is highlighted by the story of Amber and the wannabes. Amber's admittance to the shelter was not the first time that a young woman who identified as lesbian was a Fresh Start resident. It was, however, the first time that the entire shelter had been so profoundly impacted by one young woman's presence. Prior to Amber's arrival, the narratives of sexuality in the shelter assumed a collective heterosexual orientation among the resident population. Even though the *Sex, Lies and Love* curriculum addressed nonhetero-sexual identities on paper, it was inconsistently implemented by staff in practice. Amber, and the wannabes who emerged in response to her status within and out-side of the shelter, disrupted the common sense ideas that gender performances reflect sexuality, that sexuality is fixed and unchanging, and that young black women must be constrained by gender and sexuality norms that have never con-sidered their complexity and fullness of their humanity.

Amber grew up in a middle-class, predominantly black suburb of Detroit with her mother. Her parents divorced when she was four years old and her father moved to Tampa shortly thereafter. Amber has only seen him three times since. When Amber was a sophomore in high school, she realized that she was attracted to other girls even though she had a boyfriend whom she would have a child with later that year. When she became a junior in high school, she decided to tell her mother that she was gay. Amber says that her mother was "cool with it" at first but then couldn't live with the reality of seeing Amber actually involved with and displaying affection to other young women. Fighting became the routine for Amber and her mother; their neighbors got used to calling the police on their out-of-control arguments, which started to get physical around the time Amber was starting her senior year. Amber entered the shelter after her mother pulled a knife on her and told her to leave. She left, taking only her son with her, before the police could come. With no other family in the area and not wanting to stay with friends, Amber called her child's father from a pay phone and told him to drive her to GGC. She heard about GGC from a friend whose cousin stayed in the shelter years prior.

Amber is stocky and muscular. Although she is only five feet four inches, she seems much taller. She says because of her build, the way she dresses, and her low-cut fade, girls always flirt with her, mistaking her for a boy. This apparently happened at the shelter on her first day when, while standing outside smoking by the dumpster, two of the residents thought she was a boy from the neighbor-hood. Amber has a low-key confidence that is magnetic. The minute she came into the shelter the entire plane of interpersonal dynamics shifted dramatically. Amber was completely out and had just as many if not more female visitors as the other residents had boyfriends. "Mackin' hos"[23] and her overall powers of seduction were common topics of conversation when she was in the room. It did not take long, maybe a week, before the other residents started calling Amber "Pimp," "Pimp Daddy," and "Big." It was clear to me that the RAs responded to Amber differently than they did to other residents. Although she was always find-ing some way to get out of her chores—eventually managing to convince other residents to do them for her—she was hardly ever seriously reprimanded. The conversations I overheard between Amber and the shelter staff regarding rule vio-lations and missed appointments sounded playful and almost flirtatious. Amber was definitely smart and charming and quickly learned how to "mack" the shelter.

Within a month, there was a noticeable change in at least five young women in the shelter. These young women, all former divas, made a physical transformation by trading in fitted jeans and baby T-shirts for baggy jeans that hung off their behinds, oversize sweatshirts and T-shirts, and sneakers or Timberland boots. The caseworkers and RAs responded to all of this like it was a joke. "Please, they just trying to copy Amber,"[24] was what Margaret said, which seemed to be the general consensus. However, once the change moved from attire to language and behavior it stopped being treated as a joke and became a problem. The wannabes or "transformers" as they were named by the staff, started to join in when Amber made comments about the hotness or sexiness of a woman on television and started to have their own stories of attraction to young women they saw on the bus or at the mall. Two of the wannabes had boyfriends before they came into the shelter who now stopped dropping by for visits in the evening, and they all made attempts to change the way they walked by moving slower, with a wider gait. Watching the forced hypermasculine hand movements and body carriage usually reserved for male rappers (and usually only when they are in the context the choreographed music video), the only question that seemed to keep coming into our minds was: *Is this for real?*

We categorized Amber, whose performances were perhaps the most dramatic of them all, as sincere because she came into the shelter identifying as a lesbian and never gave any indication that she wavered in this identity. The wannabes, just by their name, symbolized insincerity. The assumptions we made about these young woman were a reflection of our acceptance of hegemonic notions of gender. Amber was "real" because her performance was consistent, implying a permanency that made her masculine identifications appear innate. The wannabes were not able to pull of their performances and, thus, failed to convince us. And what were we trying to be convinced of? That they were no longer sexually attracted to males? That they were questioning their sexual identity? And why was it so important to us that their intentions be apparent in their self-presentations?

Wannabes are nothing new in the residential single-sex setting. Case studies by Rose Giallombardo[25] and Ann Propper[26] talk about how butch and fem gendered roles were taken on by girls in juvenile justice settings as a way to fulfill needs that were normally met in the outside world. In some cases, girls recreated husband and wife roles to establish a fictive kin network where they provided mutual aid, emotional reciprocity, and security and protection to everyone in the family. In other cases, there was not such a strong sense of solidarity and young women were looking to fulfill their own emotional and sexual needs without making the commitment to such a large network. Girls who, like Amber, entered the facility identified as lesbian were called "trues" and the girls who got "turned out" after being in the institution were also called "wannabes." Getting "turned out" is a phrase that is still very much in rotation today among the young women in the shelter as well as those in other GGC programs who have attended Job Corps and other vocational programs. These case studies also highlight a family dynamic that existed among the thugs and wannabes that should not be ignored. A significant majority of the gay, bisexual and openly questioning young people who resided at Fresh Start found themselves homeless because, like Amber, a parent or other family member expelled them from the home. Thus doubly expelled by both society and their families, recreating a supportive, tight-knit network became essential.

The way "turned out" is used by these girls conveys more of a blurriness and sense of complication than the staff concern with the reality or fiction of the wannabes gender performances. Amber used turned out to mean that a girl, who identifies as heterosexual, develops a relationship with another girl, which can be either "just sexual or both sexual and emotional."[27] When the relationship has ended or the young woman leaves the residential setting, she may continue to be involved with other young women, be involved with men, or decide that she will be undecided and "do whatever she is feeling with whoever she is feeling at the time." Getting turned out does not necessarily mean that a young woman has taken on a new sexual identity but that she has, in Amber's words, "become open to the possibilities."

Amber discusses the nature of being turned out in a way that reveals that she views gender and sexuality as somewhat arbitrary and unstable. Talking with Amber, I learned that the Fresh Start wannabes were not being turned out. Their performances were about transgressing gender categories by seeing if they could play with the social consequences of being masculine or feminine. The catalyst for all of this was the "Amber-effect" they witnessed not only in the shelter but also outside of the agency. When they hung out with Amber, people both male and female responded to them in new ways that they found appealing. For example, one of the wannabes told me that she didn't feel like she needed to be "in petty competition with other girls to see who is like the prettiest or has the best clothes. You don't deal with that and it's like you out the game . . . you don't even have to play."[28] Amber added that "some girls don't even care about dudes thinking they are gay. They would rather be labeled gay for a minute and get some respect than be treated like a bubblehead."[29] Our curiosity as shelter staff was grounded in a conflation of sex and gender making us focus on what their behaviors and stylized appearance meant for their sexual lives more than the implications for their social lives. It also demonstrated our failure to understand the importance of respect in gaining public status, protection, and self-confidence. This type of positive injection to the wannabes self-worth could have been what the divas were looking for in their previous relationships with men whose money and attention did not necessarily translate to respect from men, even though the divas had a lot of respect for one another.

Near the end of her stay in the shelter, Amber was becoming increasingly frustrated with the wannabes. In a conversation with Amber one late night in the television/activity room she expressed anger over her perception that the wannabes do not "wanna be identified as gay" but did want to be identified with the masculine presentation of a butch lesbian identity that will let them pass as hard and earn them respect. Unfortunately, the young women labeled wannabes would agree to talk with me about all of this only minimally. The information I could squeeze out directly from them mirrored the comment about not wanting to be in competition with other young women for both male and female attention and approval based on their physical appearance. Male confusion around what their appearance signified meant that they were ignored or left alone in situations where they would normally be harassed. The opposite, however, could have easily been true if we think about the number of gay and transgendered women who have lost their lives for simply being themselves. Amber does not have a problem with their performance of masculinity, just their attempted performance of homosexuality. To Amber, the masculine performance is the ultimate artifice, the grand façade on which the entire wannabes self-presentation hinges. And it is also, as she implies, a persona mastered in the media obsession with the urban thug character and one that can be manipulated through dress and mannered behavior.

Sexuality, on the other hand, is rooted in desire and, from Amber's perspective, the acting on this desire. Amber was clearly hurt when one of the wannabes, Stacey, immediately rejected a lesbian identity when questioned by her caseworker; she took offense to Stacey's incredulous "No!" However, through her frustration, Amber is still able to consider possibilities for the wannabes behavior and in this reflection extends her discussion to include all young women who seek male validation and go to improbable lengths to earn respect. Yet Amber decides that the "male stamp of approval" and respect are not the same thing. She analyzes the female masculinity of the wannabes to essentially be rooted in their lack of validation and sense of powerlessness both within and beyond Fresh Start. Even in her annoyance, Amber understands how the wannabes get to the point where they wouldn't mind acting like a man if that means they get respect from a man.

The wannabes like the majority of the young women at Fresh Start, including Amber, seem to be striving to reach a comfortable balance between garnering respect from others without losing their self-respect in the process. Although performing respectability is ultimately about approval and validation, it can never guarantee a satisfactory outcome. Gender, like respectability, is about performativity and the imperfect reading of bodies that occurs in social contexts.[30] Therefore, although the wannabes, like the rest of us, may be intentional in their goals for presenting themselves in a particular way, their choices in achieving this are predefined, and the resulting responses are out of their control. When someone's gender is either not known to us or appears muddled in some way, this is disconcerting primarily for what it means for our behavior and presentation of self. As Betsy Lucal is able to identify through an exploration of responses to her own ambiguous gender display, gender labels enable us to interact.[31] In the case of the wannabes, it was their sexuality not their gender that posed a problem; their practices, not their displays, which were of utmost curiosity and concern among the staff. The wannabes, however, were using a gender display to gain the benefits of what the male gender symbolizes. They knew that they were not mistaken for men in the way that Amber was, so they were not gaining the prestige of men but the prestige of girls bold enough to present as male and perhaps, even more bold, not caring if these presentations lead others to question their heterosexuality. "Bending gender rules does not erode but rather preserves gender roles."[32] Lucal's observation here echoes the work of Butler and Peggy Phelan[33] and makes any subversive intent by the wannabes in terms of remaking gender norms appear impotent. But the "wannabes" are not necessarily cross-dressing and utilizing masculine behaviors to erode gender roles. Their goal is to uphold them and, instead, erode their presentation of self as gendered female in terms of all the negative social associations with being female, not the categories itself. The "wannabes" don't have the option of choosing not to do gender, but they can choose not to do femininity.

The shelter as a space and the developmental range of the young women involved may also provide insight into why the wannabes were able to make a place for them-selves to "try on gender."[34] In transitional periods of life, such as the transition from girlhood to adulthood, or transitional spaces, such as college or beginning in a new job, females may try on new gender roles. Trying-on allows us to consider the gen-dered nature of specific spaces as well as "social contexts, such as race and class, and contingencies, such as control over adolescents that shape gendered experiences."[35] Looking at gender displays in this way creates the possibility whereby the shelter can be seen by the wannabes as a transitional space where new roles and new ways of being are possible without necessarily symbolizing commitment to or permanent self-identification through these roles. The status of the wannabes as poor black girls offers another way to consider why "trying-on" is appealing. The maleness they attempt to embody through dress, language, and mannerisms has the potential to elevate their social status both within their interactions in the shelter (in the way it seems to work for Amber) and outside of the shelter where they are less objectified by the male gaze because of their rejection of the female performance. Of course, there is also the possibility that the wannabes have been turned out in the way described by Amber and have decided that they have located a new way of being and of expressing their sexuality; their physical embodiment of masculinity being a reflection of how they are attempting to display this internal shift. Nonetheless, it is important not to read any display or performance as final or wholly definitive. We are all wannabes to various degrees and demonstrate this through our performance of gender.

(RE)DOING GENDER IN THE CONTEXT OF WORK AND FAMILY

Several months after Amber entered the shelter, I ran into Trishelle, a former shelter resident, in a park in downtown Detroit. Trishelle had to call my name several times before I recognized her. The Trishelle I knew was tiny, with small delicate bones and an even tinier birdlike voice. At the time, her newborn son, although quite small himself, seemed to weigh her down when she carried him and made her look even more doll-like and breakable. This Trishelle was also called "boy crazy" and had many arguments with me about using the pay phone after the restricted hours so she could check up on the whereabouts of whatever man she was currently involved with. The Trishelle I knew was extremely proud of her "good hair" and taunted the other girls in the shelter with claims that their short nappy heads were the reason that they "couldn't catch a man." The Trishelle I thought I knew wore her long hair in corkscrew curls and would be caught dead before she would leave the shelter looking anything but fly. Her clothing choices were a source of aggravation for many of the shelter youth specialists who felt her close-fitting dresses and hot pants were "ho-ish" and trashy. The Trishell I knew was a diva.

And yet the Trishelle who stood in front of me laughing at my inability to hide my surprise and close my gaping mouth was unrecognizable to me. This Trishelle wore long baggy denim shorts that hit at her shins almost meeting the stark white athletic socks she was wearing with her Adidas flip-flops. Her striped polo shirt hung down past her behind and seemed weighted down by the huge gold medallion she wore around her neck, it swung low near her belly and looked like it could take her out for the count if she moved too quickly. This Trishelle had a close-cropped fade haircut with deep-ridged waves that signaled her careful grooming practices. She looked like a preteen male rapper. Trishelle told me that she was doing well, was on the verge of starting her own carpentry business, and was just a few years shy of being able to buy her own home. She attributed her success to the skills she gained in the carpentry trade at Detroit Job Corp after she left the shelter. When I inquired how Trishelle enjoyed her time at Job Corp she told me that "like with anything, you have to find a way to make it work for you—mugs need to learn how to get they hustle on." I had to wonder if from Trishelle's idea of getting her hustle included working a version of female masculinity[36] that would make it easier for her to gain acceptance into the highly coveted carpentry trade. Job Corp allows its participants to identify their top three vocational track choices and then places them according to a system that most of the young people and former Job Corp employees I spoke with found inexplicable and arbitrary. One aspect of the tracking that did appear systematic and purposeful was the tracking of females into the nursing and clerical vocations and males into carpentry, engineering, construction, and computer repair. This gendered tracking frustrated many of the former Job Corp participants who ended up at Fresh Start who wanted to at least have the opportunity to prove themselves in the much more lucrative fields that were apparently reserved for males. The ability to make more than the minimum wages found in the certified nursing assistant (CNA) track and the nonexistent office assistant work is critical for young women who, like Trishelle, want to get "get some property" and see "owning something and working for themselves" as the only way they are "going to get ahead."

Trishelle found a way to work the Job Corp system and get out of it what she felt would make her ultimately successful and truly independent. Whether the ultrafeminine young woman of the past or the current more masculine version in b-boy attire, one thing that remained discernibly consistent about Trishelle was her self-determination and confidence. She always gave the impression that anything she was doing at the time made sense and was the right thing to do. I imagine the Job Corp instructors and administration being just as challenged and inspired by Trishelle's tenacious self-protective tendencies as the Fresh Start staff. It is difficult to say if it is that quality alone or her decidedly masculine demeanor and performance that allowed her entry into the highly coveted carpentry track. Although during our brief conversation in the park, Trishelle mentioned her girlfriend to me and implied that she is no longer interested in dating men; it is not necessarily her identification as a lesbian or bisexual female that eases her ascension in the male track, it is her corporeality that conveys social meaning and, perhaps, may have allowed her to appear a natural fit with carpentry. In the estimation of the young women I spoke with about the Job Corp process, getting what you felt you deserved within the program meant being overly aggressive, strategically charming, or simply "boyish"—a much used term by all the young women. The options for getting ahead that these young women identified for themselves are not confined to the Job Corp setting or to the current historical moment. The angry black bitch, the cunning seductress, and the asexual, overpowering thug are tropes that have been used to constrain the ways of thinking about and potentially being a black woman. Even when the stereotype has somewhat positive connotations like the image of the superwoman, it is still a representation that requires a subjugation of the self to the interests of others and a strength that is presented as more combative and aggressive than empowering and productive. The young women I spoke with at Fresh Start resented these stereotypes while simultaneously using the different performative versions of them to advance their needs.

Young women may consciously try on versions of ultrafemininity, exaggerated masculinity, or other identities along a gendered spectrum as strategies to gain economic mobility, respect, or control in their lives. Their performances are, however, never freely chosen or experienced outside of the social scripts already provided for the ways of being within masculinity, femininity, blackness, adolescence, and poverty. In this way, we should not think of the divas, thugs, and wannabes as disrupting gender categories but can identify how their responses to social institutions can be seen as transformative work as defined by Mullings as "efforts to sustain continuity under transformed circumstances and efforts to transform circumstances in order to maintain continuity."[37] Homelessness, participation in the welfare system, and, I would argue, the ongoing consequences of living in poverty are disruptions that transform the continuity of these young black women's ability to take care of themselves. In response, they transform the predetermined nature of their circumstances by looking for ways to challenge the various urban geographies that threaten their inclusion as true citizens.

Paying close attention to the social spaces and larger economic concerns that are most prominent in their lives (such as homeless shelters, welfare agencies, limited low-wage work options) prevents the assumption, which Judith Halberman cautions us against, that female masculinities are "glorifications of men or represent a lesbian obsession with maleness."[38] In fact, if we think of the tradition of black female masculinity as tapping into empowered versions of maleness, might it not be able to consider the divas along with the thugs and wannabes as representing one type or version of female masculinity? The divas' strategic use of charm, beauty, and sexuality is based on working toward greater control and independence in their lives, and like the thugs, wannabes, and other shelter residents, they are seeking social inclusion and approval similar to that which maleness provides. Continuing in this vein of stretching the boundaries of what can be considered female masculinity, we can see how the black cultural concept of signification can be useful to think about what may be occurring in the actions of some of the Fresh Start residents. At the core of signifying behaviors is the idea of mocking a standard or norm.[39] In this case, the standard of masculinity as an ideal is, too varying degrees and purposes, imitated and, thus, held up to scorn by the divas, thugs, and wannabes. We are primarily addressing maleness here, but the project of working to be fully included in society for these young women extends to questions of race, class status, skin color, body type, and so on. In other words, there are many intersecting oppressions that may find their expression and derision within black female masculinity.

After my encounter with Trishelle, I met with a former shelter resident named Janice who had two cousins she believed were "turned out" in Job Corp. Janice praised the confidence of young women like Trishelle who were able to find a way to maneuver around the certified nursing track, which usually disappointed them with jobs cleaning rooms in nursing homes. Janice tells me that she wants to be a pharmacy technician not only because she wants to make more than a minimum wage but also because "it seems like everybody in my family is a caregiver, and then they come home and still taking care of people. Like grown folks who should be able to take care of themselves."[40] In this statement, I am interested in how Janice guides the conversation from her aunt's work as a care provider to nurturing her common-law husband, Marcus, who does not work or contribute in any other financial regard in their home. It appears that he doesn't even offer domestic assistance while her aunt is away at work all day. Janice makes the connection between her aunt's low-wage, gendered-in-the-service-sector role[41] to the gendered, mothering role she has taken on in the home as unconditional caregiver. In this regard, Janice experiences gender as an additional potential trap that, along with race and class, threatens to contain her in unfulfilling, disrespected positions both at work and in the home unless she can devise a strategy for escape. The intersection of gender, race, and class in Janet's experience influences her ability to make sense out of "acting like a dude" at Job Corp and identify the types of gendered career paths and relational roles she wants to avoid in the future. Although Janice disagree with her aunt's acceptance of the boyfriend's behavior, she tells me that her aunt's model of "working in the struggle" is both lesson and warning as she moves through gendered possibilities in the workplace, educational institutions, and at home.

Working within the structural limits of the social service agencies and the low-wage jobs that temporarily define the shape of their daily lives, the shelter residents were able to establish new definitions of family, love, protection, respect, and care. The trend of three or more residents moving out together to share childcare, domestic, and financial responsibilities became such a successful model it received support though private grant funding. Prior to my employment in the shelter, the residents mobilized to demand the mandatory parenting classes open only to the female residents be extended to their partners and other adults in the young women's lives who may at one time or another be providing childcare. These resident-led initiatives may seem small and have not undermined the underlying focus on the young women as a problematic target population in need of fixing, but they are key interventions in rearticulating the social service discourse around family structures and so called respectable lifestyles. Robin Kelley, Cathy J. Cohen,[42] and other scholars interested in locating new possibilities for resistance in marginalized communities of color have noted that young people may provide signposts for us to imagine new cultures and ways of being that have the potential for radical social transformation. Strategies for social mobility and inclusion among young black women may not only bridge the gap between what they want for themselves and what they are told is available, but they may offer creative techniques for subverting power structures through new ways of reproducing bodies and spaces.

In writing about the possibilities to create and inhabit spaces of black radicalism, James Tyner reminds us that space is produced through the "interaction of ideas and practices."[43] He also makes the case for discerning the difference between representations of space and representational spaces. Representations of space are the dominant spaces in our society and include constructed realms such as public housing projects and urban revitalization plans. These realms are "materially demarcated" and their boundaries enforced through both collective action and force. Representational spaces, on the other hand, are alternative spaces that get acted upon through resistance and protest.[44] Although Tyner specifically places artists, poets, and activists as the catalyst for these spatial disruptions, through interrogation of spaces similar to Fresh Start as well as the actions of the individuals there, new social actors with disruptive potential come into view. The strategies and critical theorizing of liminal citizens, such as the young women and resident advisors always on the verge of social expulsion or inclusion, must be taken into account if we truly want to expand the theoretical and activist potential for locating and dismantling the various, increasingly tricky, reiterations of oppression.

NOTES

1. "Hard" was used by the residents and staff to define both the physical appearance and emotional demeanor of the thugs. A hard thug was a young woman who rarely displayed her emotions in public and was careful not to don any clothing or accessories that could be categorized as feminine.
2. Katherine McKittrick and Clyde Woods, "No One Knows the Mysteries . . . ," in *Black Geographies and The Politics of Place*, ed. Katherine McKittrick and Clyde Woods (Cambridge, MA: South End, 2007), 4.
3. Ibid.
4. Judith Butler, "Performative Acts and Gender Constitution: An Essay in Phenomenology and Feminist Theory," *Theatre Journal* 40, no. 4 (1988): 524.
5. See, Leith Mullings, "African American Women Making Themselves," *Souls* 2, no. 4 (2000): 18–29.
6. "Appearances Aside," *California Law Review* 88, no. 4 (2000): 62.
7. In "Appearances Aside" (5–63), Butler discusses how although the body has incredible expressive capacities, it is never expressed or performed in a state of free will; it is always tethered to history, norms, and social scripts.
8. For more on the historical context that frames contemporary codes of respectability in black women's lives see Victoria W. Wolcott, *Remaking Respectability: African American Women in Interwar Detroit* (Chapel Hill: University of North Carolina Press, 2001) and E. Frances White, *Dark Continent of Our Bodies: Black Feminism and the Politics of Respectability* (Philadelphia: Temple University Press, 2001).

9. Exclusionary inclusion is a term with some fairly obvious connotations that has been used across disciplines including economics, political science, psychology, education, sociology, and anthropology. It is meant to define the precarious status of being only provisionally or inconsistently included in the nation state, recognized as citizens or as part of a larger mainstream community. Exclusionary inclusion has been used to characterize the status of youth, the disabled, refugees, ethnic minorities, and women. For a specific example in relation to refugee women, see Susan Kneebone, "Women Within the Refugee Construct: 'Exclusionary Inclusion' in Policy and Practice The Australian Experience," *International Journal of Refugee Law* 17, no. 1 (2005): 7–42.

10. "Deportable or Admissible?," in *Black Geographies and the Politics of Place*, ed. Katherine McKittrick and Clyde Woods (Cambridge: South End Press, 2007), 179.

11. See Barbara Cruikshank, *The Will to Empower: Democratic Citizens and Other Subjects* (Ithaca, NY: Cornell University Press, 1999) and Judith Goldstein, "Microenterprise Training Programs, Neoliberal Common Sense and the Discourses of Self-Esteem," in *The New Poverty Studies: The Ethnography of Power, Politics and Impoverished People in the United States*, ed. Judith Goode and Jeff Maskovsky (New York: New York University Press, 2001), 236–72.

12. By hip-hop culture here, I am referring to the commercialization of hip-hop musical forms and aesthetics that were most readily accessible and consistently consumed by the shelter residents. This included the music and celebrities most prominently shown on urban radio stations in Detroit, on Black Entertainment Television (BET), and on MTV. The young women additionally discussed hip-hop as filtered through the urban-oriented magazines the young women kept up with, such as VIBE, the Source, and XXL. These publications generally replicate the promotion of the popular black male rappers and black and Latina R&B singers saturating the television and radio airwaves.

13. I noted this statement from a community member who spoke during the open session of a homeless service provider network meeting in April 2002.

14. Michelle Fine, "Discourse of Desire: Sexuality, Schooling and Adolescent Females: The Missing Discourse of Desire," in *Disruptive Voices: The Possibilities of Feminist Research*, ed. Michelle Fine (Ann Arbor: University of Michigan Press, 2001), 31–59.

15. "Other mother" is a term that emerges from black feminism and refers to the role that women who are nonbiological mothers play in the lives of other, usually younger or less experienced, women. Other mothering behaviors may include providing emotional and/ or financial support, sharing wisdom and advice, and mentoring and professional skill building; in general, acting as an other or another mother. See Patricia Hill Collins, *Black Feminist Thought* (New York: Routledge, 2000), 178–83. Collins cites the "centrality of women in African-American extended families" (178) as the cultural frame for other mothers.

16. Rhonda (Fresh Start), in discussion with the author, July 2004

17. Interview with social worker in Fresh Start program, January 2004

18. Catherine Kingfisher, "Producing Disunity: The Constraints and Incitements of Welfare Work," in *The New Poverty Studies: The Ethnography of Power, Politics and Impoverished People in the United States*, ed. Judith Goode and Jeff Maskovsky (New York: New York University Press, 2001), 276.

19. Ibid., 283.

20. The twenty-four-hour residential setting is fraught with potential emergencies, especially a shelter such as Fresh Start that houses infants, toddlers, and pregnant women. Resident advisors who work after regular business hours and on the weekends have to

contend with more responsibilities, and less support, than the those staff members who work shifts were other GGC employees are present. Some of the emergencies resident advisors have had to deal with include threatening boyfriends who have managed to enter the shelter at night, residents in labor, physical fights among groups of girls, fires, a three-day blackout, stalkers on the grounds of the shelter, infants needing EMS care, and residents with mental health issues who have physically attacked other residents and staff. Being a resident advisor minimally requires incredible counseling, conflict resolution, and problem-solving skills.

21. *Outsider Within* is the title of Faye V. Harrison's book about working to expand the traditional, exclusionary boundaries of anthropology by working as an outsider (black and female) inside of the discipline. I use "outsider within" here as a black female anthropologist/activist to allude to this connotation in my own work with ethnographic work that I see as an intervention. In addition, I use "outsider within" as discussed by Patricia Hill Collins in *Fighting Words*, to describe the status of traversing various contexts and feeling as if one never really belongs to one group. This was my feeling at Fresh Start, where I never fully felt integrated into the organization as a legitimate social worker. This "outsider within" status also marked my experience in graduate school, where I studied inside of anthropology department that I always felt outside of due to my black female body and advocacy orientations. See Faye V. Harrison, *Outsider Within: Reworking Anthropology in the Global Age* (Urbana Champaign: University of Illinois Press, 2008) and Patricia Hill Collins, *Fighting Words: Black Women & the Search for Justice* (Minneapolis: University of Minnesota Press, 1998).

22. Hidden knowledge is that which is gained through oppression. Experience is foregrounded in hidden knowledge as well as the belief that people are engaged in critical theorizing all of the time as they assess the best ways to increase their life chances, gain important resources, navigate various social systems, and take care of themselves. See Collins, *Black Feminist Thought*, 8–9.

23. Amber and the other young women used "mackin hos" to mean being able to easily attain a number of attractive girlfriends and get them to do whatever you say. "Mackin hos," as used in the shelter, also implied a certain level of chivalry and respect toward women on the part of the mack.

24. This was taken from staff meeting notes on June 2004.

25. Rose Giallombardo, *Society of Women: A Study of Women's Prison* (New York: John Wiley & Sons, 1966)

26. Ann Propper, *Prison Homosexuality: Myth and Reality* (Washington, DC: US Department of Justice NIJ Publishers, 1981). Propper includes a discussion of both males and females in the adult and juvenile justice systems.

27. Amber, in discussion with the author, June 2004.

28. Interview with shelter resident, June 2004

29. Amber, interview.

30. See Judith Butler's "Gender Is a Performance and a Stylized Repetition of Acts," in *Gender Trouble* (New York: Routledge, 1990), 140. Lucal's theory of gender performativity derives from her work.

31. Betsy Lucal, "What it Means to Be Gendered Me: Life on the Boundaries of a Dichotomous Gender System," *Gender and Society* 13, no. 6 (1999): 783.

32. Ibid., 785.

33. See Butler's *Gender Trouble* (1990) and Peggy Phelan, "Feminist Theory, Poststructuralism and Performance," *TDR* 32, no. 1 (1988): 107–27.

34. L. Susan Williams, "Trying on Gender, Gender Regimes and the Process of Becoming Women," *Gender and Society* 16, no. 1 (2002): 29–52 utilized "trying on gender" instead

of "doing in gender" in her work where she talks about the gendering processes of girls in the liminal stage of adolescence. For Williams, trying on gender implies the experimental, tentative, playful, and resistant nature of the trying-on process.

35. Ibid., 31.

36. See Judith Halberstam's, "Mackdaddy, Superfly, Rapper: Gender, Race and Masculinity in the Drag King Scene," *Social Text* 52, no. 53 (1997): 104–31.

37. Leith Mullings, "Households Headed by Women: The Politics of Class, Race and Gender," in *The New Poverty Studies: The Ethnography of Power, Politics and Impoverished People in the United States*, ed. Judith Goode and Jeff Maskovsky (New York: New York University Press, 2001), 49

38. Halberstam, "Mackdaddy, Superfly, Rapper," 109.

39. For more on signification, see Claudia Mitchell-Kernan, *Signifying, Loud-Talking and Marking in Signifyin(g), Sanctifiyin' and Slam Dunking*, ed. Gena Dagel Caponi (Amherst: University of Massachusetts Press), 309–30.

40. Janice, in discussion with the author, August 2004.

41. See Evelyn Nakano Glenn, "From Servitude to Service Work: Historical Continuities in the Racial Division of Paid Reproductive Labor," *Signs* 18, no. 1 (1992): 1–43 for discussion on the historical dimensions of the racial division of labor and the consequences for women of color engaged in low-wage work in areas such as child care and health care services and food preparation.

42. Refer to Robin D. G. Kelley's introduction in *Race Rebels: Culture, Politics, and the Black Working Class* (New York: The Free Press, 1994), 11 and Cathy Cohen, "Deviance as Resistance: A New Research Agenda for the Study of Black Politics," *DuBois Review* 1, no. 1 (2004): 27–45.

43. James A. Tyner, "Urban Revolutions and the Spaces of Black Radicalism," in *Black Geographies and the Politics of Place*, ed. Katherine McKittrick and Clyde Woods (Cambridge, MA: South End Press, 2007), 218.

44. Ibid., 219.

CHAPTER 6

GRUPO OREMI

BLACK LESBIANS AND THE STRUGGLE FOR SAFE SOCIAL SPACE IN HAVANA

TANYA L. SAUNDERS

QUEER PUBLIC SPACE IN CUBA IS VERY visible and easy to find. Havana's popular gay cruising area is located along a city street called La Rampa and continues down to Havana's coastal highway, called the Malecón. This cruising area, as well as virtually all of Havana's public gay cruising areas, is located in the predominately white, wealthy, touristy area of El Vedado. Whether walking along La Rampa or sitting out at the corner of Avenues 23 and G, one will see the large numbers of gay men, men who have sex with men, and *trasvestis* (gay men who pass as women) who overwhelm the bustling touristy area where these nonheteronormative spaces are located. If one looks for women when perusing these areas, it is easy to notice that gay men far outnumber lesbians. In my estimate, as of January 2006, gay men and MTF (male-to-female) transsexuals outnumbered lesbian-identified women by at least by ten to one. When race is taken into account, there are far fewer black lesbians present in public gay scenes than black gay men.

In order to address the dearth of visible public space available to lesbians, particularly black lesbians, in the city of Havana, during the summer of 2005 about eight "out" lesbian professionals living in Havana, the majority of whom were black-identified, worked with the state-run National Center for Sex Education (CENESEX) to begin the first state-supported lesbian organization in Havana called Grupo OREMI. The group received institutional support largely because several independent, unpublished, state-recognized Cuban studies about homosexuality, conducted between 1994 and 2003, have noted the immense form of social isolation and invisibility that lesbians face in comparison to gay men (Acosta et al. 2003; Dalia Acosta, personal communication). In fact, one study showed that gay men have benefited from state efforts at eliminating homophobia, while the situation of lesbians have stagnated and, in some measures, slightly deteriorated. Unlike lesbian, gay, bisexual, and transgender (LGBT) populations in North America and Western Europe, in Cuba, as in much of the Caribbean, there is not an abundance of established social spaces (in the form of bars or community centers) for the LGBT community. There are numerous informal, and highly visible, social spaces available for Cuba's nonheteronormative population; however, these spaces are dominated by people assigned male at birth. As a result, Cuban lesbians are even more invisible than the trasvestis or the male-to-female transsexual population. I highlight this fact because this is a different situation from Euro-American histories of sexuality, where gay male and lesbian issues have been at the forefront of the struggle for sexual rights, while all the other identities (namely, bisexual and transgender) have only recently occupied a more salient role in sexual and gender-difference discourse.

Since 2003, there has been an increase in unpublished, independent documentation of lesbian experiences in Cuba; however, published accounts of homosexuality have been written by men who acknowledge that their work does not engage the experiences of lesbians because lesbian spaces are hard to access (La Fountain-Stokes 2002; Lumsden 1996). When considering the intersections of race and sexuality, Marvin Leiner (1994), Ian Lumsden (1996), and Lois M. Smith and Alfred Padula (1996) have attempted to theorize how race influences the social experiences of sexual minorities. Lumsden argued that black males are considered sexually aggressive and that being called a "black faggot" is even worse than being called antirevolutionary, an accusation that can lead to state imprisonment. Leiner and Tomás Fernández Robaina (1996) argue that Afro-Cuban religious organizations encourage particular forms of aggressive masculinity where passivity and homosexuality are abhorred.

Smith and Padula write about being a black lesbian in Cuba: "In 1994 a Cuban intellectual commented that the worst that could happen to one would be to be an Afro-Cuban lesbian, because 'although officially this is not a problem, in daily life it most certainly is'" (Smith and Padula 1996, 173). Because being (and being called) a black homosexual is one of the worst insults one could receive (which is a constant theme in my interviews and in scholarly texts on homosexuality in Cuba), I am interested in exploring one aspect of the black LGBT experience in Cuba: how and why lesbians, particularly black lesbians, have become one of the most socially marginal and invisible groups in Cuba. My interest in OREMI and the particular situation of black lesbians is a result of a chance encounter with a black lesbian professional at the Sixteenth World Congress on Sexology, held in Havana in 2003. The following is an excerpt from my field notes in 2003:

> I had arrived to Cuba to attend the 16th World Congress on Sexology. I knew that it was important to attend the congress because my doctoral research focused on Cuba's underground lesbian scene . . . While I stood wondering what to do next, I realized that a black woman, who later I learned was about 55, was walking towards me. She introduced herself. She was a Cuban professional. We chatted for a bit about the conference, the issues facing black women in Cuba, and the situation of black lesbians. In the middle of the conversation she began to whisper: "I want to start an organization just for black women." She went on to explain that there was

a grassroots-run lesbian organization for women in Santiago de Cuba. Apparently the organization had done a lot to end the social isolation of black lesbians; she wanted to see if the same thing could happen in Havana.

Two years later, this woman began working closely with CENESEX as a means of creating Grupo OREMI. Once she obtained permission to organize the group, she invited other out black-identified lesbian activists, who were also vocal activists in Cuba's underground youth culture scenes. In order to make sure that the space was a racially inclusive space, these women sought out other women who were active participants in Cuba's underground lesbian scene. "Regardless of race," one of the organizers told me in 2005, "we knew that as women, we shared a similar form of cultural marginalization." For the black-identified organizers, OREMI was also a space for racial solidarity. They felt that in order to build a lesbian community and end isolation, lesbians needed to confront their own internalized racism, sexism, and homophobia.

In this essay, my main argument is that Grupo OREMI's emergence and demise is intertwined with a racialized sex/gender system that continues to impede black lesbians' ability to participate fully in Cuban society as autonomous subjects. This is because of two main reasons. The first reason is that the racialized base of heteronormative constructions of femininity is replicated in Cuba's lesbian population, in which lesbians of all races overwhelmingly eroticize hegemonic white femininity. This is to say that in Cuba's racialized sex/gender system, black lesbians are constructed as masculine or mannish by virtue of their race and regardless of their actual gender expression.

The second issue is that Cuba's black lesbians face an intense form of social isolation resulting from Cuba's institutional discourse of national racelessness; the idealization of "la mulata," which in Cuba's three-tier racial system supports an ideology of racelessness or racial inclusion that makes it difficult for black women to develop an antiracist discourse that addresses their experiences in the postrevolutionary nation; the informal state prohibition on like-minded people (namely, lesbians) to independently organize, socialize, or work for social change; and the precarious situation in which black women find themselves after Cuba's 1990s economic crisis. All these reasons limit the ability of black women, including black lesbians, to live as autonomous, financially independent subjects.

For two months during the summer of 2005, Grupo OREMI created a safe and dependable space for antiracist social critique, lesbian empowerment, and socialization. Eventually the group ended when CENESEX began to restrict social events because of public pressure; CENESEX received a plethora of complaints from the public, which knew that the social events targeted Havana's lesbian population. There were public complaints about the visibility of women being openly affectionate, something not acceptable in public space where children could witness "low-class" behavior. Nonetheless, it is definitely important to document this grassroots effort led by black-identified women who were brave enough to undertake such an initiative.

Methodologically, in this essay, I first review the empirical (mostly quantitative) research that has been conducted on the topic of Cuba's lesbian population.

The quantitative research was given to me by two of the researchers involved in the 2002 independent study on homosexuality in Cuba, in the hope that I would publish them and bring more national and international attention to the experiences of lesbians in Cuba. I also draw from my own ethnographic data collected in Havana between 1998 and 2006 and from interview data collected from 15 OREMI participants between 2005 and 2006. Between 2004 and 2006, I spent approximately six months with six women who would become the founders of Grupo OREMI (according to the interviewees there were approximately eight lesbian activists who were part of founding the group). They were very active in Cuba's underground lesbian scene. During my discussions with the black organizers, comments about how black lesbians navigated and negotiated the underground lesbian scene were common and helped me understand better how the intersections of race and gender, in relation to Cuba's post-1959 history of homosexuality, play out in Cuba's black lesbian experience.

NOTES ON SEXUALITY IN POST-1959 CUBA

From the late 1960s through the late 1970s, homosexuality was deemed a decadent, bourgeois social ill by the revolutionary state (Arguelles and Rich 1984; Lumsden 1996). Between 1965 and 1968 those deemed homosexual, Afro-Cuban religious practitioners, Jehovah's Witnesses, hippies, rockers, and other groups characterized as "antisocial," bourgeois, and possibly counterrevolutionary were sent to forced labor camps called Military Units for the Aid of Production (UMAP; Arguelles and Rich 1984; de la Fuente 2001). The UMAP camps eventually ended in the late 1960s because of internal and international pressures.

Several years later, the 1971 Congress on Education and Culture defined homosexuality as a form of immorality that could corrupt revolutionary youth, and it mandated that known homosexuals not be allowed in educational, cultural, and other institutions that were in direct contact with them. By 1970, known lesbians were not allowed to join the country's only women's-rights association, the state-run Federation of Cuban Women. This exclusion lasted until the late 1980s (Smith and Padula 1996).

The social-policy directives of the 1960s and 1970s reentrenched cultural norms concerning femininity in which the liberation of women, as moral and feminine subjects who desired men, was encouraged, and any challenge to gender and sexuality as structures of power were condemned as an encouragement of immorality. The targeting of practitioners of Afro-Cuban religion and culture further entrenched prerevolutionary cultural norms that viewed Afro-Cuban culture as marginal, criminal, and socially deviant (de la Fuente 2001). This devaluation of Afro-Cuban culture has implicitly supported the prerevolutionary ideology that Afro-Cubans were prone to criminality as well as gender and sexual deviancy (de la Fuente 2001; Helg 1995; Kutzinski 1993).

Between 1959 and 2001, research on sexuality largely focused on heterosexual women and gay male sexuality. The dearth of work focusing specifically on lesbians is a reflection of a gender bias as well as how "hidden" Cuban lesbian life is (Arguelles and Rich 1984; La Fountain-Stokes 2002). Empirical studies and media analysis of homosexuality have tended to focus on the "gay experience" in Cuba as an experience that is exemplary of state repression (Almendros and Jiménez-Leal 1984; Arguelles and Rich 1984). Nonetheless, there are several articles and books that mention the experiences of lesbians and posit their lives improved as the overall socioeconomic situation of women improved (Arguelles and Rich 1984; La Fountain-Stokes 2002; Smith and Padula 1996). These studies were completed during the 1970s and early 1980s, before the social and economic upheaval often attributed to Cuba's post-Soviet economic downturn of the 1990s (de la Fuente 2001).

There has been some commentary about the social experiences of lesbians from Cuban American scholars; however, these authors acknowledge that their discussion and perspective of lesbians' experiences in Cuba is limited since these authors no longer live in Cuba (La Fountain-Stokes 2002). Moreover, because of the influence that US political discourse has had on empirical work on homosexuality in Cuba, print documentation of gay and lesbian experiences in Cuba has largely been framed as the plight of homosexuals against the Cuban state. The more robust analyses of homosexuality in Cuba, which consider the role of culture and gender in lesbian and gay oppression, have been in independent film.

In the films *Not Because Fidel Says So* (1988), *Looking for Space* (1993), and *Gay Cuba* (1996), lesbian oppression is linked to "homosexual" oppression. These films capture the changes in state policy concerning homosexuality, between 1980 and 1996, when the state began to focus on targeting homophobia within Cuban society in order to address the HIV/AIDS crisis. The state sought to address the crisis by reducing the social stigma concerning homosexuality and by undertaking a massive sexual-education program that targeted men who had sex with men (Acosta et al. 2003; Grupo OREMI 2005). The result of state policies has been more public space that is inclusive for gay male Cubans. These films do not address the ways in which the intersections of gender and sexuality have resulted in such a stark social distinction between lesbians and gay men, which is difficult to speak of in a gay and lesbian community, or even a "homosexual experience" in Cuba.

T Con T: Lesbian Lives in Contemporary Cuba is the first film to focus exclusively on lesbians in Cuba. *T Con T* offers more insight into the issues facing lesbians, as it focuses on the underground lesbian scene in Cuba and efforts at creating a lesbian community while navigating the decreased economic independence of women (which is a result of Cuba's 1990s economic crisis). The women in the film note the increase in gay male public space over the last twenty years, while lesbian space remains invisible. Gay male domination of nonheteronormative space is linked to the ways in which heteronormativity intersects with machismo[1] to create a particularly vitriolic and isolating experience for Cuban lesbians (Arguelles and Rich 1984).

At the 2003 Sixteenth World Congress on Sexology, researchers Dalia Acosta, Sara Más, Dixie Edith, and Mariana Ramírez Corría presented their findings from a 1994 and 2002 national study on homosexuality in Cuba. Their presentation, titled "What Do We Think About Homosexuality? / Qué Pensamos Sobre Homosexualidad?," analyzed the gender differences between how homosexuality

was viewed and accepted among the Cuban population (a summary of their findings is represented in Tables 6.1 and 6.2). With regard to gender, the summary of
their findings is as follows:

- Lesbians are generally more socially rejected than gay men.
- Women are largely judged by physical appearance, while men are valued
  primarily for personality.
- The rejection of lesbians is stronger among the women interviewed than
  men.
- Homophobia is stronger in the middle of the country than in Havana.
- People younger than thirty years of age are more accepting of homosexual-
  ity than are people 45 years and older.
- Up to 4 percent of the sample believed that there is no difference in treat-
  ment between lesbians and gays.

According to this national study, lesbians are overwhelmingly considered to be
rude, uncaring about their appearance, and unfeminine, whereas gay men are
seen as more feminine, friendly, and reserved. In comparison, lesbians are overwhelmingly judged by their physical appearance. The researchers linked this to
persisting sexism where women are not judged by who they are as individuals
but by their appearance (Más 2003). Gay men are treated slightly better than
lesbians, and between 1994 and 2002, gay men saw the greatest increase in social
acceptance.

Interestingly, the overwhelming majority of people believe that there is a difference between how lesbians and gay men are treated (only 4 percent believed
that there is no difference). Finally, the women sampled were more hostile toward

Table 6.1   Views on Homosexuality in Cuba

2002 Summary of results	Lesbians (Percentage of the sample)	Gays (Percentage of the sample)
You accept them.	14	31
You don't accept them.	86	69
Do you treat them like normal people?	58	61
Do you have a gay family member?	2	8
What are they like?		
Rude, brusque, not feminine, disheveled in appearance	97	
Reserved, introverted	32	
Delicate, refined, indiscreet, gossipy, exaggerated		95
Sociable and friendly		45

Table 6.2   Personal Treatment of Lesbian and Gays

	1993–94	2002
	(Percentage of the sample)	(Percentage of the sample)
Treat them (lesbians) / would treat them (lesbians) as normal	55	58
Treat them (gays) / would treat them (gays) as normal	56	61

lesbians than were men (Acosta et al. 2003; Más 2003). While sexuality and perceptions of it bear a strong impact on Cuban women's lives, race also has a powerful effect for Cuban women. Many black Cubans who grew up and worked during the period between 1959 and 1995, when official national discourse declared that there were "no races, only Cubans," typically did not experience the economic pitfalls of racism. The social changes of the 1990s resulted in racially based economic disparities, which forced many black Cubans (approximately thirty to sixty years of age) to acknowledge that racism existed culturally and economically (de la Fuente 2001; Fernandes 2006). For women, the economic downturn and cuts in state-run social programs resulted in limited job opportunities and an increase in caregiving duties in the home.

Further compounding their gendered experienced, black lesbians faced persisting racial ideologies that culturally constructed black women as unfeminine, masculine, sexually promiscuous, and sexually aggressive. In Cuba's three-tier racial system, where races are categorized as white, black, and mulatto, the Spanish term mulato is used to refer to Cuba's biracial category. Ideologically, Cuba's mulato population is represented by the image of the biracial Cuban woman, "la mulata" (Kutzinski 1993). The reason for this is intricately tied into Latin America's and the Caribbean's particular history of racialization. Because Latin American and Caribbean societies were predominately nonwhite and racial intermixture was common, the elites of Latin American and Caribbean nations could not easily base their racial hierarchy on the rule of hypodescent (the one-drop rule), as in the United States (Arroyo 2003; Helg 1995). The construction of a mulato category served the function of maintaining a racial hierarchy where whiteness and Europeanness were idealized as symbols of racial superiority and social advancement. In Latin American and Caribbean nations, a person of color could advance socially through obtaining wealth and by marrying someone who was lighter skinned (Arroyo 2003; Helg 1995). For readers who may not be familiar with Cuba's racial system, it is important to first address Cuba's particular race = gender system, as the existence of Cuba's third racial category, mulato, is integral to the framing of Cuban lesbians' racialized social experiences.

CONTEXTUALIZING RACE AND GENDER IN A CUBAN CONTEXT

As a result of Cuba's racial history, Cuba's mulato category symbolizes Cuban multiculturalism. La mulata is considered to be the physical embodiment of white and black, African and European racial and cultural union; she represents the Cuban nation (Kutzinski 1993). She also represents a fluid racial category in which, depending on how "European" (a reference to race and style) a biracial person appears, he or she can participate in white-only spaces and predominately black spaces.[2] La mulata serves as a way to dismiss white Cubans' historically based fears of a national race war, in which Cuba's large African and Afro-descendant population would take over the island and establish a black republic like Haiti (Arroyo 2003; Fernández Robaina 1996; Ferrer 1999; Helg 1995). Cuba's white elite began to imagine a national racial union, and an end to race, that was to be represented by the mulata's mixed-race body. Vera Kutzinski (1993) argues that la mulata symbolizes the sexual availability of black female bodies to white men. According to Kutzinski, the mulata represents sexual and gender deviance by virtue of her race. Her Africanness makes her a hypersexual woman who seduces honorable white men to act on their "deviant" sexual desires. In Cuba's racialized sex = gender system, the idealized woman is white, represents purity, honor, and motherhood, and is considered the natural and appropriate object of sexual desire. The mulata by virtue of being partially white, is socially accepted, but she represents a fallen woman because of her African ancestry. At the other extreme is the opposite of white femininity: the black woman.

The black woman represents absolute sexual and gender deviance because of her race. She was considered to be so unfeminine that she was perceived as masculine or even as a deformed male; she was likened to having the physical characteristics of a prostitute described in nineteenth- and early twentieth-century sexological literature (large genitalia, an insatiable sexual desire and libido, potentially a rapist of men and women; Helg 1995; Kutzinski 1993). In this way, la mulata is also homoerotic because, as Siobhan Somerville (2000) notes, early definition of the sexual invert (later called a homosexual) was someone who has a deviant sexual object choice: a black woman (Arroyo 2003; Kutzinski 1993).

The perception of black women as the embodiment of masculinity is internalized by Cuban women, including lesbians: Black women are not as desired as white and mulata women because they are interpolated as men. Black women are encouraged to manage perceived female masculinity or hypersexuality by straightening and elongating their hair, losing weight, and wearing clothing that minimizes the visibility of their bodies. Black women with unprocessed hair and well-defined hips and buttocks are assumed to be fat and careless about their appearance. Women openly and frequently comment on the unpleasant nature of these features and offer suggestions for women to correct them or to minimize their visibility. Strangers on the street, usually other women, often feel comfortable in making hair and weight suggestions to women they believe can make themselves appear more attractive.

In my experiences in Cuba, passing as a black Cuban woman exposed me to numerous comments that I often found shocking. Some of these comments ranged from women on the bus who whispered that I should straighten my hair (I had an Afro) to Cuban colleagues who commented that I would be a lot prettier with straight hair and a little less weight. These comments are often tied to the very corporal features that black women are often reduced to: hair, buttocks, weight, hips, and skin color (Helg 1995; Kutzinski 1993).

In Cuba, as in Brazil and other Latin American and Caribbean contexts, class can symbolically change one's race. Affluent black Cubans who are considered to be "cultured" or of a "higher cultural level" (meaning that they reject Afro-Cuban culture and embrace European culture and fashion as a cultural ideal) are often included in white and mulato social space. In the lesbian community in Cuba, especially in the white and mulata lesbian scene, desirable femininity is based on the illusion of wealth, female passivity, and lightness of skin and thin bodies. Such perceptions of beauty and femininity adversely affect the ability of black lesbians to access safe, women-centered social space.

LIVING AS A BLACK WOMAN IN CUBA'S LESBIAN SCENE

Lack of safe public space for socializing is a harsh reality for Cuban lesbians, particularly black lesbians. Though there are virtually no specifically gay clubs in Cuba, gay men still populate public spaces and often turn public spaces, such as the walkway along the Malecón, theaters, book-release parties, and other events, into informal cruising places. Such public cruising spaces for lesbians are virtually nonexistent. Women depend on informal events in the home or, frequently, attend underground lesbian parties. In order to locate these parties, one has to call a secret phone number in order to find the party's location. This number changes as the location of the party changes. Then one has to figure out how to get to the "area" where the party is occurring since an exact address is never given; instead, an oblique reference is given such as "the house close to the intersections of X and Y that has a woman with a small dog sitting outside." This then opens the path for hours of searching and transportation issues. If one is lucky or has the money, one may able to afford a taxi to get to a party location.

In comparison, gay male parties are easily found; one simply goes to the corner, park, restaurant, section of the Malecón, or other public space that has been designated as the gay meet-up point and ask, "Where's the party?" Usually informal taxis are waiting to take partygoers to distant party locations. Additionally, gay male social space is not as racially and class segregated as lesbian social space. In my experiences in attending homoerotic, male-centered spaces with male black, white, and mulato friends and colleagues, men of all races populate these spaces.

Lesbians primarily socialize at home. As a result of the economic downturn, however, working-class women and black women are less able to have events in the home as their incomes have decreased and extended family responsibilities have increased. I asked one of Grupo OREMI's organizers where women normally went to socialize. She answered,

Bueno chica, nos vemos en nuestras casitas, si es que las tenemos, las privilegiadas que las pueden tener. Nos vemos y conversamos en la calle y no sé, en algún otro concierto de alguna que otra muchacha que nos guíe. O sencillamente en las fiestas, que no son legales, pero bueno eso es parte de dónde nos podemos ver de vez en cuando y podemos bailar un poquito . . . Mira, las fiestas son siempre en lugares diferentes porque no es posible tener un espacio, digamos, fijo o un espacio que siempre sea el mismo para tener estas fiestas porque como son ilegales, quienes las dirigen, las comandan o las llevan, necesitan cambiarlas de sitio para protegerse. Digamos para no tener un problema de que lo sepan.

Look girl, we see each other in our little houses, if we have them, the privileged ones that can have them. We see each other and chat in the street and I don't know, in the sporadic concerts of the few women we have as role models. Or we simply meet in the parties, which are not legal, but is part of the places where we can go to see each other and dance a little . . . Look, the parties are always in different places, because it isn't possible to have a fixed space or a space that is always the same to have parties because they are illegal, the people that run then, what they do is that they move them or they have to change the place in order to protect themselves. We do that so that there won't be a problem that so that it would not "be known."

According to this organizer, black lesbians also have to work much harder than other Cubans to earn a living. Light-skinned wealthy women, who are able to afford their own homes or have the leisure time to create women-centered spaces, are typically unwelcoming of working-class women and black women. Therefore many women have to take their chances with the underground lesbian party scene.

These parties are "illegal" because they are often organized without a permit. Permits authorize the party organizers to profit from the event, and if the event is approved, the permit costs amount to a heavy state tax on the profits from the event. These events offer a moneymaking opportunity to a family, their neighbors, and/or a whole apartment building. Parties without a permit that are consistently loud and/or last longer than the hours of the standard noise ordinance are shut down, and the organizers are fined.[3] Therefore contemporary lesbian parties have an "illegal" feel to them because, besides the clandestine nature of finding one, permit rules and public decency codes are often strictly enforced if police are aware that party attendees are gays and lesbians.

Those who attend lesbian parties in El Vedado, the tourist and theater center of Havana, are primarily wealthy whites and mulatas who have ties to the tourist sector either as prostitutes, as wives of foreign men who live abroad, or as employees in hotels, restaurants, or other official businesses with access to chavitos.[4] In the largely white and mulata parties, attendees wear brand-name clothing such as Versace and Tommy Hilfiger. They tend to dress very "miki," a reference to the Mickey Mouse Club that expresses elitist and/or hegemonic forms of gender and sexuality. Black women have a hard time finding friends and partners at these events because oppressive social norms concerning femininity are the harshest within the lesbian community.

Hegemonic forms of femininity are strictly policed within the lesbian community so much that black women who identify on the "femme" end of the "butch/femme" spectrum have a hard time finding butch partners. At miki parties, and even at black and mulata parties, women tend to approach black women with the expectation that they will find a butch partner or a "johnny." Some women have commented that they end up feeling sexually and emotionally unfulfilled as they are expected to be the emotionally distant and sexually dominant partner by virtue of being black. However, at the predominantly black and mulata parties, there is more of a butch/femme presence than at the miki parties.

Given the particularity of how race and class intersect in Cuba, a future study as to why "white" or miki parties tend to draw a femme/femme crowd, while "black" parties tend to draw a plurality of gender representations within the lesbian community, would be an important empirical contribution. For whatever reason, given my experiences in Cuba and the existing research on how black gender and sexuality is represented, black lesbian space in Cuba seems to be a class-diverse queer space, while miki parties heavily police hegemonic norms surrounding femininity.

During interviews with former participants in Grupo OREMI, the issue of racial divisions among the lesbian population was a salient theme.[5] One black participant says this about the gay and lesbian community:

> **Interviewee:** El ambiente mucho más abierto, mucho más desprejuiciado, porque incluso entre los gays, las lesbianas, o lo que sea me parece que hay mucho prejuicio. Me gustaría que fuera un poco más pa'adelante.
> **Interviewer:** ¿Cuáles son algunos de los prejuicios?
> **Interviewee:** Discriminación de todo tipo, racial, social. No sé, hay como peldaños y hay lugares donde yo no puedo llegar y hay lugares donde ellas no pueden llegar. Es como una especie de competencia todo el tiempo y eso no me gusta porque los discriminados, debemos unirnos antes que separarnos.

> **Interviewee:** The environment is much more open, much less prejudiced because even within gays, lesbians, or whatever there is a lot of prejudice. I would like it if it were a little more advanced.
> **Interviewer:** What are some of them?
> **Interviewee:** Discrimination of every type: racial, social. I don't know. It's like there are steps and there are places where I cannot go; there are places where they cannot go. It's like a form of rivalry all the time, and I don't like it because the discriminated should be united rather than separating ourselves.

This interviewee comments on her frustration concerning the social (read: class) and racial divisions between gays and lesbians and in between miki, mulata, and black lesbians. She argues that it is ridiculous because people who are discriminated against because of their sexuality should be united, not divided. In the interviews with approximately 15 former OREMI participants, the majority of whom were nonwhite (3 white women, 7 mulatas, and 5 black lesbians), all but 2 of the respondents, when asked what their ideal woman was, indicated they liked "feminine women with long hair." The respondents stated that they preferred refined women, *mujeres finas*, which is usually code for white or light-skinned women. "Yes, feminine! The more feminine," another respondent stated, "the better I like them" (!Sí, femininas! Mientras más femininas, más me gustan).

In everyday interactions, expectations about black femininity play out in several ways: black lesbians' ability to find partners is severely truncated because, even among lesbians of color, there seems to be a strong preference for those thin, light-skinned women with long hair, and, as I have said, black lesbians are limited in their ability to find safe spaces because light-skinned, wealthy women, who are able to afford their own home or have the leisure time to create women-centered spaces, are typically unwelcoming of working-class women and black women.

MUJERES UNIDAS/WOMEN UNITED:
EL PROYECTO GRUPO OREMI

Its founders named the group OREMI after a Yoruba term used to describe lesbians, although CENESEX generally referred to the group as a "space of reflection." Though the organizers of OREMI knew that the group was being sponsored by a state institution, it meant a safe space for lesbians who have no private space to host their own events. It seems that for this reason OREMI drew a lot of black and mulata women and women who were generally socially isolated. Many of the organizers wanted to be sure that women embraced their own African heritage and the African heritage of Cuba. It is for this reason, in art shows and performances, that many of Grupo OREMI's social activities included Afro-Cuban song, dance, religious themes, and history.

The painters commented that they liked the image of the cowrie shell because in West Africa it used to be used as money. It was a reminder that African cultures had their own money, based in nature, and their own systems of exchange. The shell is painted in the image of the Cuban flag in order to symbolize the African heritage of Cuba. The women represent the racial unity of Cuban women. However, upon closer inspection, the painting is that of a black woman, with her legs open, while the cowrie shell forms the vulva and the labia of her vagina. This painting is explicitly about embracing lesbian sexuality, particularly black lesbian sexuality.

CHALLENGING MACHISMO, HOMOPHOBIA,
AND LESBIAN ISOLATION

La vida de las homosexuales cubanas permanecen en un anonimato que nos hace sentir relegadas . . . Como parte activa de nuestra sociedad poseemos problemas de aceptación de nuestra identidad que se hace evidente en las relaciones familiares y laborales, sufrimos de discriminación, desprecio, rechazo y en el mejor de los casos indiferencia. Una sociedad homofóbica como la nuestra que no ha tenido nunca una educación de tolerancia y acepción afecta notablemente el desarrollo social de aquellas personas que eligieron un estilo de vida diferente. ' En el caso de las mujeres que decidimos ser lesbiana esta homofobia se hace mayor. En una historia femenina de relegación a segundo plano con respecto al hombre donde se nos ha asignado un papel como esposas, madres de familia y dependiente del hombre, que existan mujeres que rechacen esos patrones para hacer su vida con otra mujer, "es casi una ofensa."

In the lives of homosexual Cuban women there remains an anonymity that makes us feel set aside . . . There is the problem concerning the acceptance of our identity, which is manifested in our work and family relationships, we suffer discrimination, are despised, are rejected, and in the best cases receive indifference. A homophobic society such as ours that has not had any education about tolerance and acceptance notably affects the social development of those people who decide upon a lifestyle that is "different." In the case of women who decide to be lesbian, this homophobia is the strongest. In a female history of relegation to second place with respect to men, where we are assigned the role of wife, mother, and dependent of the male, [the existence of] women who reject these norms in order to make their life with another woman, "is almost an offense." (Grupo OREMI 2005)

The organizers of OREMI note that social disdain is the strongest for lesbians. Women are devalued to second-class citizenship status "with respect to men." Lesbians are despised for their rejection of the roles assigned to them (that of wife, mother, and "dependent on the male"). The only women allowed to act "out of place" are prostitutes and mistresses, whose only purpose is to fulfill the sexual needs of men. Thus compulsory heterosexuality, feminine gender presentation, and passivity are expected of all women, with no exceptions (Rich 1993). This expectation of women is reflected in the lack of discussion concerning lesbians and/or any other constructions of female sexuality outside of (potential) heterosexual unions and adultery.

In the proposal for OREMI, the organizers note that lesbians are not a minority, meaning that they are not a group that is politically and economically disenfranchised by the state. As such, the problem they face is largely cultural. Additionally, characteristic of revolutionary discourse, the organizers argue that they do not wish to separate themselves from Cuban society. This refers to a key issue: During the early years of the Cuban Revolution, official discourse encouraged all Cubans to unite under a homogenized discourse of sameness, there were no races, no classes, and, for a while, no gender. This approach, according to the state, was taken to prevent the United States from using any divisions among Cuban citizens as a justification to overthrow the government. Moreover, state officials argued that talking about social divisions would encourage the reproduction of social inequality in the face of efforts to eliminate them.

The rejection of minority status is also a direct challenge to international discourses that reduce lesbian (and homosexual) marginalization to state repression. Such a reduction renders invisible the work of LGBT activists, such as Grupo OREMI's organizers, who work tirelessly to challenge the cultural foundations of Cuban homophobia and sexism. OREMI's organizers also wanted to challenge an implicit cultural argument that lesbians are man-haters who seek to separate themselves from men (Stoner 1991). The organizers sought to dismiss these claims as a means of establishing the group's interests as legitimate and socially inclusive.

The group was immensely popular in Havana. Participants who attended the first event commented that hundreds of women arrived. So many women arrived that many were turned away because of lack of space and resources. The event was not widely advertised and the news about the first event spread quickly by word of mouth. For OREMI's organizers and CENESEX, this was an indication of the immense need for lesbian space in Cuba. Unfortunately, CENESEX, the host institution, was not prepared for the 150 to 200 women who took advantage of having a safe, lesbian-centered space away from home, family, and neighbors. However, residents living near OREMI event locations complained about women holding hands and kissing in public. As the group grew in popularity, and to the horror of CENESEX employees and some of the lesbian activists, many women also took the opportunity of a safe space to have sex with partners in hidden corners and on rooftops.

When I asked one participant why people were having sex at crowded parties, she replied, "Who knew when we would have another chance like this to be alone." For many women the home and Cuba's racialized heteronormative public sphere continue to be places of surveillance. When a woman-centered, nonheteronormative space emerged, women felt free to engage in acts that they are unable to do in the home. The large numbers of lesbians congregating at outdoor events resulted in relentless complaints from the larger community, who were disgusted by the sight of publicly displayed, nonheteronormative female sexuality. This put CENESEX in an awkward position: as a state institution, it had a mandate to provide the services necessary for the social acceptance and support of sexual and gender minorities, but as a state institution, they were also expected to police public morality.

Ill-equipped to deal with lesbians' need for social space and unwilling to endure public reaction to seeing nonheteronormative female sexuality, CENESEX narrowed the scope of its lesbian programs to private counseling services in small groups of 25 or fewer women. The state also started recording the identification information of participants, which intimidated women who had been attending the events anonymously. For this reason, the fall of 2005 is considered by Grupo OREMI's organizers and participants to be the official end of the organization, though Grupo OREMI still exists as a counseling resource.

CONCLUSION

It is important to note that there seems to be a generational shift in which younger Cuban gays and lesbians (younger than thirty years of age) seem to express their sexuality freely and to be more racially integrated. Additionally, the state offers free gender-reassignment surgery for transsexuals, and there is an expectation that gays and lesbians will be allowed to formally marry this year. However, for the overwhelming majority of lesbians (especially for those thirty and over), it seems that one of the key issues facing them is the way in which femininity is racialized and classed. In order for lesbians, particularly black lesbians, to enjoy actively the rights guaranteed by the Cuban state, an informal space for socializing and cultural critique must be guaranteed by the Cuban state and run by locally based independent activists. Because of the limitations on people autonomously organizing to address their social and emotional needs, and as long as state-run institutions, such as CENESEX, continue to uncritically police morality and promote a narrowly defined form of femininity, lesbians, particularly black lesbians, will continue to be among the most marginalized social groups in Cuba.

REFERENCES

Acosta, Dalia, Sara Más, Dixie Edith, and Mariana Ramírez Corría. 2003. "¿Qué Pensamos Sobre Homosexualidad? Un Acercamiento a la Visión de la Población Cubana." Paper presented at the XVI Congreso Mundial de Sexología (16th World Congress of Sexology), Havana, Cuba, March 2003.

Almendros, Nestor, and Orlando Jiménez-Leal. 1984. *Mauvaise Conduite.* 110 min. Paris: Les Films du Losange et Antenne 2.

Anderson, Kelly. 1993. *Buscando un Espacio: Los Homosexuales en Cuba.* 38 min. Miami: Filmmakers Library.

Arguelles, Lourdes, and B. Ruby Rich. 1984. "Homosexuality, Homophobia, and Revolution: Notes Toward an Understanding of the Cuban Lesbian and Gay Male Experience, Part 1." *Journal of Women in Culture and Society* 9 (4): 16.

Arroyo, Jossianna. 2003. *Travestismos Culturales: Literatura y Etnografía en Cuba y Brasil.* Mexico City: Instituto Internacional de Literatura Iberoamericana.

Candelario, Ginetta E. B. 2007. *Black Behind the Ears: Dominican Racial Identity from Museums to Beauty Shops.* Durham, NC: Duke University Press.

de la Fuente, Alejandro. 2001. *A Nation for All: Race, Inequality, and Politics in Twentieth-Century Cuba.* Chapel Hill: University of North Carolina Press.

de Vries, Sonya. 1996. *Gay Cuba.* New York: Frameline Distribution.

Fernandes, Sujatha. 2006. *Cuba Represent! Cuban Arts, State Power, and the Making of New Revolutionary Cultures.* Durham, NC: Duke University Press.

Fernández Robaina, Tomás. 1996. "Cuban Sexual Values and African Religious Beliefs." In *Machos, Maricones, and Gays: Cuba and Homosexuality*, edited by Ian Lumsden, 205. Philadelphia: Temple University Press.

Ferrer, Aida. 1999. *Insurgent Cuba.* Chapel Hill: University of North Carolina Press.

Fleites-Lear, Marisela. 2003. "Women, Family, and the Cuban Revolution." In *Cuban Communism*, edited by Irving Horowitz and Jaime Suchlicki, 344–72. New Brunswick, NJ: Transaction.

Grupo OREMI. 2005. *Proyecto Grupo "Oremi" Ciudad de la Habana.* Havana: Sección de Diversidad Sexual de la ONG SOCUMES (Sociedad Cubana Multidisciplinaria de Estudios de la Sexualidad).

Helg, Aline. 1995. *Our Rightful Share: The Afro-Cuban Struggle for Equality, 1886–1912.* Chapel Hill: University of North Carolina Press.

Kutzinski, Vera M. 1993. *Sugar's Secrets: Race and the Erotics of Cuban Nationalism.* Charlottesville: University Press of Virginia.

La Fountain-Stokes, Lawrence. 2002. "De un Pájaro las Dos Alas: Travel Notes of a Queer Puerto Rican in Havana." *GLQ: A Journal of Lesbian and Gay Studies* 8 (1–2): 7–33.

Leiner, Marvin. 1994. *Sexual Politics in Cuba: Machismo, Homosexuality, and AIDS.* Boulder: Westview Press.

Lumsden, Ian, ed. 1996. *Machos, Maricones, and Gays: Cuba and Homosexuality.* Philadelphia: Temple University Press.

Más, Sara. 2003. *Lesbianas, Las Más Rechazadas: Servicio de Noticias de la Mujer.* Havana: SEMlac.

Rivera-Velázquez, C. 2008. *Monarca Absoluta, Absolute Queen: Las Krudas d' Cuba.* Miami: Tortuga Productions.

Rich, Adrienne. 1993. "Compulsory Heterosexuality and Lesbian Existence." *Signs: Journal of Women in Culture and Society* 5 (1980): 631–60. Also reprinted in *The Lesbian and Gay Studies Reader*, ed. H. Abelove et al. (New York: Routledge, 1993), 227–54.

Sanchez, Graciela. 1988. *Not Because Fidel Castro Says So.* DVD. 10 min. New York: Frameline.

Smith, Lois M., and Alfred Padula. 1996. *Sex and Revolution: Women in Socialist Cuba*. New York: Oxford University Press.

Somerville, Siobhan B. 2000. *Queering the Color Line: Race and the Invention of Homosexuality in American Culture*. Durham, NC: Duke University Press.

Stoner, K. Lynn. 1991. *From the House to the Streets: The Cuban Woman's Movement for Legal Reform, 1898–1940*. Durham, NC: Duke University Press.

T Con T Collective. 2009. *T Con T: Lesbian Lives in Contemporary Cuba*. Miami: Tortuga Productions.

NOTES

1. Marisela Fleites-Lear (2003) defines *machismo* as "the idea that men are superior to women and should dominate them socially, economically, physically, and sexually."

2. This is common in the Spanish-speaking Caribbean. For example, in her book *Black Behind the Ears*, Ginetta E. B. Candelario (2007) focuses on Dominican women's racial identity, in which being mulata is highly prized and blackness is disdained, although some Dominican women choose to identify as black depending on their social context.

3. Ian Lumsden (1996) also notes this.

4. The racial bias in the Cuban tourist sector has been well-documented (de la Fuente 2001; Fernandes 2006). The chavito is a currency in standard usage in the tourist sectors of Cuba's dual economy. Twenty-five pesos are worth approximately one chavito.

5. This interviewee was interviewed as part of the T Con T Collective, of which I am a member, for a forthcoming documentary about lesbians in contemporary Cuba.

CHAPTER 7

SEXUAL TOURISM AND SOCIAL PANICS

RESEARCH AND INTERVENTION IN RIO DE JANEIRO

ANA PAULA DA SILVA AND
THADDEUS GREGORY BLANCHETTE

WHEN IT COMES TO SEX, BRAZIL IS so exotic in Western eyes that anything can be said about it and be believed. Since the early nineteenth century, the country has been synonymous with license—a stereotype that baffles those of us who realize just how conservative Brazilians can be in sexual matters. Reality, it seems, is nowhere near as exciting as the fantasy that there is no sin beneath the equator.

These fantasies, of course, have a racialized component. Brazil has a reputation for being a country, which encourages miscegenation. If it's true, as Franz Fanon (1968) points out, that blackness is symbolically linked with carnality in racialist thought, it is also true that miscegenation is strongly associated in the Western mind with sensuality and decadence (Young 1995). The brown body is "proof" of past transgressions of the color line and the presumptive "natural sexual order," where like is supposed to mate with like. As such, "race mixing" is endlessly fascinating, even (and perhaps particularly) to those who claim to find it disturbing or repulsive. It is thus no surprise that Rio de Janeiro, Brazil's most iconic city, has turned out to be the premier sexual tourism destination of the Americas in the early twentieth century[1].

When we began our research of the sex/tourism nexus in the neighborhood of Copacabana in early 2002, we were very much aware of how the history of Western imaginings of miscegenation has deeply influenced foreign and domestic understandings of Brazil. It became apparent to us that while little was known regarding how sexual commerce and tourism interacted in Copacabana, a whole hell of a lot was imagined. We quickly found out, in fact, that some of the most florid fantasies were serving to orient public policy on how to deal with sexual tourism in our country.

The most persistent of these fantasies might be usefully labeled the "victim/victimizer stereotype." It neatly separates the people involved in sexual tourism into diametrically opposed sets. On the one hand, there are the supposedly wealthy or middle-class, white, male, middle-aged exploiters from the United States and Europe, empowered by globalism, who travel about the world in search of ever cheaper and more depraved commercial sex; on the other hand, there are the supposedly poor, black, young, female exploited living in Rio de Janeiro, who have been forced by the structural changes of the global economy to prostitute themselves.

In our first months of research in Copacabana, we learned how inadequate the victim/victimizer stereotype of sexual tourism was and how it was being used to criminalize prostitutes, most particularly lower-class, nonwhite prostitutes, in the name of saving them from evil, foreign exploiters.

To begin with, we discovered that the linkages between sex and tourism in Rio de Janeiro are extremely old and varied and produce a diverse set of prostitutions. Rio, of course, is one of the oldest port cities in the Americas. Founded in 1565, the city was a stopover for Asian- or African-bound shipping out of Europe for the better part of four centuries. As a consequence, Rio was quite international from the moment of its founding and from colonial days on, men and women of all colors and social stations could be found plying the oldest of professions in the city. Of course, many of these people have historically been poor and black or brown, but to focus on them alone (and, more particularly, to cast them as simple and passive victims of structural or economic phenomena) does not adequately explain neither their lives as individuals nor the functioning of the city's sexual market as a social aggregate.

Today, prostitution remains legal in Brazil and the sex industry of Rio de Janeiro continues to be one of the most diverse in the Americas, with prostitutes ranging from call girls charging thousands of dollars per appointment to streetwalkers working for $2.50 a pop near the Central do Brazil railroad station. Furthermore, the city boasts a booming homosexual prostitution scene (serving both genders), which is equally diversified in terms of status, costs, and work conditions. Both gay and straight commercial sex scenes are diversified in terms of race and class, though the most commonly encountered biotype is the *carioca* of indeterminate ethnicity whose skin color ranges from light to midbrown.

There is no hard evidence—or even convincing circumstantial evidence—that the city's prostitute population has increased in relative terms over the last twenty years. In fact, what evidence does exist seems to indicate that, percentage-wise, the late twentieth and early twenty-first centuries have seen an overall decrease in Rio's prostitute population from the heydays of the early 1900s. Globalization doesn't seem to have made much of an impact upon the sex trade in Rio, either, outside of spreading foreign tourists more evenly around the annual calendar.

In the heterosexual tourism scene, contact between foreign tourists and carioca prostitutes is largely confined to the neighborhood of Copacabana and its immediate environs, with some 63 percent of all reported sexual acts occurring being contracted in that region. A secondary nexus can be found in the downtown. Up to 64 percent of all heterosexual tourist contact with prostitutes is concentrated in ten venues (one disco, one restaurant/bar, one beach, one street "zona,"[2] and six saunas). Of these, all but two are in Copacabana or its immediate environs. Police estimates (and our observations confirm) that some 1,500 female sex workers can be found in this region, probably one-third of which are working the heterosexual tourism venues at any one time[3]. Significantly, in our seven years of research, we have yet to find a child[4] working in one of the ten main venues.

The prices of the main sexual tourism spots situate them at the upper end of the middle range of carioca sex establishments. The cost paid per sexual act has been floating between 75 and 150 US dollars for close to a decade now, with the women receiving anywhere from 50 to 100 percent of that. Bearing in mind that, as of September 2008, the Brazilian monthly minimum wage was around 225 USD, sexual work in Copacabana can generate more than a maid's monthly pay in an afternoon[5]. Many of our prostitute informants report wages that are at par with or higher than ours as university professors.

Working conditions in the six main venues, which actually employ prostitutes,[6] range from average to good, though as is the case with all paid work in Brazil (including that of university professors), labor laws are more often than not honored in the breach. In general, health conditions are good, with periodic AIDS testing and protected sex being the rule[7]. Sexual labor is also organized in such a fashion that the women generally feel that they are in control, at least vis-à-vis individual clients. The largest number of complaints that we've encountered so far in our (admittedly incomplete) research revolves around labor/management issues that are frankly common across the carioca job market (unpaid or late salaries, illegal docking of pay for absenteeism, deduction of labor and raw materials costs from pay, etc.).

Turning to the foreign clients, we've found them to be no more or less perverse, attractive, or emotionally healthy than men in general. The majority is white and comes from Europe and the United States. An increasing percentage (ranging from 2 to 12 percent depending on time of year and venue), however, is African American. Most are middle class, but many are working class, and a substantial number of the latter work in Brazil's growing petroleum industry. With the American war in Iraq and Afghanistan, we've also seen increasing numbers of American servicemen using Rio as a "safe" R&R destination. These men are thus hardly the unambiguous victors of globalization portrayed by so many antisexual tourism activists. Nor is the sex that they pay for appreciably cheaper than it is in most parts of the United States (where paid sex can be had for around 100 USD). Crucially, there is no hard evidence that these men are any more likely to be pedophiles or sex offenders than other men. In fact, a recent study of more than five years of calls to the sexual exploitation denunciation hotline maintained by the Brazilian federal government indicates that members of the clergy are about four to five times more likely to be accused of child molestation than foreign tourists (ABRAPIA 2004).

In short, our initial study of Copacabana (Blanchette and Da Silva 2005) concluded that, all things considered, it was a reasonably well-organized and safe commercial sexual district, with no appreciably greater incidence of violations of human or workers' rights than other, comparable segments of Brazil's tourism economy (most notably, the growing "ethnic tourism" sector patronized by black Americans in Salvador da Bahia).

In early 2003, however, it became increasingly apparent to us that a growing social panic regarding tourism and sex was brewing in the local political scene. A series of police raids were organized and carried out in the name of repressing the sexual exploitation of children (extremely rare in Copacabana) and stamping out the trafficking of women (also rare if we understand trafficking as necessarily involving violations of fundamental human rights). The organizers of these raids made ample use of the "victim/victimizer stereotype" of sexual tourism as justification for their activities, but the real purpose of police activity seemed to be to harass prostitutes and their clients, with "sexual tourism" and "exploitation of children" being mobilized as legally enabling fictions.

The most notorious of these raids was the Operation Princess series, which was supposedly motivated by denunciations of the sexual exploitation of minors. Though many arrests were made and the raids were internationally reported as being a major blow against sexual tourism and the sexual exploitation of children in Brazil, very few minors were actually encountered and the cases have not generated much in the way of legal results, due to lack of evidence. This is not to say, however, that they didn't generate any results at all: hundreds of sex workers were harassed and detained, often in handcuffs and at gunpoint, simply for being prostitutes. In almost every case, the raids generated many more violations of human and constitutional rights than they resolved.[8]

As we followed Operation Princess and other like activities, it became clear to us that the government was *not* primarily interested in protecting sex workers or even in preventing the sexual exploitation of children, rather the police were apparently seeking to repress prostitution itself. Again, prostitution is not illegal in Brazil, so in order to repress it, other illegalities needed to be alleged. The immediate motivation behind the raids seemed to be the "revitalization" of Copacabana as a "family tourism district" (a status that the neighborhood has never had in all of its history).

Our research in Copacabana led us to believe that we had uncovered a series of activities that ran counter to the received wisdom regarding sexual tourism. Far from discovering a clean divide between victimizing first-world actors and passive third-world victims, which could be further classified according to color, age, race, and class, we found much diversity among prostitutes and clients. Certainly, some generalizations could be made: Copa prostitutes were generally darker and certainly poorer than most of their foreign clients. Ethnic alterity in this nexus, however, was not so much couched in terms of (foreign) white versus (native) nonwhite but rather in terms of presumed foreign "racial purity" versus Brazilian "miscegenation."

Furthermore, most Copacabana sex workers related to us that they felt far less exploited in their current activities than they had in prior jobs. Most, in fact, had left "straight" jobs—often in the tourism industry—in order to work as prostitutes. In short, Copa prostitutes were not underaged sex slaves, "forced" into prostitution against their will or for lack of other work. Their jobs, while perhaps unpleasant, were no more exploitative than those otherwise available in the tourism sector and generated ten to twenty times as much income. The violence they reported did not usually come from pimps or foreign clients but from other prostitutes, the police, or from "good citizens" intent on eliminating prostitution.

In the public policy realm, we discovered that the social panic regarding sexual tourism and the exploitation of children was being used to construct policies, which harassed and ultimately endangered sex workers. These policies were almost always justified by recourse to the victim/victimizer stereotype of sexual tourism, with state agents claiming that their activities were necessary to protect poor, black, exploited women from the ravages of evil, white gringo tourists. However, it was precisely the poorer women working as independent prostitutes on the streets who were the preferential targets for the government's repressive activities and, although African American sexual tourists are in the minority on Copa, two of the last four heavily publicized raids resulted, almost exclusively, in the arrests of African Americans.[9] Women working the closed sexual venues (i.e., those who had, to one degree or another, bosses or pimps) and the mostly foreign white sexual tourists who frequented them were rarely discomfited by the crusade.

By late 2004, we felt that, ethically speaking, we needed to take a political stand on this issue. We no longer felt comfortable quietly listening to academic colleagues repeat received wisdom about sexual tourism when we could clearly see, in our field work, that this sort of unreflective discourse was providing the ideological justification for activities that endangered our sex worker friends and informants. We thus contacted Brazil's main prostitute advocacy group, the Brazilian Prostitutes' Network (Rede Brasileira de Prostitutas / RBP). The RBP is an NGO run by and for prostitutes, and it is extremely active in the fight against AIDS in Brazil. The group's leader, Gabriela Leite, had been one of the main public figures in the struggle for prostitute's rights since the closing years of the Brazilian dictatorship in the 1980s. Gabriela had some formal training as a sociologist before dropping out of school to pursue sex work full time and her organizational activities had helped the Brazilian federal government to decide to incorporate sex workers in safe sex education activities. It would not be an exaggeration to say that Gabriela and the national network of which she was a part were two of the main reasons the HIV crisis in Brazil was not as bad is it potentially could have been.

It was our hope that by presenting the RBP with the results of our study, we could force policy change by giving the organized prostitute movement the means to enter the debate regarding trafficking of women, and its supposed connections to sex work in Brazil. Throughout the trafficking debate in Brazil, many people had spoken *about* prostitutes, but sex workers themselves had been largely ignored as participants in policymaking. In part, this was due to the fact that state feminism in Brazil, as represented by the women's secretariat, is divided on the question of prostitution. Brazil's experience with AIDS education, however, shows that actively engaging with prostitutes as educators and agents instead of regarding them as passive victims can have extremely positive results.

Because the RBP is underfunded and overwhelmed, we felt that the prostitutes' movement was not paying attention to how the social panic surrounding sexual tourism was being used to repress prostitution. We hoped that by alerting the RBP as to how the debate regarding the trafficking of women was being used as a Trojan horse in order to repress prostitution, we could help bring about a more honest and far-reaching discussion as to how prostitution and tourism were interwoven in Brazil.

We presented our findings to the women of the RBP and have been working with them ever since. Together, we have attended national, regional, and local conferences discussing sexual tourism, the trafficking of women, and the sexual exploitation of children, providing the results of our ongoing studies of prostitution as a more rational basis than myth and prejudice for public policy and attempting to undermine the prejudices and stereotypes, which currently orient so much of Brazil's laws and police activities in this field.

Concretely, we have pushed policymakers to clearly define the concept of "sexual exploitation" in such a way that it does not automatically presume that all sex work is necessarily exploitative. We have also suggested that, in the struggle against trafficking of women and the sexual exploitation of minors, Brazil could do well by emulating its award-winning anti-AIDS program and integrating prostitutes into educational campaigns as active agents. In our experience, there is no reason to believe that prostitutes and their clients are any more accepting of the sexual abuse of women and children than the public in general. We believe that if sex workers were assured that their accusations would be taken seriously and their anonymity and citizens' rights respected, they would become valuable allies in the repression of human trafficking and the sexual exploitation of minors. Police and policymakers need to be educated regarding sex workers' rights and the stereotype of the "worthless" or "feckless whore"—frequently and openly expressed by policymakers in Rio—needs to be combated. Finally, we feel that the time has come for sex work—permitted by the Brazilian constitution and qualified as productive labor by the federal labor ministry—to be regulated. We thus support federal deputy Fernando Gabeira's 98/2003 bill (inspired by Germany's 2001 laws regarding prostitution), which would put sex work on firm legal ground. One of the effects of this law would be the repeal of Article 231 of the Brazilian Criminal Code, which literally defines any movement of prostitutes—whatsoever—as human trafficking, regardless of whether human rights were violated during said movement.

Our political work has brought us into increased contact with Brazilian policymakers and has given us a better view of how traditional understandings of race, class, and gender underpin policies regarding sexual tourism and prostitution. Basically, the Brazilian government and much of the country's media seem to have decided that, even though sexual tourism is not illegal in Brazil, it is nevertheless a menace, which must be combated. In this struggle, there are two types of Brazilian women: those who are and those who aren't supposedly threatened by sexual tourism. The first category is, of course, epitomized by prostitutes and there is a growing consensus within Brazil that this sort of woman should not be allowed in contact with foreigners "for her own good." Of course, who is a prostitute and who is not is something that's very much open to question, and this is precisely where the victim/victimizer model of sexual tourism has become codified as policy.

According to the Brazilian federal government, the victims of sexual tourism can be identified by their *vulnerabilities*. These are defined as quasiessential traits, which are based on class, race, education, and gender and which, as a rule, closely follow those adjectives stipulated by the victim/victimizer stereotype described previously. The vulnerable victims of sexual tourism are thus classified as predominantly young, black or brown, and poor women who have contact with foreigners. Police, tourism agents, and social workers are being trained to spot these *vulnerable* individuals and report any suspicious activities to local authorities.

It does not take much sociological imagination to see what this policy means in practice: poor, black and brown women, especially if they are young and frequent the same places as foreigners, are increasingly being subjected to harassment of every sort. What is sinister about this model is that it redefines class and racial profiling and social exclusion as a progressive, human rights–oriented policy.

Within this context, our goal as politically engaged researchers has been to help people see that prostitutes and their clients are actually strong potential allies in the struggle against trafficking of women and the sexual exploitation of minors. Working with the RBP, we have tried to make policymakers and civil society aware of how antiprostitution measures disguised to look like human rights initiatives in the struggle against sexual tourism—a "crime" that does not exist under Brazilian jurisprudence—actually divert resources from finding and jailing the real criminals. Finally, we have tried to bring our and the RBP's work to international audiences in order to better provide a more nuanced and balanced picture of sex work in Rio de Janeiro and its similarities and differences with similar work in other parts of the globe.

REFERENCES

ABRAPIA. 2004. *Abuso e Exploração Sexual de Crianças e Adolescentes no Brasil. Período: 01 de Janeiro de 2000 a 31 de Janeiro de 2003*. Rio de Janeiro: ABRAPIA.

Blanchette, T., and A. P. Da Silva. 2009. "Amor Um Real Por Minuto." In *The Contents of the Latin American and Asian Dialogues on Sexuality and Geopolitics*. New York: Sexual Policies Watch. http://www.sxpolitics.org/pt/wp-content/uploads/2009/10/sexualidade-e-economia-thaddeus-blanchette-e-ana-paula-da-silva.pdf.

———. 2008. "Mapeamento do Sexo Turismo no Rio de Janeiro." Presentation at the National Association of Post-Graduate Studies in the Social Sciences (ANPOCS) conference, Caxambú, Minas Gerais, Brazil.

———. 2005."'Nossa Senhora da Help': Sexo, Turismo e Deslocamento Transnacional em Copacabana." *Cadernos Pagu* 25.

CEDAW. 2003. "Brazilian Report." Paper presented at the CEDAW 29th Session, New York, New York, June 30 to July 18.

Datadez. 2006. "TJRJ Concede Habeas Corpus a Grupo Acusado de Prostituição na Barra." Last modified January 26. http://www.datadez.com.br/content/noticias.asp?id=20968.

Fanon, F. 1968. *Black Skin, White Masks*. New York: Grove Press.

Gripp, A., and E. Bottari. 2004. "Copacabana e Leme, os Mercados do Sexo." *O Globo*, February 15.

Young, R. J. C. 2005. *Desejo Colonial*. São Paulo, Brazil: Perspectiva.

NOTES

1. This affirmation comes from the analysis of some thirty thousand public reports filed by self-described sexual tourists on six different English-language sex-and-travel-oriented bulletin boards. This research is described in Blanchette and Da Silva (2009). We understand "sexual tourism" following the International Tourism Organization, which defines it as the use of the tourism infrastructure to travel to foreign lands to purchase sexual services.

2. This is Vila Mimosa, an area which concentrates several prostitution venues frequented by working class Brazilians and which is occasionally visited by foreign sex tourists.

3. This is based on the 2003 statistics of our research presented in Blanchette and Da Silva (2008). Police estimates can be found in Gripp and Botarri (2004). The number of prostitutes working Copa varies radically from month to month, but 1,500 seems to be a good average.

4. "Child" is defined here as someone from 0 to 15 years of age. From 0 percent to 2 percent of the prostitutes we observe on any given night in Copa appear to be between 16 and 17 years old. These girls are hardly ever seen inside the venues in question and tend to work the sidewalks or beach. What police arrest records have been made public after recent antiprostitution blitzes (which, it must be remembered, specifically look for minors) confirm these findings. See also Blanchette and Da Silva (2005).

5. It is worth remarking, in this context, that 20 percent of economically active female Brazilians work as domestic laborers (CEDAW 2003).

6. The disco, beach, and restaurant/bar venues do not directly employ sex workers, and sex does not occur on their premises. They simply serve as meeting places for prostitutes and clients. Only one of these three venues, the disco, charges an entrance fee. Vila Mimosa is a special case: sex workers are not employed by the venues which make up the Vila, but they do have from 15 percent to 25 percent of their earnings siphoned of by the house in the form of room rentals.

7. Both prostitutes and clients overwhelming report that unprotected anal or vaginal sex is almost unheard of, though unprotected oral sex is relatively common.

8. In one raid on an apartment brothel, for example, the apartment owner and the brothel manager were immediately released on bail while five of the brothel's employees (two telephone operators, a taxi driver, a maid, and a prostitute) were imprisoned for months as "material witnesses" until a *habeas corpus* action in their favor forced their release (Datadez 2006).

9. It's worth pointing out that these men were not involved in the sexual exploitation of minors or the trafficking of women—they were simply clients of adult, self-employed prostitutes. Under Brazilian law, they had committed no crime and, in all but one case, were immediately released.

CHAPTER 8

TRANSLATING (BLACK) QUEERNESS

UNPACKING THE CONCEPTUAL LINKAGES BETWEEN RACIALIZED MASCULINITIES, CONSENSUAL SEX, AND THE PRACTICE OF TORTURE

GUY MARK FOSTER

> What kinds of violences are necessary to consolidate the constituency designated by the pronoun "we"?[1]
>
> —Hiram Perez

GLOBAL APPROPRIATIONS OF US-DERIVED UNDERSTANDINGS OF HOW gender and sexuality operate as categories of human experience have acquired a special resonance these days. The revelation in May 2004 that US military personnel brutally tortured Iraqi male prisoners of war by employing antihomosexual taunts has placed our country's gender and sexual norms at the center of contemporary discourse. Moreover, these revelations appear to implicate contemporary gay men's own marginalization as persecuted sexual minorities in ways that, to one scholar in particular, "reads as an orientalist projection that conveys much more about the constraints and imaginaries of identity in the 'West' than anything else."[2] Indeed, as we will see shortly, not only have some gay male commentators argued that the armed forces' use of simulated forms of male-male sexuality as a method of torture strategically plays upon US gay men's (especially *white* gay men's) own identifications and desires in the service of a broad policy of national defense, but such views have sometimes also been held by those who are not gay men, and who are in fact hostile to homosexuality altogether.[3]

Such identificatory gestures position homosexuality as an overdetermined category, and they raise important questions about the nature of embodiment, affect, and the production of politicized epistemologies more generally. For instance, what modes of selective identification make possible these visceral responses to an objectified "gay" sexuality that is enacted upon and by bodies that are *neither* white nor self-identifying as "gay," but instead are visibly racialized as other? More specifically, how does white gay male outrage at the release of the disturbing photographs of Iraqi male prisoners posed in ways that *resemble* intimate acts of same-gender sexual activity, but that are in reality something quite different, function in part to unmask white gay men's own complex social positioning within US identity-based race, gender, and sexual hierarchies? In the end, whose politics and affective interests are best served by these calculated speech acts that are, at bottom, also a *mis*recognition and whose interests are foreclosed by this very same speech?

Utilizing the insights of contemporary theorists like Marlon Ross, Roderick Ferguson, and Jasbir Puar, among others, I attempt to offer provisional answers to these questions. I do so by closely examining the 2005 documentary *Ring of Fire: The Emile Griffith Story* for what I want to suggest are the conceptual linkages the film, along with the tactics engaged in by those promoting the film, shares with the Abu Ghraib prison scandal and its aftermath.

RING OF FIRE: AUDIENCE-AS-MARKET AND THE PROBLEM OF DIFFERENCE

The life and career of the former welterweight boxing champion Emile Griffith would seem to provide any filmmaker with the raw material for a powerful documentary. Arriving from the US Virgin Islands in the late 1950s, Griffith is "discovered" while working as a go-fer in Manhattan's bustling garment district. At the age of 15, his employer notes Griffith's impressive physique and brings the youth to the attention of a well-known trainer. The trainer works with Griffith for a mere two months before entering the youth into the prestigious Golden Gloves competition, where incredibly Griffith makes it all the way to the final round. A few short years later, in 1961, Griffith's growing reputation as a fighter earns him a title bout with the then welterweight champion Benny "Kid" Paret, whom he defeats in a decision. Because the fight is aired on the popular television series *Friday Night Fights*, Griffith becomes an instant media celebrity and later appears on the Ed Sullivan show. However, when Paret's handlers request a second fight, Griffith goes down in a decision. Upon losing this fight, Griffith retreats into himself. A year later, in 1962, the younger fighter is reluctantly granted a rematch with his Cuban-born opponent. Fighting with a resolve that was missing in the second encounter, Griffith is strong in the early rounds. The prefight hoopla of this rematch was marred by controversy, however, as Paret apparently began to make use of a rumor about his opponent's sexuality. At the weigh-in, Paret taunted Griffith by calling him a "*maricón*," perhaps the worst insult one presumptive heterosexual male can make to another, since the word, in Spanish, calls into question a man's masculinity by suggesting that he is a homosexual. Griffith's trainer had his hands full keeping his young fighter from throwing a punch at Paret before the bout even began. "Save it for tonight," Gil Clancy was reported to have told his charge.[4] Finally, at 2:09 in the twelfth round, Griffith lands a vicious flurry of punches to his opponent's head, 29 consecutive punches in all, causing Paret to slump worrisomely to the canvas, whereupon the referee, the famed Ruby Goldstein (celebrated for stopping fights mercifully, sometimes too soon for some bloodthirsty aficionados), finally intervenes and declares Griffith the victor. But Paret never regained consciousness and was eventually carried from the ring in a stretcher. Ten days later the Cuban fighter died in New York's Roosevelt Hospital, his young, grief-stricken wife by his side.

According to the film's narrative logic, Emile Griffith was never the same after this final fight with Paret. Although Griffith eventually returned to the ring and even won several more high-profile fights, he never recaptured the form or the wide popularity that his earlier success had garnered. As many fighters do, Griffith unfortunately stayed in the profession for far too long, finally losing a series of bouts to lesser opponents and being forced by his trainer to retire in 1977, balding and nearly forty. His earnings depleted, Griffith found a second career for a while as a trainer of promising fighters before working as a correction's officer in New York. Apparently, one night outside a Manhattan gay bar, Griffith was attacked as he stumbled onto the sidewalk drunk and was badly beaten in what the police characterized at the time as a possible hate crime. For weeks Griffith lay near death, and when he was eventually released from the hospital he had lost some of his motor skills as well as much of his short-term memory. To many observers and fans, the irony was that Griffith's condition resembled that of a punch-drunk fighter—a longtime boxer's expected fate. But the more sensational truth apparently was that the former champion's beating quite possibly occurred at the hands of gay bashers and not by an opponent in the ring.

This narrative undermines a dominant cultural assumption in Western culture, and it is that male athletic prowess and homosexuality are mutually exclusive categories. *Ring of Fire* takes up this narrative thread and attempts to unravel it with varying degrees of success. The film is the work of Dan Klores and Ron Berger, two white, Jewish, heterosexual men whose previous documentary, *The Boys of 2nd Street Park*, chronicles the ups and downs in the lives of several middle-aged men who as youngsters belonged to a Jewish basketball-playing gang. By anchoring their narrative about Griffith to the well-known trope of secrecy and revelation that has become the dominant mode of conceptualizing lesbian and gay male possibility in the twentieth century—a trope emblematized by what Marlon Ross has dubbed the "closet paradigm"—Klores and Berger ensure that their documentary will be legible within the very terms by which much of mainstream lesbian and gay discourse is presently understood.[5] However, because same-sex identities and desires are diverse in their lived realities, representational approaches that rely on this metaphor "as the essential vehicle for narrating homosexuality as a necessary progress from dark secrecy to open consciousness" often inadvertently construct universalizing narratives about lesbian and gay identities that are exclusionary.[6] One risk of any uncritical use of the closet paradigm to explore same-gender sexuality is that one "effectively diminishes and disables the full engagement with potential insights from race theory and class analysis."[7] Such an oversight may become especially problematic when the central subject of one's project is a person of color, more specifically an Afro-Caribbean, as is the case in *Ring of Fire*.[8]

The following close analysis primarily derives from two sources: (1) a screening I attended of the film in July 2005 at the Lesbian and Gay Film Festival in Los Angeles and (2) promotional materials that I received in the mail from festival organizers prior to the film's premiere as well as from the thicker, glossier program I received upon my arrival. Although I later learned that the documentary had aired on the USA television network in April of that year, the present analysis does not attempt to consider the implications of that prior broadcast but rather limits itself to trying to decipher how my own understanding of the film was shaped almost entirely by this initial experience of the film within a specifically lesbian and gay milieu. Moreover, given the concerns I raise here, my analysis engages in the interpretive critical practice known as queer of color critique. Building on the insights of scholars like Chandan Reddy and José Esteban Muñoz, Roderick Ferguson argues that queer of color analysis "interrogates social formations as the intersections of race, gender, sexuality, and class, with particular interest in how those formations correspond with and diverge from nationalist ideals and practices."[9] Because those ideals and practices have traditionally tended to "suppress the diverse components of state and capitalist formations," queer of color critique strives to "debunk the idea that race, class, gender, and sexuality are discrete formations, apparently insulated from one another."[10] In order to perform such critical work, queer of color analysis must *disidentify* with other modes of material analysis that have traditionally centered class as a privileged social formation over the simultaneous imbrication of several categories at once. For Muñoz, "Disidentification is the hermeneutical performance of decoding mass, high, or any other cultural field from the perspective of a minority subject who is disempowered in such a representational hierarchy." In short, "queer of color critique decodes cultural fields not from a position outside those fields, but from within them, as those fields account for the queer of color subject's historicity."[11]

Precisely because my own critical posture is skeptical of any epistemological stance that would preemptively see homosexuality, black maleness, and athletic prowess as necessarily mutually exclusive or as discrete identity formations, I often find myself drawn to self-consciously queer narratives that likewise aim to subvert such assumptions. From past experience, I had reason to hope that the festival's screening of *Ring of Fire* would prove to be just such a narrative. However, from the start there seemed to be a disjunction between the film I actually watched seated in the Director's Guild Theater on Sunset Boulevard and the film I had *expectations* of seeing from what I had gleaned from the promotional materials I'd read. For me, the heart of the problem centers around the question of translating the experiences of what Scott Bravmann calls "queer historical subjects" to the screen in a way that manages to remain faithful to "the specificities of the social formation" of those subjects.[12] As Julio Ortega reminds us, "Translating is the possibility of constructing a scene of mediation that frames interpretation as a dialogic exercise. Thus it is the first cultural act that places languages and subjects in crisis, unleashing a redefinition of speakers, a debate over protocols, and a struggle over interpretation."[13] In short, the practice of translation in whatever medium is never innocent, involving, as it often does, contests over the authority to name and give shape to forms of human experience that may both intersect and depart from both mainstream and folk wisdom at crucial points but that never, when all is said and done, collapse neatly into one another. The specific problems involved with *Ring of Fire* emerged most clearly when I carefully began to scrutinize the narrative logic the filmmakers employ along with how the festival organizers made use of that logic to promote—that is, *translate*—the film to their specialized niche audience—that is, men and women who are interested in seeing films with what they hope will be identifiable lesbian and gay content.

However, given the economic considerations of filmmaking and the need often to identify a niche audience for one's efforts, not everyone will constitute the target of a given film's marketing strategies. Some individuals and groups will not be targeted at all. In an essay analyzing the organizational role that film festivals play in helping to shape lesbian and gay identities, Joshua Gamson argues that such festivals become "homes or warehouses for collective identity; they involve ongoing and self-conscious decision making about the content and contours of the 'we' being made literally visible." Engaged in the business of "*identity framing*," lesbian and gay film festivals are central in "making visible particular versions of group 'consciousness and characters.'"[14] Until recently, the "particular versions" of queer subjectivity that lesbian and gay film festivals have tended to privilege were the identities and identity concerns of primarily white lesbians and gay men at the exclusion of lesbians and gay men of color. However, such practices have proven untenable in recent years, as "it has become extremely difficult to retain legitimacy as a lesbian and gay community organization without demonstrating a commitment to gender, racial, and ethnic diversity."[15] While later festivals have conscientiously responded to this criticism by diversifying their film offerings to ensure the inclusion of work by and about a wide range of *different* lesbians and gay men, much of this work has nonetheless promoted what Gamson calls the "mainstreaming and commercialization" of lesbian and gay identities. The result is that lesbian and gay cinematic identities become framed increasingly in narrow terms. Paradoxically, just as lesbian and gay male image making has begun to reach a wider audience, the view of what a lesbian or a gay man is or looks like has become *less* rather than *more* diverse. As Gamson explains it, relying on commentary from such festival insiders as Daryl Chin:

> Consolidating a market niche, typically by providing "more mainstream things that will fill up 500 seats and everything," involves affirming that same-sex desire is a coherent, shared basis for a social grouping. The accommodation of racial diversity takes place in this organizational context, primarily through a multi-culturalism that posits a plurality of lesbian and gay experiences, but does not challenge their basic commonality. The boundaries of the collective category are expanded, the "family" enlarged; racial and ethnic differences are framed as variations on a theme rather than as demonstrations of the instability of the collective. This framing prevails not so much because organizers all share this perspective—they do not—but because the characteristics of the organizational sector favor the consolidation of an audience-as-market for survival purposes.[16]

What becomes difficult to apprehend in such a context is the degree to which most lesbian and gay male communities are themselves deeply fractured by racial and ethnic division. As Scott Bravmann reminds us, "The queer fiction of the present that 'we' are 'now' a 'community' with a shared history . . . is very

deeply troubled by queer fictions of the past that powerfully refract the historically embedded, highly consequential differences among us, rightly making any
attempt to theorize or write the histories of queer heterosociality a problematic,
uncomfortable, and disturbing endeavor."[17]

THE "CLOSET" METAPHOR AS A LIMITING PARADIGM

Although actual queer communities are generally *not* founded on a "coherent,
shared basis" for understanding social identity, it was precisely this assumption
of "basic commonality" existing between all lesbians and gay men, regardless of
racial or ethnic identity, that I am suggesting was operating when I attended
the screening of *Ring of Fire* in Los Angeles. This bias could be detected in any
number of ways, but the most obvious way the festival context served to "mainstream" Klores and Berger's documentary about Griffith was in its use of the
closet paradigm in its promotional materials. For example, consider the following
passage, which was printed in the festival program I received once I arrived for
the screening:

> The year is 1962, when [as popular opinion would have it] "even Liberace was
> thought to be straight." What if—in the brutal, macho sport of boxing—the six-
> time welterweight champion of the world was really a closeted homosexual? RING
> OF FIRE, Dan Klores and Ron Berger's enthralling documentary, deftly depicts
> this very true story. During the weigh-in for a highly anticipated bout at Madi-
> son Square Garden, archrival Benny "Kid" Paret called Emile Griffith a *maricón*, a
> Spanish word for "faggot." Later, on live television, Griffith pummeled Paret, leav-
> ing him in a coma from which he died 10 days later. That match sparked outrage
> and calls for boxing reform. Griffith, who currently lives with his longtime room-
> mate and "adopted son" Luis Rodrigo, is still haunted by Paret's death. Skillfully
> blending current interviews with rare black-and-white footage, RING OF FIRE
> skewers the hypocrisy of political outrage, exposes the underside of social and cul-
> tural mores, thoughtfully provides a framework for forgiveness and bravely poses
> the question, who (or what) is really to blame for Paret's death?

This quotation is a lengthier version of the blurb that was printed in the glossy
brochure I received in the mail prior to attending the screening and that originally enticed me to want to see the film. Here, Griffith is narrativized for the sake
of its niche audience as a potential "homosexual," one who is "closeted" but who
nonetheless manages to have a "longtime roommate," a man we are told is also
Griffith's "adopted son." The fact that Griffith is Caribbean-born or black is not
worthy of mention. Only Paret, who utters the Spanish-language equivalent to
the English word "homosexual," is marginally identified by culture. Stripped of
the specificity of his ethnicity and color, then, Griffith functions in this summary
as an "abstract homosexual body," not as himself.[18] He is the ideal stand-in for the
feared and hated homosexual, a figure Jeffrey Weeks has called the "scapegoated
minority."[19] As such, Griffith becomes, in a word, a kind of "gay everyman," and
therefore someone with whom *all* gay men (and perhaps all lesbians), regardless
of race or ethnicity, can identify—that is, see as themselves, but not really.

This is because Griffith's narrative of closeted queer identity is an *anti*-identity for the film's targeted audience. For in identifying with Griffith, but in *dis*identifying with his refusal to "come out" as gay (i.e., not condoning that refusal), the film's privileged lesbian and gay viewers could then root for Griffith to conquer his fear as they, the viewers, have ideally conquered their own fear. After all, given the internal logic of the closet paradigm on which both the film and the festival organizers rely, "It [in my analysis, Griffith's 'coming out'] was an *essential* step in the evolution of a modern homosexual consciousness."[20] Not to "come out" is to give in to that fear and therefore to remain in darkness. But in being "seen" by others in such a way, "as themselves," not "dark" but "out and proud," Griffith is not "seen" as *him*self, and whatever meaning this may hold for him, as a man of color in the racially tumultuous era of postwar America. Because any "dark" body in such a cultural context becomes saturated with cultural meanings of "darkness" that preexist, and even extend beyond, his identity; that body's darkness becomes useful for others in a way that it is not seen as useful for itself.[21]

Ralph Ellison dramatized this social condition of African Americans eloquently in his 1952 novel *Invisible Man*, when he wrote, "I am invisible . . . simply because people refuse to see me. Like the bodiless heads you see sometimes in circus sideshows, it is as though I have been surrounded by mirrors of hard, distorting glass. When they approach me they see only my surroundings, themselves, or figments of their imagination—indeed, everything and anything except me."[22] In such a world, "perverse forms of anonymity" can be said to structure the social relations between blacks and whites, so that, as the Fanonian scholar Lewis Gordon has described it, "Things become what they are based on what they are not, and they become what they are not based on what they are."[23] For blacks, what such situations often translate into is farce, relations in which the following scenarios are likely to predominate: "The black is invisible because of how the black is 'seen.' The black is not heard because of how the black is 'heard.' The black is not felt because of how the black 'feels.'"[24] Such scenarios emerge for the simple reason that in white-dominated cultures whites insist on translating black experience in ways that prove palatable and undisruptive to *white* modes of seeing, hearing, and feeling. Hence "for the black, there is the perversity of '*seen* invisibility' a form of '*absent* presence'" in which the specificity of black existence is wished away in favor of narrating an existence that serves the one who is doing the seeing—in this case, the white.[25]

But what is it that white lesbians and gays presumably want to *see*, *hear*, and *feel* in Griffith's story that would require the festival promoters, and the filmmakers—who after all rely on the concept of the closet in narrating Griffith's story—to leave out crucial information about Griffith's racial and cultural identity? In other words, just how does Griffith's paradoxical racial condition of "*seen* invisibility" facilitate this very wanting on the part of contemporary white lesbians and gay men? Before I attempt to answer this question, I'd like to note that in order for such a narrative to have the explanatory power the blurb's author expects, he or she must have an inordinate amount of faith in the targeted reader's ability to draw a clear-eyed connection between the key signifiers in the passage—namely, "closeted homosexual," "*maricón*," and "faggot." Most importantly, such a reader

ultimately has to believe these signifiers to be interchangeable at the level of signification for them to experience the intended effect—that is, identification.
Moreover, that "effect" should ideally carry over from the reading of the blurb to
seeing the film for which the synopsis is merely a preview. Interestingly, whereas
the specifics of the two filmmakers' identities (racial and sexual) are suppressed in
the film's translation from "real" to "reel"—that is, Klores and Berger never appear
on screen, nor are their voices heard in the film—the sexual identities of the festival's organizers, although masked in their racial and gendered specificity, are
nonetheless accessible in other ways. That is, these individuals' mere involvement
with a lesbian and gay film festival has the effect of evoking a specific *identitarian*
affiliation, one that highlights these men's and women's real or merely affective
identification as/with gay men and lesbians, just as it does their target audience.
In so far as *Ring of Fire* purports to tell the "true story" of a Caribbean-born black
male champion boxer who was rumored to have been homosexual—but who had
not then, nor since, publicly "come out" as such—its inclusion in a contemporary lesbian and gay film festival might be said, following Gamson, to privilege a
sexual identification over a racial or cultural one. The reason for this is that both
Klores and Berger, as well as the festival organizers, in relying on the universalizing metaphor of the closet to tell and *sell* Griffith's story, flatten out that story and
its subject so as to appeal to the broadest possible audience—that is, to lesbians
and gay male filmgoers for whom a racial or a cultural identification beyond the
sexual (i.e., the queer) is superfluous. The result is the privileging of *white* lesbians
and gay men over lesbians and gay men of color, whose multi-identity concerns
are disregarded.

Because such an approach "occludes the intersecting saliency of race, gender,
sexuality, and class in forming social practices," something I am arguing a queer
of color critique works assiduously to "debunk," the film's promotional materials cannot challenge the dominant belief that these categories are "apparently
insulated from one another" and thus "disconnected."[26] In his essay, "Beyond the
Closet as Raceless Paradigm," Marlon Ross suggests an answer to the earlier question I posed as to what white lesbians and gay men want to see, hear, and feel in
Griffith's story when he writes,

> The "sphere of the body" defined by race becomes over time (moments, days,
> weeks, decades, centuries?) the model for other "new identities of bodies" defined
> by something other than race: gender, sexuality, class, criminality, etc. The abstrac-
> tion of "the body" into a further abstraction of its "sphere" currently a customary
> and necessary way of talking about these problems in academe—has the effect of
> covering over how a *single person's body* could, from the outset . . . be seen as carry-
> ing both visible and invisible markers of more than one identity discourse already
> interfused and *embodied* in that single person.[27]

If one were to replace "story" with "body" in the above passage, then it might
become clearer as to how Griffith's narrative, by analogy to the shared narrative of lesbian and gay oppression that Joshua Gamson outlines, could appeal to
mainstream—that is, white lesbians and gay male filmgoers—via the film's central

reliance on the closet metaphor. Quite simply, "race, sex, sexuality, and criminality become visible differently because different discourses are at play, even when a single body is the anatomical object."[28] And nowhere is this dynamic more on display than when black bodies are present.

UNEARTHING THE "TRUTH" ABOUT GRIFFITH'S (BLACK MALE) SEXUALITY

Of course, one thing undermining the festival organizers' effort to narrate Griffith's identity as a closeted gay man, and nothing more—not black, not Caribbean—is that Griffith himself never says with any conclusiveness that he *is* a gay man, nor do the filmmakers include any male interview subjects who were sexually or romantically involved with the athlete, neither during his heyday as a champion boxer nor as an elderly man, to corroborate this narrative. The only person who appears in the film with whom Griffith was reputed to have been sexually involved is Sadie Griffith, a Caribbean woman the boxer hastily married in the early 1970s and reportedly separated from not long after. Mrs. Griffith never utters a word about her husband's rumored homosexuality, nor is she asked. As such, she never so much as hints at what the reason might have been for why the marriage came to such an abrupt end. Was the marriage ever properly dissolved, or did the two just go their separate ways? Oddly, Sadie Griffith still carries the boxer's surname, suggesting that she and Griffith are still legally wed. But are they? Maddeningly, the documentary is sketchy in fleshing out these intimate details, just as it is equally sketchy on providing satisfying clarity around its subject's sexuality more generally.

Klores and Berger leave a number of questions unaddressed in *Ring of Fire* that eventually roused my suspicions. While answering these questions may have contributed to a more complex portrait of their subject, doing so might also have complicated the neat binary structure on which the filmic narrative depends for coherence. For instance, what did Griffith's brother, who is interviewed several times in the film, think about his older brother's rumored sexuality, or for that matter, what did his large extended family think of these rumors? Griffith's ever-present mother had already died years before the film's production in 1997, and so surely Griffith couldn't have been worried about causing her embarrassment over the scandal his possible "outing" as a homosexual would cause. The impediment the filmmakers might have come up against was simply that Griffith may not have organized his sexuality according to the model of secrecy and revelation that the concept of the closet suggests, and that *Ring of Fire* steadfastly clings to. After all, much of African American social history "indicates that intragender love has been constructed along axes not simply reducible to or easily characterized or explained by the closet paradigm and its attendant narrative of sexual evolution."[29] As such, for black men and women who engage in same-gender intimacy, whether exclusively or only on occasion, "the emphasis is not on a binary of secrecy versus revelation but instead on a continuum of knowing that persists at various levels according to the kin and friendship relations within the community."[30] As if providing a ready answer to just how Griffith might have managed to negotiate the "truth" of his sexuality with his close friends and family members, a question the filmmakers do not begin to explore (because, perhaps, it is a question that does not ultimately interest them), Ross writes,

> [I]t is impossible *not* to know something so obvious among those who know you well enough. In such a context, to announce one's attraction by "coming out" would not necessarily indicate a progress in sexual identity, and it would not necessarily change one's identity from closeted to liberated as conceptualized in the dominant closet narrative. When the question of telling loved ones what they already know does become an issue, it can be judged superfluous or perhaps even a distracting act, one subsidiary to the more important identifications of family, community, and race within which one's sexual attractions are already interwoven and understood.[31]

Ross's point is certainly timely, and intervenes quite persuasively in critical approaches that too earnestly promote a single, overarching narrative for interpreting the way diverse subjects live out their same-gender attractions. If not to shield his close family members from the "truth" of his (homo)sexuality, what then was Griffith worried about, supposing he *was* worried at all? Could the conflict have been more internal? That is, might it have been possible that Griffith, who was Caribbean-born, could not reconcile himself to the fact that he was attracted to men, supposing he was? Why is it that Griffith is so reluctant all these years later to claim his sexuality, whatever it is? What are the cultural forces that conspire to encourage him, within the framing of the documentary itself, that he should "keep his secret," so to speak? Are they, by chance, similar to the forces that may have compelled the Caribbean-born writer of the Harlem Renaissance, Claude McKay, long rumored to have been homosexual, never to publicly claim that identity for himself or to portray it openly in his work?[32]

In an article investigating homophobia in black popular culture and Caribbean literature, Timothy Chin writes of McKay, "despite the vitality and passion with which [his] protagonists are typically imbued, the forms of masculinity that the narratives inscribe do not ultimately depart from traditional notions of maleness and masculine behavior. Indeed, McKay's folk heroes reflect and even reinforce dominant sexual ideologies by asserting a masculinity that is predicated on both sexism and homophobia."[33] Moreover, I would say, these ideologies are anchored in the historical narrative of colonialism through which the West Indian gendered subject is produced. In other words, given Griffith's reticence to cooperate fully either with Klores and Berger or with festival organizers' skillful efforts at renarrativization, the documentary's spectators must "simultaneously confron[t] the patriarchal, heterosexist, and Eurocentric ideologies that constitute the particular legacy of the Caribbean colonial experience," one that perhaps, on some level, I would hazard to guess, also reflects the former champion's "*unstable* status as both a colonial subject and a homosexual."[34] In other words, might McKay's experiences as a transplanted colonial subject serve as a useful framework for trying to understand the experiences that may have drove Griffith to remain largely silent about his own sexuality, even within the context of a documentary film project seemingly designed, or at least marketed as such, to unearth "speech" about that very sexuality?

While past and present Caribbean culture has notoriously been resistant to the affirmation of same-gender identities and desires, insights into how Caribbean male and female subjects navigate that resistance are not difficult to locate. In their review essay on Caribbean sexualities, Jenny Sharpe and Samantha Pinto identify a variety of scholarly work that addresses this topic in some detail. For example, the authors cite Suzanne LaFont's 2001 essay, "Very Straight Sex: The Development of Sexual Mores in Jamaica," as a useful article that looks into colonial history to understand how sexual attitudes of the era were shaped "out of both African and British codes of sexual conduct." Because of the hybrid nature of this influence, early Jamaican notions of sexuality were likewise divided: "Th[is] creole sexual ideology approved of sexual activity as a natural part of human pleasure," however, any expression of "sexuality had to be expressed within the confines of respectability." According to the reviewers, this perspective helps to explain Jamaican culture's "tacit acceptance of a woman prostituting herself to support her children so long as she maintains a public face of respectability, while two men seen holding hands in the street can be stoned to death."[35] Sharpe and Pinto also list other works that provide useful information. Two edited volumes the reviewers cite focus specific, and much needed, attention on same-sex desire. These include Rhoda Reddock's *Interrogating Caribbean Masculinities*[36] and Linden Lewis's *The Culture of Gender and Sexuality in the Caribbean*.[37] Moreover, black gay male cultural producers like the British auteurs Isaac Julien and Rikki-Beadle-Blair have both produced film and stage work that looks closely at the virulent homophobia that has characterized much of West Indian culture in recent decades.[38] Unfortunately, the makers of *Ring of Fire* do not mention any of this scholarship, nor do they include any of these public intellectuals as commentators on Griffith's story, although they do include other commentators—such as critics Neal Gabler and Pete Hamill, gay historian Charles Kaiser, and sports writer Jimmy Breslin, as well as other assorted journalists (the novelist Norman Mailer even contributes a voice-over commentary adding to the sensationalism of the final tragic bout with Paret). But the filmmakers neglect to include a single commentator who might have addressed the role that Griffith's Caribbean birthplace and upbringing may have had on the development of his racial, gender, and sexual identities. Could Klores and Berger not have located any qualified intellectuals who might have helped to situate Griffith's compelling life within the overarching but also, given Griffith's Caribbean-born status, nuanced context of antiblack racism in postwar American society? In other words, could the filmmakers have done better than simply placing the athlete's story within the hermetically sealed boxing world, on the one hand, and, given the tightly circumscribed subject matter of the film festival itself, in the largely "white" gay world, on the other?

Contemporary social science researchers of African American sexualities have continually stressed that any strategy for elucidating the complex sexualities of *black* people, as distinct from the sexualities of whites, must resist proceeding as if racial or cultural background is irrelevant or else the same across different racial and ethnic groups.[39] Rather, as social scientist Linwood Lewis and his collaborator Robert Kertzner write in their article, "Toward Improved Interpretation and Theory Building of African American Male Sexualities," such strategies must actively seek to dispel "the belief in an essential African American (hetero)sexuality." Beliefs of this sort often "posi[t] a shared, African psychosocial essence for all persons of African descent." However, "not all African Americans have the same experiences or respond to these experiences in the same way."[40] More significantly, these revised interpretive frameworks "must account in some way for the effect on African American sexuality of living in a racialized society, a society that emphasizes race as a major organizer of life experiences and places increased significance on practices and discourses that refer to race."[41] The authors go on to state that this is especially the case for male subjects of African descent, whose sense of their own fragile gender and sexual identities must often be negotiated and reconstructed within a climate saturated with both the legacy of past as well as ongoing cultural narratives about black male sexuality as abnormal and bestial as compared to their white counterparts. With this in mind, Lewis and Kertzner conclude, "If we accept that African American men's meanings, beliefs, and emotions are in part affected by their racial and cultural background and experiences related to their background, then it is vital to allow their voices to guide interpretation of their actions."[42]

IS SIMULATED "GAY SEX" "GAY"? IS IT EVEN "SEX"? THE RISK OF TRANSLATION

At the start of this essay, I suggested that Griffith's story, especially its imaginative retelling in *Ring of Fire*, shared certain conceptual linkages with the Abu Ghraib prison abuse scandal. I would now like to make that connection more apparent. Ultimately, what Dan Klores and Ron Berger's documentary asks its viewers to consider is this: When one man calls another man a "faggot," whether in Spanish, English, or some other language that has an equivalent expression, or when one man uses another man's body against his consent in a way that invokes the widely held notion of "faggotry"—that is, homosexuality—is he commenting primarily on what this man does in bed and with whom he does it, is it commenting on this man's status as a man, or is it both? In other words, just as with the elaborately staged photographs of the abuse American soldiers inflicted upon Iraqi male prisoners of war, is this a question of gender or is it a question of sexuality? Or is it neither, and how do we tell?

After all, the two terms, gender and sexuality, name related but not identical phenomena. The way the two are related has to do with the role each term plays in conceptualizing human identity and behavior where "sex" is concerned. The term "sex" is itself part of the confusion since it has a double meaning—one of which denotes male/female difference, known as dimorphism, and the other, which denotes erotic desire/practice. As researchers Don Kulick and Deborah Cameron tell us, "Those who coined and then popularized the terms gender and sexuality were deliberately trying to get away from narrowly biological/reproductive definitions, and also to make a clear distinction between the two senses of sex. But this strategy has still not met with uniform acceptance, and the two 'new' terms, gender and sexuality, have complex histories in recent English usage."[43] While I do not have the space here to go into these complex histories, I will say that they involve historically and culturally determined notions of what the "proper" behavior is for anatomical males and females at any one time and place, as well as the "proper" forms of sexual expression these men and women can engage in both in terms of normative and nonnormative practices.

Uncritical acceptance of these understandings has come at the expense of our being able to identify and name sexuality as an important factor in a broad range of social relations, whether forced or consensual, in which gender may not always be the most privileged, or even the most salient, category in play. For instance, Marlon Ross has elsewhere reminded us that in antipornography feminist arguments in which sex is conceptualized as men's "desire for domination and power" over women, and nothing else, "it tends to spotlight the perversity of gender oppression while casting the role of race into the shadows."[44] Rather than vilifying antipornography feminists, who are hardly alone in holding such views, the point that Ross is trying to make is that this conceptualization obscures the ways in which societies with racial hierarchies in addition to gender hierarchies routinely position "men" and "women" from different racial and ethnic groups unequally in relation to these structuring gender and sexual norms so that only some men are thought to be "real men" and only some women are thought to be "real women," while other "men" and "women" are viewed as inferior, along with their sexual practices. It becomes especially difficult, then, to recognize that in such societies the oppression of "women of color," as a specific class of "women," not only involves a matter of a racially unmarked class of men exerting their dominance and control over a racially unmarked class of women but also entails, especially for black women, forms of "racial and class domination through sexualized violence from the period of slavery forward."[45] Historically, this has included white men's practice of raping black women as a calculated strategy of consolidating their gender and racial authority over both black women and black men. And as feminist analysis has illustrated time and again, rape has a complicated relationship to sex. Strictly speaking, the two are neither equivalent nor interchangeable.

Building on this theory, other scholars have persuasively argued that "we cannot ignore the question of how men in subordinate social positions in US culture, particularly African American men, become self-implicated in acts of domination through sexual violence," whether as perpetrators of that violence or as its victims.[46] After all, the subordination of black men and black women by white men within patriarchal, white supremacist regimes "collides with the cultural logic of rape."[47] This collision is one of a conceptual nature, and it emerges as soon as we realize that "graphic racial violence against black men," which is often imaged as castration or emasculation—or male-on-male rape—is sometimes equated "with an abstraction of men's sexual violence against women." Ross describes the conflation in this way:

> Paradoxically, this process of analogy and abstraction tends to keep the two acts of violence—sexual and racial—bifurcated even as they are united symbolically in the figure of race rape. It tends to construct violence against women as deriving ultimately and/or solely from sexual oppression and violence against black men as deriving necessarily from racial oppression. Sexual violence against black

men—and the sexual violence they perpetrate against others—is thus reduced to a matter of racial jousting between men of European and African descent. Racial violence against African American women then becomes exceptional, rather than symptomatic and explanatory of racial violence itself.[48]

In other words, violence that white men commit against black men is not usually conceptualized as sexual violence but only as racial violence, while the violence white men may commit against black women is always conceptualized as both sexual violence and racial violence. But for Ross, "the awful social and psychic aggression of the assault consists in the interrelatedness of exploiting sexual violation to reinforce racial subordination and simultaneously exploiting racial violence to reinforce sexual subordination." In other words, "the racial exploitation of men or women always presupposes the license—and thus the right—to exploit them sexually."[49] So the two cannot ever be disentangled; doing so, Kulick and Cameron would argue, unproductively preserves an understanding of sexuality that keeps it linked to its more narrow sexual orientation meaning so that other meanings—those beyond the biological/reproductive definitions—become difficult to theorize and to grasp.

This returns us more directly to the Abu Ghraib scandal and to the following snide comment, one authored by a black female Christian fundamentalist, whose homophobia allows her to think nothing of lumping homosexuality in with prostitution, incest, adultery, and pedophilia: "It struck me strangely that many people who were so disturbed about the abuse that happened in a prison in Iraq do some of the same perverted things in their own homes and think it's perfectly all right."[50]

To this writer, there is apparently no difference between consensual male-male sex and the brutal US torture of male prisoners by, among other heinous practices, forcing these men to simulate oral and anal sex while being bound, gagged, and having loaded AK47s pointed at their heads. This is in part because the author finds both scenarios to be repulsive to her on moral and religious grounds, and therefore any distinction between the two is unnecessary to note. While this example may be somewhat crude, given that the antihomosexual sentiment behind it prevents this writer from acknowledging any critical differences separating the two, it is nonetheless important to remember that even among progay commentators such conflations have been commonplace. One example is the following remark by gay journalist Patrick Moore. After viewing photographs of the Arab prisoners tortured at Abu Ghraib, Moore writes,

The world was stunned by these images not only because of their brutality but also because of their sexual nature. Homophobia in the American military is nothing new, but the abuse of homosexual sex as a military tactic achieves a new level of perverse ingenuity. Confronted with the use of their sexuality as the ultimate tool of degradation, gay men now have another reason to fight against the reelection of George Bush. We should be at the forefront of outraged protests against these war crimes as we will ultimately pay the price for our sexuality being further stigmatized.[51]

In this passage, Moore conflates same-sex consensual sex acts with the simulation of those acts within the context of brutal torture, and he does so in a way that makes it clear that he identifies personally with those simulated acts, as if those acts were identical to the acts he himself may engage in within the privacy of his own home with a male partner. As Moore puts it, "we," by which I imagine he means gay men, "will ultimately pay the price for our sexuality being further stigmatized."

But what is the difference, I wonder, between Moore's willful collapsing of the distinction between gay men and Iraqi prisoners and that of Ruth White, the Christian fundamentalist I quoted earlier? For starters, in White's case she collapses the two in order to condemn them both, while in Moore's he does so in order to defend one by condemning the other—that is, he defends gay male identities and desires by condemning the US military's homophobic use of those identities and desires for the sake of torture and dubious national interest. For Moore, collapsing the two proves enabling, as it mobilizes his critique against US imperialism: "We," he says, again meaning gay men, "should be at the forefront of outraged protests against these war crimes." By taking this stance, however, Moore still does not manage to escape drawing a conceptual link between consensual gay male sex practices and the practice of torture. His logic elides the specifically violent and ideological nature of those simulations, thereby suggesting that the two identities and acts—gay men and Iraqi prisoners, same-sex sex acts and simulations of same-sex sex acts—are the same and therefore interchangeable.

But how are they the same? To insist upon this sameness uncritically, even if that insistence enables critical speech and provokes outrage is not only to misinterpret the historical practice of torture itself, and the reasons marshaled for it, but it is also to place at the center of one's analysis a single defining feature of that brutal practice in a way that reveals itself to be primarily self-interested and only secondarily interested in broader matters of human rights and social justice. More important, doing so by raging at what one takes to be a recognizable, and hence familiar, form of homophobia fundamentally masks all the other features that may be just as relevant for the sake of privileging merely one. But as Jasbir Puar writes in a 2004 article exploring the Abu Ghraib controversy, "The reaction of rage misses the point: this violence is neither an exception to nor a simple extension of the violence of an imperialist occupation. Rather, the focus on purported homosexual acts obscures other forms of gendered violence and serves a broader racist and sexist, as well as homophobic, agenda."[52] Puar makes the salient point that Moore, as well as other white gay male commentators like him who have latched onto the Abu Ghraib prisoner abuse scandal because of the "'deep sense of shame as a gay man'" the images invoke within him (the quote is Moore's), "in particular sets up the (white) gay male subject as the paradigmatic victim of assaulting images."[53] Puar goes on to ask,

> Is it really prudent to foreclose the chance that there might be a gay man or lesbian among the perpetrators of the torture at Abu Ghraib? To foreground homophobia over other vectors of shame is to miss that these photos are not merely representative

of the homophobia of the military; they are also racist, misogynist, and imperialist. To favor the gay male spectator—here presumably white—is to negate the inter-sectional audience implicated as viewers of these images and, oddly, to privilege as victim the coherently formed white gay male sexuality in the West over "closeted" and acts-qualified bodies, not to mention the bodies of tortured Iraqi prisoners themselves.[54]

As with Ross's earlier point about the inadequacy of the closet paradigm, Puar's point is well taken. Notwithstanding the fact that lesbians and gay male Ameri-can soldiers might have also been among the perpetrators of the sexual abuse of Iraqi prisoners, what if some Iraqi prisoners of war at Abu Ghraib were them-selves homosexual? If so, it should be quite apparent to anyone paying even the slightest bit of attention that US military forces would not have targeted these men because of this fact; rather, they would have targeted these foreign nation-als first and foremost because they were Iraqi citizens, and therefore viewed, whether they were or not, as potential threats to our country's security. And while it may be useful at times to acknowledge that being a homosexual and being a foreign national from the Middle East are sometimes deployed by our fellow citizens in ways that seem to flaunt all human logic, as the previous examples illustrate, we must nonetheless struggle to always keep in mind that such deployments are rarely, if ever, in fact grounded in truth. Far from it. This is because, as Puar puts it, "Calling the simulated and actual sex scenes [at Abu Ghraib] replicative of 'gay sex' is an easy way for all-mass media, Ori-entalist anthropologists, the military establishment, LGBT groups and orga-nizations—to sidestep an acknowledgment of both 'perverse' proclivities in heterosexual sex and of the gender normativity immanent in some kinds of gay sex" as well.[55] In other words, "straight" sex sometimes too gets implicated in contemporary media scandals—as in the various military rape controversies that marked the 1980s and '90s more generally—but we seldom see heterosex-uals becoming enraged because "their sexuality" is being defiled by these acts. Why, then, should contemporary white gay men feel so attacked?

   This returns me to *Ring of Fire*, and to the filmmakers' decision to have Emile Griffith repeat the following statement at least twice in the documentary: "He [Paret] called me a *maricón*, and I wasn't nobody's faggot." I find myself won-dering now, is it possible that something more was at stake between the two foreign-born black men (one Latin American, the other West Indian) than simply Paret's trying to say, rather simplistically, that Griffith was a homosexual—in other words, that he was a man who willingly had sex with other men—or was he trying to say something much different? In other words, to Paret, was the fact that he called Griffith a "*maricón*" supposed to be taken by Griffith as a comment about the latter's gender, or was it to be taken as a comment about his sexuality? Both or neither? After all, is it a matter of public record that the US military was attempting to say that male Iraqi prisoners of war were homosexuals by the specific forms of sexual torture they devised to humiliate and "break" these men, or were they simply trying to let these men, these so-called enemies of the state, know who wielded the power? Always alert to the challenges of translation,

Marlon Ross reminds us that "we are dealing here with the phantom of language, with the way that language seems to make the felt swelter of realities seem both shadowy and fixed." What this means in terms of the Abu Ghraib scandal is that "in addition to the violating deficiencies of linguistic representation, we are also dealing . . . with the embeddedness of ideological formations in which race [or differences between men and nations] can be made manifest only through sexualized characteristics and behaviors."[56] In his essay, "Syncretic Religion and Dissident Sexualities," Roberto Strongman touches on this point when he argues that there is no necessary correspondence between US conceptualizations of same-sex identities and desires and those in Latin American contexts. As Strongman puts it, "The Latin American homosexual categories that find a niche" in such cultures through the use of terms like "maricónes, makomè, bichas, and ekedes . . . do not fit into the US-fabricated gay and lesbian categories. These forms of homosexuality are different from each other and from those forms of homosexuality found in the United States because they have developed within specific regional contexts."[57] Indeed, one of the greatest distinctions between the two, for Strongman, is that whereas US-derived understandings of same-sex identity and desire rely on a binary notion of secrecy/revelation, in which the image of the closet can be said to predominate, for many Latin Americans "the performance of desire is a much more defining moment than the declaration; the act is more important than the speech act."[58] Since it is not known whether Paret actually saw Griffith engaged in same-sex sexuality with another man—that is, saw him performing such desire—it is difficult to know if what he meant by calling Griffith a "*maricón*" was what other people have taken him to mean, or if he meant something else entirely. Might Paret just have been "trashing talking," that is, telling Griffith that he was going to kick Griffith's ass because he, Paret, was the better fighter—in other words, that he was more masculine? As this essay has been gesturing toward all along, it becomes imperative that we not conflate questions analytically related to negotiations of gender with those having to do with sexual identity and practice since doing so unnecessarily entangles human categories in ways that promote continual misreading rather than clarity. Nowhere is such vigilance more crucial than in sincere efforts at understanding what Fanon called the "lived experience" of people of color in a white-dominated society.[59]

This last point might be said to be corroborated in an essay black American writer James Baldwin wrote near the end of his life, in 1985, in which he weighed in on the complex matter of culture, gender, sexuality, language, and historicity, with the following insight: "The condition that is now called gay was then called queer. The operative word was faggot and, later, pussy, but those epithets really had nothing to do with the question of sexual preference: You were being told simply that you had no balls."[60] It seems to me that Baldwin's words might serve as a kind of warning to contemporary white lesbians and gay men who tend to overidentify with the various damning labels, whether pejorative or otherwise, the dominant culture has devised in order to keep the various hierarchies undisturbed and firmly in place and their own dominance unchallenged and secure. After all, if it is true that Emile Griffith is a man who prefers male sex partners to those who are female—and I for one do not know if he is or not—the fact that he angrily exclaims "I ain't no faggot" in the film is a clear indication that he does not identify with terms meant to degrade his character. And this is the case whether, for Paret, the term "*maricón*" meant that Griffith was a poor boxer or that he had disgusting sex with men. Either term, once translated into its pejorative meaning on the part of the person who utters it—in this case, Benny "Kid" Paret—"may seem to define you for others," as Baldwin well knew, and said as much, "but it does not have the power to define you to yourself."[61] This is a lesson we should all be so lucky to learn. It is certainly a lesson that Emile Griffith took to heart, but unfortunately no one seemed to be listening to him, even though he was the one speaking.[62]

NOTES

1. Hiram Perez, "You Can Have My Brown Body and Eat It, Too!," *Social Text* 84–85 (2005): 178.
2. Jasbir K. Puar, "Queer Times, Queer Assemblages," *Social Text* 84–85 (2005): 125.
3. I would like to express my gratitude to John Thurston and Angelo Robinson who commented on earlier versions of this essay, as well as Joshua Gamson, who clarified vital information in a timely manner. In addition, I would like to thank the volume's editors for their generous assistance in preparing this essay for publication.
4. Gary Smith, "The Shadow Boxer," *Sports Illustrated*, April 18, 2005, 58.
5. According to Marlon Ross, "[I]n what academics call 'queer theory,' the closet has become ground zero in the project of articulating an 'epistemology' of sexuality. Beyond political strategy and polemical tactics, the closet has become a philosophical concept grounding both lesbian-gay history and queer theory by joining them at the hips as a legitimate academic discipline. Significantly, historians and theorists of queerness stake their claims to academic centrality largely through the concept of the closet, as they argue with great rigor and sophistication that the binary between closeted and uncloseted sexual desire is a primary determinant of modernity and modernism." See Ross's essay, "Beyond the Closet as Raceless Paradigm," in *Black Queer Studies: A Critical Anthology* (Durham, NC: Duke University Press, 2005), 161.
6. Ross, "Beyond the Closet," 162.
7. Ibid.
8. I use the term "Afro-Caribbean" in the way that Linwood Lewis and Robert Kertzner do in their essay, "Toward Improved Interpretation and Theory Building of African American Male Sexualities," *Journal of Sex Research* (2003): 383–95. Lewis and Kertzner feel it is important to distinguish between diverse ethnic groups of African descent to avoid "incorrect assumptions of homogeneity in behavior" by scholars who analyze the experiences of ethnic minority populations. The authors use the term "African Americans" to denote those blacks who were "involuntary immigrants" to the United States through enforced servitude and the term "Afro-Caribbean" to denote those blacks who were "involuntary immigrants to their own country but who have immigrated to the U.S. voluntarily" (384).
9. Roderick Ferguson, *Aberrations in Black: Toward a Queer of Color Critique* (Minneapolis: University of Minnesota Press, 2004), 149n1.
10. Ibid., 3–4.
11. Ibid., 4. Also see Kara Keeling on the inside/outside status of black lesbian and gay subjects. In an essay on black lesbian cinema, Keeling writes that lesbian and gay cultural production and scholarship "demonstrate that the category 'black lesbian and gay' is

wholly inside the construction of both 'blackness' and 'lesbian and gay.' But, it also is part of what needs to be expunged vigilantly and repeatedly from 'black' and from 'gay' and 'lesbian' in order to render each category artificially coherent and discrete. Yet, any separation of 'black lesbian and gay' into two categories ('black' and 'lesbian and/or gay') presumed to be autonomous can be effected only violently." From Keeling's "'Joining the Lesbians': Cinematic Regimes of Black Lesbian Visibility," in *Black Queer Studies: A Critical Anthology* (Durham, NC: Duke University Press, 2005), 216–17.

12. Scott Bravmann, *Queer Fictions of the Past: History, Culture, and Difference* (Cambridge, UK: Cambridge University Press, 1997), 98.

13. Julio Ortega, "Transatlantic Translations," *Publications of the Modern Language Association of America* 118, no.1 (2003): 26.

14. Joshua Gamson, "The Organizational Shaping of Collective Identity: The Case of Lesbian and Gay Film Festivals in New York," *Sociological Forum* 11, no. 2 (1996): 238 (original emphasis).

15. Ibid., 246.

16. Ibid., 255–56.

17. Bravmann, *Queer Fictions,* 99–100. The compound neologism "queer heterosociality" represents Bravmann's playful effort to capture the wide diversity that makes up many lesbian and gay male communities, including differences in class, race, ethnicity, and even sexual practices, among others. The prefix "hetero," in this instance, which means "difference," is not reducible to the sexual. For a closer look at how white gay communities have participated in "othering" black gay men in particular, see Charles Nero's "Why Are the Gay Ghettoes White?" *Black Queer Studies* (Durham, NC: Duke University Press, 2005): 228–45.

18. This phrase belongs to Marlon Ross, who analyzes how people of color often function as stable, analogous bodies in some (white) queer theoretical writings designed to make visible homosexual oppression but which does not theorize whiteness as itself a racial formation. See "Beyond the Closet," 165.

19. Jeffrey Weeks, preface to Guy Hocquenghem, *Homosexual Desire*, trans. Danielle Dangoor (London: Allison & Busby, 1993), 22.

20. Ross, "Beyond the Closet," 162.

21. See Frantz Fanon's *Black Skin, White Masks*, trans. Charles Lam Markmann (New York: Grove, 1967), especially chapter 5, "The Fact of Blackness." Here Fanon writes, "I was responsible at the same time for my body, for my race, for my ancestors. I subjected myself to an objective examination, I discovered my blackness, my ethnic characteristics; and I was battered down by tom-toms, cannibalism, intellectual deficiency, fetishism, racial defects, slave-ships, and above all else, above all: 'Sho' good eatin'" (112).

22. Ralph Ellison, *Invisible Man* (New York: Vintage Books, 1990 [1952]), 3.

23. Lewis R. Gordon, *Her Majesty's Other Children: Sketches of Racism From a Neocolonial Age* (New York: Rowman & Littlefield, 1997), 37.

24. Ibid.

25. Ibid.; emphasis added.

26. Ferguson, *Aberrations in Black,* 4. The volume is ultimately focused on advancing what its author calls a "postnationalist" critique within American studies, one that would take seriously the political insights of women of color and queers of color without encouraging "the idealization" of either of these subjects or their contributing knowledge. Turning to Louis Althusser's engagement with Marxist thought, Ferguson, like Althusser, rejects categories of the abstract in favor of postulating concrete, lived experiences in theoretical formulations. "Althusser argues that as Marx turned to 'real man,' Marx turned to society. The category of 'real man' then became the impetus for historical materialism's

investigation of social formations. Althusser goes on to argue that substituting abstract man with real man results in the eventual dismissal of the category 'man' entirely." Such a critical move would usefully pave the way for valuing the insights of now marginalized knowledge producers like women of color and queer people of color without necessarily privileging "identity," per se. Ferguson writes, "Making queer of color and the woman of color [sic] subjects the basis of critical inquiry means that we must imbue them with gestural rather than emulative functions. As subjects of knowledge, they point away from themselves and to the racialized, gendered, classed, and eroticized heterogeneity of the social, summoning critical practices appropriate for that heterogeneity" (143).

27. Ross, "Beyond the Closet," 166; original emphasis.

28. Ibid., 167.

29. Ibid., 180.

30. Ibid.

31. Ibid.

32. As Ross's commentary points out, it is entirely possible that Griffith himself did not experience any type of "existential" angst over his sexuality in the way we in the sexually repressed West have come to expect. For Griffith, perhaps those individuals who "needed to know" about his sexuality—his mother, his brother, etc.—presumably already knew, and so no one else simply mattered to him. What this insight suggests, of course, is that it is the filmmakers, its distributors, as well as its various audiences, who exhibit this anxiety about pinning down sexual "truths" about other people. As such, perhaps we are the ones driven to construct elaborate narratives around someone like Griffith, all of which are designed to expose a subjective anxiety that, in Griffith's case, is in fact never really there at all; rather, it has been imposed from without, to satisfy a need that has nothing to do with Griffith himself. Taking up this critical stance allows me to argue that Griffith's behavior in the documentary itself, *as constructed and framed by the filmmakers,* interpellates the viewer in such a way as to compel our suspicion that Griffith is not being truthful about his sexuality—and this is the case whether Griffith is *actually* being truthful or not. I want to thank the editors for suggesting this reading to me.

33. Timothy S. Chin, "'Bullers' and 'Battymen': Contesting Homophobia in Black Popular Culture and Contemporary Caribbean Literature." *Callaloo* 20, no.1 (1997): 129–30.

34. Ibid., 138; emphasis added.

35. Jenny Sharpe and Samantha Pinto, "The Sweetest Taboo: Studies of Caribbean Sexualities; a Review Essay," *Signs: Journal of Woman in Culture and Society* 32, no.1 (2006): 247.

36. Rhoda Reddock, *Interrogating Caribbean Masculinities* (University of West Indies Press, 2004).

37. Linden Lewis, *The Culture of Gender and Sexuality in the Caribbean* (University Press of Florida, 2003).

38. See Isaac Julian's documentary *The Darker Side of Black* (1994) and Rikki Beadle Blair's stage play *Bashment* (2005). Both works explore dancehall reggae music and its reputation for homophobic lyrics, which are believed by many to fuel antigay violence in Britain and the Caribbean.

39. See Patricia Hill Collins, *Black Sexual Politics: African Americans, Gender, and the New Racism* (New York: Routledge, 2004); Ann du Cille "'Othered' Matters: Reconceptualizing Dominance and Difference in the History of Sexuality in America," *Journal of the History of Sexuality* 1, no. 1 (1990): 102–3; and Jackie Goldsby's "What It Means to be Colored Me," *Out/Look* (1990): 8–17.

40. Linwood Lewis and Robert Kertzner, "Toward Improved Interpretation and Theory Building of African American Male Sexualities," *Journal of Sex Research* (2003): 385.

41. Ibid., 388.
42. Ibid., 389.
43. Deborah Cameron and Don Kulick, *Language and Sexuality* (Cambridge, UK: Cambridge University Press, 2003), 2.
44. Ross, Marlon, "Race, Rape, Castration: Feminist Theories of Sexual Violence and Masculine Strategies of Black Protest," *Masculinity Studies & Feminist Theory: New Directions,* ed. Judith Kegan Gardiner (New York: Columbia University Press, 2002), 306.
45. Ibid.
46. See Michael Awkward's *Negotiating Difference: Race, Gender, and the Politics of Positionality* (Chicago: University of Chicago Press, 1995) as well as Robyn Wiegman's *American Anatomies: Theorizing Race and Gender* (Durham: Duke University Press, 1995).
47. Ross, "Race, Rape, Castration," 306.
48. Ibid., 306–7.
49. Ibid., 317–18.
50. Steve A. White and Ruth B. White, *Life Through the Eyes of an Interracial Couple: And Their Dreams of a Colorblind America* (Bloomington: Authorhouse, 2004), 586. While the couple often alternates in their narration, this particular homophobic passage is narrated by Ruth White alone.
51. Patrick Moore, "Weapons of Mass Homophobia," *Advocate*, June 8, 2004, 24; emphasis added.
52. Jasbir K. Puar, "Abu Ghraib: Arguing Against Exceptionalism." *Feminist Studies* 30, no. 2 (2004): 523; emphasis added.
53. In addition to Moore, Puar also cites two other gay male commentators who adopt a similar stance with respect to the scandal, including the Arab-American gay journalist Mubarak Dahir and Aaron Belkin.
54. Puar, "Abu Ghraib," 529.
55. Ibid., 530.
56. Ross, "Race, Rape, Castration," 308.
57. Roberto Strongman, "Syncretic Religion and Dissident Sexualities," *Queer Globalizations: Citizenship and the Afterlife of Colonialism.* ed. Arnaldo Cruz-Malave and Martin F. Manalansan IV (New York: New York University Press, 2002), 187.
58. Ibid., 181.
59. See note 20.
60. James Baldwin, *Collected Essays* (New York: The Library of America, 1998), 819; emphasis added.
61. Ibid.
62. While completing this essay, I learned that a biopic of Griffith's life has been planned by a major film studio that will purportedly grapple more thoroughly with the boxer's sexual identity. I also learned that Griffith is allegedly a longstanding charter member of the Stonewall Veterans' Association, a social and political outreach organization for GLBT individuals and their supporters. The group was founded in New York City in 1969, following the historic Stonewall rebellion. For more information on this group and on Griffith's involvement, including photographs, visit their website (http://www.stonewallvets.org/EmileGriffith.htm). As of this writing, it is not clear why the filmmakers of *Ring of Fire* did not include reference to Griffith's participation in this group in their documentary.

CHAPTER 9

"So High You Can't Get Over It, So Low You Can't Get Under It"

Carceral Spatiality and Black Masculinities in the United States and South Africa

Rashad Shabazz

I was prepared for prison.

—George L. Jackson, *Soledad Brother*

Blacks are always in one prison or another. They cannot escape imprisonment for one moment.

—Michael Dingake, *My Fight Against Apartheid*

OVER THE LAST TWO DECADES, MUCH HAS been written about the number of black men in prison. While much of this scholarship has commented on the social and economic conditions many black male prisoners emerge from and on how the criminal justice system has targeted and built a billion-dollar industry on their bodies, little has been said about the spatial geographies they lived in before entering prison. Why space? Because, like race, gender, class, and sexuality, spatiality is a central fundament of subject formation. Indeed, the human is always spatialized. We need look no further than black people's fight for social justice, which have largely been contestations over or within space—segregation, apartheid, slavery, ghettos, Bantustans—to understand its importance. Critically analyzing what philosopher Henri Lefebvre called "the production of space" reveals much about the ways in which subjects are constituted through space. This essay maps out emergent questions regarding space and the construction of black subjectivities. It explores the ways black quotidian space and prison space interact. Examining the spatial geographies of poor and working-class black men preincarceration reveals how prison has been for many, an ubiquitous reality, not only in terms of the rapid acceleration of black men entering and exiting prison, but, more precisely, in the deployment of carceral techniques (surveillance, policing, and containment) into the quotidian lives of poor and working-class blacks. But the prisonization of black spaces fostered an even more egregious formation: the emergence of prisonized subjectivities. Ubiquitous carceral structures, what South African antiapartheid activist and former prisoner Michael Dingake called the prison blacks cannot escape, compounded with the circularity of black men between prison and black quotidian spaces, proved to be a destructive combination. It gave rise to subjects who are, to use the late George Jackson's formulation, "prepared for prison."

This essay explores the connections between carceral space, race, and black masculine gender performativity. My argument is simple yet provocative: drawing on the insights of black prisoners, I contend that carceral forms organize the living and working space of many poor and working-class black men in the United States and South Africa. I use the Robert Taylor Housing Projects—a notorious project on Chicago's Southside—and South Africa's mining compounds, as my case studies. The prisonization of these quotidian spaces profoundly shaped black male subjectivity, thus giving rise to a carcerally inflected black masculinity, made visible through the performance of prison masculinities, the embodiment of carceral aesthetics, and the transference of sexual politics from prisons to other carceral sites.

ROBERT TAYLOR HOMES, APEX OF CARCERAL MISE-EN-SCÈNE

The Robert Taylor housing project emerged as the Second Word War closed. Located on Chicago's Southside, they were seen as the answers to the horrific tenements (kitchenettes) blacks lived in. Robert Taylor was the epitome of carceral mise-en-scène. Its construction was buoyed by the postwar "racial break"; a period where white supremacy was reformed rather than destroyed (Winant 15). Of all the high-rise projects built in the postwar period, it resembled prison the most. Constructed between 1960 and 1962 on 95 acres of land, the one-quarter-mile wide, two-mile long project consisted of 4,400 units—making it the largest housing project in the world. Units were contained in 28 identical 16-story buildings, grouped in a U-shape formation, encircled with "cages of meshed wire" (Wilson 25). It was built within a contained field of city blocks with railroad tracks to the east and siphoned off from a white, middle-class community to the west by the Dan Ryan Expressway. The buildings faced each other, with a "yard" for recreation in the center. Grouped in threes, the anonymity of the buildings forced residents to remember which "stack" they lived in. An autocratic management style centralized all operations, enabling the Chicago Housing Authority to control things like the heat, leaving residents with relatively little individual agency in their own homes (Bowly 128). The *coup de grace* of its carceral architecture was the entrance to the complex. Vehicles drove along a U-shaped road, which gave police easy access to monitor resident activity (Venkatesh 126).

John Woodland, a philosophy student at Maryland State Penitentiary, reveals the subtle ways carceral power organizes the projects. Woodland's geography of the West Baltimore projects provides an important framework to think about Robert Taylor. Using Michel Foucault's *Discipline and Punish*, he examines the continuities between the prison and the high-rise projects he grew up in.

> One thing I noticed when I first came to the penitentiary is that the penitentiary is similar to the high-rise projects in West Baltimore or wherever. In prison, it's the tiers; in the projects, it's different floors. You have this limited space between a fence and where you live, and the room that you live in is also kind of confined—you know, big enough for maybe a couple of people. In prison, the cell is not really big enough for one person, but they put two in there. Same thing with the projects— they're not big enough for entire families, but they put entire families in there. (James 208)

His careful observation of the spatial limitations in both prisons and projects illuminates the way confinement is built into project landscapes. Like prison cells, projects jammed people into spaces unfit to house them. Yet, when they were built in Chicago, black residents rejoiced. The projects in general, and Robert Taylor specifically, gave the appearance that the state heard black people's demand for adequate and safe housing. In spite of the burgeoning hope, projects like Robert Taylor continued the ugly history of black confinement. In time, residents came to see this one-time paradise as a "prison" (Meincke).

Robert Taylor residents were also physically set apart from the rest of the city, even within the mostly impoverished community where it was located. This was a direct result of city planning. European modernist designers—most notably, Le Corbusier—who stressed the importance of "openness" inspired Robert Taylor's construction. But Robert Taylor's open spaces were "dead spaces" with no trees, pathways, or playgrounds; tons of concrete isolated residents from the surrounding black community. Robert Taylor's landscape gave the appearance of openness, while concealing its carceral logic. Residents had no physical contact with the semiaffluent, white, and resource-rich community to the west, known as Bridgeport. This mostly Polish neighborhood housed the stadium where the Chicago White Sox played, which brought significant revenue and jobs into the community. But it was on the west side of the Dan Ryan Expressway. The Dan Ryan plays an important role in the matrix of black spatial order on the Southside. As whites fled to the suburbs, expressways emerged to service their entrance in and out of the city. Opened in 1967, five years after Robert Taylor, the mammoth expressway was a physical barrier that kept Black Belt residents on the "low end" away from Bridgeport's citizens and resources.

And so it went. To the east of Robert Taylor was a train yard, to the south, poverty. North was downtown, a place where many blacks did not feel welcome and an expressway to the west. All four sides of the project were marked with physical boundaries, hazards, poverty, and dead spaces that worked to fix residents in their place. The entire mise-en-scène of Robert Taylor expressed a restrictive, prison-like containment, which was underwritten by a "periphrastic" spatial order.[1]

The project's isolation and poverty also conspired to regulate services as basic as food distribution. As the project packed tens of thousands of poor people into dead zones, grocery stores and healthy food establishments did not move into the area. With inaccessible transportation and large grocery stores located miles away from the project, it was difficult for residents to have their subsistence needs met. Moreover, many did not accept food stamps, which was the way many residents purchased food. This scenario left residents at the mercy of the corner store; small convenient stores located around the project. They sold food and toiletries, mostly, and all accepted food stamps (and eventually EBT cards). There was a twofold problem with corner stores: first, they sold unhealthy foods at inflated prices. Lean meats and fresh vegetables were hard to come by in these stores. Instead, residents had to make due with processed foods and fatty meats. We can attribute the levels of obesity in large part to this phenomenon (Will). Second, through using these commissaries, residents were also familiarized with routine forms of carceral order when they shopped. Fear of robbery or worse prompted many storeowners (many of whom were not black) to enclose cashiers in bulletproof encasements. Reminiscent of the way death row prisoner Mumia Abu-Jamal talks about the prison visiting room, a space that prohibits prisoners from having physical contact with visitors, residents often could not touch store employees—they could only speak to them through Plexiglas walls and receive their merchandise through turnstiles.

POLICING AND SURVEILLANCE

The ubiquity of policing and surveillance is yet another example of the entrenchment of carceral devices in poor and working-class black communities. In response to increasing levels of violence in the early 1980s, then mayor Jane Byrne commissioned a study of security at the high-rises. Cabrini-Green, a Northside high-rise was used as a case study. The report offered recommendations for planning and security to stem escalating crime rates. It was heavily influenced by the work of Oscar Newman, a planner, who emphasized "defensible space" (Venkatesh 123). "Defensible space" referred to the need to make habitable spaces open, visible, and cooperative to surveillance. Proposed changes for Robert Taylor included placing enclosures at the ground floor to force pedestrians to enter through a central entrance, video surveillance in the lobbies, lighting systems, metal detectors and turnstiles in the lobbies, and "perimeter patrols" (123). One of the more egregious and paternalistic measures was the "resident identification system" (123–24). Residents received ID cards, which included name, building number, and apartment, that they had to carry with them at all times; they could not enter the building without it. Luckily, only some of these changes took place (physical changes to buildings never materialized). In spite of this, the commissions' recommendations normalized encroachment onto the lives of residents through a host of technologies.

Chicago Housing Authority (CHA) security tactics in effect augmented resident feelings of isolation from the larger Black Belt. Calls for a "special" police force for Robert Taylor along with state of the art surveillance equipment, controlled visitation, and curfews did not make the one-time paradise feel like a home but instead like a prison. This feeling was cemented when CHA chairman Vincent Lane instituted a controversial plan to root out crime. Labeled "Operation Clean Sweep," the program sought to enact "mass arrests" in the towers (Venkatesh 129–30). The arrests followed surprise searches of apartments, without warrants. Conducted before dawn, the special Robert Taylor security units raided apartments looking for illegal activity, gang members, and drugs. It's no wonder that during this period, residents began to refer to Robert Taylor as a "vertical prison" (Meincke).

MINING COMPOUNDS: PRISONIZING BLACK LABOR

Prisonizing the Robert Taylor homes unfortunately was not the final word in deploying carceral forms into the quotidian spaces of black people. On the other side of the Atlantic Ocean, black South Africans, like the residents of Robert Taylor, were also confronted with the realities of racialized containment. Mining compounds were flagrant expressions of the deployment of carceral devices into black quotidian life. Like African reserves,[2] the mining compounds were archipelagic sites reflecting the prisonization of black South Africa. Mining compounds emerged at the end of the nineteenth century when gold was discovered in Johannesburg and diamonds in Kimberly (Thompson 115). Industrial capitalists, eager to mine the precious resources, established mining compounds to house blacks, who traveled from the reserves to work. The mining compounds served one major function: exploit the cheap black labor for the purpose of extracting South Africa's most coveted natural resource. The majority of workers traveled hundreds of miles and work and lived in compounds sometimes called hostels. Over the decades, and with the aid of the state, mine compounds established a sophisticated system of surveillance and coercion (Crush 828). Jonathan Crush, quoting Stanley Cohen, argues the compounds were "spaces within which individuals were observed, partitioned, subject to timetables and disciplines designed not as ostentations signs of the mining industry's wealth and power, but as a forms of moral architecture of the fabrication of virtue and hard work" (831). These totalizing institutions, which actively controlled the lives of workers, were effective because like the Robert Taylor housing projects, they were laden with architecture, techniques, and rules that circumscribed workers' mobility. Mines used police to keep workers in line. Coercive spatial arrangements were deployed to ensure in the minds of workers that the management was always watching. Disciplinary architectural forms created a panoptic system that allowed management to monitor workers. Moreover, women and children were barred from the compound, which made the many months men spent away from their families difficult. And as a result, resembling the way prisoners negotiated their estrangement and homosociality, men in the mining compounds established alternative structures of masculine performance.

The architecture, space, and landscape of the mining compounds reflect a carceral logic. Many South African scholars have turned their attention to the way compounds harnessed and deployed carceral power.[3] In his study of mining compounds, Dunbar Moodie quotes the deputy commissioner of the Johannes-burg police: "The compound must be suitably constructed to contain the natives and I know of no better attempt at this than the City Deep compound" (77). The deputy goes on to say the compound is equipped with a "high galvanized iron fence," with "turnstiles" to force workers into single file lines. Pulling the cloak off the compound's carceral construction, he says, "The buildings are so constructed that from the compound manager's office he can see down any direc-tion along the lines of the huts. The buildings are arranged like spokes on a wheel with the office as a hub [and] by that means they are able to see exactly what goes on in the compound and practically almost in the rooms." Panoptic in its form, the Deep City compound is a lucid example of the restrictive architecture that underwrote their construction. From its inception, the compound drew on the logic of carceral punishment.

Workers' living space further illustrates the flagrant employment of car-ceral structures in compounds. Mine owners wanted to create "closable" spaces throughout compounds, packing large numbers of workers into tight spaces (Moodie 78). In a communiqué to a colleague, a compound manager who was actually trying to demonstrate that his compound housed workers comfortably, wrote, "The Compound has 52 rooms of 60 bunks each, 2 rooms of 40 bunks each, 260 bunks each (total bunks, 8,400). The 60 bunk rooms accommodate an average of 54 Natives per room" (Moodie 77). More than prison-like, this example demonstrates how compounds also drew on the spatial practices that undergirded slave ships. Workers had no privacy from the forced gaze of others or from the disciplinary gaze of management.

By the 1970s, mine management began to implement more nefarious and coercive measures to ensure control over worker movement. Like the Robert Taylor housing projects, the mines began to implement electronic identifica-tion badges. These badges, however, were equipped with an electronic barcode that had to be swiped into a reader to gain access to the kitchen, the common rooms, and the recreation rooms within the mining compound. Upon swiping their identification badges, data of the employee's location are stored in a central computer. Management can not only see where employees have been but can also calculate the time, date, and how many times the employee visited the room. This form of "superpanopticism" has the ability to survey the lives of employees "without windows, towers, wall or guards" (Crush 833).

POLICING

Like the Robert Taylor housing projects, police were central to the exercise of carceral power in the mining compounds. Police were a normal part of the labor practice. The point of having them was not to keep workers safe. Rather, police power keeps workers in line and nullifies worker political mobilization. Accord-ing to Mandela, the guards on Robben Island were used by prison authorities to carry out the prisons' plan of breaking the "sprit" and "resolve" of prisoners. "To do this," says Mandela, the authorities attempted to exploit every weakness, demolish every invite, [and] negate all signs of individuality" (390).

Mine police were in many cases black. This was a strategic move. It was thought that black police officers would do a better job of "maintain[ing] order" (Moodie 79). These officers had the legal authority to send miners to "mine lockup"—a jail on the mine site (Moodie 79). Many of these cases went before the Native Affairs Council and carried a punishment of two or three days in lockup with no food or water. The presence of police, and the existence of on-site jails, if nothing more, makes the existence of carceral punishment all the more normal. Moreover, the police had the ability to search barracks for contraband (alcohol, smoking and gambling paraphernalia, or knives). And they had the ability to monitor men to make sure they were not engaging in sexual relationships (Moodie 246).

Mining and the Quarry

In the literature from Robben Island political prisoners, the lime quarry stands as a central motif in prisoner's characterization of prison life.[4] For some political prisoners, like Mandela, working at the quarry were moments where they escaped the isolation of the prison and could see other parts of the island. For people like antiapartheid activist Moses Dlamini, who served many years on Robben Island, the quarry was a mix of pain and resistance. But for everyone, the quarry was backbreaking, incredibly strenuous labor. Prisoners worked in the hot sun nine hours a day crushing large rocks into smaller ones. They were loaded on a truck and driven off, only to become the material to build roads and expand the prison.

The exploitation of mostly black labor to expand island infrastructure resembles the way black workers in the mines were overworked and underpaid. Like the quarry, working in the mines was an incredibly laborious process. Long hours and dangerous working conditions were standard (Moodie). Both the quarry and the mine figure centrally in late nineteenth- and twentieth-century South African culture and politics as sites of labor organizing, violence, racism, resistance, and, crucially, carceral punishment. As black men labored under exploitative conditions, they were being prepared/trained in the ways of prison life. Both the state and mine owners used this symbiosis to their benefit. A ready reserve of laborers trained in mining enabled both Robben Island and the mines to continue their labor process without missing a beat.

The techniques, architecture, and practices used to organize the mine compound and the Robert Taylor projects were at once similar and distinct. The mine contained workers in large rooms; workers were frequently subjected to the gaze of each other, management, and police. While the people in the project were contained in large individual residences, physically isolated by a train station and an expressway, they were confronted with the ubiquity of policing, their food distribution was centralized, and residents were forced to wear identification badges. Both the project and the mine, however, drew on forms of superpanopticism (identification badges that tracked movement) to monitor the movements of residents and workers. These total institutions succeeded in deploying carceral forms into the quotidian lives of black people. Moreover, they succeeded in its normalization. Indeed, landscape, space, police, and surveillance form the interactive network that prisonized black mine labor and black life in the projects.

Understanding the ways in which this network of carceral apparatus shaped the subjectivity of inhabitants further elucidates the oppressiveness of caracal space. The carceral regulations and architecture already embedded in both the project and compound's landscape provided fertile ground to cultivate carceral subjectivity. The importation of prison culture by former prisoners and the project's and mine's own system of carceral punishment, primed the men for prison life. In this "world without women," aggressive hypermasculinities dominated how masculinity was performed (Walker, Reid, and Cornell 66). Project and mine culture, which privileged the performance of prison masculinity, became the new grammar in the writing of black men's lives.

SPACE AND THE SUBJECT: CARCERAL CIRCULARITY AND PERFORMANCES OF PRISON MASCULINITY

Who we are as subjects is significantly informed by our relationship to physical space. Indeed, spatiality, like gender, sexuality, class, and race, is central to our existential makeup.[5] Human geographer Kathleen M. Kirby makes this point when she writes, "space and where we are in it . . . determines a large portion of our status as subjects, and obversely, the kinds of subjects we are largely dictates our degree of mobility and our possible future locations" (Kirby 11). When applied to the prisonization of black quotidian space, Kirby's insights allow for a radical reading of the projects and mining compounds. It demonstrates not only that subjects are prisonized through spatiality but that the production of those subjects "dictates" their mobility and prepares them for "future" interaction with carceral space. This becomes clear when we examine the performances of black masculinity in these spaces. Black men who dwell in the projects and mines have their performances of masculinity shaped by the ubiquitous carceral world that surrounds them. Indeed, they are "prepared for prison" through the deployment of carceral forms into their everyday life (Jackson 4). And with no real or abstract power in a hostile, often-violent world, these men learn how to negotiate this world by performing prison masculinities. Moreover, the accelerating rates of black male incarceration, which has fostered the circulation of black men from these spaces to prison and back again, has worked to normalize the performativity of prison masculinity and to imbue the black male body with a carceral logic.

POSTINDUSTRIAL CARCERAL MASCULINITY

The prisonization of poor and working-class black masculinity in the United States was aided by the demise of the postwar economy. Black feminist Patricia Hill Collins argues that black men in the postindustrial city are "urban prisoners" (90). According to Hill Collins, "African American reactions to racial segregation in the postcivil rights era, especially those living in hypersegregated, poor inner-city neighborhoods, resemble those of people living in prison" (90). For Hill Collins, this prison-world of the ghetto produces a context where, like prisoners, black people "simply turn on one another, reflecting heightened levels of alienation and nihilism" (90). This is especially the case with respect to black men. Faced with few job possibilities, insufficient schools, drugs, and easy access to guns, black men kill each other over seemingly inconsequential things. She maintains that the politics and performance of black masculinity is shaped by a geography of carceral punishment, poverty, and adoption of prison masculinity. For many men, this meant taking on a carcerally bound performance of masculinity, what I term *postindustrial carceral masculinity*. Emerging out of a period of massive deindustrialization, economic and political disinvestment, and increased policing and prison construction resulting in accelerations in the number of black men in prison, the postindustrial carceral subject ushered in an era where performances of black masculinity were deeply informed by carceral space.

Robert Taylor residents were very attuned to how the exercises of carceral power were influencing how young men performed masculinity.[6] In the carceral yards that surround the Robert Taylor housing project, young men learned to perform masculinity contiguous with the political, economic, cultural moment. In his book *Brothers*, Sylvester Monroe narrates his life growing up in Robert Taylor during the 1970s. Like many youth, Sylvester and his friends learned to read, write, do math, sing, and play ball in the confines of the project. At the same time they learned to "jive girls," hustle, make money in the underground economy, steal, drink, and fight with sticks, bricks, stones, knives, and, eventually, guns. From his earliest days, Sylvester and his friends thought of life in Robert Taylor as a preparatory prison. According to his friend Honk, "if you came from trey-nine (thirty ninth street) . . . prison was just a change of address" (Monroe 41).

Honk's analysis attests to the circularity between the prison and the projects and demonstrates the way young men learned to perform masculinity. During the 1970s (the period of Honk's youth) black men were moving between the cities and rural prisons at supersonic speeds. As geographer Ruth Wilson Gilmore notes, states like California relied heavily on prisons to soak up postindustrial surpluses that left black, brown, and white bodies out of work. White bodies soaked up jobs in the new prison industry and black and brown bodies were its raw material. Robert Taylor became part of this new circular system of black bodies vacillating between prison and black living space. But this circulation was made possible by increased carceral order within black living space. Both the carceral space of the project—cages, isolation, policing, and surveillance "meshed" with performing a type of masculinity that centered on negotiating and surviving violence—and a reliance on physical toughness were useful in "preparing" these young men for prison. In short, their performance of masculinity was prisonized.

Race and class profoundly influence prison masculinity. The circulation of men of color, particularly black men, between carceral spaces and prison effectively linked the performance of prison masculinity with black (and brown) men. Prison masculinity is characterized by "ultramasculine" hyperaggressive performance. It relies on physical toughness and the willingness to negotiate and survive violence (Sabo, Kupers, and London 3). According to Don Sabo, Terry Kupers, and Willie London, prison masculinity takes its cue from hegemonic masculinity. This performance of masculinity is the "prevailing, most lauded, idealized, and valorized form of masculinity in a historical setting" (Sabo, Kupers, and London 5). In the United States, hegemonic masculinity emphasizes "male domination, heterosexism, violence, and ruthless competition" (5). Moreover, hegemonic masculinity posits femininity as "compliant," "passive," "sexually receptive," and "fragile" (5).

In American culture, hegemonic masculinity is always associated with heterosexuality and whiteness. White masculinity—particularly white, middle-class masculinity—has access to real and abstract forms of power, such as financial power, political power, and workplace authority. Black men do not have access to these forms of power. Instead, black men use their bodies and the threat of violence to gain financial status and street credibility. This is demonstrated in the lyrics and hypermasculine performance in hip-hop, for example (I will elaborate on this in more detail in the following section; Hurt). Without material or abstract power, black men use their bodies to present themselves as being worthy of respect. It's not a coincidence that this logic governs many men's (and some women's) prisons. Sculpting the body into a seemingly impenetrable machine garners respect, admiration, and even fear among other prisoners. The hypermasculine logic of prison demands toughness and the willingness to use violence if necessary—characteristics that spilled over and shaped performance of masculinity in postindustrial ghettos. This was accelerated by two factors: (1) higher levels of people entering prisons during the late 1970s and early 1980s, as a result of systematic violence and repression,[7] and (2) the increasing prisonization (spatial isolation, surveillance, underground economics, and centralizing of a population's diet) of poor black communities. These factors worked together to effectively fuse postindustrial masculinity with prison masculinity.

MASCULINITY AND CARCERAL AESTHETICS

An important element of the circularity between prison and black masculinity is perhaps the most unassuming and yet most pervasive—aesthetics. Characterized by baggie pants, exposed boxer shorts, large T-shirts, and bandanas, this aesthetic formulation, although it emerged from prison, has infused hip-hop culture (Harris 66). Prisoners wear baggy clothes because in prison they don't receive clothes that fit nor do they receive belts. So their pants sag. It's nearly impossible to walk down an urban street or watch a rap video and not see this style repeated. The question is why?

Cultural critic and hip-hop historian, Kevin Powell, explains that to understand the emergence of prison culture within hip-hop, we must be attentive to broader social and economic changes that gained traction under Reagan/Bush. Public housing subsidies diminished, urban schools received less funding, industrial jobs continued to decline, interest rates skyrocketed, and states prosecuted drug addicts and dealers to the fullest extent of the (increasingly harsh) law. As blacks entered and exited prisons, prison (and gang) culture congealed into the lyrical content of hip-hop music. Although he does not explicitly state it, this set of circumstances also transformed the urban male culture in general and hip-hop specifically (Hurt). The revolving door between poor black communities and prison, what I have been calling the symbiosis between prison and black communities, transported its culture and aesthetics into the "hood." Not to be mistaken as a critique, this genealogy of the prisonization of hip-hop culture is another example of prison's ubiquity and the symbiotic relationship prison has with the ghetto.

Another example of the prisonization of the hip-hop aesthetic is the transformation of black male physiques. Beginning with Tupac Shakur and continuing with rappers LL Cool J, Ja Rule, Lil Wayne, Rick Ross, and 50 Cent, the black male physique has endured a remarkable transformation. For over a decade, the covers of hip-hop publications, such as the *Source*, *XXL*, and numerous rap videos depict bulkier, more muscularly defined, and tattooed bodies. These transformations, to some, are nothing more than fashion, which I concede is in part correct. When read against the profound social and political upheavals that placed tens of thousands of black people behind bars, however, trends don't explain the entire story. Black prisoners, in fact, illuminate the more complex carceral picture beneath the muscular black male physique.

In *Life in Prison*, the late Stanley "Tookie" Williams tells of his experience learning about prison as an adolescent. A friend's older brother's pictures of black men in a prison yard help Williams imagine himself in prison: "There were times when Rock would pull out his wallet and flash some pictures of him and his homies standing in a prison exercise yard, the men in the photos were big and buff, flexing their muscles and smiling into the camera. Iron weights and benches were in the background. I would stare at those pictures and say, 'Wow. Look at all them muscles.' I told myself that one day I wanted to have a big chest and large arms and have my picture taken in the prison yard" (Williams 14). Williams's admiration for the men in the photos illuminates the complex symbiosis between black men's physique, prison culture, and desire for patriarchal power. He admires them, not because they are "cool" per se but because they embody power. It is true that men (and women) in prison lift weights to escape boredom and stay fit; however, it cannot be denied that the imposing figure of a muscular frame renders a sense of power. Given the fact that prisoners, and the communities they come from, have no real or abstract power, it's not surprising they use their bodies to get it. Prison activist and scholar Don Sabo writes "men cultivate their bodies to send a variety of messages about the meaning of masculinity to themselves and others" (Sabo, Kupers, and London 65). One message articulated for sure through bulking up is "I'm not to be messed with." In the context of the hypermasculine and hyperviolent world of prison, building the body is a way to keep safe; it enables the articulation of power by physically dominating another. (But this sense of power is not "real." That is to say, there's no direct correlation between being physically intimidating and being safe.) This logic is replicated in the "yard" of the "inmate society" as well.

"To Change One's Character": Carceral Masculinity in the Mines

In South Africa, like the United States, carceral spatiality and the deployment of carceral techniques transformed worker subjectivities, as well. And like black men in the projects, the carceral world of the mines dictated their (lack of) mobility and future interaction with prison. Two factors contribute to the prisonization of black masculinity in South Africa: One, the ubiquity of carceral forms that orga-nized the mine, detailed previously. Two, the circularity of black men between mines and prison, what human geographer Teresa Dirsuweit refers to as the migra-tion of male prison culture from prison to the mines and back again (Dirsuweit 72). According to one mineworker, "to be a miner is to change one's character." When examined through the lens of spatiality and carceral circularity, the trans-formation of mine worker identities reflects the influence of prisonization. We can see this in how they perform masculinity. Loud talk; boisterousness, physical toughness; lewd remarks to women; claims of "taking" young boys for wives; physical violence; institutional regulations (new employees had to strip naked in a room full of men in order to be examined by a doctor); and fear typified mine masculinity (Moodie 13). While a measure of this performance may seem normal for blue-collar work, the restrictive architecture, carceral regulations, and explicit injection of prison culture made it anything but typical.

Prison is an "ultramasculine world," where men are hailed to perform exag-gerations of masculinity and where hypermasculinity is always being codified. On one level, the hierarchy created among prisoners to garner power and or recog-nition fosters prison masculinity. On another level, prison masculinity emerges in relation to the architecture and to the prison administration, which uses and reinforces the hierarchy created among prisoners to normalize hypermasculinity.

Like the United States, South Africa's prisons suffer from this exaggeration of masculinity as well. We see this in the writings of antiapartheid political prison-ers. In his memoir of his incarceration on Robben Island, Pan African Congress activist Moses Dlamini writes that hypermasculinity was a key element of prison punishment. Upon entering Leeuwkop prison, Dlamini saw men who'd been damaged by what he called "apartheid justice" (23). According to Dlamini, the men in Leeuwkop had hard stares, "scars on their heads and faces, tattoos on their chests and arms," and faces that had seen much pain (23).

In Dlamini's memoir, the performance of prison masculinity was expressed primarily through sexual abuse by guards and prisoners. For example, when Dlamini arrived at the prison, all the new prisoners were put on display in front of guards and other prisoners. White prison guards turned this into an oppor-tunity to evoke racist sexualized fantasies regarding black men's genitals. Guards also remarked to other prisoners that they could "get a good wife" from this new crop of prisoners (Dlamini 23). The guard's participation in sexualized racism was expressed in and through feminizing new prisoners, by placing them at the bottom of the gender and sexual hierarchy. Moreover, the guards and the prison-ers who watched the display of new prisoners positioned themselves at the top of the masculine hierarchy. This hierarchy enabled sexual violence. Those at the top violated those men at the bottom. Dlamini notes that despite his efforts, he and his comrades could not resist the sexual advances of prison gangs (111, 155).

So as not to pathologize sex in men's prisons, it's important to note that not all sexual relationships were the result of coercion. A desire to have companionship also fostered relationships between men. One of the few openly gay antiapartheid activists, Simon Nkoli, pointed out that several men had consensual sex and some were involved in relationships with other men. Nkoli's openness about his sexual-ity, however, led to his marginalization by the "High Organ," the antiapartheid leadership present on the island. "I was exposed as one of those and left to suffer from severe suppression, loneliness and isolation," says Nkoli (Buntman 245). Although men's prisons are saturated with hypermasculinity, the homosocial order enables men to develop fluid sexual practices. As noted previously, these practices are sometimes coercive; there are nevertheless cases where men find deeply caring and emotionally fulfilling relationships.

Mining compounds borrowed in part from prison's hierarchy of masculinity. Like prison, mining compounds were homosocial spaces. Also like prison, the gerontocracy positioned older men at the top of the male hierarchy (Moodie, Ndatshe, and Sibuyi 122–28). Older men held power over newer workers, which extended beyond simple work perks. As Dlamini illustrates, in prison, older prisoners, and those willing to use violence, had their pick of younger or newer prisoners who were at the bottom of the prison hierarchy. Like prison, older men in the mines held the power in the relationships. For example, older men "proposed" to younger men and performed the role of the "head of the household," they bought gifts for "wives," and sexually, older men "penetrated" them (through the thighs; Moodie, Ndatshe, and Sibuyi 128–34). Like prison, sex and intimate relationships between men in the mines were not based entirely on hypermasculine performance. Indeed, a longing for companionship underwrote many "mine marriages" (Moodie, Ndatshe, and Sibuyi 128).

What this demonstrates is that mines provided a way for black men to have alternative arrangements for sexual practice and masculine identity, what Moodie refers to as "variations of the patriarchal theme" (Moodie, Ndatshe, and Sibuyi 119). As in prison, the mine's spatial order worked to foster new ways of imagining sex and sexuality. Miners used this to negotiate between the carceral community they inhabited and a desire for sexual and emotional connection. Where sex and/or longing for companionship between men in the larger society of South Africa, and in particular among blacks in the homelands, was both taboo and criminalized, the mines provided a space for exploring same-sex relationships without breaking laws or social taboos.[8]

Nevertheless, carceral practices underwrote this arrangement. While there is something to be said about the way black men had the opportunity to have alternative ways of practicing masculinity, we must also grapple with the fact that it emerged out of a set of social arrangements that was informed by the violence and punitive spatial order of prison.

CONCLUSION

The production of black spatial arrangements unearths the ways in which carceral techniques have played a role in how black spaces are organized. Moreover, this reading of black people's relationship to ubiquitous forms of carceral punishment illustrates how these spaces primed black men for prison. Exploring black oppression across geopolitical frontiers reveals one undeniable fact: spatial exclusion has and remains a major expression of black subjugation.

In *Black Skin, White Masks*, revolutionary thinker Franz Fanon wrote that living in a racist society negates the ability of blacks to ontologically have an "independent self-consciousness," for blackness, he argued, is always experienced "in relation to the white man" (Fanon 110). This Fanon called the "fact of Black-ness." Drawing on Fanon's generative analysis, it is clear that spatial constriction is also a fact of blackness. The racial spatial ideologies of apartheid, segregation, and slavery, with its techniques of racial management—ghettos, mining com-pounds, reserves, projects, and prisons—that fix black bodies and form black subjects in space, constitute the network that blacks have politically resisted for centuries. Parliament Funkadelic playfully referred to this battle in the song "One Nation under a Groove." Over a funky rhythmic beat, George Clinton and Bootsy Collins belt out "so wide you can't get around/so low you can't get under it/so high you can't get over it/this is a chance/this is a chance /to dance your way out of your constrictions." Indeed. But the stubborn persistence of this network demonstrates that the battle is far from over and that black people must not only dance their way out of their constructions, but they must also destroy the system that forces them to dance.

ACKNOWLEDGMENTS

I would like to thank my mentor and dissertation advisor Angela Y. Davis for her tireless support and feedback in the completion of the project. I would also like to acknowledge my other committee members Bettina F. Aptheker, George Lip-sitz, and Tricia Rose for all their support. I want to thank Pascha Bueno-Hansen and Marco Mojica for their brilliant feedback while this project was being con-structed. Finally, yet importantly, I want to thank Glen Elder for suggesting that I write this article.

WORKS CITED

Bowly, Jr., Devereux. *The Poorhouse: Subsidized Housing in Chicago, 1895–1976*. Carbondale: Southern Illinois UP, 1978.

Buntman, Fran Lisa. *Robben Island and Prisoner Resistance to Apartheid*. Cambridge: Cam-bridge UP, 2003.

Coetzee, Jan. K. *Plain Tales from Robben Island*. Hatfield: Van Schaik, 2000.

Crush, Jonathan. "Power Surveillance on the South African Gold Mines." *Journal of Southern African Studies* 18.4 (1992): 825–44.

Dingake, Michael. *My Fight against Apartheid*. London: Kliptown, 1987.

Dirsuweit, Teresa. "Carceral Spaces in South Africa: A Case Study of Institutional Power, Sexu-ality and Transgression in a Woman's Prisons." *Geoforum* 30 (1999): 71–83.

Dlamini, Moses. *Hell-Hole, Robben Island: Reminiscences of a Political Prisoner in South Africa*. Trenton: Africa World, 1984.

Fanon, Frantz. *Black Skin, White Masks*. New York: Grove, 1967.

Forman, Murray. *The 'Hood Comes First*. Middletown: Wesleyan UP, 2002.

Gevisser, Mark, and Edwin Cameron, eds. *Defiant Desire*. New York: Routledge, 1995.

Gilmore, Ruth Wilson. *Golden Gulag*. Berkeley: U of California P, 2007.

Goldberg, David Theo. *Racist Culture: Philosophy and the Politics of Meaning*. Cambridge: Blackwell, 1993.

Harris, Keith M. "'Untitled': D' Angelo and the Visualization of the Black Male Body." *Wide Angle* 21.4 (1999): 62–83.

Hill Collins, Patricia. *Black Sexual Politics*. New York: Routledge, 2004.

Hurt, Byron, dir. *Hip Hop: Beyond Beats and Rhymes*. 2006.

Jackson, George. *Soledad Brother: The Prison Letters of George Jackson*. Chicago: Lawrence Hill, 1994.

James, Joy, ed. *The New Abolitionists*. New York: State U of New York, 2005.

Johnson, E. Patrick. *Appropriating Blackness: Performance and the Politics of Authenticity*. Durham: Duke UP, 2004.

Kirby, M. Kathleen. *Indifferent Boundaries: Spatial Concepts of Human Subjectivity*. New York: Guilford, 1996.

Lefebvre, Henri. *The Production of Space*. Cambridge, UK: Oxford, 1991.

Mandela, Nelson. *Long Walk to Freedom: The Autobiography of Nelson Mandela*. Boston: Little, Brown, 1994.

Massey, Doreen. *For Space*. London: Sage, 2005.

Mbembe, Achille. "Necropolitics." *Public Culture* 15.1 (2003): 11–40.

Meincke, Paul. "Last of the Robert Taylor Homes Comes Down." *ABC News* 15 May 2007. http://abclocal.go.com/wls/story?section=news/local&id=5308437.

Monroe, Sylvester. *Brothers*. New York: Ballantine, 1989.

Moodie, Dunbar. *Going for the Gold*. Berkeley: U of California P, 1994.

Moodie, T. Dunbar, Wivienne Ndatshe, and British Sibuyi. "Importance and Male Sexuality on the South African Gold Mines." *Journal of Southern African Studies* 14.2 (1988): 228–56.

Naidoo, Indres. *Robben Island: Ten Years as a Political Prisoner in South Africa's Most Notorious Penitentiary*. New York: Vintage, 1983.

Sabo, Donald F., Terry Allen Kupers, and Willie James London, eds. *Prison Masculinities*. Philadelphia: Temple UP, 2001.

Sanders, G. Rashaad Shabazz. "'They Imprison the Whole Population': U.S. and South African Prison Literature and the Emergence of Symbiotic Carcerality, 1900–Present." Diss. U of California, Santa Cruz, 2008.

Thompson, Leonard. *A History of South Africa*. New Haven: Yale UP, 1990.

Venkatesh, Sudhir Alladi. *American Project*. Cambridge: Harvard UP, 2000.

Visher, Christy, Nancy G. La Vigne, and Jill Farrell. 2003. "Illinois Prisoners' Reflections on Returning Home." 9 Sept. 2003. *Urban* Institute. http://www.urban.org/publications/310846.html.

Walker, Liz, Graeme Reid, and Morna Cornell. *Waiting to Happen*. Boulder: Lynne Rienner, 2004.

Will, Katherine E. W. "Regional Diet, American." *Diet.com*. 2007. 10 Aug. 2008 http://www.diet.com/g/regional-diet-american.

Williams, Stanley. "Tookie." In *Life in Prison*. San Francisco: Chronicle, 1998.

Wilson, David. *Race and Cities: America's New Black Ghetto*. New York: Routledge, 2007.

Winant, Howard. *The New Politics of Race*. Minneapolis: U of Minnesota P, 2004.

Young, Vershawn Ashanti. *Your Average Nigga: Performing Race, Literacy, and Masculinity*. Detroit: Wayne State U, 2007.

Zwelonke, D. M. *Robben Island*. London: Heinemann, 1973.

NOTES

1. According to philosopher David Theo Goldberg, periphrastic space "implies dislocation, displacement, and division. It has become the primary mode by which the space of racial marginality has been articulated and reproduced" (Goldberg 188).

2. The reserves were the most visible expression of South Africa's prisonization. They were archipelagoes of carceral punishment. Developed to sequester Africans into the nation's most isolated areas, the reserves are a flagrant exercise of carceral power. The reserves enabled the exploitation of black labor power and acted as a physical barrier to keep blacks out of the white gene pool. A network of carceral characteristics—the pass laws, banning, and police—that worked to fix Africans in their place, echo back to my examination of carceral punishment in the United States. They served three purposes: they isolated blacks into the far reaches of the country, away from the resource rich urban centers; they physically contained them; and they provided a cheap readily available source of labor. The organization of space, specifically as it applies to land distribution, was critical to the stability of apartheid. According to postcolonial theorist Achille Mbembe, at its heart, colonial occupation was a matter of "seizing delimiting, and asserting control over a physical geographical area." Moreover, he stresses, colonial occupation was a relentless practice of "writing on the ground a new set of social and spatial relations . . . tantamount to the production of boundaries and hierarchies, zones and enclaves; the subdivision of existing property arrangements . . . ; [and] resources extraction." According to Mbembe, space was the "raw material of sovereignty," and violence was how sovereignty was exercised.
3. See Ibid; Dirsuweit; Moodie; Moodie, Ndatshe, Sibuyi.
4. See. Coetzee; Dlamini; Mandela; Naidoo; Zwelonke.
5. See Forman; Kirby; Massey.
6. My use of "performance" is informed by the work of performance theorist E. Patrick Johnson and the literary theorist Vershawn Young. For Johnson, performance "facilitates the appropriation of blackness." Drawing on Johnson's work, Young suggests that black people endure what he calls the "burden of racial performance." For Young, the performative elements of blackness demand that black people perform those tropes. According to Young, not doing so risks skepticism or exclusion (Johnson; Young).
7. According to Urban Institute researcher Nancy G. La Vigne, "The return of so many prisoners to a handful of Chicago communities is only half the story . . . The other half is the high rate of people being sent or returned to prison who come from these communities. This cycling in and out of prison can have significant social and economic impacts on the residents in these neighborhoods." (Visher, La Vigne, Farrell).
8. As I note in my dissertation, "'They Imprison the Whole Population': U.S. and South African Prison Literature and the Emergence of Symbiotic Carcerality, 1900–Present": "Glen Retief writes that sexual repression was central to apartheid regulations. Keeping the white population 'pure' and white fostered the regulation of sex between racial groups. This was expressed in the 1957 Immorality Act. Though the law did not directly reference gays and lesbians, it was extended to them. According to Retief, the Nationalist Party used the existence of 'gay parties' to strengthen its repression of sex and sexuality. See, 'Keeping Sodom Out of the Laagar: State Repression of Homosexuality in Apartheid South Africa' in, *Defiant Desire*, ed. Mark Gevisser and Edwin Cameron (New York: Routledge, 1995). Dirsuweit writes that in the face of the repressive carceral structures that underwrote the mine, men could escape the taboos of same sex intercourse and explore other possibilities. See, Dirsuweit, 'Carceral Spaces in South Africa: A Case Study of Institutional Power, Sexuality and Transgression in a Woman's Prisons'" (131).

CHAPTER 10

CAN YOU BE BLACK AND WORK HERE?

SOCIAL JUSTICE ACTIVIST ORGANIZING AND BLACK AURALITY

ASHON T. CRAWLEY

If I can't say a . . . word
If I can't say a . . . word
If I can't say a . . . word
I'll raise my . . . hand
If I can't say a . . . word
If I can't say a . . . word
If I can't say a . . .
I'll raise . . . my . . .

—Congregational Song

ACKNOWLEDGEMENT

Powerful. This song. I remember.

THIS SONG IS POWERFUL BECAUSE I REMEMBER—BEING born and raised in the BLACK Pentecostal denomination named the Church of God in Christ (COGIC)—that one time as we sung it, someone, instead of merely raising their hand in praise, threw a handkerchief to the floor. The "word" that they could not say, but certainly could sing, literally took flight and eventuated on the ground. The word "hand" transformed from noun to verb, from its "hyptostasis, paralysis, and arrest suggested [as a] *noun*" to "the domain of action and the ability to act suggested by the *verb*" (Mackey, *Discrepant Engagement* 266). The singer corporeally performed an improvisation, literally rupturing the song by casting off the "word" and word that could not be said.

Powerful. This song. I remember.

This song is powerful because I remember—as I am an organist and pianist and often accompany church services with instrumental music—that "if I can't say a," it is followed by a caesura, a brief but pronounced break, before "word" is sung. Typographically, I used ellipses to represent this break, this pause, this interruption as what, following a quote from Ralph Ellison, Jennifer Brody says are "a suspended space and space of suspense where 'the unheard sounds came through, and each melodic line existed in itself, stood out clearly from all the rest, said its piece, and waited patiently for the other voices to speak,'" which allows one to hear "'not only in time, but in space as well'" (Brody 689). The way the song was sung created a different time and space in and through which one could have a sacred encounter.

Powerful. This song. I remember.

This song is powerful because I remember—as I learned to sing, learning about rhythm and time, melisma and falsetto, wails, and groans and moans, from this tradition—that there were times when the singer would, unlike the brief caesura, cease singing altogether before saying "word" or the word. This literal lack for a better term is performative, it is the arrival of the "accretional 'yes'" heard just underneath the repetitious chorus—repetition being a staple in BLACK music (Mackey, *Bedouin Hornbook* 20). This chorus "annexes the trace of its historical locus" and, thus "[constructs] . . . an otherwise unavailable Heaven" (Mackey, *Bedouin Hornbook* 20), as instruments play to fill in the emptied vocal space; this refusal or inability to continue singing "[suggests] a continuum, a complementarity, between human voice and instrumental voice, an interchange between speech and song, verbal articulation and nonverbal articulation" (Mackey, *Paracritical Hinge* 195).

I have an activist impulse birthed through my religious tradition that privileged the body as a sacred thing, a thing that should clap, raise hands, dance, vocalize exhortations, speak in tongues, and lay hands for healings. Simply, I learned that in order to perform sacred acts, one must, as Bayard Rustin encouraged, "act and act with your body" (Kates et al.). This activist impulse compelled me to do activist organizing work that could bring together critical conversations about race, gender, sexual orientation, class, ability, and religion in ways that do justice to the world.

As such, from September 2007 to August 2008, I worked for the Gay, Lesbian, and Straight Education Network (GLSEN) in New York City. The organization's mission is "to assure that each member of every school community is valued and respected regardless of sexual orientation or gender identity/expression." However, my final day with the organization, having experienced institutional inequities, racisms, sexisms, and hierarchies of oppression, I sent an email letter to the entire staff titled "Brief Notes and Goodbye, or Can You Be BLACK and Work at GLSEN?" (Crawley).

This writing reflects on the corporeal-sung experience of "if I can't say a word" as but one example of the various ways BLACK aurality structures BLACK life.

From reflection, this writing likewise anticipates how BLACK aurality can invade structures, systems, institutions and how BLACK aurality can, hopefully, shift the dominant narratives of racisms, sexisms, classisms, and homophobias.[1]

RESOLUTION

During my tenure at the well-funded, well-resourced, medium-sized nonprofit organization GLSEN, I began wondering if, in fact, "social justice" ever survives its own institutionalization; its processual stricturing, particularly given our society's capitalist impulse; and the historicopresent entanglements with racism, classism, sexism, and willful ignorance. When a particular marginalized identity is selected as the *one* to address, when that identity is the rationale both for the organization's existence and institutionalization, how does the selection itself instantiate the marginalization of others, as is the case with GLSEN? GLSEN, founded in 1990 as a group for teachers and volunteers, established its mission to make all K–12 schools safe spaces for all students, particularly LGBTQ (lesbian, gay, bisexual, transgender, and queer) persons. As their website states, "Since homophobia and heterosexism undermine a healthy school climate, we work to educate teachers, students and the public at large about the damaging effects these forces have on youth and adults alike" (GLSEN, "2003–2008"). They have recently launched a public service announcement campaign to eradicate the phrase "that's so gay" from usage by K–12 young people. However, though GLSEN touts—and I believe sincerely believes it has—a social justice posture, their inattention also occasions the blind spots through which social justice for *all* is elided by categorizing and prioritizing homophobias, with BLACK people exoticized as "more homophobic" than white people. And the (imperialist, hegemonic, classist, racist, sexist) beat goes on . . . *dun, dun, dun.*

This essay will attempt to do two things. First, it will rehearse the letter sent to the organization to set a foundation for the subsequent argument regarding BLACK aurality and activist organizing. As such, I will reproduce sections of the letter in the following, editing out names of individuals and cutting for length. Second, the essay will make a case for BLACK aurality, or what I term the BLACK sonic framework (BSF). Engaging Arthur Jafa, Nathaniel Mackey, Fred Moten, and Frederick Douglass, I posit that there is a "sound and subjectivity" evinced in cultural productions, "Brief Notes," the letter sent to the organization, notwithstanding. This framework privileges the rubrics of BLACK aurality as "the site of improvisation," resists rigidity, and uses a variety of culturally produced moans, hollers, cries, melisma, falsettos, and stutters (Moten 179). Finally, I'm interested in how we can infuse the sonic materiality, the phonic substance, of BLACKness into activist organizing to both inform and deform—that is destabilize, decenter, deconstruct—white, capitalist, patriarchal, antifeminist, antitransgender, and antiqueer organizing. What remains when black phonic materiality meets with and engages queer activism?

In terms of typography, I use "BLACK" both in the initial letter and in this writing. I use BLACK to foreground BLACKness as a concept that should not be overlooked; rather, it is a conceptual frame of thought that bears pause, it is a typographic *ritenuto*, calling for an immediate reduction in tempo, an instantiation of the overlookedness and undervaluedness of BLACKness. It is the "[re]appearance of the disappearance" of BLACKness enfolded in textual occlusion in terms like "multiculturalism" and "diversity" (Moten 200). I argue for the "ontological condition" of BLACKness as that which works against; that which resists; and that which is obscure but is supra-abundant and bears mentioning, not(at)ing, and engaging (Moten 18).

With the current political correctness that would rather subsume BLACKness under the monikers of multiculturalism, cultural diversity, and intersectionality as a means of disrupting BLACKness as that which need be contended with and engaged, the typographic usage of "BLACK" claims that BLACKness is real, or more directly, that people live the materiality of BLACKness daily. Similar to how a musical note functions on a score as a device to structure musical thought and around which a musician can improvise, "BLACK" is a textual notation, letters "sounding out" the irreducible materiality of BLACK performance; it must be heard, the letters scream, whether loudly as a wail or softly as what Mackey calls the whisper, a "laminated shout" (Mackey, *Bedouin Hornbook*).

Some may argue that this call for and attention to the irreducible materiality of BLACKness is essentialist. However, I err on the side of Arthur Jafa as being an "antiessentialist" in that I believe there are retentionist strains in the materiality of BLACKness. He goes on to describe this as the belief that there are "certain levels of cultural retention" wherein "people carry culture on various levels, down to the deepest level, which I would call a kind of core stability." Moreover, he says, "The middle passage is such a clear example of this, because you see Black American Culture particularly developed around those areas we could carry around in our heads—our oratorical prowess, dance, music, those kinds of things" and that "we have to be able to look at these arenas to see how Black people have intervened to transform them into spaces where we can most express our desires." Similar to material retention, Joseph Roach describes "orature," which "comprises a range of forms, which, though they may invest themselves variously in gesture, song, dance, processions, storytelling, proverbs, gossip, customs, rituals" are "modes of communication [that] have produced one another interactively over time" (Roach 11). As such, it appears appropriate, if not necessarily provocative but powerful, to turn to the BLACK sonic framework to (in)form normative notions of activist organizing. Asking, what do BLACK people desire, we can answer, recognizable, audible personhood.

Activist organizing that takes seriously the BLACK sonic framework is "a summons, a call-to-arms as it were, an invitation into an area of *un*common sense" beckoning the "gut-level realization" found in BLACK sound that bears "the primacy of intensity over etiquette" (Mackey, *Bedouin Hornbook* 27). Was "Brief Notes" unprofessional, inappropriate? Was it a "taunt" of sorts (23)? I caution against that reading as knee-jerk and reactionary. Some actions are simply trying to voice what refuses to be heard and rather "taunts . . . our inclination to hear it as taunt," as unprofessional, and as inappropriate. Rhetorical arguments of unprofessionalism and inappropriateness easily elide racisms, maintaining the primacy of the hierarchic structures of organizations and render antiracist work secondary to (white) queer activism because charges of racism must be stated decorously and proven by *proper* channels. Part of the challenge for activist organizing in white social justice institutions is to hear for hearing's sake, not to *mis*hear by disavowal and reproach.

Refusing generalizability, accounting for the BLACK sonic framework "makes hesitation eloquent" and utilizes the "inarticulacy" of scat to open for subtle nuances in varied experience without denigration (Mackey, *Discrepant Engagement* 274). This hesitation is the "stuttering quality suggestive of a discomfort with any pretense of definitive statement" (44). "One of the reasons [BLACK] music so often goes over into nonspeech—the moaning, humming, shouts, non-sense lyrics, scat—is to say, among other things, that the realm of conventionally articulate speech is not sufficient for saying what needs to be said" (Mackey, *Paracritical Hinge* 193). In this way, inarticulacy is not so much the inability to speak coherently as it is a demand to hear differently—with new ears, as it were—varied patterns of utterance. Attending to this sonic framework attends to "that buzz, that vibration, that multiply-aspected vocality" of BLACK sound, and to "worrying the note" indicating the "indeterminate, inherently unstable sonic frequencies" of racist, classist, sexist, homophobic, antitransgender, and antiqueer normativities (Jafa; Mackey, *Paracritical Hinge* 197). BLACK sound informs and deforms white institutions because it is "notoriously a critique of social reality, a critique of social arrangements in which, because of racism, one finds oneself deprived of community and kinship, cut off" (Mackey, *Discrepant Engagement* 234). This cutting off, this wound to community and kinship, is about life and personhood, and BLACK sound is "a form of social and epistemological dissent" (Mackey, *Discrepant Engagement* 9). This audible dissent, disruption, and decentering must transform the politics of social justice organizing and, subsequently, will be life affirming and will yield to the viability of multiple ways of existing in the world.

How can social justice organizations organize without marginalizing identities; concurrently, how can they tend to the blind spots that arise when intersectional identities are not taken into account? I believe BLACK music, with its rudimentary foundation in BLACK sound, gives a framework for organizing without institutionalization, structuring without strictures. Aurality of BLACK sound resists: moans, hollers, shrieks, cries, falsettos, melisma, modulations, inversions, choruses, repetitions, and improvisations and rhythms defy limitation, the strictures of subjectivity, structures of power, and demeaning discourses. This essay gestures toward a theory of social justice praxis based on BLACK aurality. Social justice organizations should be intentionally attentive to the aurality, in this case, of BLACK sound because this sound voices the problematics of institutionalization supposed and purported in seemingly race neutral spaces. BLACK sound creates "dark points of possibility" for insurgent action and for social justice activism that fully accounts for the intersectionalities white social justice organizations often occlude and that must be *heard* outside the bewildered gaze of white, gay normativity—that is, privilege and power that structures who is and is not visible and heard (Brooks 8).

PORTIONS OF "BRIEF NOTES AND GOODBYE OR CAN YOU BE BLACK AND WORK AT GLSEN?"

The simplistic analysis would render either a yes or no answer without nuance or depth of thought. I would answer the question by saying: "it depends," or, at the very least, gray areas abound. What I do know is that I couldn't be BLACK and work for the organization. What I mean, simply, is this: I was not allowed to bring my whole self, my full self, my BLACK self to work without fear of retribution or consequence. A shame, really. As a brief note, I will say that I speak only for myself in this writing. Any BLACK person or person of color (or ally of ours) working at GLSEN who feels that any of this brief note resonates closely with his or her experience, I stand in solidarity with you.

[. . .]

GLSEN touts that it is a social justice organization and that it has a nonoppressive work environment, yet the perpetual silencing of my thoughts, ideas and contestations—in the guise of GLSEN's purported needs for "unity," "diversity" and "multiculturalism"—created a work setting that was not conducive to mutuality, learning, openness, honesty, truth-telling or, ironically, social justice. Rather, my experience has dictated that GLSEN functions in ways that perpetuate institutional inequities, institutional racisms, institutional sexisms, hierarchies of oppressions. It is because I am a BLACK, queer-identified, male-gendered person that I was able to see, feel and hear the conflictual postures of GLSEN as an organization. (Others, undoubtedly, see it too from their vantage.) Outside the organization, GLSEN represents a beacon of hope for the ending of bullying and harassment in educational settings, giving educational professionals the tools necessary to combat those gross, erroneous wrongs against young people. Yet, what I saw, felt and heard within the organization saddens me: concerns of BLACK people are dismissed as inconsequential, noted as coming from an "angry" space, are thought as "too preachy" and are believed to conflict with the overall goals and mission of the organization.

"Intersectionality" and Occlusions

BLACK people are fetishized and tokenized both with the resources provided by the organization and with staff who try to dedicate themselves to the mission of GLSEN internally. Need examples? "Ashon, you have tunnel-vision with regard to race" [stated by my boss]. When I first joined GLSEN, I was most excited about the opportunity to work at an organization that joined the rigorous activist work of social justice with concerns for young people, pedagogical strategies and education. I wanted, in earnest, to use all that I had learned from a theoretical, academic viewpoint in the creation of curricula that challenged the multiple ways people are oppressed, the "intersectionality" of race, gender identity/expression, sexual orientation, class and ability. In October, 2007, I opened the No Name-Calling Week Resource Guide, read the lessons and was not surprised by the lack of analysis with regard to race; I was informed that many of the resources provided to educators needed to be reworked in order to take seriously the "intersectionality" we so often name (GLSEN, No Name-Calling).

I read Lesson 9, "What's in a name?," a lesson used to "increase students' awareness about the impact of names and slurs in their lives; encourage students to reflect on their own experiences with name-calling; provide students with a greater understanding of the derivation and usage of common slurs; challenge students to consider ways that they can reduce name-calling in their schools" (GLSEN, No Name-Calling 91–98). The slurs listed are: Faggot; Retard; Nigger; Bitch. After reading the entire lesson, I was very concerned with how BLACK people were represented in the final two readings. In both the Nigger and Bitch readings, BLACK people are named as the ones who perpetuate their harassment through those terms.

The Nigger reading, for example, does not ever use the words "racism" or "slavery" or anything castigatory about the group from which the word gained cache in the West: white people. "Nigger is a term rooted in hatred, used to belittle blacks and degrade African American culture" (GLSEN, No Name-Calling 96). No mention of racism there. No mention of white people. No mention of exploitation. I wonder if the description is even correct—that it is a term rooted in "hatred"—because it appears to me that "hatred" isn't possible in an in institutional climate that says BLACK people are non-human. BLACK people during enslavement (and today, even?) were (are?) the categorical definition of everything it meant to be human alterity. Simply, can one have "hatred" for non-being, non-human substance? The piece also states that "black comedians have been subject to criticism for playing on the N-word in their skits, yet they receive only a fraction of the criticism that whites receive when using the term in public," implying that whites should not ever be criticized for using the term because, well, black people do it too (GLSEN, No Name-Calling 96). The Nigger reading begins its final paragraph with this query: "But is there an intelligent way to use [the term]?" and closes by stating that it can only be stated intelligently "when used for academic purposes" (GLSEN, No Name-Calling 97). So, not only throughout the piece are BLACK people blamed for its perpetuation, we are also questioned about the limits of language and intelligence. BLACK people who are not in the academy, who are not scholarly, who are not learned cannot possibly understand the nuance of language usage and redeployment. Only those with access to a particular knowledge base can and should use terms like Nigger. This classist, racist assumption is appalling.

The Bitch reading, though shorter, doles out damage to BLACK people as well (GLSEN, No Name-Calling 98). It states that the continued usage of the term is because of hip hop and rappers like Missy Elliot.

My concern, beyond the offensive tethering of perpetual oppression to the group of people towards which the oppression was targeted, was with the audience for the resource guide. Simply, what are we teaching those who have access to capital, who attend suburban schools? Do these declarations instantiate dismissals of BLACK people because, as the lesson implies, we are our worst enemy?

[. . .]

After I began developing lessons based on a plan that would include BLACK, Latino/a, Asian/Asian-American people, I was told that the curriculum focused too much on race issues and that, instead, the curriculum should be much broader in scope and appeal. I was told that, for example, I could create a lesson plan for young people who have military parents that move from place to place. Though I fully understand that young people in this position often lack the ability to create long, healthy friendships because they often move and may have difficulty socially if a parent dies in combat, "military children" are not a historically oppressed group, from my estimation. It was this meeting that first introduced me to how notions of diversity and multiculturalism at GLSEN erased discourse of particularities, of how GLSEN names "intersectionality" as the work of intersectional analysis itself, rather than the actual doing of it in any way that is serious and rigorous.

After [these lessons were] put on hold, I began writing a lesson plan for the National Day of Silence 2008.[2] The reading I created for students was about silent protests and I specifically wrote about the sit-ins at the Woolworth counter in 1960 in North Carolina. I used the words, in the original iteration of the reading, "racism" and "racist" to describe the conditions under which BLACK people in NC were fighting but was told that the words "racism" and "racist" would "turn off" our potential audience. I guess there is something about truth that is off-putting to people. It is sad that an organization that asserts its dedication to diversity, multiculturalism and intersectionality cannot find within itself the ability to speak truth to power. Beyond naming Martin Luther King, Jr., and Bayard Rustin, we rarely delve into the topic, and if we do, it is an appendage to our work, not taken up as part of the overall mission of making schools safer for all students. I question, then, who is the all in "all"? It was in that meeting that I was told that I have tunnel-vision with regard to race issues and that GLSEN is an organization that focuses on "sexual orientation and gender identity/expression" and further, if I wanted to do what I am passionate about, which is clearly "race stuff," that there are many other organizations I could join to do just that.

I was also told that I write in a particular voice and that it was not the "GLSEN voice" and that everything needed to be in that "GLSEN voice." Questions loom. Who is this non-raced, non-gendered, non-classed "voice of GLSEN" and have I met him? To be sure, there is no way to avoid race, gender, class. My assumption, then, is that this "GLSEN voice" is that of whiteness, maleness (non-transgender, but of course) and is middle-classed.

[. . .]

But alas, work at GLSEN has truly been an endarkening experience;[3] I have learned much! Working here is the first time I experienced what I had theorized in academic papers and conversations: the imbrications of institutional racism, sexism, classism and anti-religious sentiments. I have seen, heard and felt the inequitable distributions of benefits, of oppressive silencing that arises from fear when dealing with manager/directors. This is not social justice. Rather, the notion that this is a social justice organization actually creates the blindspots through which many of us cannot see, in which many of us operate, of which many of us remain willfully and woefully unaware. (Crawley)

Though I have received communications from several staff members/colleagues that worked with me at the organization, at the time of this writing, there has been no official communication from the executive staff to me personally regarding "Brief Notes." There was a sluggish response from the executive staff to remaining staff members a month after my initial message, and one portion reads,

So the remaining question is why didn't [the executive staff] or the management team as a whole send out an all-staff email immediately. Given the number of times that particular question has been raised by different members of the staff, an all-staff response now seems important. Frankly, [the executive staff of GLSEN] thought that sending a general message about such important and serious issues on one's last day, 15 minutes before the end of the work day and then leaving, was not a professional, constructive or appropriate approach. We were further frustrated and confused that these very serious allegations were not raised in the various venues established to produce corrective action—such as the DWG, workplace grievance processes (internal or external via ADP) and Ethics Point. And responding to the email in kind, to all staff, could be seen as validating or reinforcing that approach. All of us on the management team are committed to providing a healthy and productive work climate, and we care about all of you as colleagues, so we want to move past this specific issue to the core important questions for all of us on staff. Bottom line—I and all of my management team colleagues take the allegation that GLSEN is a racist organization extremely seriously. And that is entirely a separate issue from any written response to one email. It is crucial that we work together to strengthen existing avenues for addressing this kind of extremely serious issue, in order to eliminate barriers that thwart effective communication and the full partici-pation of any member of our staff community in our collective work.[4]

The message sent from the executive staff to the remaining staff members points to how institutionalization and organizing limits the ways one is supposed to respond to grievances. Because my response—an email on the last day—diverged too much from the norm, it was read as unprofessional and inappropriate. Their message implies that there is a norm toward which we all aspire—respectability—and that I was behaving by a lesser standard; I was BLACK as hell at that moment. Notwithstanding the fact that I raised my issues through many of those channels, the overarching theme from the executive staff was that issues raised because they were done in a purportedly inappropriate manner, undercut the charac-ter and integrity of the sender and, as such, could be dismissed rather easily. It was only after staff members continually asked the same question, "Why is there no response?," that administrators felt compelled to respond en masse. The ruminations of an angry BLACK man certainly were not enough. The organiza-tion "temporarily position[ed]" and indict[ed] my particular brand of dissent as unprofessional and inappropriate (Alexander 75). Because my dissent was "frustrate[ing]," it was read as a terrorizing act, a terrible moment and a threat for the overall goals of the organization (Alexander 75).

"Brief Notes" was improvised, written in about twenty minutes and sent three days later, on my last day of work. I sent it after standard congratulatory moments when I was thanked for my work by several members of the staff. I was also given a $50 gift card to Borders Books and Music and, I suppose, I should have been happy and content. Because things seemed to be ending on such a high note and with a sentiment of rapport, "Brief Notes" was unexpected (to its audience), to say the least. I had stated concerns I detailed in my letter to managers, in the Diversity Working Group's monthly meetings and in my exit interview. No one should have been surprised, yet the executive staff acted aloof and put-off by my show of unprofessionalism, sending such a terse message on my last day. It wasn't fair! The nerve! Anger, of course, ensued.

"Brief Notes" is BLACK musicality, a constant refrain, a familiar chorus for many people of color that work at that organization and many others like it. It is BLACK aurality: dissent and ascent function as call and response, pas-sionate response to impassioned utterance. As BLACK sound, the unexpected, unprofessional, inappropriate response to a racist call "seemed structureless and incoherent" and was "put down as unmelodic" (Mackey, *Discrepant Engagement* 38). The overarching goal for the letter was to give concrete examples of how the very notion of social justice that does not seriously wrestle with intersectionality is problematic. I wanted to improvise the standard "good-bye letter" with their nor-mally saccharine, false, and lied thank-yous; I wanted it to scream BLACKness, for the text to perform a caesura. The letter also intimates that "cultural diversity *is* cultural" meaning "it is a consequence of actions and assumptions that are socially—rather than naturally, genetically—instituted and reinforced" (Mackey, *Discrepant Engagement* 265). M. Jacqui Alexander's text, *Pedagogies of Crossing*, was very useful in my meditation before writing "Brief Notes." She elucidates:

"Allegiance to multiculturalism usually takes a form that evades an analysis of power, cathecting all difference onto the bodies of people of color in a way that avoids developing a commitment to antiracist practices" (Alexander 113). What happens when culturally situated notions and assumptions (e.g., respectability, professionalism, race, class) prevail or go unchallenged? If we do not interrogate, for example, the idea of BLACK criminality, how does this concept find its way into organizing efforts that append BLACK people into their organizational efforts? Are BLACK people working in these organizations "function[ing] as players" or have we "affected other aspects" of organizing (Jafa)? How and why are we expected to "fall in line" with parascribed (i.e., preprescribed) futurities and how does this go against social justice for *all*?

It appears that the organization, and others like it, long for coherence with a system already predetermined. Queer activist organizing at GLSEN seemed to function similarly. Speaking about queer theorists, but quite applicable to (white) queer activists and organizations, Omise'eke Natasha Tinsley says, "theorists have a tendency to wait (figuratively) for queers of color to arrive . . . in the hopes that they will join the sexuality-centered signifying games already set up . . . in the hopes they will take up theories . . . and rework them through race, for example" (Tinsley 206). Though the scholarship of queers of color such as E. Patrick Johnson, Gayatri Gopinath, Jose Muñoz, and M. Jacqui Alexander are welcome additions to queers of color critiques, it appears that Tinsley's assertion that non–people of color queer theorists pause with regard to rigorous intersectional analysis is well founded and documented by these queer of color theorists.

This pause, this caesura, and this waiting was my experience at GLSEN. This particular caesura in some cases and denial in others of a queer of color critique in places like GLSEN denies BLACK musicality, it denies BLACKness, it denies resistance and improvisation. Rather than accounting for how the control mechanisms set in place at GLSEN did not yield fully to the "discovery" of ongoing racisms at the organization—so much so that I had to respond in a seemingly unprofessional manner and felt so marginalized that I had to speak in a way that appeared excessive and certainly unwanted by the organization—the naming of professionalism and appropriateness washes the organization's hands clean of the tenor, tone, and texture of the message.

PURSUANCE

The "heart-rending shrieks" of Frederick Douglass's Aunt Hester physically and metaphorically awakened him—physically by piercing his ears, metaphorically by his knowledge of enslavement taking place at that moment (Douglass and Blight 42). Douglass notes that the sounds of the enslaved had the ability to "impress some minds with the horrible character of slavery;" that "they were tones loud, long, and deep" and that these tones were "a testimony against slavery" (Douglass and Blight 47). There is an implicit musicality in BLACK cultural productions that Douglass ingeniously anticipates: an epistemology of BLACK aurality. This sound both witnesses and witnesses against injustice, continually comments on and critiques the present state of the world, and optimistically hopes for a different world anew. Or, as Nathaniel Mackey aptly puts it, "Like the moan or the shout . . . the falsetto explores a redemptive, unworded realm . . . where the implied critique or the momentary eclipse of the word curiously rescues, restores and renews it: new word, new world" (*Bedouin Hornbook* 42).

Activist organizing can benefit from the framework with BLACK aurality, especially "the site of improvisation" at its core (Moten 179). That is, organizing efforts need to be open to multiple interpretations from racialized subjects and must constantly attend to how the work they do instantiates injustice with their normativizing impulses. They must allow for improvisation—that is, contend with the unrehearsed narratives and rigorously engaging disagreements rather than occluding dissention for the cause of "unity." From working with a "social justice organization" that is funded by and has an executive staff predominantly lacking people of color, the discussions of race and racism were surface-level, lacking depth, and shallow, lacking critical reflection and intervention. Internal staffing tensions, disagreements, and disparities of any organization can affect how it engages external communities—and this was my experience with GLSEN.

More, organizations of this kind use figures like Martin Luther King Jr. and Bayard Rustin because of their extraordinariness and assert that the modern-day fight for civil rights of gays and lesbians is an extension of and engagement with the BLACK civil rights movement in the United States, without heeding their misappropriations of these persons or moments. Though there are indeed parallels that can (and should) be drawn, what nags is how the insouciant, glib linkage disavows how modern-day LGBTQ arguments for "civil rights" are racist and classist at the core by erasing "black inventiveness" by way of "white appropriation" and is done "with condescending, romantic-racist, appropriative attitudes that have done nothing to radically change the [organization's] founding racial assumptions" (Mackey, *Discrepant Engagement* 8, 266). Moreover, as they are also cultural, these institutions find "a cultural use of marginal identities to imagine a new kind of community" without realizing their instantiation of marginality of those very identities by way of misappropriation, glib dismissal, and disdain (Roach 17). These white queer folks imagine themselves as *the* extension of the BLACK civil rights movement through "surrogacy," fitting themselves "[i]nto the cavities created by loss through death or other forms of departure" of figures like King and Rustin, imagining a "collective memory [that] works selectively, imaginatively, and often perversely" (Roach 2).

Perverse, indeed. These organizations reproduce and reimage people of color through fetishistic and voyeuristic imaginings. Thus this essay is not a fanciful engagement of in-vogue theories or a set of obfuscatory locutions written to wow the reader. Rather, this essay is about personhood and the varied ways BLACK people must insert our voices into institutions and systems that only can *hear* us insofar as we *cohere* with their parascribed normative narratives. This essay is very much an engagement of spirit and is theoethically concerned. That I had to assert my personhood by way of an email—an email that stated bluntly that I could not be fully human and that there were limits to what I was allowed to say—is a testament to how "theorizing . . . becomes an existential necessity" (Alexander 106).

PSALM

Sweet Jesus, sweet Jesus
He's the lily of the valley, the bright and morning star
Sweet Jesus, sweet Jesus
He's the god of every nation bless his name
How I love him, how I love him . . .[5]

This song, for me, bears in it the trace of homophobia rooted in religious, Christian rhetoric. I was called a faggot as I sang about sweet Jesus during a choir rehearsal when I was but ten years old. The song is tethered to that moment, that naming of faggot—a literal call, with damaged personhood, the impassioned response. This call and response was "an encounter, the mutual, negative positioning" of the flawed logic of Christian community where I was in that world but not of it (Moten 21). Additionally, this encounter "is appositional [and] is shaped by a step away that calls such positions radically into question;" this encounter, intriguingly, allowed for an acceptance for and love of myself as a queer individual, faggotry, and all (Moten 21).

Still, I cannot sing the song without a feeling overwhelming me almost to the point of tears as that moment, etched in times past, has that sound connected to it that I feel deep in my body, in my stomach, in my bones. That sound is the irreducible materiality that animates how I move through the world and, consequently, renders visible my existence as a musician, singer, songwriter, preacher, activist, scholar, son, friend, and lover. I am forever in relation to that phonic materiality and that materiality must be redeployed to critique injustice. Joining a queer community that dismisses its own members by way of racism is similarly unjust. Giving attention to sonic materiality to animate social justice activist organizing can account for the ocular centrism—that is, the over- and underlooking—of particular identities at the behest of others. The activist organizing I argue for "attends to the participatory nature of music—the way it makes listeners respond through singing and dancing" in such a way that this organizing is never closed but is always open to interpretation, improvisation, and use of BLACK sacred sound in such a way that makes both callers and responders "speak back" and also "recognize their responses as part" of the organizational efforts (Obadike).

Queer activist organizing that takes seriously the intersectionality of race, gender, class, sexual orientation, ability, and religious expression is necessary and the scene I recount in this section speaks across these various identities. GLSEN's mission that aspires toward training educational professionals in order to make all students in K–12 schools feel safer and accepted members of their respective communities, when rigorously wresting with the intersectionality beyond its mere naming as important, would prove effective in curbing situations like this from occurring in the future. The work of intersectional analysis requires attention to diverse registers of knowledge and I believe hearing BLACK aurality, not simply as noise, taunt, or complaint but as an episteme, gestures toward this important process. I did not feel safe at home, at school, or at church. My feeling of safety and acceptance was not simply relegated to how I related to my classmates. Indeed, my feelings of being misplaced and mishandled followed me from place to place. That is, my intersectionality was affected, not just my "religious" sense of self or my "racial" sense of self. Queer activist organizing must follow this trajectory of intersectionality and be responsible to them all.

WORKS CITED

Alexander, M. Jacqui. *Pedagogies of Crossing: Meditations on Feminism, Sexual Politics, Memory, and the Sacred Perverse Modernities*. Durham: Duke UP, 2005.

Brody, Jennifer. "The Blackness of Blackness . . . Reading the Typography of *Invisible Man*." *Theater Journal* 57 (2005): 679–98.

Brooks, Daphne. *Bodies in Dissent: Spectacular Performances of Race and Freedom, 1850–1910*. Durham: Duke UP, 2006.

COGIC, West Angeles. *Little Saints Celebration Medley: Kum Ba Yah/Sweet Jesus/Joy Bells/Ye*. Sparrow, 1990.

Crawley, Ashon. "Brief Notes and Goodbye or Can You Be Black and Work at GLSEN?" Email correspondence. 2008.

Douglass, Frederick, and David W. Blight. *Narrative of the Life of Frederick Douglass, an American Slave*. Boston: Bedford/St. Martin's, 1993.

GLSEN. *No Name-Calling Week Resource Guide*. New York: GLSEN, 2001.

———. "2003–2008." *GLSEN*. 2009. Gay, Lesbian, and Straight Education Network. 1 January 2009 http://www.glsen.org/cgi-bin/iowa/all/about/history/index.html.

Jafa, Arthur. "69." *Black Cultural Studies*.1992. Black Cultural Studies. 21 Sept. 2008 http://www.blackculturalstudies.org/a_jafa/69.html.

Kates, Nancy, Bennett Singer, Independent Television Service, National Black Programming Consortium, and California Newsreel. *Brother Outsider: The Life of Bayard Rustin*. California Newsreel, 2002.

National Day of Silence. 2012. http://www.dayofsilence.org.

Mackey, Nathaniel. *Bedouin Hornbook*. Callaloo Fiction Series. 2. Charlottesville: UP of Virginia, 1986.

———. *Discrepant Engagement: Dissonance, Cross-Culturality, and Experimental Writing*. Cambridge Studies in American Literature and Culture. 71. Cambridge: Cambridge UP, 1993.

———. *Paracritical Hinge: Essays, Talks, Notes, Interviews*. Contemporary North American Poetry. Madison: U of Wisconsin P, 2005.

Moten, Fred. *In the Break: The Aesthetics of the Black Radical Tradition*. Minneapolis: U of Minnesota P, 2003.

Obadike, Mendi. *Music*. Westport: Greenwood Press, 2003. 22 September 2008 http://www.blacknetart.com/morrison.html.

Roach, Joseph R. *Cities of the Dead: Circum-Atlantic Performance*. New York: Columbia UP, 1996.

Tinsley, Omise'eke Natasha. "Black Atlantic, Queer Atlantic: Queer Imaginings of the Middle Passage." *GLQ* 14.2–3 (2008): 191–215.

NOTES

1. The use of poetics in this section is to hallucinate the aurality toward which my theorizing aspires. This piece not only should be read graphically but should be heard and should be read aloud. This is consistent with my own theorization that there are different

registers of knowledge, various ways to learn. Some are more attune to the visual while others are more attune to the aural.

2. For more information about the National Day of Silence, please visit the website http://www.dayofsilence.org. Generally, "the National Day of Silence brings attention to anti-LGBT name-calling, bullying and harassment in schools" and "is a student-led day of action when concerned students, from middle school to college, take some form of a vow of silence to bring attention to the name-calling, bullying and harassment—in effect, the silencing—experienced by LGBT students and their allies" (National Day of Silence).

3. "Endarkening" is a term I first heard used by a mentor, Dr. Alton Pollard, which explores the richness of BLACKness and the learning of knowledge as endarkening rather than en*light*ening.

4. This is part of an email sent to all-staff a month after I sent "Brief Notes." I choose, intentionally, not to "cite" this message because I do not want to indict the colleague who sent the message to me. The colleague still works for the organization and has a position to maintain there, whereas I do not. As I do not want to put my colleague's position in jeopardy, I find it inappropriate to "cite" the day and time this message was sent as well as the sender.

5. This is a traditional hymn. For a sample recording see COGIC, West Angeles.

CHAPTER 11

FEMINIZING LESBIANS, DE-GENDERING TRANSGENDER MEN

A MODEL FOR BUILDING LESBIAN FEMINIST THINKERS AND LEADERS IN AFRICA?

ZETHU MATEBENI

INTRODUCTION

IN FEBRUARY 2008, THE COALITION OF AFRICAN Lesbians (CAL) hosted the third Leadership Institute on *Building Lesbian Feminist Thinkers and Leaders for the 21st Century: Feminist Response to Patriarchy and Homophobia in Africa*. LAMBDA, the Mozambiquan Association for Sexual Minority Rights, and member of CAL, the Coalition of African Lesbians, facilitated the logistics for hosting the institute in Maputo, Mozambique. The institute attracted more than sixty delegates from all regions in the African continent, with the majority from South Africa. CAL, a network of organizations, is the first African body that seeks to be "the voice and face" of African lesbian, bisexual, and transgender women. The leadership institute is one of the ways in which CAL aims to "build the capacity of African lesbians and organisations." CAL does this through utilizing "African radical feminist analysis in all spheres of life" (Coalition of African Lesbians 2006).

Participants were invited through various organizations across Africa that are affiliated with the coalition or are part of the broader LGBTI (lesbian, gay, bisexual, transgender, and intersex) sector. While the institute remained specific to lesbian and feminist participants, various individuals and/or groups who did not identify as lesbian or feminist were present. Included in the groups were transgender men, commercial sex workers, and bisexual women.

The location of the institute, Maputo, was selected for political reasons. Mozambique, a neighboring country to South Africa, is one of the many African countries where homosexuality is illegal. The September 16, 1886, penal code's articles 70 and 71 impose security measures on "people who habitually practice acts against the order of nature" and is still in existence. The penal code criminalizes both male/male and female/female sex. CAL and LAMBDA's move to host the institute in Maputo was to create lesbian presence and visibility.

Given the diversity of the participants, the institute proceeded in English, French, and Portuguese, three of the many languages spoken on the continent. The hotel reception and halls were full of large posters and banners of the institute and its content. It was impossible for any patron of the hotel to miss the aim of this gathering. The institute kicked off with a reflection and dialogue on the Charter of Feminist Principles for African Feminists, a product of the first African Feminist Forum (AFF) held in Accra, Ghana, in November 2006. The AFF, which meets every two years, brings together African feminist activists to deliberate on key issues critical to the women's movement. The charter, which the AFF (African Feminist Forum 2008) presents as a "mobilisation tool and instrument to review feminist organising at different levels and in different locations," sets out a set of codes of conduct / ethical guidelines for individuals, organizations, collectives and institutions. These conduct codes can be used for monitoring institutional development as well as peer review with other feminists.

For many at the Maputo institute, this charter was new, which meant that the discussion was not an easy one to follow. Participants seemed unaware of the charter and silence loomed when it was time to interrogate and move toward its adoption. There was a strong disjuncture between the participants present at the institute and the people to whom the charter speaks. The charter does not foreground women's diverse sexual orientations and gender identities, while CAL puts lesbian women at the forefront, and to some extent bisexual women and transgender women. Both are silent about transgender men.

While I had not attended the African Feminist Forum in Accra, Ghana, in November 2006, which laid the foundation of the adoption of this charter, attending the Maputo institute reminded me of a newspaper article emanating from the Accra conference. Like the Maputo institute, this conference attracted participants from all parts of the continent. The day after the conference ended, *The Heritage*, a newspaper in Ghana, had as its headlines and front-page article "After Blockade of Gay Conference LESBIANS MEET IN ACCRA. They Meet as NGO for Women's Empowerment" (Karimatu 2006). Outside the journalist's description of the conference as an "abominable meeting," it is unclear what the conference content is. The author continues to give a description of the participants in the conference. Of the eighty participants, lesbian women from South Africa are singled out and described as "beautiful and ugly, tall and short" and come from a country where they claim their rights are violated. The author's reference and portrayal of lesbians can only be understood as sensationalist. In the entire article, there is no mention or reference to feminism, feminists, or the actual focus of the conference. The silence of the participants in the Maputo institute compels me to wonder about the position and relevance of such feminism in the diverse African context, both visible and absent in the room with sixty participants.

In the next few pages, I wish to engage with the model of "building lesbian feminist thinkers and leaders in Africa" deployed at the Maputo institute and the numerous questions, many of which have been contextualized and problematized by various African feminists, which it evokes. This is not an attempt to engage or even pretend to engage with African feminism as a discourse but rather a reflection and an engagement with a process and model, taking place within this framework. What emanates from such a model is that feminisms are being negotiated in Africa, and it seems to still be exclusionary in its conception and practice.

LESBIAN FEMINISM IN THE AFRICAN CONTEXT: A MODEL FOR REVISION?

The Charter of Feminist Principles for African Feminists starts by naming and defining feminists. According to the charter, those who name themselves feminist are engaged in the deeply political fight for women's rights. The naming recognizes the diversity of those who call themselves African feminists, "We have multiple and varied identities as African Feminists. We are African women—we live here in Africa and even when we live elsewhere, our focus is on the lives of African women on the continent. Our feminist identity is not qualified with 'Ifs,' 'Buts,' or 'However.' We are Feminists. Full stop." This was the first contention in the meeting. Participants were unhappy about the rigidity this conceptualization of a feminist identity proposed. Some participants were concerned that an adoption of feminism intimates abandoning other identity categories or that a feminist identity (or rather an attachment to feminist ideology) was more valued than other identity categories. "Ifs," "buts," or "however" was translated to mean that one is only feminist to the exclusion of all other identities, and this identity has to stand alone. One participant articulated, "I agree with some of the principles of feminism, BUT from what I've seen with regards to feminists, I do not want to call myself that." This participant's sentiments were not isolated. While many women in Africa carry out a broad feminist agenda, many eschew the label "feminist" for different reasons (Frenkel 2008). Some suggest that those reasons might include: feminism, as a named category, lacks significance for many; how it represents a foreign concept; and for some, how it enacts exclusions (Reddy 2004). We cannot dismiss that the word itself, as well as the discourse and practice that constitute feminism, are deeply political.

The discussion on the charter continued with definitions of feminism and patriarchy. This section of the statement was subject to much scrutiny. A number of participants were not familiar with the language in this discussion and especially the term "patriarchy" (all were second- or third-language speakers in English, Portuguese, and French) and could not understand why they had to spend their time and energies "dismantling patriarchy" when they could "barely survive." Many of the participants were black women and transgender men from low socioeconomic backgrounds. A majority of them have been volunteering in their country's organizations for a number of years, sometimes even without stipends. Many narrated stories of lack of funds for transport from their homes to their organizations. Some could not afford to buy food, clothes, or take care of their families. Everyone had received a grant to travel from their country to Mozambique and accommodation had been paid for by CAL. However, many people struggled to pay additional airport taxes as CAL was unable to offer stipends. There was a general sense that participants struggled to "make ends meet" due to economic and political situations in both their organizations and wider countries. A facilitator, a director of a black lesbian (feminist) organization in Johannesburg, South Africa, was tasked with "breaking down patriarchy." She did this with a useful exercise and lesson on power. By the end of her session, many were keen to identify as feminists and with the fight against patriarchy. Within the same discussion, a voice from the transgender men's group could not be ignored. He argued that the underlying theme of this form of feminism—heavily debated, but not resolved—is that it places "women" at the center of its fight and agenda. The charter is clear in its feminist mandate and regulates spaces, which are "created to empower and uplift women." It further prescribes that "women's organisations and networks should be led and managed by women. It is a contradiction of feminist leadership principles to have men leading, managing and being spokespersons for women's organisation." The contentions here were strong and obvious. Transgender men were sidelined and strongly rejected, as they were not only "men" but also part of the system being dismantled. Furthermore, while many are both part of and leading organizations, this statement seemed to challenge their positions. Other voices present (for example sex workers and lesbians who did not identify with feminism) were not heard during this discussion. The charter does not single them out, but is also silent about them, with the exception of an interpretation of the clause on freedom of choice and autonomy.

Much has been written about the contours of a United States based "women-only" feminist movement and how antimale sentiments alienated many poor and working-class women. Such movements were criticized for suggesting that all men belong to one category and all "share equally in all forms of male privilege" (hooks 1984). Transgender men as well as lesbians who presented forms of masculinity at this institute articulated abusive experiences they encountered in society, including within lesbian circles as well as in their relationships. They related stories of how their partners coerce and force them to portray a particular type of masculinity within relationships; how the lesbian movement has used them to push a particular agenda focusing only on lesbian women, excluding transgender issues. Many claimed to be resisting this coercion and hegemonic masculinity for a different way of being men and transforming or creating masculinities that are sensitive to what it means to be women (as they themselves are former women).

The discussions accomplished a few tasks, one focused on defining the boundaries of who is feminist: she is African; she lives/works/comes from Africa; she is not male. The latter continues to still be contentious. It was agreed that CAL and its affiliates are inclusive of transgender people while the charter isn't. Adoption of the charter implied, although not stated, adopting the principles that exclude transgender individuals.

While such "universal simplicity" was useful for many, we are working against producing a type of feminism, like that from the West, that has been problematized by those inside and outside its borders. It is dangerous to say that all feminisms are homogenous. Feminisms are diverse and it is "incorrect to assume discourses of feminism that constitute 'Africa' adequately represent theory, practice and experiences of those who constitute themselves African" (Reddy 2004). While the institute attempted to break down the two concepts, it clearly failed to interrogate the category "lesbian" in the African context. In its failure to define, there was an unarticulated rejection of lesbians whose behaviors and sexual styles do not conform to the feminist agenda and the "ideal" woman: specifically butch-femme lesbians, masculine women, as well as female-to-male persons. This rejection was perpetuated by the assumption that butch-femme couples, masculine women, and female-to-male persons are oppressive and represent patriarchy. Generally, masculine women were frowned upon, especially when they were in a relationship with feminine women. While seeking to liberate all women (reliant on the assumption that all women are the same and that there is an essential female identity), lesbian feminism has oppressed those lesbian women seeking to be different. This resonates with lesbian-feminist movements in other parts of the world, which have disregarded class, race, sexuality, and gender differences, as well as the different cultures experienced by women (Calhoun 1995).

Participating in this institute surprisingly revealed to me that even within (certain) lesbian circles, there are hegemonic generalizations and essentialisms that assume a particular interpretation of the category "lesbian" and the category "woman." Such generalizations efface the problems, perspectives, and political concerns of women marginalized because of their class, gender, race, religion, ethnicity, and sexual orientation. This model raised two pertinent questions in relation to feminism in Africa. Only partly answered, they did injustice to the lives of many African women whose identities are multiple and constantly in flux. Who is this lesbian subject that such an institute relies on? What is the kind of intervention that such an institute promotes? The lesbian subject that such a model intimates is one who cannot accommodate a multilayered experience, a subject whose identity is rigid and frozen, to be thawed by exposure to a particular feminist ideology. This is clearly in contradiction to the narratives of many of the participants present at this institute and to the lives of the diversity of African women. The institute was not keen to discuss the classed and racialized experiences, which both create distance and in many ways divide women. Rarely can such difference be transcended (hooks 1984). I had hoped that this intervention could dismantle such differences and offer new ways in which feminism can work for many in Africa.

CONCLUSION

While the organizers and many participants at the Maputo leadership institute were impressed with the outcomes of the experience, there were a number of shortfalls, mainly articulated during the tea breaks and in the evaluation forms. The institute attempted to cover a great deal, which is indicative of the diversity of women and women's experiences in Africa. A clear take-away from the gathering is that the notion of feminism is still both problematic and contentious. It may require more than a week's training to build lesbian feminist thinkers and leaders. There is certainly a strong move toward feminism, with its form, shape, and practice still under construction. The model deployed there claimed lesbian and/or feminist identity to be hermetically sealed, while in reality, they are heavily contextual, diverse, and fluid.

Similarly, the Forum for the Empowerment of Women (FEW), a black lesbian organization based in Johannesburg, has been struggling with the version of feminism that it has recently deployed. FEW was started in 2003 by a group of black lesbians who were concerned about issues affecting black lesbians in South Africa. The organization was then formed with programs and campaigns to increase visibility, provide safe spaces, as well as address violence targeted at black lesbians. The organization was well known for its "Rose Has Thorns Campaign," which was crucial in addressing all the issues the organization was concerned about. In 2006, under new leadership, the organization changed its focus and deployed a feminist ideology. The organization framed itself as a feminist and activist organization focusing on building activism and raising consciousness among black lesbians (Forum for the Empowerment of Women [FEW] 2009). The campaign that the organization had established was soon replaced by a leadership program and a campaign focusing on violence toward all women. In framing itself feminist, the organization included in its constituency lesbian, bisexual, and transgender women. However, as the chairperson of FEW states "the programs that the organisation develops are targeted only at lesbian women. They are not targeted at bisexual and transgender women, but the latter are not excluded from the organisation" (Pereira 2009).

The chairperson of the organization argues that there is a disjuncture between what resides in the governance of FEW and the organization's constituency. It appears that what the organization wants to achieve through feminism is not in line with what black lesbians need. The version of feminism existing within the work of FEW can be perceived as developmental because it focuses on building consciousness and leadership among black lesbians. The organization also sees its role as transforming black lesbians from being nonactivist, uninformed, and apolitical to being an informed, politically conscious, and activist constituency. One criticism that the chairperson lashes out on this model of feminism is that it is heavily reliant on deconstructing power within a heteronormative framework. Furthermore, it neglects speaking about lesbian identity as a whole and in relation to power (Pereira 2009). Once again, even under this model of feminism that is aimed at addressing lesbian women's interests, the identity lesbian disappears and transgender experiences fall out. FEW, like the Maputo institute, may need to revisit their stance on feminism and their approach to lesbian and transgender experiences.

Clearly, organizations in Africa are faced with the challenge to search for better ways of making lesbian feminism and feminism in general more easily accessible and relevant to the lives of women (and transgender men) in Africa, whose daily experiences are those of marginalized persons. This goes beyond counting distribution of T-shirts printed "feminist" and having large numbers of participants at conferences and such institutes. If such interventions continue without a thorough reading of the context, then they would even miss the telling sentiments of many participants of such meetings: "We're not feminists, but we'll take the free T-shirts!"

REFERENCES

African Feminist Forum. 2008. "Concept Note." Accessed January 9, 2009. http://www
.africanfeministforum.org/v3/files/AFF%20Concept%20Note-2008.pdf.

Calhoun, Cheshire. 1995. "The Gender Closet: Lesbian Disappearance under the Sign
'Women.'" *Feminist Studies* 21 (1):7–34.

Coalition of African Lesbians. 2006. "Constitution of the Coalition of African Lesbians."
Johannesburg, South Africa: CAL.

Forum for the Empowerment of Women. 2009. "Interview with Dawn Cavanagh by Mpumi
Mathabela." Last modified January 27. http://www.few.org.za.

Frenkel, Ronit. 2008. "Feminism and Contemporary Culture in South Africa." *African Studies*
67: 1–10.

hooks, bell. 1984. *Feminist Theory from Margin to Centre*. Boston: South End.

Karimatu, Ana. 2006. "After Blockade of Gay Conference Lesbians Meet in ACCRA." *The
Heritage* 20 (4).

Pereira, Bronwynne. 2009. Personal interview with chairperson of FEW. January 30.
Johannesburg.

Reddy, Vasu. 2004. "Sexuality in Africa: Some Trends, Transgressions and Tirades." *Agenda*
62: 3–9.

CHAPTER 12

BLACK FEMALE SEXUAL IDENTITY

THE SELF-DEFINED

ANNECKA MARSHALL AND
DONNA-MARIA MAYNARD

IN 2008, A SURVEY WAS CONDUCTED TO gauge Barbadian and Jamaican women's views about the manner in which their sexuality is perceived by Caribbean society. The survey also helped gauge the extent that the lives and sexual identity of black Caribbean women have been influenced by historical sexual stereotypes and to identify alternative images of Caribbean women's sexualities.

The notion of black women as immoral, lascivious, and diseased has been used to legitimize their subordination since the sixteenth century. The historical depiction of sexually aggressive breeders has contributed to contemporary images of Caribbean womanhood. During slavery, portrayals of African women as hypersexual and licentious were used to justify oppression. The belief that Africans were animalistic, with uncontrollable sexual appetites, served to legitimate the exploitation of their labor and their abuse by white men.[1]

The portrayal of black women as prostitutes was long used to gratify the sexual and economic needs of white male slave owners.[2] Exotic mythology of promiscuity continues to be articulated in contemporary Caribbean society in exploitative sex tourism whereby Western tourists assert racial and sexual privilege. Black women are sexually denigrated by notions of inferiority and corruption.[3] Patricia Mohammed criticizes the rigid ordering of Caribbean societies whereby women are defined as seductive temptresses who need to be controlled by men. Mohammed states that although female sexuality is regulated by religion, popular culture, and language to satisfy male pleasure, women are negotiating their sexual needs.[4]

M. C. Holmes describes black female sexuality as historically being a "site of contestation," resulting from "centuries of slavery exploitation, force, and victimization."[5] Hence contradictory stereotypes of black women as either hypersexual and promiscuous or asexual "Mammy" types exist. The literature suggests that there is a relationship between stereotypes, the social construct and the sexual self-concept, and the psychological construct in men and women. A number of published studies have investigated sexual identity in nonblack North American samples using quantitative methodology to decipher which specific characteristics men and women perceive their sexual self-concept as being composed of. Glynis Breakwell and Lynne Millward employ the term "sexual self-concept" to describe those aspects of sexuality that individuals endorse as descriptive of the self. They identify some central dimensions of sexual self-concepts, including the degree to which one is romantic, passive, willing to experiment, ignorant about eroticism, responsible for contraception, likely to exploit, and faithful. They argue that the structure of the sexual self-concept is significantly influenced by dominant social representations of gender differences and relationships. Additionally, L. T. Garcia and D. Carrigan look at sexual self-knowledge and find that the differences between men and women reflect prevalent gender stereotypes. They suggest that women and men internalize conventional social expectations in their views of self. Elsewhere, Garcia investigates men's and women's sexual self-view and finds that they reflect traditional beliefs about men and women.[6]

Caribbean feminist studies on women's sexual identities challenge Western myths by focusing on the ways that gender, class, race, and ethnic inequalities influence erotic agency. Such research emphasizes that heterosexual women reassert control of their sexual meanings and expressions within the context of cultural expectations about chastity and purity that attempt to subvert the hypersexual stereotype. It demonstrates that Caribbean female sexuality is socially dominated by men's sexual desires, but, as our study confirms, it is also autonomous and fluid. Caribbean women's sexualities are generally characterized by serial monogamy, fidelity to men, procreation, and financial requirements. Lesbophobia and diverse sexual realities that transgress heterosexual intimacy are underresearched areas that our research addresses.[7]

Previous research recognizes that stereotypes coupled with one's past experiences influence one's current sexual identity to some extent. Hence we decided not to impose the components of sexual self-concept that have arisen from North American nonblack samples on to Caribbean women, in a quantitative study. Instead, we used a qualitative methodology that would be sensitive to the fact that sexual identity is influenced by history, politics, and society. The present investigation explores how sexual self-conceptualizations are cast against historically situated stereotypes of black Caribbean women, accessing their sexual identities from their perspective.

A qualitative methodology of questionnaires with open-ended questions was employed with the intention of capturing whether Caribbean women have incorporated or redefined stereotypes of hypersexuality that existed since slavery. The questionnaires were completed by 153 female university students ranging in age from 19 to 55. Of these, 101 women were in Jamaica, and 52 were in Barbados. Most defined themselves as black (143) and heterosexual (146). The data were analyzed using content analysis of the themes that arose from them, which indicated that Barbadian and Jamaican women believe that the general view of female sexuality in society is one of heterosexual promiscuity. Most of the women surveyed claimed that they felt happy, comfortable, and secure about their sexual self-concepts and experiences. Some are proud, ecstatic, and elated by their great sex lives. Only eight respondents mentioned indifference or worry about their sexual self. In general, the findings demonstrate that Jamaican and Barbadian women assert liberating self-perceptions and partnerships in the sexual arena, despite prevailing stereotypes.

THE SEXUAL MYTHS LIVE ON

It is evident from the majority of the respondents that the stereotypes of hyper-sexuality exist. However, young women do appear to be creating their own definitions of sexuality as a reaction to the stereotypical images of black women that are portrayed in popular culture.

Participants explain that Caribbean women are resisting and redefining derogatory myths that have existed since slavery. Women are expected to be monogamous, docile, sexually restrained, and modest. Female sexuality is viewed as changing in positive ways as a reflection of the increase of women in leadership roles in Jamaican society and throughout the Caribbean. The participants believe that women are increasingly strong-minded, demanding, and in control of their sexual realities. They argue that independent and liberated women are competently exploring the freedom of choice to say and get what they want but that men feel threatened by this. They believe that women who do not value themselves allow men to dominate them.

However, women are still affected by myths that portray them as sexual objects, desirable, wild, sensuous, promiscuous, prostitutes, and sexual-reproductive machines whose goal is to satisfy men's desires. Respondents state, "I think the general view of female sexuality in the Jamaican society centres around the female being submissive to the male. There is the notion that females need to 'please their men' and so as to achieve this they must go to any length achievable to give satisfaction. People's views about female sexuality aren't changing in Barbados. Women are still seen as submissive sex slaves and sex symbols." Participants consider the ways that social and religious attitudes influence women's self-perceptions and choice of sexual partners. Most participants argue that they resist hypersexual stereotypes through chastity, fidelity, and celibacy. Rearticulating sexual myths, they create their own self-definitions. These respondents rebel by not conforming to dominant societal opinions. Instead, they choose moral, responsible, and sensitive men who treat, respect, and understand them as equals. An inherent alternative interpretation of these findings is that the women are still controlled by those stereotypes, especially if they in fact desire to be sexual but are consciously deciding not to be.

Carol Vance asserts that sexuality is an ambiguous and complex set of power relations.[8] Sexual power operates at different levels whereby both men and women assert social control. Women experience restriction, repression, and danger. Women also encounter pleasure, agency, exploration, and safety. Vance maintains that women internalize conventional cultural norms of acceptable sexual attitudes and behavior. Women who do not conform to coercive expectations of heterosexuality, marriage, and motherhood are deemed as "bad" women. This legitimates stigma, violation, and punishment by state, religion, medical profession, and public opinion.

Respondents describe divergent self-concepts of sensuality and power struggles for male dominance and female independence in the sexual realm. They argue that sexually liberated women are chastised because they are deemed as threatening to patriarchy and heterosexuality. Caribbean men often resent independent women because they think that they are aggressive and hard to deal with. This image may be a legacy from slavery that reveals a nonsensical desire for submissive women.

Respondents assert that depending on women's socioeconomic positions, men tend to control female sexual behavior. In such cases, women modify their sexuality to suit men. However, financially independent women do what they please to a large extent. Respondents assert that through compromise, women partly control their sexuality. This is evident in women choosing their sexual partners, experiences, and clothes. They reason that there is immense pressure from society, family, and religion for women to meet men's sexual needs and ignore their own. Participants think that a significant amount of female sexual liberation is achieved by women who reject mainstream social values. These women dictate their sexual preferences, initiate sexual intercourse, choose contraception, and use sex toys. Eighteen respondents believe that women continue to please men sexually and allow men to make decisions about their appearance and sexual conduct to their own detriment. As one participant argues, "I do think that a lot of men control women's sexuality because many women are dependent on men for their sense of identity."

RELIGION

From an Adlerian perspective, religion plays a number of important roles in Caribbean women's sexual identity. It functions to encourage behavior that is conducive to survival and to discourage behavior that is not. Hence many religions contain sanctions against nonreproductive sexual behavior. The Caribbean is a very religious region, with Christianity dominating in its many denominations. Church and Sunday school are prominent features of socialization and socializing in the Caribbean.

Religion and sexuality are linked for black women. As M. C. Holmes observes, greater religiosity predicts more conservative sexual behavior in black women. This relationship between religion and sexuality was expressed by many of the Barbadian respondents, who noted, "[female sexuality] . . . is considered to be value based." "My own perception [of my sexual identity] and choices [of sexual partners] are mainly guided by my religion." "The bible says it's better for a man (or woman) to marry than to burn."

SEXUALITIES

Most participants support bell hooks's assertion that black women embrace diverse self-perceptions and relationships that are based on equality, mutual respect, and lustful fulfillment that transform their lives.[9] Respondents explain that women want healthy sexual adventures. Many participants want to be self-actualized, with sexually mature and open-minded partners who respect them. Respondents debate the comfort and security of emotional, social, and sexual gratification, and most believe that they are sexually satisfied but that there is also some room for improvement.

Perceptions of lesbianism and bisexuality are very negative in Caribbean culture. Participants observe that lesbians and bisexual women are seen as abnormal and chastised, especially in Jamaican culture.[10] Respondents maintain that deep prejudice against lesbians and bisexual women is institutionalized in Caribbean societies. Some acknowledge that lesbophobia reinforces heterosexuality and divides women. Most of the respondents are deeply opposed to lesbianism for religious reasons. They regard lesbianism as an abomination. Offering biblical objections, they stress that lesbianism is unnatural, disgusting, and perverted. Most think that lesbians are psychologically bruised women who are scared of men. Six respondents held extreme views suggesting that lesbians should be killed. These views reflect those of Jamaican society, which is renowned for rampant violence against gays and lesbians. Indeed, Barbados still criminalizes homosexuality, and most of the rest of the Caribbean also has a long history of intense homophobia.[11] Nevertheless, other respondents opined that individuals should have the right to choose their happiness and sexual preferences: "I think people have free will but they do not have power to influence others sexual preference." "I think it is wrong, but women have the power to choose."

Most participants maintained that bisexuality is horrid for religious reasons. They perceive bisexuals as searching for their heterosexual identities. Most respondents condemn bisexual women because they think that they are nasty and disturbed, requiring urgent psychological and spiritual help. Participants assert that bisexuality is dangerous to health by increasing exposure to STDs and HIV/AIDS.

TRANSFORMING ATTITUDES TOWARD
CARIBBEAN FEMALE SEXUALITY

Audre Lorde writes that sensuality has personal, socioeconomic, and political power. It is important that women transcend suppressive portrayals of femininity and reclaim erotic inspiration.

Most respondents believe that social expectations about women's sexual freedom are changing due to the influence of migration, the mass media, and the Internet. They argue that people are becoming more progressive about sex as a result of dialogue. Resocialization in the home, school, and mass media enables women to increase awareness about how to gain sexual control. Greater choices are available to women as they stand up for themselves and express their needs for sexual satisfaction and respect their bodies. Respondents explain, "When a woman has detached herself from the narrow mind of society only then will liberation come. Not that I am saying every woman should live a life of 'looseness' but we are all a product of society and thus have the conscience of society. Sexual liberation comes firstly from how we think as females and the choice we make. Women as a group have to become more aware and take control of their sexuality." Respondents believe that generally women's ideas about sex are not shaped by men. Many participants are optimistic about new constructions of female sexualities leading to sexual confidence, happiness, and autonomy. The liberalization of women encourages sexual assertiveness, self-love, and sexual diversity. This is especially evident in single women being more expressive in their personalities, clothing, attitudes, and approaches toward relationships they claim. A respondent asserts, "I believe that women's liberation lies in their minds. I believe that social expectations about women's sexuality can be changed. By allowing women to be more aware of their own sexuality, let them know that we have the power and not men." Women expect recognition of all their attributes and not just sexual ones. Respondents explain their liberty to demand how they wish to be treated sexually. Women have sex whenever and wherever they want: "Women are more sexually liberated and they have more of a say in their sexual relationships."

Respondents believe that women are equally in control of sex activities. Students argue that women are experimenting with sex toys and are less dependent on men for sexual satisfaction. However, several participants state that stereotypes of sexuality are moderately revised in ways that meet men's needs:

> I don't believe there are new definitions of female sexualities. Just recycled concepts put forward first by men are now being presented and supported by females.
>
> I think many people believe that women are simply obligated to sexually satisfy men in the society.
>
> These myths and female sexual subordination will not significantly change until women initiate mental and social changes.
>
> West opined that shame and repression of sexual feelings of black women was a way of them trying to distance themselves from those negative images.
>
> I try to stress on personality, I like people not to see me as attractive physically but attractive personality wise.
>
> It [the hypersexual stereotype] makes you uncomfortable and conscious of your sexuality and your choice of sexual partners are rated closely.

Opposing the stereotypical image of black women may serve to enhance the black woman's functioning in a social context. Indeed, black women may find it empowering to not be representative of such a stereotype.

Although the majority of the respondents reported that the prevalent stereotype that exists with regard to Caribbean women's sexuality is one of promiscuity, none of them accepted this as a fair portrayal of their own sexuality. In fact, most of them not only emphasized their religious beliefs but also advocated a monogamous union, regardless of one's sexual persuasion.

None of the respondents spoke of femininity, romance, or sensitivity in relation to their own sexuality. Hence this reinforced the decision that had been made to utilize a qualitative approach in this study rather than imposing the characteristics of sexual identity from the findings of research on nonblack North American women.

Although it is evident that Barbadian and Jamaican women have knowledge of the sexual stereotypes believed to have been established during slavery, they do not appear to be embracing them. This research indicates that they have distinguished their sexual identity as strong, assertive, liberal, sexy (without being overtly sexual), and in control and that they recognize the importance of personality. However, they have failed to dispel the hypersexual stereotype. Breakwell and Millward find that women with an assertive sexual self-concept are more likely to be sexually active and have more sexual partners, which could explain the extended life of the hypersexual stereotype of black women, who often are perceived as being assertive in all realms of life, and self-reported a very assertive sexual self-concept.

It appears that some Caribbean women are using their fictional goals of chastity, monogamy, and abstinence as tools in dealing with their sexuality. One's sexual identity is open to societal influences; hence it is embedded in the ethos of the time. Alternatively, while most participants argue that they resist hypersexual stereotypes through chastity, fidelity, and celibacy, the very choices they make also represent acquiescence to societal interpretations of black women's sexuality. Therefore just as emancipation did not give the black man instant and complete freedom, neither did it release black women's sexuality; instead, it may have left the legacy of a hypersexual, promiscuous stereotype.

CONCLUSION

The transforming attitudes of Caribbean women toward their own female sexuality have clearly emerged in this study. Female students in Jamaica and Barbados reveal diverse sexual self-concepts. Respondents provide alternative ideas that counteract repressive culturally imposed definitions of appropriate sexual lifestyles. The findings of this qualitative study demonstrate that Caribbean women create their own independent definitions of sexual empowerment. They address the impact of social, religious, and moral expectations on their sexual freedom. Refuting historical stereotypes of hypersexuality and promiscuity, participants convey an increase in Caribbean women's self-esteem and assertiveness in the sexual realm.

NOTES

1. B. Bush, *Slave Women in Caribbean Society, 1650–1838* (Kingston, Jamaica: Ian Randle, 1990).
2. P. H. Collins, *Black Feminist Thought: Knowledge Consciousness and the Politics of Empowerment*, 2nd ed. (New York: Routledge, 2000).

3. K. Kempadoo, "Sexuality in the Caribbean: Theory and Research (with an Emphasis on the Anglophone Caribbean)," *Social and Economic Studies* 52, no. 3 (2003): 59–88.

4. P. Mohammed, *Ruminations on Sexuality* (Kingston, Jamaica: Women and Development Studies Programme, 1992).

5. M. C. Holmes, "Mental Health and Sexual Self-concept Discrepancies in a Sample of Young Black Women," *Journal of Black Psychology* 28, no. 4 (2002): 347–70.

6. See B. L. Andersen and J. M. Cyranowski, "Women's Sexual Self-Schema," *Journal of Personality and Social Psychology* 67, no. 6 (1994): 1079–100; Glynis M. Breakwell and Lynne J. Millward, "Sexual Self-Concept and Sexual Risk-Taking," *Journal of Adolescence* 20, no. 1 (1997): 29–41; L. T. Garcia and D. Carrigan, "Individual and Gender Differences in Sexual Self-Perceptions," *Journal of Psychology and Human Sexuality* 10, no. 2 (1998): 59–70; L. T. Garcia, "The Certainty of the Sexual Self-Concept," *Canadian Journal of Human Sexuality* 8, no. 4 (1999): 263–70.

7. See Kempadoo, "Sexuality in the Caribbean"; Mohammed, *Ruminations on Sexuality*; D. D. Reddock, D. R. Douglas, and S. Reid, *Sex, Power and Taboo* (Kingston, Jamaica: Ian Randle, 2008).

8. C. S. Vance, *Pleasure and Danger: Exploring Female Sexuality* (London: Routledge, 1984).

9. See bell hooks, *Feminism Is for Everybody: Passionate Politics* (Cambridge, MA: South End Press, 2000).

10. Audre Lorde, *Sister Outsider: Essays and Speeches* (Fremont, CA: Crossing Press, 1984), 45.

11. Tim Padgett, "The Most Homophobic Place on Earth?" *Time*, April 12, 2006.

CHAPTER 13

AIN'T I A MAN

GENDER MEANINGS AMONG BLACK MEN WHO HAVE SEX WITH MEN

RENEE MCCOY

ACCORDING TO THE CENTERS FOR DISEASE CONTROL and Prevention (CDC), there are over one million persons living with HIV/AIDS in this country. Almost half (49 percent) of these are blacks, who contract this disease at a rate seven times higher than whites. Among blacks with HIV/AIDS, 48 percent report male-to-male sexual behaviors, making this the predominant risk factor.[1] For more than 25 years, public discourse throughout this country has stressed prevention through protection. One must ask, then, what happened for a disease that has decreased within other groups to have remained so disproportionately devastating among blacks? Culturally, blacks are not known for willingly flirting with danger. We are, after all, the ones who scream, "Don't go in there!," knowing the killer always lurks behind the door. We instinctively know to hit the floor when shots are fired rather than raise our heads to find the smoking gun.

Perhaps the most absurd mystery for the twenty-first century is why anyone, especially black men who have sex with men (MSM), would risk contracting a disease with such monumental risks for morbidity and death. To understand this absurdity we must explore the cultural baggage blacks pass from one generation to the next, making black MSM expendable, discounting their lives, and marking down their futures. Efforts to stem the spread of HIV/AIDS have been severely hampered by stigmatization and misinformation about MSM culture and identity. It is commonly thought that black MSM are simply darker reflections of the larger LGBT (lesbian, gay, bisexual, and transgender) community. Such is not the case. First and foremost, the lives of black MSM unfold within a cultural context shaped by racism on the outside and conservative religious values and shades of homophobia within their own communities. In order to survive, many turn blind eyes and deaf ears to targeted prevention messages focused on labels such as "gay" or "down low." In this process, black MSM who are not "label identified" are also not encouraged to explore the risks of the behaviors in which they engage. They identify as black men, nothing more and, certainly, nothing less. Although the black community has rewarded them with acceptance for this voluntary invisibility, HIV/AIDS prevalence among black MSM has steadily increased. Prevention efforts that have ignored the significance of gender identity, racial pride, black masculinity, and male responsibility when targeting black MSM have, as a result, been unable to contain the spread of HIV/AIDS.

A popular argument justifying negative attitudes about MSM has been that their male and masculine identities are somehow incomplete or flawed, that their sexual identity somehow diminishes and skews their worth as men. This perceived incompleteness has been used to justify exclusion and perpetuate disparities in health care and disease prevalence. Researchers, however, have long known that cultural beliefs about masculine identity influence health behaviors among men and as such can contribute to strategies to improve health and combat disease.

This article is a discussion of one component of a larger study of meaning, identity, and risk that examined and described cultural beliefs of twenty black MSM living in Detroit. It departs from the position that in order to understand sexuality involving two men it is essential to understand the designation of "man" itself. Toward that end, participants responded to the question "What does it mean to be a man?" Data analysis identified two significant categories of meaning: personal character and social expectations. Findings suggest that black MSM share traditional cultural beliefs of American society about gender, which are rooted in responsibility, dependability, and the centrality of the family, regardless of their public persona and sexual orientation Also, in light of the salience of racial identity in this country, it appropriately introduced racial identity as a necessary dimension of any investigation of gender. Accordingly, participants were asked to weigh the relationship between their racial identity and sexual orientation. Together, these findings provide valuable insight into the future design and implementation of programs to improve health among this group.

The meanings of being a man that were presented by the participants in this study emphasized actions taken to enact masculinity rather than personality traits. A man is a man if he does the things a man is supposed to do, such as providing for his family or being responsible in his business affairs. To be a man in America is to enter a realm of stereotypes and expectations that have survived for centuries. Historically, models of the ideal male have represented him as hunter, fighter, leader, and custodian of all living things. In the frontier tradition upon which this country was founded, a "real" man is someone who can take a punch and still ride his horse. Few have withstood more punches in this country and remained on their horses as a black MSM. Yet HIV/AIDS is, today, his most formidable opponent, the one punch from which he just may not recover.

Analysis began by identifying key themes in the responses, essential characteristics attributed to the term "man." Two significant categories emerged, characterizing a man as a matter of (a) personal character and (b) social expectations. Participants offered 76 responses, which were assigned as relevant.

A MATTER OF PERSONAL CHARACTER

Up to 47 percent of the responses were categorized as "personal character." Responses representative of the individual's inner self and personal temperament were placed in this category and identified through words such as "respected," "trustworthy," "honesty," "truth," and "integrity." One participant reported,

> As I'm moving into my forties I understand being a man or my manliness as the essence of who I am so which is why it's important that I'm honest with myself . . . so I maintain a flowing of truth in my life because I'm finding that that is the essence of my manhood. . . . So as I embrace the truth . . . causes me to be a man of integrity for what I'm doing. So I think being a man is the sum total of my experiences. Realized through my actions and my gestures and my personality.
>
> Through the acknowledgement that I am attracted to man I am attracted to women. I do love to sing. I am this. I am that. I can do this. I think that's the sum total of all that."

In the previous response, the participant, one of three men who self-identified as a bisexual, pointed to truth and honesty as essential qualities for a man. He connected age and wisdom as guides for his life. Interestingly, he said that self-discovery is the first criteria for being a man. In his comments, he expressed deep regard for his relationships with men and sentimentally presented his feelings for women. He did not, however, talk about men as sexual partners, but rather said he is "attracted" to them, suggesting a connection deeper than mere sex.

Similarly, another participant (as follows) said a man is driven by integrity and responsibility. He expanded his meaning to include perceptions of family and friends as witnesses to his integrity, his manness. Not only is he a man, but he is also a man that everyone likes and affirms: "Somebody who's—one of the words I try to live by is integrity. All the time, when I'm at work, when I'm with my family, my friends, I try to live by being a responsible person and to me integrity is my word. And I think that's what it is . . . [S]omebody who can be really responsible and dependable. That's why I think I have such a wonderful group of friends and they think a lot of me. Of course, I think a lot of them too. I think that's why. They know they can depend on me."

In the following response, others are again enlisted to validate gender identity. Comments introduced a degree of defiance against stereotypical definitions and revealed a sense of self inclusive of personal struggles and victories. This respondent is a thirty-year-old man who openly identifies as "homosexual." He offered a litany of character traits and components of personal identity: responsible, respectful of women and children, respected by other men, masculine persona, independent, and a responsible parent. The "whatever" at the end was an indication of how "man" does more sexually than procreate.

> A man is a male who is the opposite of a woman. That's a hard question to answer. I'm a grown man who takes care of my responsibilities. I respect women. I support myself. I respect children. I demand my respect from other people. I don't demand

my respect . . . I expect to be respected by people of the same sex or opposite sex. I believe in letting everybody live.

I can't really identify what a man actually is without thinking about it.

A man is masculine, not aggressive but be . . . to carry your own weight, accept responsibility, not just go out there and use your sexual organ to procreate or whatever.

Additional comments in this category related to men as being self-assured, mature, independent, self-supportive, and confident. An abiding notion was that a man takes care of himself, his family, and his community.

A MATTER OF SOCIAL EXPECTATIONS

Almost half (46 percent) of the comments also addressed role or cultural expectations. These were placed in the "social expectations" category. In the following, for example, the participant discussed how the expectations of his family shaped certain internal values. "My father and my grandfather, the women in my life, my mothers, my . . . the people in my life have all contributed to who and what I feel is the man that I am now." This single parent and pastor of a church introduced the important influence of others, particularly his grandfather, mother, and other women. Earlier in the interview he used the word "transparent" to describe the way he felt men should be in the world. He suggested that integrity demanded disclosure of one's sexuality and could potentially dilute negative consequences.

Conflicting expectations about what men ought to be doing surfaced in the following response in which the word "supposed" is presented five times, suggesting this participant may not agree with the strict criteria society establishes for men. "First it means having certain role identities placed on you by the culture. Expectations. Supposed to wear certain clothing, carry yourself in a certain manner. Role expectations that you're supposed to play out. . . . Usually you're supposed to be the bread winner; you're supposed to be assertive if not aggressive; you're supposed to be the provider role." This respondent, who is a transvestite who earns a living performing as a female impersonator, takes a different approach, prefacing his response with a declaration that he is a man. In spite of his professional persona and his decision to wear women's clothing most of the time outside of his workplace, he was adamant about being identified as a man all the time.

Additional responses placed in this category included the following:

- Expectations of dependability
- Community expectations to be a role model
- Familial responsibilities for family members
- Expectations of fiscal responsibility
- Expectations to amass material goods

Surprisingly few comments (20 percent) related to physical characteristics. It is suspected that this was because biological differences are so obvious. One respondent said, "Besides certain genitalia and cultural expectations it gets real nebulous." This comment combines both the physical and the cultural aspects of being a man. Another respondent said, "A man has a penis and a woman has a vagina." He pointed out that regardless of how a man acts (feminine, dressed in drag) he is still a man because of his genitalia.

THE IMPORTANCE OF RACIAL IDENTITY

When the interviews shifted to racial identification, respondents felt race was more important than sexual orientation. Participants were asked whether they identified as gay/homosexual/bisexual black / African American men or as black / African American gay/homosexual/bisexual men. Up to 80 percent of the participants said that the order of terms used to describe them was important and placed racial identity before sexuality. "I consider myself Black and gay, but not necessarily a gay black or Black. I've never put that label on myself. So . . . a Black gay man." Reluctance to being labeled was a common thread running throughout the data. In the following response, the participant tells us that if he is pressed to make a choice, race comes first. "If I was gon' put a label on it I would consider myself an Black gay male." The man who offered the following response has a history of gay activism. He was over fifty years of age, making him a member of a dwindling group of elders within the gay rights movement. "I use Black gay man . . . yeah . . . Black because politically, outside of America, if you're not white you're black in most countries of the world and because it kind of embraces the struggle that Third World countries are dealing with. And then 'gay' because it's succinct. It lets you know that I am politically and sexually attracted to other men. And for me 'black' first because primarily my desire goes toward other black people, black men specifically." His response was reflective of attitudes expressed throughout this study. Accordingly, black MSM deal with issues typical of the black experience: racial oppression, kinship with the struggles of other minorities, and racial pride and allegiance. These responses were expected given the hundreds of years during which blacks faced racial discrimination. Their sexuality has not placed them within a supportive and caring sexual community. They have, rather, remained on the periphery of the gay rights movement as well. A black MSM is a black man with an additional dimension of oppression and rejection and, ultimately, less motivation to choose life and health over risk and sexual satisfaction.

DISCUSSION

Contrary to initial expectations, few men mentioned "power," a lynchpin of American masculinity, or made comments that could have been coded as such. One participant commented, "It [being a man]means that I have power. That's what it means to be a man. Like I have a power structure that means I can pretty much do whatever I put my mind to." In this response, the participant said he has power; men have power; society provides support for men (power structure); and "power" means the absence of limitations on one's actions. This may suggest that although black MSM adhere to many traditional values, they do not perceive themselves as powerful. It is certainly an area that deserves further attention.

It was mentioned earlier that one respondent linked integrity to disclosure of one's sexuality. The "down low" phenomenon of the past few years continues to challenge black MSM to tell and to live the whole truths of their lives. Within the context of HIV/AIDS these black MSM have painfully demonstrated that lies kill. This study points out that many black MSM strive to be "real" men. We must remember, however, that those who limit honesty to convenient truths fail to be authentic men as they risk the survival of the entire community. In their attempt to demonstrate their "realness," these men have unleashed weapons of mass destruction throughout the black community under the guise of protecting the people they love from the pain of stigmatization.

To many, being a black MSM is an attack against the fundamental principles of black culture, a rejection of the God who liberated us from slavery and elevated us to imagined positions of power and privilege. The emergence of HIV/AIDS in our communities has driven blacks to aggressively attack same-sex behavior as an embarrassment that diminishes worth and devalues life. We tend to want to believe that real men do while black MSM get done and that *ain't* pretty. This study determined that first and foremost, black MSM are men—no more, no less—and to understand sexual risk for this group, one can start by exploring gender meanings. It discussed how black MSM perceive themselves as men who embrace traditional values and respond to traditional expectations. As men, they are driven to be the all-American male. It is in that representation that black MSM are afforded a taste of liberation, where they can feel freedom brush across their tongues if only for a moment. Real men are responsible, dependable, family-oriented, powerful, trustworthy, and action centered.

This study did not consider the meaning of "woman" for black MSM. Addressing the meaning of female identity is critical for the black community in general and has serious implications for black MSM. Typically, when black men are questioned about their rationale for negative attitudes about homosexuals, they will respond by saying, "Because they act like women." Rarely do they respond to lesbians with the same sentiment. In fact, the sexual stimulation men receive from the mere thought of two women having sex with one another has long been accepted and encouraged. The challenge for blacks is to explore our tendency to lessen the value and power we assign to women in this society, to urge one another to move beyond the oppressive view that men do and women get done. Given the role women have played in the advancement of blacks throughout history, it is madness for black MSM to be relegated to a lesser position in our communities because they "act like women." We engage in this madness nevertheless, and it just makes no sense. Intellectually, we acknowledge the role of women as pivotal to the civil and human rights blacks have won in this country. In practice, however, our responses have been quite the opposite. The reality and health of black MSM would be so much different if the roles of women were not so diminished and subservient.

IMPLICATIONS FOR THE FUTURE

The implications for HIV/AIDS prevention from the discussion begun in this article are considerable. First, it suggests that prevention efforts to address risk among black MSM may be effective if they proceed from a position of male responsibility rather than sexual orientation and labeling. Black MSM, especially those who resist labels and disclosure to themselves as well as to their loved ones, may respond to prevention messages that acknowledge their value as contributors to the future and welfare of the black community as a whole. We must begin to consider prevention messages that encourage safe behaviors because that's what real men do. "Real" black MSM strive to be responsible to themselves, to the people they love, and to their race. Prevention messages must also begin to hold black men accountable for their behaviors regardless of how they name themselves.

Second, we are challenged to consider how the value we place on women is detrimental both to them and to black MSM. Since HIV/AIDS first surfaced, women have consistently composed almost a quarter of the total number of persons with the disease in this country; most of these have been black women. Globally, that representation is much more drastic; women are almost half of the people with HIV/AIDS in developing countries. Within a moral context, our lack of attention to HIV/AIDS among women reflects our willingness to cleanse our race of the "bad girls" who put themselves at risk through drugs and sex. Our reluctance to address their prevention and care needs indicts the moral fiber of this society as we declare by our silence and absence that both women and black MSM are expendable.

The information presented here is but a beginning in understanding how to better respond to the disproportionate impact of HIV/AIDS on blacks, especially black MSM. One of the most volatile insults one can hurl at a black man is to call him a "sissy" or a "punk." Embedded in those words are centuries old challenges to the very core of male identity; to be "called out" can be painfully threatening to black men. They live in a world that has historically rejected their manhood because of the color of their skin. Sexuality introduces a new dimension of vulnerability that can further diminish self-worth and demote black men to an even lower status. This article has sought to initiate discussion about the insidiousness of believing that black MSM are removed from identifications with traditional role designations, have distorted senses their own self-worth, and have replaced loyalty to their race with sexual obsessions. There is no justification whatsoever for the dismissal of the prevention and care needs of black MSM by black religious and civic leaders, families, and individuals on the basis that they are not "real men." There is no justification for arguments that black MSM are only tangential contributors to the future and well-being of the race. HIV/AIDS is about health and humanness. Blacks throughout this country are called to understand that there can be no healthy black community without initiatives to address and upgrade the health and future of black MSM.

NOTE

1. Centers for Disease Control and Prevention, "Cases of HIV Infection and AIDS in Urban and Rural Areas of the United States, 2006," *HIV/AIDS Surveillance Supplemental Report* 13, no. 2 (2006), accessed January 30, 2009, http://www.cdc.gov/hiv/topics/surveillance/resources/reports.

CHAPTER 14

PERFORMANCE AS INTRAVENTION

BALLROOM CULTURE AND THE POLITICS OF HIV/AIDS IN DETROIT

MARLON M. BAILEY

I see Ballroom as an artistic community that can connect with youth on issues of HIV/AIDS prevention, and the relationship between drugs and unsafe sex.[1]
—Wolfgang Busch, Filmmaker, *How Do I Look*

Despite the feelings of some in Black communities that we have been shamed by the immoral behavior of a small subset of community members, those some would label the underclass, scholars must take up the charge to highlight and detail the agency of those on the outside, those who through their acts of nonconformity choose outside status, at least temporarily.[2]
—Cathy J. Cohen, "Deviance as Resistance"

The house structure is geared specifically toward the ball scene (particularly in Detroit). As far as its purpose, houses provide a source of family nurturing that often times a lot of kids don't get at home.
—Prada Escada from the House of Escada in Detroit

INTRODUCTION

"WHAT'S GOING ON IN THE USA? GEORGE Bush got us in a disarray. We got soldiers in Baghdad; we should be fighting AIDS instead," chanted Chicago ballroom commentator Neiman Marcus Escada.[3] Usually spoken in front of a captive crowd of black queer members of the ballroom community during a ball, Escada's words serve as an astute critique of both US imperialism in the name of "national security" and its unwillingness to take appropriately aggressive measures to curtail the spread of HIV/AIDS infection among black gender and sexual marginals locally and abroad. Consisting of black and Latina or Latino LGBTQ (lesbian, gay, bisexual, transgender, and queer) people, ballroom culture is a minoritarian social sphere where performance, queer genders and sexualities, and kinship coalesce to create an alternative world. Thus within and through performance at balls, Neiman Marcus Escada contributes to the creation of a counterdiscourse of HIV/AIDS. This is but one example of the important role that performance plays within ballroom culture and how it is a part of a critical practice of survival in which many of the members of this community are engaged.

Ballroom culture, sometimes called "house ball culture," is a relatively clandestine community consisting of African American and (in some locations like New York, Miami, and Los Angeles) Latino or Latina LGBTQ people. Although Jenny Livingston's popular documentary film, *Paris Is Burning* (1991),[4] provides only a glimpse into the world of ballroom culture, it was the first exposé to bring mainstream exposure to ballroom practices in the late '80s in New York City. Since its beginnings in Harlem more than fifty years ago, ballroom culture has expanded rapidly to every major city in the United States, including Chicago, Atlanta, Baltimore, Charlotte, Cleveland, and Philadelphia. Notwithstanding the popular media coverage of ballroom culture in recent years, from its members appearing in Madonna's music video, *Vogue* (1990), to the deaths of two of the community's most prominent icons, Pepper LaBejia (2003) and Willie Ninja (2006), to date, this unique and generative culture has received scant scholarly attention.

Perhaps more important, out of the limited scholarship on ballroom culture, the disproportionate impact of the HIV/AIDS epidemic on its members has barely been mentioned let alone examined. An increasing number of community-based organizations (CBOs) have received federal, state, and/or local funding for their prevention programs that target ballroom communities.[5] Yet the funding support for these prevention programs has yet to garner comprehensive studies that can help determine their overall effectiveness in reducing HIV/AIDS infection among ballroom communities. As a result, little is known about the sociocultural challenges that members of this community face and how social practices that are organic to ballroom culture assist its members in withstanding the scourge of the disease and challenging the stigmatization associated with it.

Therefore, in this performance ethnography[6] of ballroom culture and HIV/AIDS in Detroit, I delineate three aspects of ballroom culture that are potential strategies for HIV/AIDS prevention that already exist within the community. First, I highlight three core dimensions of the ballroom community: the gender and sexual identity system, the kinship structure, and the performances at the ball. Second, I argue that, generally, HIV/AIDS prevention programs that target black communities have relied on research and intervention models that are based on individual sexual behavior and are void of cultural analyses. As a result, the organic practices and strategies of prevention that emerge from within so-called at-risk communities have been woefully neglected. For instance, even though HIV/AIDS infection is disproportionately high among black men who have sex with men (MSM), a substantive portion of black MSM remain HIV negative. More research needs to be conducted to identify and support strategies deployed by black MSM that protect them from infection. Drawing from Friedman et al., I argue that these strategies are forms of *intravention*. Intravention describes HIV/AIDS *prevention* activities that are conducted and sustained through practices and processes within so-called at-risk communities themselves.[7]

Finally, I delineate three forms of *intravention* that are rooted in black performance traditions and are integral to ballroom culture: (1) the creation of a social epistemology, (2) social support, and (3) prevention balls. These three aspects demonstrate that the black queer members of the ballroom scene are communities of support rather than simply communities of risk.[8] Looking to performance and other cultural work, in theory and in practice, not only will yield more socioculturally nuanced theories, methods, and models for HIV/AIDS prevention but also can help guide CBOs to forge more effective and sustained programs aimed at reducing HIV infection in black communities in general and black queer communities in particular.

BLACK QUEER PERFORMANCE AND HIV/AIDS

I approach this examination of ballroom culture using the methodology of performance, emphasizing research and community activism in HIV/AIDS prevention. My nine years of performance ethnographic research on ballroom culture and HIV/AIDS consist of my participation in the very performances and cultural practices that I analyze.[9] Hence as I describe later in this essay, I competed in balls as a member of both the Detroit and Los Angeles Chapters of the House of Prestige. Accordingly, my performance approach involved me being a member of the ballroom community and working for two CBOs that collaborated with the ballroom community.[10] I have also been engaged in extensive HIV/AIDS prevention research and activism among black gay men and transgender women. Given my particular vantage point, this essay seeks to forge a conceptual framework and a language between public health and (black) cultural studies that can illuminate the central role that performance plays in the lives of ballroom members as it relates to the epidemic.

By and large, the research on HIV/AIDS and culture has been produced in disparate domains of scholarship. Research on the disproportionate impact of HIV/AIDS on black communities has been beset by a failure to employ truly interdisciplinary approaches to HIV/AIDS prevention studies to explicate the multifaceted nature of this epidemic and to identify innovative strategies to combat it. More or less, HIV/AIDS research has been dominated by biomedicine, epidemiology, and social science.[11] Calls for radical interdisciplinarity and cultural criticism have been only marginally addressed at best and outright rejected at worst.[12] As a result, the topic of HIV/AIDS among black queer communities falls through the cracks, so to speak, of several disparate intellectual conversations that fail to account for the multifocal contexts in which black queer people live.

As a site of cultural inquiry, African American studies has been markedly absent from discourses and sites of inquiry and advocacy in HIV/AIDS prevention studies. With the exception of Cathy J. Cohen's groundbreaking work *The Boundaries of Blackness: AIDS and the Breakdown of Black Politics,* published in 1999,[13] African American studies has failed to sufficiently theorize or even address the social and cultural dimensions and implications of AIDS among black communities, particularly since its epidemiological profile has become primarily black and queer. Founded on the principle of creating theoretical and practical knowledges that can effect social change in the lives of everyday people, remarkably, African American studies has not translated its fundamental intellectual and political principles into a praxis to confront the AIDS crisis on the ground. Of note, in "Deviance as Resistance: a New Research Agenda for the Study of Black Politics," Cathy J. Cohen calls for a "paradigmatic shift" in African American studies that builds on black queer studies that attempts to reduce, if not eliminate, the superficial distance between researchers in the academy and the communities from which many of us hail and purport to study.[14] Indeed, any sociocultural site of inquiry or "studies" should both emerge from and be applicable to the experiences of everyday people.[15]

Recent trends in performance studies, however, have opened a space to examine not only the theatrical and quotidian dimensions of performance but also the relationship between performance and social change as well. According to D. Soyini Madison and Judith Hamera, performance studies has been concerned with analyzing how, through performance and performativity, human beings fundamentally make culture, affect power, and reinvent their ways of being in the world, especially those who have limited or no access to state power.[16] Perhaps most germane to this study of the ballroom community and HIV/AIDS is Dwight Conquergood's argument that performance is at once a radically multi-disciplinary and embodied approach to examining an object of inquiry and an active participation in performance as "tactics of *intervention*" in spaces of alterity and struggle.[17]

Theorizing HIV/AIDS through performance, or what Robin D. G. Kelley refers to as cultural labor,[18] necessarily shifts the emphasis in HIV/AIDS research away from individual sexual behavior that supposedly leads to infection to a focus on culture as an arsenal of resiliency strategies upon which marginalized communities rely to survive the social crisis. For instance, in his analysis of the forms of cultural expression among black urban youth on the street, Robin D. G. Kelley suggests that black urban youth undertake cultural labor within an increasingly politically powerless and economically deprived urban sphere.[19] Likewise, in my larger project on ballroom culture, I frame its members' reconstitution of gender and sexual subjectivities, family/kinship, and community as a form of cultural labor as one way to withstand and creatively respond to the sociocultural and economic forms of exclusion that they experience. And as I elaborate in the following, in the ballroom community, these forms of cultural labor are inextricably linked to performance.

Performance studies scholars such as José Muñoz, David Román, and Barbara Browning have made invaluable contributions to the study of HIV/AIDS, queer communities of color, and performance.[20] Since there is scant research on the Ballroom community and the epidemic, in general, and almost no literature on this topic within public health, this ethnographic study of ballroom culture in Detroit is an appropriate basis from which to forge cross-disciplinary dialogues and research. For instance, one of the core concepts in HIV/AIDS prevention theory and practice is *intervention*. Within public health, intervention models are designed programmatically to facilitate behavioral change in order to reduce incidents and prevalence of HIV infection among targeted communities that have been identified as "high risk," or as "risk communities." In "AIDS: Keywords," Jan Zita Grover defines "risk groups" as an epidemiological concept that serves to isolate identifiable characteristics among certain communities that are predictive of where infection is most likely to occur so as to contain and prevent it.[21] In other words, within public health, the aim is to identify, isolate, and contain infection within a particular risk community so that the general population remains safe from infection.[22]

There are two useful critiques that a cultural studies analysis of HIV/AIDS prevention research and practice offers. First, it is important to problematize how public health discourses construct risk and attach disease to particular bodies and communities based on a range of biased assumptions. Hence the category of "communities of risk" is almost always used to stereotype and stigmatize people who are already viewed as "outside the moral and economic parameters of 'the general population.'"[23] "Communities of risk" becomes a common sense notion that is, in part, produced by public health and is often reinscribed by researchers working with dispossessed communities. Second, the public health concept of interventions, which is designed to facilitate individual behavioral change among groups of risk, relies on assumptions about the population with whom they work. Public health officials and CBO workers assume that only they know how best to reduce HIV prevalence within these communities and that the members of so-called risk groups do not possess sufficient knowledge about prevention. Consequently, in most cases, prevention practices are imposed on communities that are often socially and culturally inappropriate and ineffective.

To address the aforementioned concerns, performance theory undergirds my ethnographic engagement with ballroom culture and HIV/AIDS. As Dwight Conquergood argues, performance is transdisciplinary and boundary breaking, and it has the potential to help produce an understanding of social problems in more nuanced ways.[24] Unfortunately, performance has yet to be taken seriously within public health. And although performance may be recognized by some CBOs, research on HIV/AIDS prevention and treatment using performance as both a method and an object of study has not occurred. Instead, studies in HIV prevention overemphasize the sexual behaviors of gender and sexual marginals, and most do not adequately investigate the interplay between the discourses of AIDS and the social conditions that drive the epidemic, especially among communities that are marginalized in a variety of ways. Consequently, there is a gap in the majority of the research on HIV/AIDS and its impact on and prevalence within so-called high-risk communities; this gap prevents researchers from attending to the social/sexual behavior and the sociocultural and politicoeconomic context in which such behavior occurs.

Conceptually, I call for a move from *intervention* to *intravention* in HIV/AIDS prevention studies to capture what so-called communities of risk do, based on their own knowledge and ingenuity, to contest, to reduce, and to withstand HIV in their communities. In my critique of the concept of intervention that is so prevalent in public health and prevention studies, I draw from the work of performance theorist David Román, who suggests that cultural performance is, indeed, an act of intervention into the cultural politics of race, sexuality, and AIDS.[25] Such cultural politics pathologize black sexuality and represent black queer men as vectors of HIV infection. Thus I join performance (as it is an arena in which minoritarian communities engage in social struggle) with Friedman et al.'s notion of "communities of *intravention*."[26] In their study of HIV/AIDS prevalence among communities of injection drug users (IDU), Friedman et al. further argue that "[c]ognitive-behavioral theories that focus on the individual may not provide sufficient understanding for such efforts because they lack the concepts and methodologies needed to identify, understand or intervene in structures and processes that are at the cultural system, community network levels."[27] My analysis here attends to the ways in which such communities of risk deploy strategies to address the correlative social factors that make people more vulnerable to the epidemic such as, but not limited to, social isolation, low self-worth, violence, and poverty. Thus the concept of *intravention* is a key point of entry for performance into the analysis and development of targeted HIV/AIDS prevention programs within a black queer cultural context.

In what follows, I delineate the aspects of performance that are central to the ballroom community that intravene in the HIV/AIDS epidemic. Instead of referring to the ballroom community as a community of risk, I suggest that ballroom is a community of support. In the ballroom community, performance is the means through which members create a counterdiscourse (through a social epistemology), provide social support (kin labor) for its members, and produce prevention balls in order to reduce black queer people's vulnerability to HIV/AIDS infection through competitive performance. Thus ballroom cultural practices are a form of intravention, deploying protective and prevention efforts that emerge from within the culture itself, efforts that the larger black community as well as overall society, fail to do. This community constitutes a site of refuge where its members have the opportunity to be nurtured, to experience pleasure, and to access a better quality of life in the face of the AIDS epidemic, particularly for those that are located at the very bottom of society. Clearly, enhancing the quality of life is a precondition to reducing the spread of HIV in the community.

BALLROOM CULTURE: A COMMUNITY OF SOCIAL SUPPORT

Although ballroom culture had existed for decades prior to Livingston's documentary, the film has become the primary prism through which this rich and longstanding cultural practice is recognized and understood. Even in some of the more recent glances of ballroom to which the American public has been exposed, very little has been revealed about the day-to-day lives of the people involved and the multiple purposes that the social structures within the community serve.[28]

The community is sustained by two inextricable features: flamboyant competitive ball rituals and houses, the anchoring family-like structures that produce these rituals of performance. Ballroom subjectivities and familial roles are based on an egalitarian gender/sexual identity system that offers more gender and sexual identities from which to choose than available to members in the "outside" world (see the following).[29]

GENDER/SEXUAL IDENTITY SYSTEM

Ballroom Culture: Three Sexes

1. Woman (one born with female sex characteristics)
2. Man (one born with male sex characteristics)
3. Intersex (one born with both male and female sex characteristics or with sex characteristics that are indeterminate)

Six-Part Gender/Sexual Identity System

1. Butch queens (biologically born male who identify as gay or bisexual and are and can be masculine, hypermasculine, or effeminate)
2. Femme queens (male-to-female transgender people, who may be at various stages of gender reassignment, i.e., hormonal and/or surgical processes)
3. Butch queens up in drags (gay males that perform drag but do not take hormones and who do not live as women)
4. Butches (female-to-male transgender people, who may be at various stages of gender reassignment; masculine lesbians; or females appearing as males regardless of sexual orientation)
5. Women (biologically born females who are gay, straight identified, or queer)
6. Men (biologically born males who live as men and are straight identified)

House Parents

1. Mothers: butch queens, femme queens, and women
2. Fathers: butch queens, butches, and men

Because gender performance is central to self-identification and can imply a whole range of sexual identities in ballroom culture, the system reflects how the members define themselves largely based on the categories that they walk or perform. All members of the ballroom community identify as one of the six categories in the gender/sexual identity system. If or when one "walks a ball," that participant competes in the competitive categories that coincide with their gender/sexual identity within the ballroom community. For instance, a femme queen can only "walk/perform" in categories that are listed under femme queen on the ball flyer. The intensely competitive performances at the ball events create a space of celebration, affirmation, critique, and reconstitution in the everyday lives of its black queer members.

It is worth noting that there are no balls without houses, and there are no houses without balls. And in the kinship system of ballroom culture, houses are led by "mothers" (butch queens, femme queens, and women) and "fathers" (butch queens and butches), who, regardless of age, sexual orientation, and social status, provide a labor of care and love with or for numerous black queer people who have been rejected by their blood families, religious institutions, and society at large. Houses, for instance, are one of the core features of the ballroom community, and houses serve as social, and sometimes literal, homes for its members.[30] Thus the ball, combined with the social relations within the houses outside of it, are mutually constitutive and, taken together, make up the world of ballroom culture.

No doubt, technology has played an integral role in the expansion of ballroom culture, allowing the members of this national network to stay connected through the World Wide Web. For instance, the national ballroom scene uses various websites such as http://www.walk4mewednesdays.com, http://www.thehouseofballs .com, and http://www.getyourtens.com as well as websites, Yahoo! groups, listservs, and blogs that are set up and maintained by houses and individual members in order to connect with the community at large and to communicate with their chapters throughout the country. In addition, there are magazines devoted to ballroom culture such as *CLIK Magazine*. The National Confederation of Black Gay Prides is an umbrella organization that works with citywide black gay pride festivities, bringing together black and Latino LGBTQ members of the community to participate in national balls. Albeit transient, the ballroom scene is large and growing, providing a world for black and Latina or Latino LGBTQ people to reconstitute, affirm, and celebrate their queer gender and sexual identities.

I believe that it is important to bring ballroom culture into scholarly focus within the context of the AIDS epidemic and to examine the complex conditions in which many of the black LGBTQ members of the ballroom community live daily, such as sociocultural exclusion and isolation, poverty, and violence and abuse. By and large, the multiple forms of marginalization that black queer people experience make this community more vulnerable to HIV/ AIDS infection.[31]

BALLROOM CULTURE AND HIV/AIDS

I begin this portion of my examination by situating ballroom culture and HIV/ AIDS within the context of Detroit.[32] Given the disproportionate impact of HIV/ AIDS on black communities across the country and its particular devastation of black people in Detroit, and given that the ballroom community is embedded in black communities in the city, HIV/AIDS and its effects on ballroom is an instructive case study. Invariably, the interlocking oppressions of race, class, gender, and sexuality shape black queer people's experiences as they exacerbate the suffering of marginalized groups at the hands of the virus.[33]

In Michigan, although African Americans compose only 14 percent of the total population, according to HIV epidemiological data for 2008, new infection rates for African Americans were 59 percent; this was compared to a 35 percent infection rate for whites. By race and gender, HIV infection rates for black men were 41 percent compared to 29 percent for white men. And it is worth noting that African American women make up 73 percent of all HIV cases among women in Michigan.[34] HIV infection rates among MSM were 45 percent compared to 13 percent for heterosexual transmission.[35] Based on this epidemiological data in Michigan, we can infer that black MSM have increasing disproportionate rates of new HIV infections (e.g., there are higher HIV infection rates among blacks, among black men and black MSM, and among men; the primary route of HIV transmission is male-to-male sexual intercourse).[36]

Detroit carries the majority of HIV prevalence in Michigan.[37] Known as both the "chocolate city" and the "motor city," Detroit has the most distinct racial and class demographics of any large US city. According to the 2000 US Census, Detroit is the largest city with a black majority population in the United States. Out of approximately 951,270 residents, 83 percent identified themselves as black or African American. In socioeconomic terms, Detroit has one of the poorest populations in the country, as between 26.8 percent and 33.4 percent of the city's residents live in poverty.[38] Like many other cities with large black populations, Detroit is one of the places hardest hit by the disease.[39]

HIV/AIDS workers in Detroit, some of whom are HIV positive, have a unique vantage point when considering the intersections of gender, sexuality and HIV/AIDS. The prevention workers that I interviewed suggested that the dominant discourse on HIV/AIDS, one that pathologizes and sutures the disease to homosexuality and that disallows a candid dialogue about sexuality and HIV risk reduction, hampers their ability to reduce infections rates in the city. Compounded by the disturbing socioeconomic conditions, most HIV/AIDS cases among men in Detroit are black MSM. Black people infected with HIV/AIDS in large cities like Detroit do not have access to AIDS prevention and treatment resources that are equal to their white counterparts.[40] Thus black MSM who are infected with or are at high risk for HIV/AIDS infection experience a simultaneity of oppression, structured not only by and through race, class, gender, and sexuality but also through HIV/AIDS.

For example, when I asked Tino Prestige, a butch queen and a case worker at the Horizon's Project, an HIV/AIDS prevention and services agency in Detroit, why he thinks the HIV/AIDS epidemic is so severe among African American men in Detroit, he said, "There's a lack of information in the school system, NO discussion of sexuality, and no discussion of how to be sexually responsible even if you are heterosexual. People have a whole lot of ignorance about LGBTQ issues, and people still think that it's wrong because of their religious views." Similarly, Noir Prestige, also a butch queen, described how once, while he worked for the Men of Color Motivational Group (MOC), a now defunct HIV/AIDS prevention agency in Detroit, he delivered a presentation on HIV/AIDS, and a school administrator insisted that he not encourage homosexuality, as if HIV/AIDS was "naturally" linked to homosexuality and as if talking about homosexuality would lead to young people adopting it. That is why Noir reiterated the need to "de-gay" or "de-homosexualize" HIV/AIDS so that all people will take the problem seriously. A public discussion of HIV/AIDS, especially among young people, requires this delinking of HIV/AIDS from homosexuality in order to ease homophobic fears held in society. At the same time, prevention workers are faced with a conundrum of sorts because when homosexuality is not discussed, black MSM and/or gay men are rendered invisible while still viewed as the primary vectors of HIV/AIDS infection.

Both Tino and Noir attest to that fact that explicit and implicit homophobia resulting from familial and cultural expectations to adhere to hegemonic gender and sexual norms directly influence the information that black queer people receive about HIV/AIDS. As Lester K. Spence argues, in general, the larger black community's knowledge about HIV/AIDS, black people's perception of their own risk of contracting the virus, and their preferences concerning HIV/AIDS policy are all intrinsically linked to their views on homosexuality.[41] Ultimately, the treatment and policing of sexuality that black queer people endure from the outside create deep-seated internal struggles that influence the way they self-identify and interact with others, both gays and heterosexuals.

As Spence suggests, black queer people constitute an "out-group" and are therefore shunned more than any other group in the United States.[42] And in effect, for black people in Detroit, what should be a consensus issue, HIV/AIDS, is instead what Cathy J. Cohen calls a crosscutting issue.[43]

According to Cohen, crosscutting issues disrupt the imagined consensus that disguises hierarchies and inequities as a collective community consciousness. Many of my interlocutors suggested that "the Black community" tends to imagine itself as "straight" and that AIDS has impacted a few sexual deviants within the community who have lost their way. Noir Prestige stated that the family and community that he grew up in believed that "if you weren't gay, you wouldn't get it [AIDS]." Therefore, crosscutting issues pose challenges for marginal groups disproportionately, and they directly affect a particular segment *within* the marginalized population.[44] It is no surprise, then, that black communities' response to HIV/AIDS by linking it to homosexuality is an instance of what Cohen terms secondary marginalization where select, privileged members of black communities determine the priorities and regulate and police the margins in order to shape a public image that disavows and disciplines the less privileged members or those who do not conform.[45]

Therefore, ballroom culture is compelled to be proactive and multifaceted in its struggle against the disease and the "othering" discourses that accompany it. As David Román aptly points out, AIDS cannot be separated from the discourses that construct and, in fact, "sustain it."[46] Discourse regarding AIDS informs the specific priorities (defining those whose lives are worth saving) that public health institutions devise regarding prevention. Recalcitrant racism, sexism, homophobia/heterosexism, poverty, and other forms of disenfranchisement are inextricably linked to scurrilous representations of AIDS as a black gay disease.

In Michigan, the scant HIV/AIDS reduction strategies consist of the distribution of brochures, condoms and other safe sex materials, discussion groups, and safe sex training,[47] but they ignore the crucial role that cultural values play in shaping the stigmatization associated with race, class, gender, sexuality, and AIDS. Directly related to this issue, few CBOs create programs that move beyond simply reducing individual "risk behaviors," by addressing the social conditions that contribute to them.

For instance, as Noir emphasized firmly, "HIV kills, why? Stigma. The people living *with it* have to make others comfortable living around it; that's a lot of work. And folks die trying to accomplish that because you end up living in secret. Support is key and very essential in living with the illness or around it." Noir demonstrates how a vicious cycle of stigmatization undermines any prevention program. Unwittingly or not, CBOs extract their prevention techniques from these hegemonic discourses that overdetermine black MSM as a risk population.

While I was conducting fieldwork, the two organizations that focused on the black queer community in Detroit enacted prevention programs buttressed by convergent racialized, classed, gendered, and sexualized discourses of risk. But it is the isolating of certain black groups within the black community on one level, and the characterization of black people as a high risk population on the other, that keeps ballroom members from utilizing the prevention and treatment resources offered by these organizations. For example, Tino Prestige underscores this when he says, "The Community Health Awareness Group has a mobile testing unit. But when the unit shows up to a ball, people won't be willing to go to it cause people will think something is wrong with them, so they don't want to be seen that way." Simply put, ballroom members are already stigmatized, the prevention efforts themselves are stigmatized, so our utilization of the services stigmatizes us even more.[48]

BALLROOM COMMUNITY PRACTICES AS HIV/AIDS INTRAVENTION

What do black queer members *do* about such conditions? How does the cultural work of creating an alternative minoritarian sphere help refract feelings of worthlessness caused by stigmatization and oppression? How does ballroom culture provide a space to forge alternatives realities for its members? Part of what is at stake in the ballroom community here is a struggle for alternative community representation and community preservation in midst of a health and social crisis.[49] In what follows, I delineate three forms of intravention that are organic aspects of ballroom culture or what Friedman et al. refer to as collective risk-reduction reinforcement.[50] Members of the ballroom community create a counterdiscourse of HIV/AIDS that recast its members as people with lives worth saving, not merely risk groups; the structure of the community provides social support; and the community produces prevention balls that are based on ballroom community values and practices in an attempt to destigmatize HIV/AIDS so that its members can be more receptive to messages of risk reduction.

SOCIAL EPISTEMOLOGY OF BALLROOM CULTURE

First, I highlight the ways in which ballroom members construct a social epistemology as a critical aspect of the overall work of creating an alternative social sphere. This alternative social sphere is a crucial source of value for ballroom members. I emphasize key characteristics of ballroom culture/spaces that are strategies for addressing HIV/AIDS that reflect its members' desire for recuperative forms of self and collective representations.[51] I contend that ballroom practices and their potentialities unveil the difference between *prevention* approaches and the on-the-ground practices of cultural *intravention*.

In his study of the *milieu*, a homosocial underground scene in Abidjan, Côte d' Ivoire, Vinh-Kim Nguyen suggests that social knowledge informs the "social relations and the tactics used to navigate them for individual and collective benefit."[52]

This social knowledge is usually contained within dispossessed communities and subaltern spaces and allows its members to comment on their conditions as well as to develop strategies to alter them. For example, social knowledge in the ballroom community views gender and sexuality as fluid and mutable, kinship/family as not necessarily biological, and performance as integral to community affirmation and preservation. Hence the creation of a social knowledge is how ballroom members reconstitute themselves in the midst of the HIV/AIDS crisis in an attempt to change the social consequences of it.

All of my informants agree that doing HIV/AIDS prevention work within the ballroom scene is difficult; however, some believe that it is a cultural space of hope. One such possibility is the notion of self-renewal, a way of reconstituting the self within ballroom to contend with the negative representations in the outside world. For instance, ballroom is what Diva D from the House of Bvlgari calls a "fictitious existence." When I asked him whether "low self-worth" was a motivating factor for black queer people to join the ballroom scene, he responded, "Yes, it gives them a brand new identity; it gives them a brand new slate. If your family don't care about you because you are gay and what not or if you can't get a job, the Ballroom scene helps you start a-new. It creates a brand new identity that you can feel comfortable with." The social knowledge of ballroom links the balls to the community-fashioned kinship system that both sustains the community and facilitates HIV/AIDS prevention.

Therefore, ballroom social knowledge enables effective HIV/AIDS prevention that is based on the values and norms established by its community members as opposed to those imposed on it from the outside.

Kinship and Social Support

As the house mother of the Detroit chapter of the House of Prestige and former HIV/AIDS prevention worker at the time of the interview, Duchess suggests that ballroom is built on social relations that redefine prevention work. He stated further that "[t]he structure of the [Ballroom] community already allows for familial prevention work, you know, just in the fact that someone can say to you, 'now you know you need to wear a condom' and it be from someone that you have built that trust factor with. People in the community do prevention work all of the time." Within these houses, members consult with their house parents and their siblings on issues that, either by choice or by necessity, they do not discuss with their biological kin. House mothers and fathers, in particular, provide daily parental guidance for ballroom kids on issues such as intimate/romantic relationships, sex, gender and sexual identities, health, hormonal therapy, and body presentation, just to name a few.

Siblings in houses provide support for HIV prevention among those not infected, but they also play an integral role by supporting those already infected with HIV as well. For instance, a very thin and increasingly frail looking Noir Prestige began one our many interviews by excusing himself to go to the bathroom, apparently to throw up. "Excuse me," said Noir in the living room of his small, tidy apartment that he shares with his boyfriend of eight years. "I just started new meds; this shit is horrible but I shall survive." Noir went on to describe how his very close relationship with Tino Prestige has helped him cope with his condition.[53]

Noir remarked that he and Tino Prestige have very similar life experiences. They were both infected with the virus in their teens. They are both in long-term relationships (eight years) with partners who are not infected, partners who struggle with the difficulties of loving someone who is HIV positive and/or living with AIDS. They are both treatment advocates at the Horizon's Project. At the balls, they walk in butch realness categories, thug realness, and schoolboy realness.[54] Most importantly, they provide treatment for each other. It is worth mentioning here that in ballroom life, one's age is not based on necessarily one's years on earth; rather, it is based on how long one has been in the ballroom scene and/or been out in the gay world. Hence the "big" brother reminded his "little" brother to take his meds, and he often drove him to his appointments with his doctor. They cared for one another especially in moments when each of their partners did not rise to the occasion. In a separate interview I conducted with Tino Prestige, he said, "We are truly brothers." Clearly, these siblings help each other endure the psychic trauma that comes along with HIV/AIDS in ways that their partners could not.

In many cases, house members express love for one another; serve each other when needed, and undoubtedly they add overall value to each other's lives, especially when facing desperate situations. In general, houses provide what Cornel West describes as nonmarket values: love, care, and service.[55] Not only do these values constitute a labor of care that becomes intensified when the community decides to deal with HIV/AIDS collectively, but they also exist in the quotidian aspect of ballroom life.

BLACK QUEER PERFORMANCE AND HIV/AIDS PREVENTION BALLS

Despite the inability of some public health departments to devise and sustain effective HIV/AIDS prevention strategies for so-called high risk communities, some ballroom houses have joined forces with a few CBOs to create "prevention houses" and "prevention balls." As I argue previously, ballroom houses, in general, are spaces of social support that often reinforce messages of HIV/AIDS prevention either directly or indirectly. But prevention houses usually have formal funding from and/or programmatic ties with CBOs, and they engage in HIV/AIDS prevention activities and coordinate balls based on HIV/AIDS prevention themes.

Again, since there are no houses without balls and there are no balls without houses, part of the important discursive work of prevention houses occurs at prevention balls. On the one hand, the importance placed on image and status in ballroom makes HIV/AIDS prevention work difficult because members distance themselves from the topic of HIV/AIDS for fear that it will tarnish them. But on the other hand, competitive performance, image, and status are used to disseminate and promote messages about HIV risk reduction among ballroom members. Out of the numerous balls that I attended and/or participated in, most of them were packed with hundreds of black queer people from all over the country. As Francisco Roque from The Gay Men's Health Crisis, Inc., said, "The Ballroom community is a captive 'at-risk' population and modeling behavior is built in the community." Albeit imperfect, it is a necessary strategy to use competition and image within a ballroom cultural context to disseminate information and simultaneously reduce stigma.

A hallmark of ballroom culture, competition is another means through which image and status are formed and repaired. Since individual members and houses can gain recognition and status only by "snatching trophies,"[56] competition is an integral aspect of the social world of ballroom that offers possibilities for effective HIV/AIDS prevention. Former father of the House of Infiniti and the executive director of Empowerment Detroit, an HIV prevention agency targeting black gay youth, Jonathon Davis confirmed this when he said, "In terms of the Ballroom community in Detroit, if it ain't got nothing to do with a trophy, these girls don't care." And when I asked Pootaman, a twenty-year-old member of the House of Ninja and an HIV/AIDS prevention worker at MOC at the time of the interview, why he became interested in walking balls, he said, "I enjoy the competition, the feeling of sitting someone down to prove a point, that I could take home a trophy." Father Infiniti and Pootaman speak to the centrality of the trophy, the accoutrements that come along with it and how both represent the attainment of value and affirmation that ballroom members are usually otherwise denied in the outside world.

Lastly, in order to illustrate more vividly how prevention balls work, I describe my experience as a performance participant and witness. In March 2005, I competed in the annual Love is the Message Ball in Los Angeles.[57] As a member of the Los Angeles chapter of the House of Prestige at the time, I walked, along with Pokka, the father, in the "school boy realness versus executive realness" category for the mini grand prize. The description of the category on the flyer read, "School Boy Realness—Let's see if U were paying attention in Sex Ed. Bring us School Boy realness w/a safe sex production. Props a must and you will be graded on your project and knowledge. VS. Executive—U have been promoted to CEO of a condom company of your choice. U must have a prop and be prepared to sell your product to the board." Pokka planned our performance and was determined to win the trophy and the $100 cash prize. Since Pokka and I walk executive realness, I dressed the part and played the role of a CEO and Pokka was the president of the board of directors for the Lifetime Condoms Corporation. He had spent time and money to prepare everything we needed to mount this mini production.

When Kodak Kandinsky, the commentator for the evening, announced our category, members from various houses came out as school boy realness wearing clothes with several condoms attached to them. Because I was in the waiting area of the hall, I could not see them perform their mini production. When it was our turn, Pokka walked out ahead of me, dressed in an all-black suit and carrying his laptop computer case. As he approached the judges' table, he read a statement about the crisis of HIV/AIDS in the black community, stressing that condom use is an effective strategy in the fight against the spread of the disease. "Now I bring to you Professah Prestige, our new CEO, to make a brief statement," said Pokka. I came strutting down the runway in a navy blue suit carrying my laptop computer in a black leather computer bag in one hand and a large black portfolio case full of billboards in the other. When I got to the judges table, I took the microphone and said, "My name is Professah Prestige, the new CEO of Lifetime Condoms. We have new durable condoms that do not reduce sensation. I hope that you all will give them a try. Be safe and use condoms." After my statement, the commentator asked the judges to score me. "Are they real? Do you see it? Judges score him (all of the judges flashed their cards with "10" written on them). Ok, tens across the board. Prestiges step to the side. Next contestants please," said Kodak. "Thank God, I did not get chopped," I thought.

After other competitors were eliminated or what we call, "chopped," there were only five competitors left, Pokka and me from the House of Prestige and three members from another house (these members walked school boy realness). Then someone from the Minority AIDS Project posed the following question to all of us: "What is a dental dam?" Each of us was told to whisper the answer in Kodak's ear. When he came to me, I explained that a dental dam is used for oral sex, and it provides a barrier of protection between the mouth and the anus or the vagina. Then Kodak announced that only two of us said the correct answer, a school boy realness kid from the other house and me. Apparently, Pokka gave him the wrong answer. I felt kind of bad because Pokka had done most of the preparation for our production.

Finally, the judges had to choose who looked more real between the realness kid and me. "Who is realer?" said Kodak. When Kodak got to the final two out of the seven judges, one of them pointed at me and said, "He look like a real executive." At the end, I won the category. I was shocked and thrilled at the same time. They gave me a trophy and the $100 prize. I kept the trophy and gave the money to the house mother to put in our house fund. I had won the category for the House of Prestige. Most importantly, within the competitive spirit at the balls, members of the ballroom community were exposed to knowledge about safe sex without individuals being singled out and stigmatized. Clearly, performance, kinship and the social knowledge function as cultural practices that allow ballroom community members to radically intravene in the AIDS crisis, as the practices are derived from within the community itself.

CONCLUSION

Ballroom members perform the labor of caring for and the valuing lives that are integral to building and sustaining a community in the midst of crisis. Ballroom practices are important alternatives that attend to the multifarious challenges that HIV/AIDS poses, especially the attendant public and scientific discourses that render black queer people dysfunctional and dangerous and further stigmatize them as vectors of disease. These values sustain the community and constitute a critical component to any form of intervention aimed not only at reducing the spread of HIV/AIDS but also at attempting to cultivate the necessary systems and structures (within ballroom) that redress the violence done to black queers. This is violence at the hands of not only the HIV/AIDS epidemic but also the "other-ing" discourses that coproduce it.

The focus here is the ballroom community's creation of "communities" and of new and counter modes of self-representation and self-identification that offer possibilities for members of the minoritarian communities to alter the conditions for themselves. And those of us who are ensconced in notions of "at-risk" com-munities know that HIV/AIDS—the disease itself—does not discriminate. It has no boundaries. On the contrary, it is the health and sociopolitical responses to it—on a local, national, and global scale—that do. This fact marks the difference between *prevention* (from the outside) and *intravention* and the dialectic between the two that is necessary to ameliorate the epidemic.

I do not romanticize performance by suggesting that it can totally overhaul or transform the social and material conditions in which ballroom members live. Some members fall through the cracks, many die, but some survive and they do so with the assistance of fellow ballroom members. Ballroom culture demon-strates how performance can add value and meaning to the lives of those rendered valueless and meaningless. But as cultural critic and homo-hip-hop artist Tim'm West aptly argues, since there are few safe spaces for black queers, especially those suffering from HIV, many of us must claim all spaces as salvageable in whichever ways it supports our breathing.[58]

NOTES

1. I interviewed Wolfgang Busch on November 30, 2003, in New York City. He is the director of *How Do I Look*, a recent documentary on ballroom culture in New York City released in January of 2006. Wolfgang said that he wants the proceeds from the film to be dedicated to HIV/AIDS prevention. *How Do I Look*, directed by Wolfgang Busch (2006, New York: Art From The Heart, LLC) DVD; for more information and updates go to http://www.howdoilooknyc.org.

2. Cathy J. Cohen, "Deviance as Resistance: A New Research Agenda for the Study of Black Politics," *Du Bois Review* 1, no. 1 (2004), 27–45.

3. This chant by Neiman Marcus Escada was taken from a CD of house music mixes called "Bamabounce."

4. *Paris Is Burning*, directed by Jennie Livingston (1990, Burbank, CA: Off White Produc-tions, Inc., Miramax Home Entertainment, Buena Vista Home Entertainment, 2005) DVD.

5. Currently, the Gay Men's Health Crisis (GMHC) has the longest standing HIV/AIDS prevention program that focuses on the ballroom community. The House of Latex of the GMHC has held its annual Latex Ball (an HIV/AIDS prevention ball) for 18 years. The Latex Ball is by far the most popular ball in the country, usually drawing between 2,500 to 3,000 audience members/participants. Ironically, this program is not recognized by the CDC as an intervention and it is not federally funded.

6. Performance or performative ethnography is a method of data collection that requires that the researcher actively participate in the very performances and cultural practices that he/she is analyzing. Simply put, for the performance ethnographer, performance is the object and the method of study, as well as the theoretical framework through which the data is analyzed. More discussion on performance ethnography can be found in D. Soyini Madison's *Critical Ethnography: Method, Ethics, and Performance* (Thousand

Oaks, CA: Sage, 2005), Norman K Denzin's *Performance Ethnography: Critical Pedagogy and the Politics of Culture* (Thousand Oaks, CA: Sage, 2003), and E. Patrick Johnson's *Appropriating Blackness: Performance and the Politics of Authenticity* (Durham, NC: Duke University Press, 2003).

7. Samuel Friedman et al., "Urging Others to be Healthy: 'Intravention' by Injection Drug Users as a Community Prevention Goal," *AIDS Education and Prevention* 16, no. 3 (2004): 250–63.

8. Ibid.

9. E. Patrick Johnson, *Sweet Tea: Black Gay Men of the South (an Oral History)* (Chapel Hill: University of North Carolina Press, 2008), 8.

10. In 2003, I worked for Men of Color Motivational Group Inc. (MOC) in Detroit, Michigan. MOC had a CDC funded program that emphasized HIV/AIDS prevention among the ballroom community. The program lost its funding, and the organization eventually closed in the midst of controversy. For more information see Brent Dorian Carpenter, "Sexual Harassment Allegations Rock Men of Color: Funding Could Be at Risk," *Between the Line*, June 2003, 12–18, http:// www.pridesource.com.

11. It is worth noting that most qualitative studies that are conducted on HIV/AIDS within public health are not ethnographic. In my experience working with and among other HIV/AIDS researchers, I am usually the only ethnographer involved in any given research project.

12. Carlos Ulises Decena, "Surviving AIDS in an Uneven World: Latina/o Studies for a Brown Epidemic," in *A Companion to Latina/o Studies,* ed. Juan Flores and Renato Rosaldo (Malden, MA: Blackwell, 2007), 276–96.

13. Cathy Cohen, *The Boundaries of Blackness: AIDS and the Breakdown of Black Politics* (Chicago: University of Chicago Press, 1999).

14. Cathy J. Cohen, "Deviance as Resistance: A New Research Agenda for the Study of Black Politics," *Du Bois Review* 1, no. 1 (2004): 27–45.

15. Ki Namaste, "The Everyday Bisexual as Problematic: Research Methods beyond Monosexism," in *Inside the Academy and Out: Lesbian/Gay/Queer Studies and Social Action*, ed. Janice L. Ristock and Catherine G. Taylor (Toronto: University of Toronto Press, 1998), 110–35.

16. D. Soyini Madison and Judith Hamera, "Performance Studies at the Intersections," in *The Sage Handbook of Performance Studies*, ed. D. Soyini Madison and Judith Hamera (Thousand Oaks, CA: Sage, 2006), xi-xxv. For more elaboration on theories of performance and cultural formations and/or deployments of performance as resistance see José Muñoz, *Disidentifications: Queers of Color and the Performance of Politics* (Minneapolis: University of Minnesota Press, 1999).

17. Dwight Conquergood, "Performance Studies: Interventions and Radical Research," *The Drama Review* 46, no. 2 (2002): 145–56.

18. Robin D. G. Kelley, *Yo' Mama's Disfunktional! Fighting the Culture Wars in Urban America* (Boston: Beacon Press, 1997), 45.

19. Ibid.

20. David Román, *Acts of Intervention: Performance, Gay Culture, and AIDS (Unnatural Acts: Theorizing the Performative)* (Bloomington: Indiana University Press, 1998); Barbara Browning, *Infectious Rhythm: Metaphors of Contagion and the Spread of African Culture* (New York: Routledge, 1998).

21. Jan Zita Grover, "AIDS: Keywords," in *AIDS: Cultural Analysis, Cultural Activism,* ed. Douglas Crimp (Boston: MIT Press, 1998), 17–30.

22. Cindy Patton, *Fatal Advice: How Safe-Sex Education Went Wrong* (Durham, NC: Duke University Press, 1996), 23.

23. Grover, "AIDS: Keywords," 27.

24. Dwight Conquergood, "Of Caravans and Carnivals: Performance Studies in Motion," *The Drama Review* 39, no. 4 (1995): 137–41.

25. Román, *Acts of Intervention,* 155.

26. Friedman et al., "Urging Others to be Healthy," 250.

27. Ibid., 260.

28. Karen McCarthy Brown, "Mimesis in the Face of Fear: Femme Queens, Butch Queens, and Gender Play in the Houses of Greater Newark," in *Passing: Identity and Interpretation in Sexuality, Race, and Religion,* ed. María Carla Sánchez and Linda Schlossberg (New York: New York University Press, 2001), 208–27.

29. What I call the "gender/sexual identity system" is typically called the "gender system" within ballroom culture. My outline of the six subjectivities within the system is drawn from my ethnographic data that include my attendance/participation in balls, my analysis of numerous ball flyers, and interviews that I conducted with members from all over the country over a nine year period. Despite a few discrepancies among different sectors of the community, the general components of the system are standard throughout the ballroom scene. The gender/sexual identity systems is separate but inextricably linked to the competitive categories that appear on ball flyers. At balls, competitive performance categories abound, but the gender and sexual identity system serves as the basis upon which the competitive categories are created. For an example and an analysis of a ball flyer/program, see David Valentine's *Imagining Transgender: an Ethnography of a Category* (Durham, NC: Duke University Press, 2007), 78–84.

30. Emily Arnold and Marlon Bailey, "Constructing Home and Family: How the Ballroom Community Supports African American GLBTQ Youth in the Face of HIV/AIDS," *Spec Issue: The Journal of Gay and Lesbian Social Services: Issues in Practice, Policy, & Research* (forthcoming): 1–34.

31. Sel Julian Hwahng and Nuttbrock, "Sex Workers, Fem Queens, and Cross-Dressers: Differential Marginalizations and HIV Vulnerabilities among Three Ethnocultural Male-to-Female Transgender Communities in New York City," *Sexuality Research & Social Policy: Journal of NSRC* 4, no. 4 (2007): 36–59.

32. While I acknowledge the participation of Latina/o queer people in ballroom culture in some locations, the majority of ballroom members are black queer people. Since my primary site of examination is Detroit, Michigan, where the ballroom scene is almost exclusively black, all of my interlocutors and the communities to whom I refer are black queer people.

33. Brett C. Stockdill, *Activism against AIDS: At the Intersections of Sexuality, Race, Gender, and Class* (Boulder: Lynne Rienner, 2003), 4.

34. All statistics cited here are from the "Home Page," Michigan Department of Community Health, last modified 2008, http://www.michigan.gov/mdch.

35. In a five city study of HIV infection among black MSM conducted by the CDC in 2005, it was estimated the 46 percent of black MSM are infected with HIV/AIDS and 64 percent of those who tested positive were unaware of their status. Centers for Disease Control and Prevention, "HIV Prevalence, Unrecognized Infection, and HIV Testing among Men Who Have Sex with Men—Five U.S. Cities," *Morbidity and Mortality Weekly Report* 54 (2005): 597–601.

36. One of the critical problems with the reporting of HIV epidemiological data by local health departments is that the data is not often disaggregated by race, gender, and "sexual risk categories." As a result, most of the data collected on the local level does not provide specific numbers on black MSM.

37. "Home Page," Michigan Department of Community Health, last modified 2008, http://www.michigan.gov/mdch.
38. "Census 2000 Gateway," US Census, last modified April 1, 2000, http://www.census.gov/main/www/cen2000.html.
39. Cathy J. Cohen, "Contested Membership: Black Gay Identities and the Politics of AIDS," in *Queer Theory/Sociology*, ed. Steven Seidman (Cambridge, MA: Blackwell, 1996), 372.
40. Roy Cain, "Gay Identity Politics in Community-Based AIDS Organizations," in *Inside the Academy and Out: Lesbian, Gay, Queer Studies and Social Action*, ed. Janice L. Ristock and Catherine G. Taylor (Toronto: University of Toronto, 1998), 200. More elaboration on this can be found in Cathy Cohen's *The Boundaries of Blackness: AIDS and the Breakdown of Black Politics* (Chicago: University of Chicago Press, 1999); Steven Seidman, ed., *Queer Theory/Sociology* (Cambridge: Blackwell, 1996); and Brett C. Stockdill, *Activism Against AIDS: at the Intersections of Sexuality, Race, Gender, and Class* (Boulder: Lynne Rienner, 2003).
41. Lester K. Spence, "Uncovering Black Attitudes about Homosexuality and HIV/AIDS" (paper presented at the National Conference of Black Political Scientist in Alexandria, Virginia, 2005, 1–30).
42. Ibid., 6.
43. Cathy J. Cohen, *The Boundaries of Blackness: AIDS and the Breakdown of Black Politics* (Chicago: University of Chicago Press, 1999), 70.
44. Ibid.
45. Ibid.
46. Román, *Acts of Intervention*, xxiii.
47. Nancy E. Stoller, *Lessons from the Damned: Queers, Whores, and Junkies Respond to AIDS* (New York: Routledge, 1998), 2.
48. Cain, "Gay Identity Politics," 200.
49. Stuart Hall, "What Is This 'Black' in Black Popular Culture?," in *Black Popular Culture*, ed. Gina Dent (Seattle: Bay Press, 1992), 1–21.
50. Friedman et al., "Urging Others to be Healthy," 251.
51. Kim D. Butler, "Defining Diaspora, Refining a Discourse," *Diaspora* 10, no. 2 (2001): 189–218.
52. Vinh-Kim Nguyen, "Uses and Pleasures: Sexual Modernity, HIV/AIDS and Confessional Technologies in a West African Metropolis," in *Sex in Development: Science, Sexuality, and Morality in Global Perspective,* ed. Vincanne Adams and Stacy Leigh Pigg (Durham, NC: Duke University Press, 2005), 245–68.
53. Noir Prestige died from complications of HIV/AIDS, May 4, 2005, in Detroit, Michigan.
54. In ballroom culture, "realness" refers to a fundamental set of criteria for performance. These criteria have been a part of ballroom culture throughout its more than five decades of existence. Realness requires strict adherence to certain performances, self-presentations, and embodiments that are believed to capture the authenticity of particular gender and sexual identities. I argue elsewhere that these criteria are established and function based on a schema of race and class that give realness its discursive power in both the Ballroom scene as well as in society at large. Thus the performance criteria for schoolboy realness and executive realness include not only "looking like" a school boy or an executive, but also performing gender as a man with normative masculinity that signifies "straight" sexuality.
55. Cornel West, "Nihilism in Black America," in *Black Popular Culture,* ed. Gina Dent (Seattle: Bay Press, 1992), 37–47.

56. In ballroom lingo, "snatching a trophy" means winning the category and being awarded a trophy and/or a cash prize. This term is also referred to as "slay and snatch: slaying the competitors and snatching the trophy."

57. This annual ball is cosponsored by the House of Rodeo and the Minority AIDS Project in Los Angeles.

58. Tim'm West, "Keepin' It Real: Disidentification and Its Discontents," in *Black Cultural Traffic: Crossroads in Global Performance and Popular Culture*, ed. Harry J. Elam Jr. and Kennell Jackson (Ann Arbor: University of Michigan Press, 2005), 162–84.

CHAPTER 15

IN THE HEAT

TOWARD A PHENOMENOLOGY OF BLACK MEN LOVING/SEXING EACH OTHER

H. SHARIF WILLIAMS (HERUKHUTI)

Black men loving black men is [a] revolutionary act.

—Joseph Beam

So to live in a Black male body and to desire other Black male bodies is to move about daily on a physical, psychological, and spiritual battleground.

—Ibrahim Abdurrahman Farajaje (formerly Elias Farajaje-Jones)

These moments open our eyes to the walls that have been constructed to constrain our pleasures, desires, passions, and bodies . . . We can choose to draw power from these moments in service to our growth and liberation. We can choose to make [them] moments of erotic agitation in the struggle for our sensual empowerment. The choice is ours on a personal and a social level.

—Herukhuti

IN THE UNITED STATES, BLACK MEN WHO seek to feel each other sexually and/or emotionally encounter a number of historical and contemporary obstacles to doing so. From a historical context, as early as the beginnings of the European colonial project and the enslavement of African people, black male sexuality was managed and policed by the social structures of the day—social policy, law, and commerce (Bennett 297–325; Farajaje-Jones 327). These systems of management and policing served to organize black male sexuality in ways that maintained the good order of capitalism, white supremacy, and patriarchy. In the contemporary context, black male sexuality is managed and policed by contemporary social structures, for example, heterosexism, sexism, white supremacy, and capitalism. Contemporary systems of management and policing differ in certain ways from the historical. Now hip-hop hypermasculinity and hyperheterosexuality, a throwback to the Hollywood-produced black buck archetype of black manhood (Bogle

10); Obama-era politics of respectability, a throwback to the Duboisian talented tenth agenda; and HIV/AIDS prevention, as a sociological, psychological, epidemiological, and spiritual phenomenon that has come to be associated with behavior surveillance and modification, function to constrain the possibilities of feeling and being felt by another black man and marginalize the spaces for such feelings, emotional and physical, to transpire.

So what's a brother to do when he's working to understand these temporal and spatial environs in which black men have sex with other men? I, a doctoral student at the time, was faced with this question as a graduate research assistant employed at the HIV Center for Clinical and Behavioral Studies in New York City and working on my own pilot study of the role of pleasure, emotions, and gender performance in the sexual decision making and risk taking of black and Latino men who have sex with men. I was interested in learning, at the level of ethnographic understanding, about the sexual choreography of black and Latino men who have sex with men—from the moment of contact until the moments just after sex ends. I wanted to be able to say ethnographically that I could feel these men.

I say ethnographically because at the level of the personal I already did feel these men. As a black man who had sex with men and women, I knew and practiced the sexual choreography of finding an interested and desired partner, establishing a mutual sexual understanding, securing a location, and having sex. But in the knowledge production and management context of the US HIV industrial complex, personal knowledge and experience in sex is subjugated knowledge. Like those who criticized the centering of critical self-reflection in the second wave feminist movement resulting in the response "the personal is political" (Hanisch), the HIV industrial complex requires the subversion of personal knowing in legitimate discussions of sexuality and the denial of the concept of the personal being the social except in matters of transmission vectors or disseminations of HIV prevention strategies. A sample size of one is looked upon with great skepticism, particularly if that one is the self.

Therefore, I sought to find other men who could help me develop a sense of our sexual choreography that would be scientifically legitimate. I knew from my previous experiences talking with black people about sex that they oftentimes provide very little detail about the actual sex acts. A somewhat detailed story of how people met often degenerated into a quick summation of the actual sex, "we fucked." That truncated form of narrative is fairly useless from an ethnographic perspective. Choreography of any form comprises numerous choices, decisions, actions, reactions, and responses. It is important to have as much of these elements in view to be able to grasp the choreography as an entire system or script.

Script theory of sexuality has been found to be a useful approach for social scientists and cultural theorists to engage sexuality (Kimmel ix). Here is a basic articulation of the sexual scripts concept from *Sexual Conduct, 2nd Edition*:

> Our use of the term "script" with reference to the sexual has two major dimensions. One deals with the external, the interpersonal—the script as the organization of mutually shared conventions that allows two or more actors to participate in a complex act involving mutual dependence. The second deals with the internal, the

intrapsychic, the motivational elements that produce arousal or at least a commitment to the activity.

At the level of convention is that large class of gestures, both verbal and non-verbal, that are mutually accessible. Routinized language, the sequence of petting behaviors . . . the conventional styles establishing sexual willingness are all parts of culturally shared, external routine. These are the strategies involved in the "doing" of sex, concrete and continuous elements of what a culture agrees is sexual. (Gagnon and Simon 14)

By exploring these scripts and their meaning to the actors, one can understand the phenomenology of sexual experience for the actors. With that as my goal, I chose the specific methods—storytelling and narrative—and tools for the study (Williams 3).

THE MEANS TO MEANING

The means I took to access the intrapsychic and interpersonal scripts of the black men in my study was to engage them as storytellers. In individual, one-on-one interviews, I asked them to tell me a story about men having the most satisfying sex—specifically anal intercourse—possible. I asked the men to tell me the story in the third person. This third person storytelling technique was adopted from a narrative protocol used in *The Storytelling Project: Participant Manual.*[1] I primed the men prior to the storytelling by asking them questions about each of the "characters" involved in their story. After the characters had been developed, I asked the men to tell me the story. I rarely interrupted the men while they told their story and only did so to ask a clarifying question if I didn't hear them or understand a word or phrase. After each man told his story, I asked a series of *probe questions* to enlist each man in the analysis and exploration of his story.

The third person storytelling and enlisting the storyteller in the analysis and exploration of his story created a partnership relationship between the research participants and me in the context of the interviews. We were both engaged in the examination of this thing out there—the story—in ways that are different than when a researcher looks at the research participant as the objectified subject. And yet, at the same time, I maintained some level of the interested yet detached posture of traditional researcher. This was in part due to the context in which I was conducting the study—as a junior researcher under supervision at a tier one, large research institution.

This was not a community-based research context by any means even though I considered myself a member of the community in which the research took place. Each of the men that I interviewed I saw as my brothers. Although I knew only a few of them from the community prior to their participation in the study, I could recognize them as representatives of a community in which I had friends, associates, and lovers. I hoped this translated into a demeanor that in addition to being the interested, neutral researcher also said, "I see you. I feel you. I am of you."

I cleaned the data of identifiers and substituted Afrocentric names as aliases for names the interviewees used in telling their stories while using a numerical code for each interviewee. My research team coded the data from the interviews for emergent themes using content analysis (Lieblich, Tuval-Mashiach, and Zilber 112). Approximately 29 coding nodes were generated (e.g., "being a bottom," "being a top," "the body and bodily fluids," "childhood sexual abuse or inter-generational sexual contact during childhood," "communication," "drug use," "effeminacy," "expectations," "HIV/AIDS," "hook up choreography," "mas-culinity," "partner choice," "partner description," "passion, lust, and desire," "penetration," "places where sex happens," "pleasure and ecstasy," "preparation for sex," "race," "reasons for condom use," "reasons for no condom use," "reasons to have sex," "relationship to sex," "self-concept," "sexual initiation," "sources of sexual knowledge," "stories," "timing of condom introduction," and "women as referent").

For the purpose of this chapter, I selected specific nodes (e.g., "pleasure and ecstasy," "love and intimacy," and "passion, lust, and desire") to explore the affec-tive elements of the data most relevant to the book. I then conducted a second level of content analysis to the data provided by the black men (17 in total) in the study to construct the discussion provided in this chapter. I used the word *construct* because I believe that research is a constructed narrative.

Good qualitative research is a self-aware and critically self-reflective storytell-ing and construction of narrative. I don't purport this work to be the absolute truth but rather a truth—a true reading—of the data generated from the study. I ground my discussion, therefore, in the data, my experience, and existing theory so as to make meaning of what I experienced as a researcher in this context. I hope my understanding is useful to you in your journey to understand—to feel me and these men through me.

Of the 17 men whose data were analyzed for this chapter—ranging in ages from the early twenties to the midforties, 32.5 percent were primarily/exclusively anal insertive (i.e., tops) and believed themselves to be HIV negative or primar-ily/exclusively anal receptive (i.e., bottoms) and believed themselves to be HIV positive. Based on the epidemiology of HIV transmission and assuming their knowledge of their HIV status was accurate, these men are least likely to expose their partners to the HIV virus during condomless anal intercourse. Another 32.5 percent of the men were men who believed themselves to be HIV positive and either were primarily/exclusively anal insertive or had anal intercourse practices that varied considerably between anal insertive and anal receptive (i.e., versatiles). These men were most likely to expose their HIV negative partners to the HIV virus during condomless anal intercourse should they be the insertive partner. A third category comprised 35 percent of the men. These men who believed them-selves to be HIV negative either were primarily/exclusively anal receptive or had practices that varied between anal receptive and anal insertive. Assuming their beliefs about their HIV statuses were accurate, they were, therefore, most likely to be exposed to HIV by an HIV positive insertive partner during condomless sex. All the men had to have indicated that they engaged in condomless anal inter-course at least once within the three months prior to being screened for the study.

This epidemiological context is important for a number of reasons. Black sexuality research is currently funded because of the pathology paradigm—epistemological fetish in examining pathology. A basic (social) science of black sexuality is virtually nonexistent. Instead what we have are scientific incursions into black sexuality through studies of HIV and sexually transmitted infection prevention and unplanned/unwanted pregnancy (e.g., teen pregnancy). Our, black people's, basic and critical understanding of our sexuality is an area that receives little to know support financially or theoretically unless it can be produced through an examination of pathology in our communities.

The study that contributed the data for this discussion was funded to examine HIV prevention questions. The rationale that led to the funding of the study was rooted in the pathology paradigm. Although I am not an adherent of the pathology paradigm, I had to advance such a rationale in order to receive funds to engage in a thoughtful examination of black (male) sexuality. Living, working, and loving in a society that is governed by white supremacy and normativity, we, black folks, are constantly navigating and negotiating our access to resources to be able to do what we need to do for ourselves.

If—in reading the discussion of the data—you feel as though you are twisting and turning your perception to understand what I am saying about the phenomenology of black men loving/sexing each other, that is as it should be. I purposely organized the discussion of the data for that purpose—to give you the experience of the phenomenology as you are reading. It is a phenomenology that is twisting and turning—not easily experienced or understood. We, black men, twist and turn to meet each other in spaces of physical and emotional feeling. At least as early as our earliest introductions to white supremacy in the Americas, we have been twisted and turned by it and have twisted and turned in our navigation and negotiation of it. Our access to our bodies and our emotions has, in this context, been contested and confounded. The complexities and challenges of these dynamics will hopefully be obvious to black male readers with same-sex sexual experience and become apparent to readers without such experiences of blackness, maleness, and homosexual desire.

IN THE HEAT: DO YOU FEEL MY PLEASURE?

The men I interviewed used pleasure as a language that connected them to other men in deep and meaningful ways. Pleasure was the means through which the men could feel and be felt by each other. These men literally spoke in tongues, fingers, lips, dicks, and asses to bear witness to their own humanity and the humanity of others. They provided useful examples of how black men loving/ sexing each other provide pleasure through physical connection and intimacy, release of and freedom from pressure and stress, and facilitation of another man's pleasure and how these experiences define the nature of pleasure.

In the data, physical connection and intimacy are linked with pleasure at a very fundamental level. During the probe question section of our interview, Interviewee 014[2] and I had the following exchange regarding the story he shared with me:

> **326:**[3] PI (Principal Investigator): Tell me what, specifically, during the experience was pleasurable for Jahiem?

327: 014: I, probably the closeness of another human being. Mmm.

328: PI: When you say the closeness, what do you mean?

329: 014: Physically.

330: PI: Why, why was the closeness pleasurable?

331: 014: I guess that's one of the things that turns him on. That's what it is. That's one of the things that turns him on, the physical closeness.

Later, in exploring his version of ideal sex, Interviewee 014 and I have this exchange:

546: PI: During an ideal sex situation, what would be specifically pleasurable?

547: 014: During an ideal sexual situation, what would specifically be pleasurable? I guess, the sense of intimacy would be pleasurable.

548: PI: Ideally, that would be?

549: 014: Yeah.

550: PI: What would be specifically pleasurable.

551: 014: Yeah. Yeah. A sense of intimacy.

552: PI: Why, why a sense of intimacy? Why would that be pleasurable?

553: 014: For me, that's what sex is all about, so.

Other men I interviewed shared this desire for and pleasure from physical connection and intimacy. Interviewee 002 and I talked about the pleasure in his sex:

323: PI: What specifically is pleasurably about the sex you usually have?

324: 002: Yeah, OK, all right. Then honestly it is just, I think the end of it a lot of times. You know what I mean? After I get over washing myself and the person actually stays. Just to have that person lay down because I don't know, like I used to always sleep with my mother, then when I get sick up to the age of 20 probably, and I'm 22. I used to always go into bed with my mother if I had a cold or anything. I would jump into bed with my mother and just having a warm body to lay up next to and to cuddle with basically. That's the most pleasurable thing for me.

The physical reality of the pleasure created by a black male body against another black male body is a psychological, sociological, spiritual, and political statement. It writes against the genocidal compression of the transatlantic slave ship experience, backbreaking labor of the slave plantation, marginalizing slander of Jim Crow segregation, and physical conformity of neoliberal capitalism. Farajaje-Jones wrote, "Our bodies have been colonized and treated as though they were someone's occupied territories, with all sorts of projections and fears mapped out across them" (328). Therefore, when black men reclaim the territories of their bodies in being close to each other and feel each other, they write large the fundamental connection we have to our humanity.

In two of the interviews, Interviewees 020 and 064 articulated the vital nature of such physical connection. With Interviewee 020:

194: PI: Tell me what was specifically pleasurable for Sharif, in the experience.

195: 020: The feeling of, of being, being penetrated, being entered, having within [inaudible] having himself a part of someone, a vital part. Being close to as two people could possibly get. That's what it was.

With Interviewee 064:

> **482:** PI: Mmm-hmm. What was specifically pleasurable?
> **483:** 064: Being connected to somebody. Having somebody. Having, feeling whole, or whatever. Being connected to somebody, I think.

As black men in the United States, we live in a society in which we are inundated with messaging and structural violence that dehumanizes us. The pressure and stress of blackness and subordinate masculinity in Eurocentric and patriarchal society as well as the pressure and stress of class exploitation in a capitalist society make it necessary to carve out sites of humanization for black men. These spaces are contexts in which black men can remove themselves, even momentarily, from the pressure and stress.

Sex can be one of those contexts—spaces in which black men remove themselves from the brunt of the pressure and stress of experiencing structural violence and microaggressions. In our discussion of the feeling of ejaculation, Interviewee 024 and I had this exchange:

> **390:** PI: In that moment of ejaculation, what would you ideally be feeling?
> **391:** 024: I would feel, actually, I, I would feel good. Just coming makes me feel good.
> **392:** PI: "Good," what do you mean?
> **393:** 024: I want to say, "Lift a burden." I'm not, I'm not going to use those words again. I would say it's, it's just a good feeling that you get. At least it's for me. I can't say for anybody else, only for me. It makes me feel good, once I cum.

We can do this for each other and ourselves. The sexual space can become the place where we lay our burdens down as the gospel song, *Down by the Riverside*, suggests. But unlike in the song, in this context we lay our burdens down by the rivers of our orgasmic fluid or by the press of our flesh. Interviewee 016 put it thus in his discussion of pleasure:

> **216:** 016: The kissing, you know, the, the rubbing, the foreplay. You're, you're trying to make that person feel like he's somebody that he's wanted. And you're just using the, the sex acts to make that person feel that he's somebody.

Here, Interviewee 016 expands the field of Jesse Jackson's famous slogan, "I am somebody" to include ways of supporting another black man's personhood through the body. And there is a particular pleasure derived from the fact that it is the body that serves as the agent of the acknowledgement. Interviewee 035 said the following:

> **398:** 035: The freedom of it, I guess. Just the fact that my body's doing something that brings me pleasure. I don't know.

We acknowledge each other's personhood and feel pleasure. We seek to facilitate the pleasure of another black man and in so doing we are pleased. This erotic extension of the *Nguzo Saba* principle of *Ujima*—the Kwanzaa principle of collective work and responsibility, which makes our brothers' problems our own—makes our brothers' pleasure our own.

This was evident in the interview with Interviewee 009:

> **274:** PI: During foreplay, what are you usually feeling?
>
> **275:** 009: What am I usually feeling? A hunger. I'm usually feeling a hunger. It's, it's like a, it's a sexual hunger. It's a hunger to do things other than the actual penetration. Like to please you. You know what I mean. It's a hunger to explore your body, with, in all sorts of ways. By using my tongue and my hands. You know what I mean? That's what the hunger is.

In his interview, Interviewee 069 made concurring acknowledgments of the interconnected relationship between his pleasure and the pleasure of his brother:

> **447:** 069: So if I'm not seeing that you're satisfied, I'm either going to stop or rush through it, get my nut, and stop and just leave. Because it's, you know, it's sex. Supposed to be pleasurable for both of us, not just me. So if you're not enjoying yourself, you're taking away from the joy that I'm going to—that I should be feeling. Because I like to please my partners. And if I'm not pleasing you, I feel horrible! [laughs]
>
> **488:** PI: What specifically is pleasurable about the sex you usually have?
>
> **489:** 069: Making my partner cum.
>
> **490:** PI: Why that?
>
> **491:** 069: Making my partner cum is like—because if I don't, I don't feel that I'm doing my job right. And that's not a good feeling.
>
> **492:** PI: Mm.
>
> **493:** 069: And of course, I mean, ejaculating, myself, that's always a great thing. I mean, like I don't—I've gone days with sexual partners that I was just like, "OK, you got yours? Good! All right. We can stop now." Because like me cuming isn't; I can cum any time. Me making someone else cum, that's the purpose that I don't get every day, all day. So, excuse me, so I really take a lot of joy in that.

The men I interviewed talked to me about pleasure—the pleasure of sex and the pleasure in sex—in ways that connected me to their experience of pleasure. While maintaining the pose of an interested, disinterested researcher, I saw within myself the truth of the men's phenomenology of pleasure. We were able to *touch* each other through the act of storytelling and story listening in ways that mainstream sociomedical scientific research fails to do and therefore were able create a theory that heals, in addition to, informs. Our touch, while not physical, provided what Stallings called "the link that keeps both parties conscious of feelings, despite uncomfortableness" (110) and therefore "a location for healing" that hooks described as the healing potential of theory in saying, "I came to theory desperate, wanting to comprehend—to grasp what was happening around and within me. I saw in theory then a location for healing" (Stallings 59). By being with these men and understanding our experience via the process of theoretical and analytical interrogation, I was able to experience my own healing and cocreate a space of partnered investigation that held the possibility of healing for the men I interviewed.

In the Heat: Do You Feel My Intimacy?

While the men I interviewed found ways to feel other men physically—to make the physical connections that fostered physical intimacy—they struggled to find emotional connections and intimacy with the men with whom they had sex. In some cases, it was as if the intensity of the physical connection and intimacy established through sex was too much for the neurological circuitry—causing a short circuit to the emotional infrastructure of one or more of the parties. Short-circuited, the man would withdraw or flee from the connection. In other cases, the dearth of opportunities to connect emotionally with other men, to feel them at that level, left the black men in the study frustrated, pessimistic, and feeling a sense of loss.

This is profoundly paradoxical. Men possessing the capacity to establish such powerful and intense physical connections and intimacy find themselves wanting when it comes to establishing or maintaining powerful and intense physical connections and intimacy. One reason for this may be in their investment in maintaining the *cool pose* of black masculinity. Framing the concept of the cool pose, Majors and Billson wrote, "Coolness means poise under pressure and the ability to maintain detachment, even during [in]tense encounters. Being cool invigorates a life that would otherwise be degrading and empty. It helps the black male make sense out of his life and get what he wants from others. Cool pose brings a dynamic vitality into the black male's everyday encounters, transforming the mundane into the sublime and making the routine spectacular" (2). The experiences of the men in the study demonstrate how the cool pose can function as a barrier to feeling, life, achieving desires, and experiencing the sublime and spectacular at the level of the emotional. In our interview, Interviewee 002 and I had this exchange illustrating these dynamics:

> **235:** PI: How close to your dream sex or ideal sex is the story?
> **236:** 002: Well, um ideal sex it's pretty close. Just the whole, I don't know if it's the let go part, the fact that dude was kind of freaky and he didn't hold back a lot so that's like my dream sex. Just for you to let go as much as I let go and we try to both, we try to satisfy each other instead of just getting a nut, you know.
> **237:** PI: Let go of what?
> **238:** 002: Um.
> **239:** PI: [inaudible] let go of?
> **240:** 002: Just like restrictions or "I don't do this" or "I don't do that" or, um, let go of, um, just feeling like, um, you got to put up like a big front or some shit as far as like when you having sex. Like you don't like, dig, being smacked in your face or you don't like nut on your face and all that. He was the type of dude that would like bust on my face so it was like OK. You know so it was interesting you know.

By telling us what was ideal about the sex in the story—the letting go of the cool pose, the detached maintenance of poise, Interviewee 002 directs our attention to what he defines as a fulfilling connection. Lest we think that the desired connection is merely physical, there is this exchange between Interviewee 002 and myself:

277: PI: You said there was only one time where it was love or it felt like love?

278: 002: Yeah.

279: PI: Say that again.

280: 002: It was only on time I was dealing with a dude for like a year and I don't know if it was love. I don't know if it was love on his part but with me I was doing a lot of cheating.

281: PI: Say it again.

282: 002: I did a lot of cheating [laughter] and it ultimately came to an end after I cheated with the wrong person. And it was, it was like fucking with him was like no other and it was a whole year. You know how shit get boring after you fuck with somebody and we never had a bad time fucking. You know what I mean we was like, we were just like there. We was mentally connected, spiritually we was there. Emotionally we was there. It was nothing like the nut that I bust with him and everybody else that was just like two different; it's two different things all the way.

283: PI: What was different about it?

284: 002: I mean I guess.

285: PI: Or better yet, what was that nut like?

286: 002: That nut was like, the nut, it was like, I don't know. That's my baby. It was like, it was like OK um, I don't know. I don't know what the nut was like it was just like I love this nigger you know what I mean. Like I care for this nigger, there's a certain amount of respect for this nigger. You know what I mean like you won't have for other niggers. It's like and it was like you're making love. You're not just fucking. I mean y'all, y'all, I don't know. It was, it was a good feeling. It was like everything was right after we fucked. Right after I nutted, everything was cool. Whatever problems I was going through, whatever struggles I had it was like oh I could take on the world right now because me and my baby got up, we chilled, we did ours and it was cool.

In our interview, Interviewee 021 and I had this exchange that supports the notion that desires for connection reached beyond the physical for men in the study:

385: PI: Is there anything else that you're feeling, in addition to wanting more?

386: 021: I guess, to connect. Like, to have this sort of spiritual connection, like—to connect, that's all. That's the only best way I can put it.

The same was true in the interview with Interviewee 035:

259: PI: What would you change in the story to make it more ideal?

260: 035: They didn't have sex so soon. They would really get to know each other, and determine, to really see it, who that person is, what they're like, what their likes are, what their dislikes are. So when they do have sex, it will be, it will be more romantic. That's, that's what it would be.

261: PI: How would it be more romantic?

262: 035: I don't know. I just think you getting to know someone is a lot more romantic. I mean, it be, you know, that, and because they, you know, when you're having sex with a person, it's, [inaudible], it's on a deeper level. And especially because you're really, you're not just making love to that person's body, you know. I mean, in a sense, kind of, like, cliché, but you're sort of making love to that person's, you know, soul or spirit. You're more, there's more of an emotional connection, which is more romantic than it just being a physical connection or, "I, I like this person," "I like how they talk," or whatever. Or, you know, like, how they dress. You know, it's more of a, "well I really [inaudible] this person nice." Who they are as an individual. Who they are as a, as a person, you know. And and, you know, that turns me on even more than just the physical, you know?

Working with these data and witnessing the anguish communicated by the men in my study, I question the degree to which men who live the cool pose can experience the emotional connection that they seek. Does the coolness of the pose chill and make brittle the emotional infrastructure needed to maintain these desired emotional connections? In our interview, Interviewee 046 calls forth these questions so brilliantly in his analysis of the story he told me, which was based on his lived experience:

160: PI: What was Kareem feeling and thinking after the sex?

161: 046: It was great. It really was. It was great. I felt a sense of fulfillment, not just for myself, for—but for the other person. A sense of bonding. And some of what. And a sense of, sense of growth between the two people.

162: PI: What's the end of the story of Kareem and Abdul? How does their story end?

163: 046: Tragic. A sense, a sense of loss.

164: PI: Why? How was it tragic?

165: 046: I think tragic because I think Abdul never really got hold of the fact that he had someone who was giving him just what he needed, as far as the nurturing, the loving, the way the person treat him as a—as a man, as a—just a person—a person who didn't want to be; what's the right word? I don't want to take more time getting it out. Just in a sense, just didn't want to make the person feel left than—less than.

166: PI: And you said Abdul never got over that. That was a bad thing for Abdul?

167: 046: Well, for him it was, yeah, because he didn't, in his mind, because he never had those kind of feelings before for another guy, or another guy never give him those kind of feelings, it was hard for him to be able to deal with those kind of feelings and put them into perspective, and to realize that just it can be like this. It doesn't have to be what he's used to. So.

168: PI: So what did Abdul end up doing?

169: 046: Breaking it off, breaking off the relationship. So it was just a little too mu—it was a little too emotionally—it was too a little bit emotional for him to deal with what was going on in his—in his mind and, and the feelings he were having—was having.

170: PI: Mmm.

171: 046: It was easier for him to go back to dealing with guys that would be more what he's used to. That way he—he can focus on, "OK, well, I already know what's going to happen." He don't have to worry about putting himself out there. And so if it goes bad, it goes bad. But it's something that, that he knows is good. So it'll be harder to challenge itself. And it wasn't enough of a challenge.

172: PI: Where did that leave Kareem?

173: 046: Knowing that that's just some of the things that can happen. It's, it's just something that can happen in, you know, in relationships, especially when you have someone who is emotionally; I don't know the right word for it. Maybe emotionally beaten down, something like that.

In my previous work, I've discussed the painful challenges of establishing a deep emotional and spiritual intimacy—such as the one described and desired by the men in the study—through or during sex without having had a foundation for nurturing that connection after the sex. In *Conjuring Black Funk, Volume 1*, I said,

> In most of my relationships, the point at which we decide to have sex is sooner rather than later. That's partly because most of my relationships have started when I developed an emotional attachment to someone with whom I only initially intended to have sex . . . In part because of my internalization of social messages, I forget how profound and intimate an immediate sexual encounter with someone can be. In forgetting that reality, I frequently underestimate the potential of those encounters then I wake up next to someone and a deep emotional, spiritual connection has been made without any other aspects of the foundation of an ongoing relationship . . . It can be very, very painful too. You've already established a significant bond/connection and now you have to discover if you and the other person(s) know how to maintain and support the connection, are capable of maintaining and supporting the connection, and are interested in maintaining and supporting the connection. Damn!
>
> Coming to terms with the answers to those questions can work you the fuck out. (129)

While we may seek and appreciate connecting, what Interviewee 020 called, the "vital part[s]" (line 195) of each other, we, as black men loving/sexing each other, are confronted by the emotional and spiritual consequences of our attempts to feel each other. The men in the study suggest that it is easier for us to feel the physical pleasure of each other than it is to feel intimacy with each other. The poise and detachment of the cool pose may not be, particularly when it mediates between our sharing of emotional intimacy, as useful and empowering as it has been constructed in other contexts.

In the Heat: Do You Feel My Desire?

Desire and lust among the men in the study offer an interesting countermetaphor to the cool pose. Over and over again, the men in the study used the metaphor of *heat* to talk about the desire, lust, and passion they felt in their sexual choreography. They talked about being *turned on* by lovers who moved them to arousal. The men referred to *chemistry* being shared in ways that were undeniable, immediate, and compelling.

Like pleasure and ecstasy, desire, lust, and passion functioned as connective tissue between the men in my study and their sex partners. The heat of desire, lust, and passion bonded them in the choreography of sex. Desire, lust, and passion were the language spoken, sometimes with words and other times with bodies.

In our interview, Interviewee 009 and I had this exchange:

322: PI: Do you usually let the men you're having sex with know that you're feeling pleasure?

323: 009: Yeah, by moaning. But sometimes I don't. Because I want them to work harder.

324: PI: Explain.

325: 009: Sometimes, when you're having sex with a person, and then when they're all into it, sometimes you can sense that they have more to offer, and they might be holding back. So sometimes I hold back, and I moan. And it'd be like, "Come on, baby. Be a freak with me. Be a freak with me." And it forces them to work harder. And then you give them a little bit by simply moaning. Or you, you simply make the booty spin or bounce back on the dick or something like that. Or you do some sweet that's going to blow their fucking mind like, "That's the fuck I'm talking about!" And then they start working even harder, like, "Yeah!"

326: PI: Sweet like what?

327: 009: Huh?

328: PI: Something sweet like what?

329: 009: When I say sweet, something like fun or something like hot.

In his interview, Interviewee 003 discussed the passion and lust of the men in his story:

205: 003: Khafra' legs were shaking, and he was ejaculating; stuff like that. Khafra was hot, his eyes. His eyes looked very determined; his eyes were just focused on just fucking the hell out of me, out of Seneferu. [laughs] Oops. [laughs] Out of Seneferu; stuff like that. And so, Seneferu just felt very; Seneferu just felt very freaky, and Seneferu just felt very, "this guy . . . this guy's doing a good job." And Khafra just looked very sweaty and nice, and he came on top of Seneferu's back.

The heat of our passion, lust, and desire can melt the cool pose, even to the point of shaking our legs and making our bodies sweat. In our interview, Interviewee 002 and I also explored the phenomenology of being in the heat:

403: PI: In an ideal situation, how would you know that you're feeling these things?

404: 002: I don't know, your heart will race. I mean I don't know. You're feelings just start. I mean you feel the tension in the air, you feel the sexual heat between y'all and the heat is good too. Like when both of your bodies are at a degree of heat bumping together.

It is noteworthy that it is in the heat that "you're feelings just start" (line 404). It is those moments of heat that inspired me to write the following in the poem *The Kiss*:

> when desire wrests itself free
> moves from the heart cavity
> lips part to release,
> breath previously trapped by possibility
> whispers lust's secret into the space
> between lovers,

and need builds a bridge that curiosity
planned a long time ago (1).

Interviewee 046 acknowledged the erotic epistemology contained in the passion of a kiss:

181: 046: And when they first kissed, they knew it was something there. There was definitely some chemistry there, a very passionate chemistry.

The chemistry, heat, and turn on of the passion, desire, and lust created the context for the men in the study to feel each other and the potential for them to know each other in that feeling. Passion, desire, and lust were the instigators of feeling as feeling was the gatekeeper of pleasure.

IN THE HEAT: CRUCIBLE FOR NAKED (R)EVOLUTION

In the heat of black men loving/sexing each other, there exists epistemological and liberatory resources, for example, passion, lust, and desire; intimacy; and pleasure and ecstasy. Farajaje-Jones wrote, "So much has told us that we are evil because we do not have sex for the sole purpose of reproduction; so much has told us that we are incarnations of evil because we like sex. As Black queer male bodies, we struggle against the image of us as too libidinal, too lust driven, too sexually criminal, and this struggle has given us other ways of viewing sex and bodies" (331). Yes, we are libidinal and lustful. We seek out and relish in the pleasures our corporeal selves can provide. We hunger for the intensity and heat that our flesh produces against the right body with the right knowledge of how to encourage our ecstasy. And some of us feel these lusts and passions at multiple levels of being—physical, emotional, and spiritual.

Perhaps, same-sex sexuality, for black men regardless of sexual identity, represents a site of potential liberation from the emotional restrictions of the cool pose. Same-sex sexual experience could provide an emancipatory language of the body and affect that black men can use to step outside of the confines of socially accepted and acceptable black male embodiment—outside the politics of respectability—in a society that is simultaneously patriarchal, white supremacist, and capitalist.

Within the heat of black male-male sexuality, there exists an opportunity for feeling (e.g., desire, lust, connection, vulnerability, security, power, etc.) and affect. This opportunity can serve as a warming call to reimagine and reconfigure black male embodiment. The challenge is to retrofit our emotional infrastructures to be as resilient in response to the heat of our emotional connections and intimacy as our bodies have been to the heat of our physical connections and intimacy. If we accomplish that task, we will be able to see each other, feel each other, see ourselves, and feel ourselves, which is was that make our love/sex with each other truly revolutionary.

That is what I mean by naked revolution. When we are able to be as comfortable being emotionally nude with each other as we are being physically nude, we will be better able to practice a revolution—a social movement for social justice—that is intimate and local and at the same time intensely transformative.

WORKS CITED

Beam, Joseph. "Brother to Brother: Words from the Heart." *In the Life: A Black Gay Anthology.* Ed. Joseph Beam. Boston: Alyson, 1986. 230–42. Print.

Bennett, Lerone, Jr. *Before the Mayflower: A History of Black America.* 5th ed. New York: Penguin, 1982. Print.

Bogle, Donald. *Toms, Coons, Mulattoes, Mammies & Bucks: An Interpretive History of Blacks in American Films.* 4th ed. New York: Continuum, 2001. Print.

Farajaje-Jones, Elias. "Holy Fuck." *Male Lust: Pleasure, Power, and Transformation.* Eds. Kerwin Kay, Jill Nagle, and Baruch Gould. New York: Harrington Park, 2000. 327–35. Print.

Gagnon, John, and William Simon. *Sexual Conduct: The Social Sources of Human Sexuality.* 2nd ed. Piscataway: Aldine Transaction, 2005. Print.

Hanisch, Carol. "The Personal Is Political." *CarolHanish.org.* N.p., Feb. 1969. Web. 20 May 2010.

Herukhuti. *Conjuring Black Funk: Notes on Culture, Sexuality, and Spirituality, Volume 1.* New York: Vintage Entity, 2007. Print.

———. "*The Kiss.*" 2009. Unpublished poem.

Kimmel, Michael. *The Sexual Self: The Construction of Sexual Scripts.* Nashville: Vanderbilt UP, 2007. Print.

Lieblich, Amia, Rivka Tuval-Mashiach, and Tamar Zilber. *Narrative Research: Reading, Analysis, and Interpretation.* Thousand Oaks: Sage, 1998. Print.

Majors, Richard, and Janet M. Billson. *Cool Pose: The Dilemmas of Black Manhood in America.* New York: Simon and Schuster, 1993. Print.

Stallings, L. M. *Mutha Is Half a Word: Intersections of Folklore, Vernacular, Myth and Queerness in Black Female Culture.* Columbus: Ohio UP, 2007. Print.

The Wheel Council. *The Storytelling Project: Participant Manual.* Flagstaff: The Wheel Council, 2005. Print.

Williams, Hameed S. *Journeying through the Erotic: Narrative and Storytelling in New Millennium Sex Research.* 2006. Unpublished manuscript.

NOTES

1. My dissertation chair, Dr. Annabelle Nelson, developed the narrative protocol for her organization The WHEEL Council. She introduced me to third-person storytelling as a research method.

2. Because of the sociomedical science context of this study, research participants were given numbers to maintain their anonymity.

3. These numbers are line numbers for the text of the written transcript for each interview.

Figure 16.1 Mizz Jade (Davon Chance) from Cryptofemme series by Chloé Zetkov

CHAPTER 16

FOR "THE CHILDREN" DANCING THE BELOVED COMMUNITY

JAFARI SINCLAIRE ALLEN

seeking a now that can breed futures
like bread in our children's mouths

—Audre Lorde

WE STUMBLE, GRACEFULLY, OUT OF THE BLUE-BLACK club light. Walls painted with black acoustic tile and heavy velvet blackout curtains have cocooned our nascent comings, goings, and carryings on. "We are exhausted. [And] afraid of the passion that briefly consoles us."[1] Much has happened as time stood still—while we conjured moments of rapturous faggotry. In the harsh glare of leaving and forgetting, we get distorted glimpses of our present. And I wonder about this current moment—half-past, or thirty 'til. This time 10, 15, 25 years too late? And I wonder. I want to look for what we have forgotten, inside. J. Halberstam writes, "I am in a drag king club at 2:00 a.m. . . . and the people in the club recognize why they are here, in this place at this time, engaged in activities that probably seem pointless to people stranded in hetero temporalities. Queer time for me is the dark nightclub, the perverse turn away . . . a theory of queerness as a way of being in the world and a critique of the careful social scripts that usher even the most queer among us through major markers of individual development and into normativity."[2] But as Halberstam demonstrates elsewhere,[3] turning away from the "the careful social scripts" have wildly disparate meanings and consequences for subjects for whom access to the scripts—and to status as subject, citizen, person, or any normativity whatsoever—is always already troubled.[4] Indeed, the iconic sexualized black body is "so boundlessly imagined" that the black person discursively "loses meaning."[5] Some are multiply vulnerable, in a land with no people, "cut off from among their people," and in graves unmarked. While my larger project attempts to take up the charge to draw blackprints of collective resistance by folks whose lives "are indicative of the intersection of marked identities and regulatory processes, relative powerlessness and limited and contradictory agency,"[6] here I want to linger on one site of grace imagined and experienced in order to point toward other sites, experiences, and instances of freedom in collectivity. I offer the underground black queer club as a key site for an exploration of not only individual desire and autonomy but also community. This intervention is made within a particularly "queer time"—past and present, futures yearned for and denied—and "queer place"—the club, the black queer page, stage, and canvas of everyday life. Beyond encouraging an orientation toward a black queer studies that is at once about material effects and resonant affect, I also hope to sketch some ways we might rethink recent debates on the child, relationality, and futurity in queer studies, which have proceeded without the voices of "the children." Although Edelman writes, convincingly, "Fuck the social order and the Child in whose name we're collectively terrorized; fuck Annie; fuck the waif from Les Mis; fuck the poor innocent kid on the Net; fuck Laws both with capital ls and with small; fuck the whole Symbolic relations and the future that serves as its prop."[7]

I do not mean, here, the constructed white, middle-class child in whose name the symbolic orders itself and for whom legislatures craft law, which Lee Edelman strategically poses as opposite queer in his recent book, *No Future: Queer Theory and the Death Drive*. By "the children," I mean of course, Dorothys, or, in more recent black gay parlance, same-gender-loving—gay, bisexual, lesbian, transgender, queer—people of color. These children's temporal, spatial, and relational orientations and on-the-ground politics are certainly distinct from the gay world divorced of relationality, politics, and reality that Lee Edelman theorizes, following Lacanian psychoanalytic theory. But my objective is not to quarrel with Lacan, or psychoanalysis more broadly. Hortense Spillers and, more recently, Antonio Viego have already argued for what Spillers calls "the proper . . . contextualiz[ation] and confrontation between 'psychoanalysis' and 'race,'"[8] and Viego holds that there is an antiracist charge in Lacanian theory.[9] My contention is that although Edelman forcefully recaptures some of the innovative potential of queer theory by tracing cultural shifts of white, middle-class gay men toward the so-called mainstream, his attempt to universalize this argument beyond its limited borders at once disappears black feminist theory and attempts to "dispense with" the utopic impulse of radical queer-of-color critique,[10] which has much to offer his theorization and thus enervates the real radical potential of refusal, negativity, and ruthless questioning of futurity that he suggests. Edelman proceeds without an analysis of the differences between and among those queered by the coconstitutive dominative mode of racial, sexual, and gender hierarchies. Further, following Lacanian theory, in which the "real" is an effect of language and not to be confused with reality, everyday suffering and death is not his concern in *No Future*. Here, I am looking very differently at death and subjectivity. I am writing for the children of color—the kids routinely harassed, criminalized, and targeted for destruction, displaced from the small shelters they had built. Thus it is more aligned with the queer-of-color critique of Audre Lorde, Joseph Beam, Essex Hemphill, Barbara Smith, Gloria Anzaldúa, and others and reflected in the utopian hermeneutics of José Esteban Muñoz. He writes, "The queerness of queer futurity, like the blackness of a black radical tradition, is a relational and collective modality of endurance and support . . . It is a being in, toward, and for futurity."[11]

We must recognize that normative assumptions of futurity are dangerous. In *Homos*, Leo Bersani brilliantly calls out gay and lesbian resignification of family and citizen for often having "assimilative rather than subversive consequences."[12] Still, while it is true that for many the price of citizenship is costly and valued since normative family accrues only with tremendous sacrifice, for others, the unruliness of excessive blackness precludes this altogether. Extending M. Jacqui Alexander's theorization of the state's simultaneous sexualization, racialization, and gendering of particular bodies, "not just (any) body can be a citizen any more,"[13] not every child—and almost no black child—resembles the child in Edelman's polemic. Indeed, *No Future* might be productively read against the 2008 passage of Proposition 8 in California. Although diametrically opposed politically, each show a related brand of white gay refusal to recognize the complexity of the life-worlds of those for whom "sexual liberation" alone will not guarantee freedom just as much as it "reveals" (for those outside of black communities) religious conservatism in black communities, which takes heterosexism as doctrinal.

COMING/OUT WITH YOU

Pearls clutched and wide-eyed with amazement, I called myself brave, riding the Long Island Railroad to the city, hoping that indeed something would happen. That the safety that my particular home represented would be temporarily interrupted by thick danger and wet excitement. Donald Woods has already told our story: "ladies-in waiting gasp . . . shoulder to shoulder sissies/on the crest of manhood / twirling like tomorrow is certain / dipping and diving / like the future / like forever."[14] A combination of privilege and cowardice prevented the lure from being completely irresistible for James and me, 17-year-olds with Queens addresses, absent "bridge and tunnel" self-images. Experiences like ours are quite different from the reality of so many of the children we passed on Christopher Street, or the Piers, with no homes to which they could return. "For the embattled," Audre Lorde has already reminded us, "there is no place / that cannot be home / no is,"[15] which says therefore that there is no one that cannot be family, or is.

The night and the club thus provide an essential and unique space to lose the minds one uses all week, to find small cracks and crevices to call home. In some ways resonant with the nonpolitics that Edelman advocates, the kinds of "coming/out" that I participated in required no parade and no declarations outside of our cocoons of recognition. Samuel Delany offers coming/out as a way to understand the accretion of events and relationships that shape the "process of becoming who we are" in his luminous essay of the same name.[16] While to be a homosexual is pitched as if it is about individuality and "coming out" of established heteronormative structures and logics, but not necessarily into anything at all, what if we think of queer as precisely not about individualism and moving outside but as a continual, dynamic project of constituting a collection of interstitial outsider perspectives? Getting our lives (together). "Yonder they do not love your [body] . . . Here in this place, we flesh . . . flesh that weeps, laughs; flesh that dances on bare feet in grass. Love it . . . This is flesh that I am talking about here.

Flesh that needs to be loved."[17] Toni Morrison is audacious in her insistence that former "slaves" in the post–Civil War Midwest claim their own bodies and bodily pleasure as their own. Black lesbians and gay men in the current late capitalist moment are no less transgressive. No less flesh that needs to be loved than the reconstructed subjects in her *Beloved*, gathered together "here, in this place" to hear an old woman preach amid the trees. Reading Morrison, I hear electronic claps, djembe drums, and cowbells. Tambourines and whistles shout. Sweat pours off my face and hers. His body, mine. A choir hums as Sylvester sings/preaches Baby Suggs's words to a hard-hitting house beat.

The club is the central institution of black queer communion. Here we assert bodies, putatively and dangerously riddled with disease and threat of violence, not only as instruments of pleasure but also as conduits to profound joy and, perhaps, spiritual bliss and transcendent connection, interstices or conduits that connect, perhaps, to utopias.

BABY POWDER LINES CONSECRATE THE SPACE

We are the veve. Going back to these spaces, the club, the memory, the nostalgia, is the line of the drawing . . . It manifests that world. This world.[18]

In this statement, visual artist Wura-Natasha Ogunji references the sacred cornmeal drawings made on the grounds of Voudun ceremonies—another place in which there is also always dancing, communal feeling, and personal and group transcendence—as one of a number of acts that consecrate the place necessary to transport the Lwa (natural spirits or gods) from Ginen, a sort of "Africa," to embody or "possess" dancers/worshippers. We lay claim to this understanding of dynamic, continuous time and space, which brings together *bembe, lime,* ring shout, and the club. Each of these collective practices of love reach toward spiritual connection to each other and to the divine, while simultaneously constituting a utopia—that is, a no place. This is the "steal away" of enslaved ancestors who, in order to claim ownership of themselves, temporarily "escaped" to clearings like Morrison describes or merely took a moment to remember their humanity. Place must be reimagined, but also temporally recalibrated. In the *GLQ* special issue on "queer temporalities," Halberstam, likewise, talks about arrested queer time, and Boellstorff suggests that queers "fall off" the rigid heteronormative temporal structures.[19] In all these cases, our time is too often cut short. Thus for us, an instance of futurity must be contained in a fleeting and fraught now.

It is approximately 4:00 a.m. on a Saturday at the Octagon, a predominantly black gay and lesbian underground dance club in New York City, and I am at an event held each Friday night by a group of black gay entrepreneurs, U Men/U Sweat.[20] Emile Durkheim might call this form of sociality collective effervescence, rituals of assembly wherein groups author and reauthor themselves though exuberant collective practices. Victor Turner would call this liminal space in which newly imagined perspectives unfaithful to the status quo emerge, *communitas.* With *communitas*, we can start thinking in terms of what follows the read, the critique, the protest, or the transgression of the norm. Here the in-between spaces we occupy feel less lonely, atomized and vulnerable.

The DJ had moved quickly through club remixes of pop and R&B early in the evening to underground club music. Now tribal house predominates. At the end of the "evening," he will play disco classics for the faithful few, like me, who do not mind dancing while folks sweep and stack clean glassware. The music peaks with a Latin-inspired jungle cut, "Love and Happiness," where Cuban American underground dance music diva La India sings a Yoruba praise song to the *Orishas Yemaya* and *Oshun*. Dancers respond to the rhythm and the background chanting vocals, some attempting to follow or mouth the words. The crowd is peaking— some moving in rumba hip movements, shoulders roll and shake, heads move and turn as one might see in a bembe at the moment when a change in drum beat signals the end of the explicitly religious portion of the service. La India repeats—or the DJ mixes, for this is just as much his performance as hers—"love and happiness . . . love and happiness . . . love . . . love and happiness." Then for nearly thirty seconds we are left on the dance floor with no more words, no more electronic strings, only the bass beat and the sound of hundreds of syncopated feet, stomping the dance floor. DJ Fred Pierce introduces another vocal in the soundscape. It is Kenneth Bobien's high tenor backed by a choir singing a familiar gospel song, "I shall not be moved." Some of the children raise their hands outstretched above their heads. Some hug other dancers or, where there is room on the packed dance floor, run around in apparent ecstasy or twirl. More look absently off into the distance as they dance. Others close their eyes—singing or mouthing the words, as a few dancers jump up and down in rapture. Two young men, each in their midtwenties, saunter to the center of the dance floor from just behind my position in front of one of four eight-foot speakers at the edge of the slightly raised dance floor. Earlier, they had been swaying and shimmying conservatively, scanning the crowd as they sat perched at the bar. Now as they approach the center of the floor, their hands are high above their heads with palms upturned and fingers pointing behind them. Their heads are slightly upturned as they enter the dance floor. The crowd parts. The two resplendent butch queens are singing high notes in response to the call of Bobien's Hammond organ, which has now been complemented with piano, bass, and guitars. Here is a ground for, if not instantly coherent "community," certainly congregation, which suggests "free your ass and your mind will follow."

It is now about 4:30 on Saturday morning, and church has become the central activity of this dance floor congregation. There are bars and dark corners—folks are making dates, drinking alcohol, and a few giving graphic description to the biblical phrase man shall not lay with man nor woman lie with woman, in this space marked as profane yet practiced and felt as sacred sanctuary. E. Patrick Johnson explores just this sort of ecstatic experience in his beautiful work "Feeling the Spirit in the Dark."[21] He directly challenges the false dichotomization of body and soul that currently holds sway in increasingly conservative and fundamentalist Christian churches. Further, he questions the effectively excommunicated position of black gay men in the church. By excommunicated, I refer to both the Catholic understanding of being deemed outside of the body of the Church (understood as the body of Christ), or not "in communion," and the sense of being unable to speak or be heard, made mute, moot. Johnson argues that the place of the church is "narrativized in advance," while the space that is created in the dark of the club makes more allowances for improvised performance. He shows the transgressiveness of the space of the underground club, which challenges the prescriptions, or prescripting, of the performance of church and proscriptions of the church "place" as opposed to the space that is created in the club.

GET YOUR LIFE

This space is one in which there is the felt experience of a common union and a nurturing of individual projects and common experience. Here transcendence can take place. That is, you can get your life. You got to get your life before you, or it, can be transformed. Transformation comes from being "turned out." To get your life through an experience of ecstasy, or "losing" your "mind," your received "identity," on the dance floor. To "get your life" means to recover something that you profoundly need—perhaps parts of yourself, gathered together for once. All laid down together, side-by-side. To find a deep and authentic truth of existence. Getting your life means stepping outside of your current pretension to a life, to see where yours may be hiding—what grace you might imagine—and then help others see. I am not describing here what some simplistically call "coming out," but rather coming inward: "going up" or "going in," in black gay parlance. The club is one place where many have begun to feel the outer edges of this divine life. Again, with no guarantees. That the club is the space in which black queers celebrate this oneness means that the club is also politics. After all, M. Jacqui Alexander reminds us that "the fact of the matter is that there is no other work but the work of creating and re-creating ourselves within the context of community."[22]

As E. Patrick Johnson and others have shown, and Reginald Harris testifies to, the black gay club may in fact be the only place a transgender person, gay man, or lesbian—shut out from other spaces of divine communion—may witness or participate in a vision of beloved community. This vision is not a substitute for church any more than it is a substitute for organizing. In fact, it represents a more ecumenical, democratic, honest, and expansive ethic of humanity than religion or formal politics. Classic house/club refrains implore the dancer to "free your body," "move your body," "give it up," and "let yourself go," which may be interpreted as sexual innuendo but is also understood in the space of the dance club as an exhortation to a deeper psychic and spiritual freeing that only takes place through the pleasures of the body. This social transcendence, or at least temporary respite, is related to the legendary spiritual transcendence that so many underground house partiers (in)cite. The transformation takes place through collective effervescence evoked by the music, the people, and the safer space for spinning and spiraling. This may be for only a moment. The club children are aware of the ephemeral state of their *communitas* and the precariousness of (our) family making. Most do not come to the club explicitly to sign on to some enduring political-cum-metaphysical movement. They come out to the club to "feel the music . . . take you higher," to a place of embodied well-being that extends beyond the physical place or time.

Consider that, at least for black same-gender-loving persons, to be lesbian, bisexual, transgender, or gay, or more to the point, queer, is to build loving friendships and networks of friends and family not only outside symbolic discourse in which they are always already invisibilized or muted but also outside of cultural institutions and often once removed from extended heteropatriarchal biological families, where the violences of traumatic racialized pasts very often resound, echo, and reproduce themselves in homes where protection cannot be assured. That this work is most commonly done in the dark of the club—sweat pouring and with pleasure in mind—is an ironic (attempt at or) reminder of selfhood for those whose historical (and paradigmatic) experience is precisely and uniquely marked by expropriated labor in chattel slavery, in which black bodies were (are) not owned by those who inhabit them. Thus Bernice Johnson Reagon tells us, for black people, jook joints, rum houses, house parties, beach limes, fish fries, and the like constitute "sacred territory . . . the only way you know who you are sometimes has to do with what you can do when you go home from work, change clothes . . . and dance all night long."[23]

The beat (at clubs such as Tracks DC, Better Days, Loretta's, The Warehouse, and The Garage), the word (for instance, in anthologies such as *This Bridge Called My Back*, *In The Life*, *Brother to Brother*, *Does Your Mama Know?*, and *Sojourner*), and the flesh (ah, the flesh) are thus inextricably connected and continuous with my own erotic subjectivity. In the harsh Atlanta sun, when I temporarily lost sight of the grace I could own, and where later, the darkness of Loretta's provided an incubator for Doug and Kara and me, I imagined it was Joseph Beam's voice that first called me by my new name, before putting his lips on mine, his hand in mine. Many years passed before I confessed my schoolboy crush. I learned I would never meet Joe. He had been gone for two years by then. So when in the original 1991 introduction to *Brother to Brother: New Writing by Gay Men* Essex Hemphill writes, "If I had read a book like *In the Life* when I was fifteen or sixteen, there might have been one less mask for me to put aside later in life," he was talking about me and those like me—turned out by my club twirling and inspired by Joe's beautiful soulful eyes and chocolate skin on the back cover of a book kept hidden in my basement with (straight) porn stolen from my older brother. After Friday night Gay Men of African Descent (GMAD) meetings, James and I would find ourselves on the corner outside the Gay and Lesbian community center, at Rafaellas, or Keller's—as if the meeting had been officially adjourned there—all of this prelude to but also inclusive of "the club."[24] From our positions—perched at the bar, twirling on the dance floor, shamelessly flirting, testing our sexual power—we easily found our ways to parades and protests and letter writing and workshops and interventions and civil disobedience and consciousness-raising and spiritual reconciliation with new goddesses and new languages and new lands where we connected with those on similar paths. For queers of color, this is not an either/or proposition, but a both/and, living as we do in the interstices, or what Gloria Anzaldúa would call *nepantla*, "una tierra desconocida" (a land unknown). This life in-between, constrained as it is, is also a site of potential freedom, most centrally because it has to be.

IS IT ALL OVER MY FACE?

By sacrificing our melancholic memories and making them public, I think we can make our mourning visible (as well as our analysis and our anger) and use this to produce something better for the future.[25] This is, of course, partly about my own nostalgic longing. What and who has passed before my own eyes. But unlike discrete, individual melancholia, my longing is connected to that of a number of black and other queers of color whose dreams were nurtured by experiences of common union at the club. Today I hear "I Can't Forget," by Mr. Lee, mixed with "House Nation." I remember Better Days on Fiftieth Street in Manhattan. Neon dicks on the walls five-feet tall and men grinding on the dance floor threatened to disrupt the comfortable domesticity that I had briefly escaped via the Long Island Railroad and a nervous subway ride two stops uptown. The flyers I receive on my way out, the smell of the man who held my waist then moved my shoulder and locked his arm tightly . . . , the taste of his neck on my cheek and lips—that "burdensome knowledge of carnal secrets" Essex Hemphill extolled—all ephemeral evidence. That which I could deny if I had to. Forget and begin adolescent life anew. Evidence, however, which also held a promise, and called out to me later. "In the beginning was Jack. And Jack had a groove."[26] Jose´ Estéban Muñoz is certainly correct that "instead of being clearly available as visible evidence, queerness has instead existed as . . . fleeting moments, and performances that are meant to be interacted with by those within its epistemological sphere,"[27] which he glosses as ephemera. Ephemera is for me the trace, the taste, the print that lingers, but most often not long enough to show or prove, and while not concrete, that which inspires. Here I am not claiming ephemera as "evidence" as much as a resolute commitment to those with whom Reggie Harris reminds us, we are still dancing. What is the promise in an archive that sees "the spaces where others ought to be"[28] on the dance floor at the club? What about an archive that remains in mourning's memory, recollected stories and the ache of yearning lodged in our bodies (and our) politic(s)? If the classic Chicago house music cut by Todd Terry is right—that "house is a feeling," nowadays, for black queers of a certain age and experience, that feeling is nostalgia—queer black morning. Certainly we must all pick up the weapons and pens and tools—and steps of our sisters and brothers. Perhaps to remember is also to spin where he or she shimmied—rewrote, corrected, altered, improved—palimpsest. Lithe, fierce G. Winston James, theorizes the feeling as follows:

> walking the tracks of those better days
> I came across children dancing
> Dead
> Voguers killed in kanzai dips
> striking old-style poses
> On the glossy fingernails of Death
> fluttering eyelashes and my flailing arms
> removed the AIDS dead from the ceilings
> placing them gingerly in bus-stop formation
> by their fashions—

Bringin' it hard, laughing
Twirling to the same beats
through twenty-five years of dying
to be seen, to be fierce
Finally to be loved
Like the classics[29]

The records—compact discs—still "spin" and children continue to twirl in pockets all over the world, but Nickel Bar, Better Days, Tracks and Garage in New York, Chicago's Warehouse, Tracks in DC, and kindred clubs have all closed. Much to my chagrin, I found that, as in many remaining legendary black gay clubs, in Chicago's Prop House, deep house music is often relegated to the small room to make way for hip-hop and pop mixes. What do we risk losing in the shift from (now Bishop) Carl Bean's "I Was Born This Way" to Beyoncé's exhortation to formalize property relations through marriage—that is, to "put a ring on it"? Today, I am still thinking of my after-party talk with Marvin K. White—incredulous that we are now the older men at the club—tickled by the twists, drops, turns, and intrigues of the J-Setters and other southern expressions of faggotry; the Jiggin' of the young transmen, studs, and butch young women and their ultrafemme partners. Meanwhile, Edelman has asked us to turn our backs on sociality. This we refuse. The current moment speaks just as loudly and clearly to the need to radically alter fundamental assumptions about community, family, politics, and connection to what Audre Lorde called "that deep place of longing" within each person, as our pasts impel us to reconsider this.

(T)RACE FOR THEORY

Black queer critique—rooted in the black feminist and black liberation movements of the 1970s and responding to the important political and social shifts of the 1980s and early 1990s—first revealed spaces within blackness that had previously been concealed and silenced, "yield[ing] unexpected ways of intervening and . . . mak[ing] space for something else to be."[30] More alarming than the fact that Roderick Ferguson's "something else" certainly has yet to be realized, the current structure of feeling seems to announce that political pragmatics must win over dreaming, imagining, or "trying on" ways of being someone else. I agree with Bersani's illumination in *Homos* that gay men and lesbians have "estranged ourselves in the process of denaturalizing the epistemic and political regimes that have constructed us."[31] And like Muñoz and Halberstam, I have great sympathy for Edelman's provocative turn away from reproductive futurisms and embracing of the ascription of negativity. The difference is the lens through which he perceives the local and shared political present. As Halberstam, Muñoz, and Rodriguez[32] argue, this is in part due to Edelman's narrow archive. But it is not only a problem of archive or memory but also a textual absenting or conscious forgetting through studied ignorance of work by radical people of color. Incisively reading the moment in the early 1980s, when "theory" began to be reconstituted and codified as a very particular and rarified site, Barbara Christian's famous commentary "Race for Theory" was also prophetic: "For people of color have always theorized . . . how else have we managed to survive with such spiritedness the assault? . . . My folk, in other words, have always been a race for theory—though more in the form of the hieroglyph, a written figure which is both sensual and abstract, both beautiful and communicative."[33]

If in fact my people of color are a "race for theory," my black queer people are sensual, abstract hieroglyphs in motion, seen best in black light—disco balls mirroring and refracting their complex facets. The poet's visions, the artist's eye, and the dancer's movement represent our courage to imagine a grace that would transcend stultifying hegemonies and abstractions that pretend to tell us who we are. Especially, in fact, if the answer is no one; absent(ed) in the symbolic; connected to no one and nonpolitical, as Edelman suggests. Edelman writes as if black feminist theorists, artists, and activists had not already elaborated a politics of negativity or refusal, which included, for example, working with black men on racisms and "against" us on our sexism,[34] all the while attempting to work on realms of consciousness and material change—in some cases, revolutionary—at the same time. While there was no deep investment or I should say, expectation, of reparative action by the state, work on several fronts and in a number of sometimes contradictory sites goes on simultaneously. Here family and the child are pertinent, but certainly not in the ways Edelman imagines.[35] Moreover, these activist intellectuals—most of whom were located outside of academe—chronicled and theorized various ways in which the notion of the black (woman) as subject is always already in question. Queer black and people-of-color critics have taken the mantle of developing reading and writing practices that refuse both positivist science and postmodern theoritism (and here I want to make the distinction between theorizing and the fetishization of theory), which suggests that knowledge is not situated but lodged somewhere far from where black queers live and whose pretensions to universalism only serve to further marginalize us. Still, recognition "that there are other terrains for the interrogation of sexuality . . . that do not begin and end with queer studies"[36] too often seems to have little purchase in academe, where black studies and queer studies compete for smaller and smaller corners of the margins. Black queer studies thus requires movement toward memory, personal yearning, and political resistance to very real and increasingly globally interconnected sites of black genocide.[37] Following João Costa Vargas, then, "rather than adopting the self-proclaimed detached social-scientific gaze, I argue for an analytical approach that gains insight and depth precisely because it is informed by grassroots efforts, past and present, to analyze and intervene." The locus of critical inquiry for us will have to turn to those Cathy J. Cohen's work so aptly places in a single frame of analysis—those in fact pushing at the boundaries of black politics—"punks, bulldaggers and welfare queens," the imprisoned, immigrants, and transgender individuals.[38] As Thomas Glave reminds us, the scholar, the archivist, the advocate, and the activist—often also artists, poets, and visionaries ourselves, "All of us, in continual quest of language that honors, testifies to, inscribes experiences dishonored and distorted, when they are mentioned at all . . . an art of the impossible. An art that, at its most essential core, insists only that we listen deeply to ourselves; that we attend

ourselves first . . . to move with equipoise and gallantry through the selves of others in these enormous adventures we refer to as life, literature, invention; spirit,
feeling, and vision."[39] This art of the impossible—or everyday witnessing to the
extraordinary work of survival in the face of genocide, with verve and hope—is
illustrated in Marvin K. White's "Anthem," through the mundane processes of
getting ready for the club. He begins:

> misread everything
> bathroom scale
> belt holes
> swoll feet and waist
> Cinderella Snow White Jones you a mess
> But it's a look
> Be convinced
> Find the belt and pumps to match it . . .
> Carry

Later, he moves on to poetically theorize the moment of erotic transcendence that
follows his process of tuck/tarry/carry/catch/ . . . push:

> night is not about
> the man you play all week
> but about banshees
> and haints finding crawlspace in your back
> djs paging a house music god to the floor
> over crackly p.a. system
> it's about waiting by black speaker box burning bush
> for sign
> for word
> that only comes to the children who lose their minds on this dance floor
> who come to lay their burdens down
> and get blessed on this music
> it's about never having been called
> or chosen for anything except this
> this dance
> and not being welcome in any house
> except this one
> where we blur
> push

So the process of "tuck / tarry / carry / catch / push," regarded by most as
"putting on" artifice or fantasizing a world in which, for example, it is OK for a
three-hundred-pound black man to push and twist and serve and carry in silver
hot pants and go-go boots (or some such combination I have witnessed hundreds
of times) is recognized as the real, or at least most important, reality here in the
club. It is no wonder that so many people experience Holy Ghost conversions
on the dance floor, and meet among the most significant folks in their lives at
clubs. No wonder that Brian Williamson, the Jamaican activist brutally killed at

his home, whom Thomas Glave remembers as courageous and loving, was a club owner. His club, Entourage, Glave reports, became a beacon for same-gender-loving people in Jamaica, where the global scourge of homophobia is expressed not only in negative representation and legally supported discrimination but also in relentless public violence and killings. Thus precisely, "in our private spaces, we will continue to love and make love to one another . . . tell jokes, play cards and watch TV . . . nyam our curry goat and brown stew chicken . . . and tek bad tings mek laugh."[40] That is, for the children, to carry on at the club (the lime, the get together, the fiesta) is in fact to carry on—that is, get on with the stuff of life, to get our lives (and protect our lives and those of our friends, family and children) even in the midst of wars inside and out. White ends "Anthem" this way:

we make our hips circle into peace
Clap and raise dust
And spirit give nations notice . . .
Dance is good
And we who are children
Its children
Are good
Even in the time of war
Children
Thank you
For dancing with me
For watching my front lines[41]

ACKNOWLEDGMENTS

This essay is lovingly dedicated to my friend James Andrew Jefferson (December 31, 1969–July 2008), who made all the difference. An earlier version was presented at the 2008 LA Queer Studies conference, where I was influenced by resonances with the presentations of Gayatri Gopinath, Jack Halberstam, Juana Maria Rodriguez, and Rinado Walcott. I am grateful to Shaka McGlotten, Vanessa Agard-Jones, and Dána-Ain Davis for their kind guidance and keen editorial eyes.

NOTES

1. Essex Hemphill, "Tomb of Sorrow," in *Ceremonies: Prose and Poetry* (New York: Plume, 1992).
2. Judith Halberstam, *In a Queer Time and Place: Transgender Bodies, Subcultural Lives* (New York: New York University Press, 2005), 7.
3. R. L. Caserio et al., "The Antisocial Thesis in Queer Theory," *PMLA* 121, no. 3 (2006): 819–28.
4. I will not rehearse here arguments of subjection and paradigmatic racial terror already theorized by Frantz Fanon through Hortense Spillers, Orlando Patterson, Joy James, Saidiyah Hartman, and Frank Wilderson, for example.
5. Hortense J. Spillers, "Interstices: A Small Drama of Words," in *Black, White, and in Color: Essays on American Literature and Culture* (Chicago: University of Chicago Press, 2003), 152–75.

6. Cathy J. Cohen, "Deviance as Resistance: A New Research Agenda for African American Studies," *DuBois Review: Social Science Research on Race* 1, no. 1 (2004): 27–45.

7. Lee Edelman, *No Future: Queer Theory and the Death Drive* (Durham, NC: Duke University Press, 2004), 29.

8. Hortense J. Spillers, "'All the Things You Could Be by Now if Sigmund Freud's Wife Was Your Mother': Psychoanalysis and Race," in *Black, White, and in Color: Essays on American Literature and Culture* (Chicago: University of Chicago Press, 2003), 376–427.

9. See Antonio Viego, *Dead Subjects: Toward a Politics of Loss in Latino Studies* (Durham, NC: Duke University Press, 2008).

10. Edelman writes, "Since spatial limitations preclude my rehearsing and responding to each of the papers, I'll dispense with the queer utopians at once . . . not to dismiss their position but simply to suggest that I've already addressed that position." Lee Edelman, "The Antisocial Thesis in Queer Theory" (paper presented at the MLA Annual Convention, Washington, DC, December 2005).

11. José Esteban Muñoz, "Cruising the Toilet: LeRoi Jones/Amiri Baraka, Radical Black Traditions, and Queer Futurity," *GLQ: A Journal of Lesbian and Gay Studies* 13, nos. 2–3 (2007): 353–67.

12. Leo Bersani, *Homos* (Cambridge, MA: Harvard University Press, 1995), 5.

13. See M. Jacqui Alexander, "Not Just (Any)Body Can Be a Citizen: The Politics of Law, Sexuality and Postcoloniality in Trinidad, Tobago, and the Bahamas," *Feminist Review: Sex and the State* 48 (1994): 5–23.

14. Donald Woods, "We Be Young," in *Brother to Brother: New Writing by Black Gay Men* (Washington, DC: RedBone), 70–73

15. Audre Lorde, "School Note," in *Black Unicorn* (New York: Norton, 1978), 16–18.

16. Samuel Delany, "Coming/Out," in *Shorter Views: Queer Thoughts & the Politics of the Paraliterary* (Middletown, CT: Wesleyan University Press, 2000), 67.

17. Toni Morrison, *Beloved* (New York: Knopf, 1987), 88.

18. RedBone Press Writing Workshop, personal communication, 2006.

19. Carolyn Dinshaw et al., "Theorizing Queer Temporalities: A Roundtable Discussion," *GLQ: A Journal of Lesbian and Gay Studies* 13 (2007): 177–95.

20. Octagon has closed, holding a few special events only intermittently after 1999.

21. E. Patrick Johnson, "Feeling the Spirit in the Dark: Expanding Notions of the Sacred in the African-American Gay Community," *Callaloo* 21, no. 2 (1998): 399–416.

22. In "Remembering This Bridge Called My Back, Remembering Ourselves," in her *Pedagogies of Crossing* (Durham, NC: Duke University Press, 2006), M. Jacqui Alexander offers another way to see the wide-ranging processes of friendship between women. It offers an archeology of experiences and knowledges that seem to ineluctably connect to this consideration of friendship in the life.

23. This appears in *Dancing*, PBS, 1993.

24. Beyond the clientele of any one place, the circuits of race, desire, and belonging found black and other men of color interacting across class (with the fewer middle-class and upper-class men having the most mobility in these circuits, of course).

25. Alexandra Juhasz, "Video Remains: Nostalgia, Technology, and Queer Archive Activism," *GLQ: A Journal of Lesbian and Gay Studies* 12, no. 2 (2006): 319–28.

26. Mr. Fingers, *Can U Feel It*, backed with Martin Luther King Jr., "I Have A Dream," Trax Records TX-127, 1986.

27. José Esteban Muñoz, "Ephemera as Evidence: Introductory Notes to Queer Acts," *Women and Performance* 8, no. 2 (1996): 6. In *Disidentifications: Queers of Color and the Performance of Politics* (Minneapolis: University of Minnesota Press, 1999), Muñoz critically takes up the work of the cadre of cultural workers of the late 1980s and 1990s who, he reminds us, retold "elided histories that need both to be excavated and (re)imagined"

through "powerful and calculated set of deployments of ephemeral witnessing to Black queer identity" (57).

28. Reginald Harris, personal communication, 2007.

29. G. Winston James, "At the Club (for Ronald Lemay, Daniel Revlon, Grace, Moi Renee and All the Legends of Old)," in *The Damaged Good* (New York: Vintage Entity), 94–97.

30. Roderick A. Ferguson, *Aberrations in Black: Toward a Queer of Color Critique* (Minneapolis: University of Minnesota Press, 2004).

31. Bersani, *Homos*, 4.

32. Juana Maria Rodriguez, *Queer Latinidad: Identity Practices, Discursive Spaces* (New York: New York University Press, 2003).

33. Barbara Christian, "The Race for Theory," *Cultural Critique* 6 (1987): 51–63.

34. From a statement by the Combahee River Collective.

35. While the future needs of the Symbolic Child he poses are held above the present needs of adults who fall out of heteronormative time and place, in the real world of queer-headed families of color, family figures in the recognition of interdependence between, for example, queer children and parents or extended family members in need, biological and adopted children, and kids in need.

36. Ferguson, *Aberrations in Black*, 85.

37. The necropolitics referred to here is echoed by black activists and artists. Essex Hemphill emphasizes in "The Tomb of Sorrow," "everyone wants a price for my living."

38. As Matt Richardson has observed, scripts of participation in the time and space of black life, or any other space other than that which they make for themselves, are never extended to black transpeople, who exist as spectral presences haunting (these and other) margins.

39. Thomas Glave, "Fire and Ink: Toward a Quest for Language, History, and a Moral Imagination," *Callaloo* 26, no. 3 (2003): 215.

40. Thomas Glave, *Words to Our Now: Imagination and Dissent* (Minneapolis: University of Minnesota Press, 2005), 76.

41. Marvin K. White, "A Letter that Looks Like a Poem for a Dance Floor that Feels Like an Altar," in *Last Rights* (Washington, DC: RedBone, 2002), 69–72.

About the Contributors

Marlon M. Bailey is an assistant professor at the University of Indiana, Bloomington. His research interests include African diaspora studies, queer diasporas, race, gender and sexuality, queer theory, black queer studies, theater/performance studies, ethnography, and HIV/AIDS. Currently, Dr. Bailey is completing a manuscript that expands his performance ethnographic study of ballroom culture, a black and Latina or Latino queer culture in North America: *Butch Queens Up in Pumps: Gender, Performance, and Ballroom Culture in Detroit*. The book is forthcoming from the University of Michigan Press. He is also an accomplished professional actor, director, and performance artist.

Thaddeus Gregory Blanchette has a PhD in social anthropology from the Brazilian National Museum. Since 1999, he has researched the immigration axis between Brazil and the United States and has, in particular, concentrated on the English-speaking communities of Rio de Janeiro. His current project looks to sex and tourism in Rio.

Dána-Ain Davis is an associate professor at CUNY Queens College. Her areas of specialization include black studies, family and sexual violence, reproductive rights, poverty and welfare policy, and women's studies. She has published one book, *Battered Black Women and Welfare Reform* (SUNY Press), as well as a number of articles on women and welfare policy. She served as president of the Association of Black Anthropologists, executive director of the ADCO Foundation, board chair of the New York Foundation, and she currently serves as a consultant to a number of foundations that fund projects involving women's issues.

Simone C. Drake is an assistant professor of African American and African studies at Ohio State University. Her research interests are broad and interdisciplinary, focusing on critical race, gender, and legal studies; transnational black feminism; black masculinities; visual and popular culture; and the literature of the African diaspora in the Americas. Many of these research areas intersect in Drake's manuscript, *Transnational Negotiations: Critical Appropriations in Black Women's Cultural Productions* (under review) and in her second project, *Imagining Grace: Black Men's Lives Between the Poles*. Drake has published numerous articles on race and gender in literature, film, and culture. She serves on the editorial board for *Spectrum: A Journal on Black Men* (Indiana University Press).

Aimee Cox is an assistant professor of African American and African studies and an urban anthropologist. She received her PhD in cultural anthropology from the University of Michigan where she also held a postdoctoral fellowship with the Center for the Education of Women. Professor Cox's research and teaching interests include urban youth culture, public anthropology, social mobility, black feminist thought, and performance. Her most recent work explores the strategies young women in low-income urban communities use to become economically and socially mobile. She is currently completing a book titled *OutClass: Black Girls and the Politics of Self-Improvement.*

Ashon Crawley is a doctoral candidate in English at Duke University. His research focuses on the performance of race, gender, sexuality, and religion. His dissertation project, tentatively titled "Historicity and Black Studies: the Aesthetics of Pentecost," is about the theological-philosophical force of blackness, given in the historicity of practices such as the ring shout (dancing flesh), testimony service (enunciating voice) and whooping (eclipsing breath). More than the "merely aesthetic," he argues that these practices are philosophical, critiquing the disciplining of and resistance to (black) sociality that animates Enlightenment philosophy. He received his BA from the University of Pennsylvania and a master of theological studies degree from Emory University.

Guy Mark Foster teaches at Bowdoin College. His critical essays and short fiction have appeared in such places as *African American Review, Empowerment versus Oppression: Twenty-First Century Views of Popular Romance Novels, Symbiosis: A Journal of Anglo-American Literary Relations, A Companion to African American Literature, Ancestral House: The Black Short Story in the Americas and Europe,* and *Brother to Brother: New Writings by Black Gay Men.* He is currently finishing up a book project titled *Waking Up to the Enemy: Towards a New Ethics of Interracial Intimacy in Contemporary Literature and Popular Culture.*

Roberta Hunte is an instructor at Portland State University in conflict resolution; women, gender and sexuality studies; and child and family studies. She is completing her doctorate in peace and conflict studies from the University of Manitoba in Winnipeg, Canada. Her dissertation is focused on the ways black women negotiate the intersections of race and gender in long-term careers as tradeswomen. She is on the board for OPAL Environmental Justice Oregon, and the Oregon Peace Institute.

Ethan Johnson is an associate professor in the Black Studies Department at Portland State University. He has published in the journals *Race, Ethnicity and Education, International Journal of Qualitative Studies in Education, Souls, Ethnography and Education,* and *Oregon Historical Quarterly.* He is also the coeditor along with Professor Kassie Freeman of the book *Education in the Black Diaspora,* in which he wrote several articles. His work focuses broadly on the educational experiences of youth of African descent concerning how they negotiate and interpret racial identity and racism. In addition, his scholarship compares and contrasts mainstream/white and black people's representations of blackness in both popular culture and the mass media. Currently, he is working on two projects. One considers how students in an Afrocentric after school program make sense of their racial and cultural identities. The other examines the Afro-Ecuadorian educational movement.

Annecka Marshall is a lecturer in gender and development studies at the University of the West Indies, Mona Campus, Jamaica. Her research interests address sexual diversity, variance, and paraphilias.

Zethu Matebeni is a faculty member in the Institute for Humanities at the University of Cape Town. Her works focuses on black lesbian sexualities and identities in postapartheid Johannesburg. She worked previously as a research manager for the South African Government's National Campaign on HIV and AIDS, TB, and STIs and has lectured at the University of Pretoria. She is actively involved in organizations that promote the lives and rights of LGBTQI people.

Donna-Maria Maynard is a lecturer in clinical and counseling psychology at the University of the West Indies, Cave Hill Campus, Barbados. Her current research interests focus on relationships, depression, anxiety, and sexuality.

Shaka McGlotten is an assistant professor at Purchase College-SUNY, where he teaches course on ethnography, digital culture, and queer studies. Dr. McGlotten's research focuses on the intersections of media technologies with categories of gender, sexuality, and race in particular. Dr. McGlotten also works in what might be broadly called "affect studies," or the study of the ways feelings are central to our individually lived and shared social experiences. Dr. McGlotten has recently completed a manuscript that explores these themes. *Virtual Intimacies: Media Cultures and Queer Sociality* examines a range of media sites—DIY porn, online gaming, gay chat rooms—to examine the mutual intensification between digital media culture and the creativity of queer sociality. His writing on gaming, chat rooms, zombies, and porn have appeared in anthologies and journals such as *Transforming Anthropology*.

Ana Paula Da Silva has a PhD in cultural anthropology from the Federal University of Rio de Janeiro. She mostly researches race and gender issues and was one of the first scholars to conduct research on the impact of affirmative action policies in Brazil. Currently, she is working on a book outlining the history of the myth of the hypersexualized Brazilian woman.

C. Riley Snorton is an assistant professor at Northeastern University. Snorton earned his PhD in communication from the Annenberg School of Communication. Snorton's academic and teaching interests include media anthropology, Africana studies, gender and queer theory, cultural studies, performance studies, ethnographic film, media production, and media activism. Snorton is the director of a short documentary titled *Men at Work: Transitioning on the Job* and has published or has articles forthcoming in the *International Journal of Communication*, *Hypatia: A Journal of Feminist Philosophy*, and *Souls: a Critical Journal of Black Politics, Culture, and Society*. Snorton has also contributed to numerous edited volumes, including *The Comedy of Dave Chappelle: Critical Essays, Homophiles, and Trans[gender] Migrations*. Before beginning a PhD program, Snorton worked as a media relations manager for the Gay and Lesbian Alliance against Defamation and the Gay, Lesbian and Straight Education Network. His dissertation, *Trapped in the [Epistemological] Closet: Black Sexuality and the Popular Imagination*, examines the concept of the "down low" in news and popular culture.

Dr. Tanya L. Saunders is an assistant professor of sociology and anthropology at Lehigh University in Bethlehem, Pennsylvania. Her research examines the ways in which black artists, intellectuals, and activists throughout Latin America and the Spanish-speaking Caribbean employ cultural aesthetics, such as hip-hop and contemporary art, to work for social change locally, nationally, and transnationally. She is currently completing a book about the underground hip-hop movement in Cuba and on a handful of articles that address the themes of social change, artistic movements, and transnational black identity. Dr. Saunders appears in the journals *Souls: A Critical Journal of Black Politics, Culture and Society*, *Black Women Gender and Families*, *Feminist Media Studies*, and *Caribbean Review of Gender Studies*. She is a 2011–12 Fulbright Scholar Award recipient for Brazil, where she will expand the regional focus of her work. Her research interests are in the areas of sociology of culture, Latin American and Caribbean studies, African diaspora studies, political sociology, social identity and inequality (race, gender and sexuality), sociology of music, sociology of art.

Rashad Shabazz's work brings together theories of race and racism, black cultural studies, gender studies, and critical prison studies within a methodological framework that draws on history, human geography, philosophy and literature. He is currently an assistant professor at the University of Vermont. His research explores the ways in which race, class, sexuality, and gender articulate through geographies of antiblack racism. Currently Dr. Shabazz is working on a book manuscript that examines how black identity, culture, and antiblack racism are produced and disciplined through spatiality. His scholarship has appeared in *Souls* and *Spatial-Justice Journal*.

H. Sharif Williams (Herukhuti) is a clinical sociologist (with a specialty in sexology), cultural worker (media, theater/performance arts, creative writing, and visual arts), cultural studies scholar (focusing on sexuality, gender, and spirituality within the African diaspora), and traditional African shaman (*Khmt* and *Dagara*). Dr. Herukhuti is the founder of Black Funk: The Center for Culture, Sexuality, and Spirituality; editor-in-chief of http://www.blackfunk.org; and the author of *Conjuring Black Funk: Notes on Culture, Sexuality, and Spirituality, Volume 1*

(Vintage Entity Press). Dr. Herukhuti holds a PhD in human and organizational systems and a MEd in curriculum and instruction. Dr. Herukhuti's work has been published and anthologized in various academic and popular contexts including *Sexualities*, *Journal of Bisexuality*, *ARISE Magazine*, and *Ma-Ka Diasporic Juks: Contemporary Writings by Queers of African Descent*.

Index